CRYPTODAD

CRYPTODAD

The Fight for the Future of Money

J. Christopher Giancarlo

WILEY

Published by John Wiley & Sons, Inc., Hoboken, New Jersey.
Published simultaneously in Canada.

For general information on our other products and services or for technical support, please contact our Customer Care Department within the United States at (800) 762-2974, outside the United States at (317) 572-3993 or fax (317) 572-4002.

Wiley also publishes its books in a variety of electronic formats. Some content that appears in print may not be available in electronic formats. For more information about Wiley products, visit our web site at www.wiley.com.

Library of Congress Cataloging-in-Publication Data

Names: Giancarlo, J. Christopher (James Christopher), 1959- author.
Title: CryptoDad : the fight for the future of money / J. Christopher
  Giancarlo.
Description: Hoboken, New Jersey : Wiley, [2022] | Includes index.
Identifiers: LCCN 2021036636 (print) | LCCN 2021036637 (ebook) | ISBN
  9781119855088 (hardback) | ISBN 9781119855101 (adobe pdf) | ISBN
  9781119855095 (epub)
Subjects: LCSH: Cryptocurrencies. | Digital currency. | Finance—United
  States.
Classification: LCC HG1710 .G53 2022 (print) | LCC HG1710 (ebook) | DDC
  332.4—dc23
LC record available at https://lccn.loc.gov/2021036636
LC ebook record available at https://lccn.loc.gov/2021036637

Cover Image: Mike McGregor Inc.
Cover Design: Paul McCarthy

SKY10029872_091621

This book is dedicated to three wise teachers:
Ella Jane, my mother, who taught faithfulness in living;
Henry, my professor, who believed liberty is the goal of learning; and
Regina, my wife, who shows kindness as the essence of love.

Contents

Foreword

Cryptocurrency, or "crypto" as it is colloquially known, is a pretty big deal. In our opinion, a bigger one than the Internet itself. And we believe it has the potential to have as great an impact on personal freedom as the printing press, the personal computer, and the early, open Internet. Why? Because crypto makes decentralization possible, which is to say its center of gravity is you, the individual.

Prior to the invention of Bitcoin, the idea of a decentralized network, in which unrelated computers around the world could reliably reach agreement with each other on something (e.g. who owns what), was thought to be entirely theoretical. The challenge lies in the possibility that one or more computers in the network could be bad actors trying to confuse the others.

In computer science, this agreement problem is known as The Byzantine Generals' Problem. When Satoshi Nakamoto, Bitcoin's pseudonymous creator, published the Bitcoin white paper in 2009, she, he, or they presented the world's first ever solution to this hitherto intractable problem. As described, the Bitcoin mining algorithm ensures that a network of computers that don't know each other will in fact reach agreement with each other in a reliable manner. And that this agreement or consensus—what today, we call a blockchain—would be immutable and verifiable.

Historically, such agreement had to be entrusted to a central party or ended up concentrating toward one. Money has long been the purview of governments and finance the domain of big banks. Tim Berners-Lee's original, utopic vision for the commercial Internet—an open network of interconnected computers—has become a closed, dystopic oligopoly of data cartels. When you log on to the Internet today, you're really logging on to one of five companies: Facebook, Amazon, Apple, Netflix, or Google, aka the FAANG companies. Has there ever been a more appropriate acronym?

The problem with centralization of power was captured best by Lord Bryon: "Power corrupts; absolute power corrupts absolutely." These sectors are centralized, not because it is the best approach, but because it has been the only approach ... until now. Satoshi's break-through not only made the decentralization of money possible, but it also provided a blueprint for the decentralization of anything.

We now can envision a future where the Internet, finance, and money will not be controlled by a few, but by the many. Where the value of these social networks (they are all social networks) will not accrue to just a handful of CEOs and companies, but to all of us, their users. Where you no longer need someone's permission to invest, borrow, or build. A level playing field with no inside baseball.

Bitcoin was the first cryptocurrency as we have come to know them. It has created an entirely new economic sector we now call crypto. This sector, like the Internet, has grown from total obscurity into one that can't be ignored. While today, it still appears to most as a niche technol-ogy, tomorrow it will be everything. When Jeff Bezos was first pitching Amazon to potential investors, the first question he was always asked was, "What's the Internet?" Crypto's story arc will be no different.

Crypto is not just a technology; it is a movement. One that offers the possibility of greater choice, independence, and opportunity for all. It can achieve things that our current systems can't even begin to con-template. It allows our money to work like email. Its barriers to entry are low—requiring only an Internet connection and a smartphone. It has the power to redesign the Internet, the financial system, and money in a way that fosters and protects the rights and dignity of the individual.

These are quite awesome possibilities and embody the ethos and founding principles of our country. Crypto is very American.

It would have been hard to predict the sheer economic opportunity of the Internet back in the early 1990s. Not long ago, many of the Internet companies that today are the biggest economic drivers of the global economy were seen as novelties or didn't even exist. The majority of these companies are American and their economic growth and prosperity was captured primarily by Americans. America won the Internet.

This was not a coincidence or the result of a lucky accident. This can be traced entirely back to the pro-entrepreneurial culture that America has long established through its rule of law and thoughtful regulation. These choices that we made gave rise to sophisticated capital and credit markets that provided nourishment to start-ups and solidified America as both the cradle and hotbed of innovation. Entrepreneurs came to America to build because they could do so with a clarity and pace that was impossible to match in any other country in the world. And once this ecosystem was established, it became both self-reinforcing and self-perpetuating.

But while the race for the Internet is more than three decades underway and America's leadership position is firmly entrenched, another one has begun—the race for the Internet of Money. It's still early, but unlike the race for the Internet, the United States is not the leader. To date, the biggest crypto companies are being built offshore. In many cases, they are being built by US citizens who have left America because the regulatory environment is too slow, opaque, or draconian to keep up with the global pace of innovation. And for perhaps the first time ever, US customers are flocking to offshore financial platforms because they simply can't get what they want here, at home.

This sad irony is painful to admit. America is not where the majority of crypto entrepreneurs go to build. The land of the free and the home of the brave, the bastion of democracy and free markets, now, all of a sudden, has an uncertain future as the host country for the greatest technology revolution of the last quarter century. America has been operating under the false pretense that a global, decentralized, permissionless technology movement that transcends borders is going to wait around for America's permission. It won't. America has gotten complacent. It has confused the Internet boom with the crypto boom, assuming that because we won one, we will win the other. Our past success will not be an indicator or causation of our future success.

But alas, all is not lost. It is still early, and our fate rests entirely in our own hands. Our country has leaders like Chris Giancarlo who understand the vast promise of cryptocurrencies. Under his tenure as chairman of the Commodities Futures Trading Commission (CFTC), Giancarlo championed crypto throughout the halls of government and left behind a pro-crypto legacy at the CFTC that lives on to this day. His dedication to our country becoming a leader in crypto, as we have been in the Internet, earned him the nickname "CryptoDad" on Twitter and legions of Internet followers. And his sense of duty and patriotism that led him to serve in our government for five years similarly motivates him to make sure America is not left behind. Giancarlo is a true American.

Our sincere hope is that many will read this book and begin to better understand not only the enormity of the opportunity that stands before us, but also that our ability to prosper from it is not guaranteed. Our hope is that this book will give you an insider's view into where we are as a country with respect to our regulatory approach to crypto and where we need to be. Armed with this knowledge, we can then start working together toward a solution. We can build an ecosystem with the proper ingredients and nutrients that will allow crypto to flourish here, on our shores. Together, we can ensure that America becomes the undisputed best place for entrepreneurs to build in crypto. That America remains the land of opportunity where you go to make your dreams come to life.

We hope you will join us and CryptoDad as we fight for this future. We won the space race, we won the Internet. Now, let's go win the fight for the future of money.

Onward and upward,
Cameron & Tyler Winklevoss
July 16, 2021

Preface

July 14, 2021

En route to Big Moose Lake, New York

I wrote this book to tell a story. A story of a five-year journey around the globe through the centers of financial power. A true story from my eyes and ears. Of what I saw and what I experienced, what was said and who said it. Much of it is serious, some of it funny, a bit of it is revealing about the way decisions are made at the highest levels that affect the lives of each one of us.

It is a story of real events that took place during the later portion of the twenty-teens: 2014–2019. It is a story of real people, many of whom are wonderful, some are dear to me, a few disingenuous, most of them important in more or less obvious ways to how the US and global economy are run.

I am telling this story to interest readers who may wonder what it is like to be in the setting of political power over financial affairs in Washington and, occasionally in London, Brussels, Basel, and Hong Kong.

I trust readers will enjoy the ride. I hope so, because along the way I have a more important message to impart. The message is that something big is going on all around us. Something bigger than one person's accidental and quixotic experience through the halls of power. It is a change that comes not once in a generation, but perhaps once every few centuries.

This change is being driven by a new wave of the Internet—the Internet of Value—that permits the instant transfer of things of value over the worldwide Web directly from person to person without the need for intermediaries.

The revolutionary change that I am talking about is in the way society experiences holding and sharing things of value, including the most valuable thing of all: money. Soon, moving money will be as simple, immediate, and cost-free as sending a text message, whether across a supermarket counter or around the globe.

Why is this revolutionary? Because up to now money has been limited in space and time. The ability to move money far from home is somewhat slow and costly and limited to banking hours by those who can afford it. Now, for the first time in human history, the use of money will transcend space, time and, importantly, social class.

Here is the deeper story that I will tell: how money is changing right before our eyes. And, that you, the reader, must take hold of that change. You and your fellow citizens must speak up and effect that change.

Money is as much a social construct as it is a government one. Together, we must make sure that the values that are enshrined today in the US dollar and the currencies of other democracies—values like individual liberty, freedom of speech, personal privacy, free enterprise, and the rule of law—are encoded in the digital money of the future.

Money is too important to be left to central bankers. You and I must assert a voice in the rapidly coming change in money. We must make sure that our financial privacy and economic liberty are safe and secure. If we do not, the people I tell you about in this book will make those decisions for us. We can't let the promise of the convenience of digital money blind us to the threat of the loss of our liberty to unelected technocratic and government elites, however noble their intentions.

Without inviolable protections for such civil liberties as freedom of speech, free enterprise, and individual economic privacy, digital Dollars, digital Euros, or other forms of digital currency would be no more worthy of a democratic people than the currency of authoritarian ones. Free societies have everything to gain by encoding into sovereign and non-sovereign digital currency stout protections for individual liberty and privacy. Free people have everything to lose by neglecting it. The choice is essential to the future of civil society.

This book is not a technical book about the complexities of Bitcoin and other cryptocurrencies or their underlying distributed ledgers, although it does try to explain those things in simple terms. It is not a guide to Bitcoin trading strategies. This book will not tell you whether crypto is a good or bad investment. It is not even an appeal for the creation of a digital dollar, although it does explain what is at stake in doing so. No, this book is more basic than that.

This book is written to take a stand for the future of economic privacy and financial liberty. We must harness this unstoppable wave of digital money—the Internet of Value—to advance greater economic inclusion, financial and economic freedom, and human aspiration for generations to come. We must be bold, not timid. Ultimately, we must insure that the future of money is determined by a free society of fearless people, philosophers and farmers, teachers and musicians, fast-food cashiers and hotel cleaners, doctors and dreamers, and accidental regulators like me.

And people like you.

Introduction

"Dreams I had just yesterday
Seem to all have passed away in time
And, once again, I have a memory
Another treasure in this life of mine,
This life of mine.
"Fate shows no mercy to love
And so, I pack my wheels once more
'cause there's so many
Backroads in life yet to explore
Yet to explore
"I know I can't ever change
My lone person or my mind
And so, I have to be on my way
And leave those realities behind
Yeah, leave 'em behind
"And now, the sun is shining down
Upon a road
Twisting and unwinding
For this, I gave my all
I gave my all.
"I'm lookin' for a road
I'm lookin' for a road
I'm lookin' for a road
Again."[1]

Thank you for opening the pages to this book. I'll tell you why I wrote it.

The future of the US economy—and, indeed, the world's—will be determined at the dynamic intersection of markets, technology, and politics. The interplay of these determines the cost and availability of the food we eat, the energy that heats our homes, the electricity that powers our smartphones, our mortgages and auto loans, and, ultimately, the money we use to pay for all of these. It determines the continued affordability of the vaunted "American way of life."

I have spent a 37-year career in that economic intersection, first as a Wall Street lawyer and later as a finance executive. I then served for 5 years at its center at one of the world's least understood yet most important market regulators, the US Commodity Futures Trading Commission, known as the CFTC. It was there that, quite unexpectedly, I glimpsed the most profound change in generations: The rise of the Internet of Value, Bitcoin, and cryptocurrencies.

So this book is, in part, a personal one about how I have navigated my professional path in a radically changing world. But I hope it is much more than that. It is also a call to arms. Based on what I have seen, I believe democratic society faces an urgent need to courageously confront the extraordinary transformations wrought by the Internet of Value that will intimately affect the daily lives of each and every one of us. They must be shaped by a free people.

Here's why I say that. Let me begin with three key observations about financial markets.

Antiquated Infrastructure

First, consider that America's physical infrastructure—its bridges, tunnels, airports, and mass transit systems—that were cutting edge in the last century but have been allowed to age and deteriorate in the current one.

Sadly, the same is true about much of our financial infrastructure, both in the United States and in many developed Western economies. Systems for check payment and settlement; shareholder and proxy voting; investor access and disclosure; and financial system regulatory oversight—once state-of-the-art and global models in the twentieth century—have fallen behind the times in the twenty-first century. In some cases, embarrassingly so.

This aging financial system puts developed economies like the United States at a competitive disadvantage to the likes of China that are building new financial infrastructure from scratch with twenty-first century digital technology. Here's a good example: it typically takes days in the United States to settle and clear retail bank transfers. In many other countries it takes mere minutes, if not seconds. It also takes days to settle securities transactions and weeks to obtain land title insurance. It is still often faster to move money around the globe by stuffing cash in a suitcase and carrying it on a plane than it is to send a wire transfer.

Nothing better reveals the limits of our existing financial system than the US government's initial financial response to the COVID-19 pandemic in the spring of 2020. Tens of millions of Americans had to wait a month or more to receive relief payments by paper check. More than a million payments were made to people who were dead.

Internet of Value

A second observation is that these aging financial and regulatory systems are struggling to adapt to the next wave of digitization that I and some others call the "Internet of Value."[2]

The first wave was the Internet of Information. Wikipedia is an example and emblem of that first wave: a massive decentralized, online reference authority composed collaboratively by volunteers. That initial wave took information written, owned, and controlled by elite publishers like Encyclopedia Britannica and democratized it, rendering it easily accessible at a keystroke, anytime, anywhere, and for free.

That first Internet wave was superseded by another: the "Internet of Things." Thanks to this wave, seemingly every place we shop and dwell, everything we wear and drive, and every device we engage with is connected to the Internet.

We are now on the cusp of the Internet's next wave: the Internet of Value.

As remarkable as were the earlier waves, the Internet of Value will be an even deeper transformation of our economic selves than the earlier waves combined. This wave will do to currency, financial instruments, and economic activity what the Internet of Information did to knowledge: reduce costs, increase speed, transcend barriers, improve accessibility, enhance certainty, and decrease bottlenecks to instantaneous transactions across the globe.

In this wave, things of value—such as contracts for energy, agricultural, and mineral commodities; stock certificates, land records, and property titles; cultural assets like music and art; and personal assets like birth records and drivers licenses—will be stored, managed, transacted, and moved about in a secure, private way from person to person, without third-party intermediaries. This next wave of the Internet will shift the medium of trust from large centrally managed institutions to person-to-person digital handshakes powered and secured by cryptography, tokenization, and shared ledgers carried across a network of personal computers and smartphones. Think of the ability to send money or confer ownership over property by mere text message without having to go through an intermediary—a powerful bank or a credit card company—to authenticate who you are and the person you are sending it to. The opportunities will be no less transformative than what Uber did to mobility, Airbnb did to lodging, and Amazon did to commerce. We are only in the middle innings of what will be a decades-long digital revolution.

Ask yourself: When was the last time you mailed a stamped letter rather than sent an email? When was the last time you pasted photos into an album instead of stored them on your mobile phone? When was the last time you played a CD, cassette tape, or vinyl LP rather than listened to Pandora or Spotify? If the Internet could transform letter writing, photography, and music in one generation, it is naïve to think the Internet will not do the same to financial services and money. In a few years' time, writing a paper check will be as archaic as sending film to Kodak to be developed. So will sending money by wire transfer—or even via mobile apps like Venmo or Square Cash—since all these ostensibly "digital" methods still rely on costly intermediaries, such as banks and credit-card companies. Just over the horizon is a world in which we will soon send things of value directly to the recipient, mobile device to mobile device, without any third-party needing to assist—or take a cut.

Nowhere will the Internet have a more dramatic impact than in the realm of money. Sir Jon Cunliffe, the widely respected deputy governor of the Bank of England, once commented to me that, every several generations, society re-asks the question: "What is money?" He thinks this latest Internet wave is prompting society to ask that question once again.

He's right. Society has been questioning the nature of money for over a decade now. Bitcoin[3]—rising from the ashes of the last financial crisis in 2008—was the first digital asset. Since its advent, the private sector has launched thousands of budding, non-sovereign cryptocurrencies of lesser or greater promise.

Clearly, the private sector is way ahead of governments and central banks in exploring digital money. But lately, governments are starting to react. Most of the world's central banks are now taking a serious look at a sovereign form of cryptocurrency, called central bank digital currency.

The world as we know it today is one of competing currency zones in which monetary systems, banking, and foreign accounts are generally oriented to one reserve currency or another. Think of the US dollar zone and the "Eurozone." As I will explain in this book, those old currency zones may well be replaced tomorrow by widely networked and integrated national digital currency zones. There likely will be a Chinese digital currency zone and perhaps a Digital Euro zone. In these zones, central bank digital currencies will be networked through distributed ledgers with all important financial functions and transactions—including retail credit and business lending, domestic and global payments, securities and commodities trading, and central bank monetary policy—under the control and watchful eye and sway of powerful central banks. The increase in speed, efficiency, and velocity of money could turbocharge economic growth. Such centralized economic and financial control for major world economies would be unprecedented. It would be the utmost expression of the Internet of Value: fully-integrated, networked, digital economies.

The Digital Future of Money

My third observation is that the standards, protocols, and rules for the digital future of money are being established today. If we act now, we can make sure that democratic values—freedom of speech, individual economic privacy, free enterprise, and free capital markets—are encoded in the digital future of money. In so doing, we can harness this wave of innovation to maximize financial inclusion, capital and operational efficiency, and economic growth for generations to come.

If we do not act wisely and quickly, however, this new Internet wave will lay bare the shortcomings of America's aging, analog financial systems. Worse, it will mean that the values of our nondemocratic economic competitors—state surveillance, social credit systems, law subservient to the state, and centrally planned economic activity—will be embedded into the future of money, diminishing the vibrancy and health of the global economy, individual liberty, and human advancement.

This book is about the digital transformation of money and how it will change the lives of everyone in the global economy. But it is also a more personal story. It's about how I, a Margaret Thatcher–admiring, free market Republican, helped build one of the world's leading derivatives trading platforms only to find myself in the epicenter of the 2008 financial crisis. That experience led me to support the financial market reforms in the Dodd–Frank Act—a law that I now view as the last major "patch" of the long-standing analog, account-based financial system.

Those experiences led to my appointment to the CFTC by President Barack Obama. They also led to my subsequent elevation to CFTC chairman by President Donald Trump—after confirmation by a unanimous Senate.

Like Jimmy Stewart in *Mr. Smith Goes to Washington*,[4] I went to Washington as a political naïf with reformist goals. My immediate objective was to complete and improve reforms to the swaps market. Yet, halfway through, I found myself staring at the first ripples of the next wave of the Internet—a wave that will soon shake the existing financial system to its core.

The immediate challenge was a product called Bitcoin futures, which I will discuss in more detail later. I faced significant pressure to hamper its debut. But I resisted that pressure—not without a few moments of self-doubt. Instead, I led the agency to encourage financial innovation, prepare for the Internet of Value, and oversee the development of crypto derivatives. Braving political risk, we reduced regulatory uncertainty for financial market innovators. The decision laid the groundwork for the emergence of an enormous new ecosystem of retail and institutional cryptocurrency greater than anything I could have anticipated. For that, the online cryptocurrency community dubbed me "CryptoDad." This book is my story.

★★★

Undoubtedly, the continuing evolution of the Internet of Value will come in fits and starts. There will be bubbles, crashes, mistakes, and successes. There will be fiascos and criminal behavior as with any profound change. There will be enormous business disruption and even more business innovation that still cannot even be imagined.

Yet, the technology will not be stopped. Suppression in any one jurisdiction will just move the evolution to another. The direction of travel for this innovation is increasingly clear and, frankly, amazing. Bitcoin is just the tip of the iceberg. The question for American policy makers is whether they have the courage to let this new wave of innovation take place here in an intelligently regulated fashion that contributes to our economic benefit or irresolution to force it to happen elsewhere.

The question for a free people is whether they will make their voices heard in the design and operation of the digital future of money. Will the reasonable expectation of privacy from both commercial and governmental surveillance provided by paper money be found in digital money? Will a digital dollar or non-sovereign forms of digital money secure individual economic privacy against government surveillance guaranteed by the US Constitution and expected by the American people? Who will decide?

I am convinced—and I hope to persuade you in this book—that the ongoing evolution of the Internet will revolutionize money and banking in the same way it has revolutionized communications, photography, retail shopping, business meetings, and entertainment. It is naive to think that it will not. Yet, the venerable global financial services industry and its central bank overseers have been slow to even acknowledge its arrival. Some have a vested interest in the old infrastructure. The western economies will not keep pace if the matter is left to politically browbeaten bank executives, political protectors of the status quo, a few snarky financial journalists, and rigid central bankers. We need officials with courage, determination, foresight, and the willingness to take risk.

If we fall behind the curve, then the future rules, protocols, and values of digital money will be set by our nondemocratic economic competitors. Instead, a free society must show the courage of its bedrock convictions. We must fearlessly lead the digital revolution in money and finance and not cede leadership in the Internet of Value to autocratic economic competitors. That's the only way we can counter the values of authoritarianism with democratic values: individual economic privacy, rule of law, and markets free of state control.

That battle is being waged today. It will take daring and determination to regain the initiative. This book is about summoning that courage—both socially and governmentally—to overcome political inertia, institutional complacency, and societal fearfulness in the fight for the future of money.

PART I

OPENING LAPS

Chapter 1

Down in the Swaps

If everything seems under control, you're just not going fast enough.
—Mario Andretti (champion auto racer), *Interview with Sam Smith*

Red Light

Thursday, November 6, 2014 (CFTC Headquarters, Washington, DC)

"You cannot speak at SEFCON V."

I looked at my senior legal counsel, Marcia Blase, for a moment and let that sink in.

"What? I thought that we were good to go? What happened?"

SEFCON, which had launched in 2009, was the annual Swap Execution Facility Conference. To many readers that must certainly sound like some obscure Wall Street gathering—and a boring one at that. But it was then the premier industry event focused on the important and growing category of trading platforms—swaps execution

facilities—that were defined and mandated by Title VII of the Dodd–
Frank Act. Dodd–Frank was the landmark financial industry reform legislation passed in the wake of the 2008 crash.[1] (More about this swaps
business momentarily.)

This conference was organized by a trade association I had helped
form a few years before: the Wholesale Markets Brokers Association
Americas (WMBAA). I was a past-chairman of WMBAA, stepping down
in 2013 when the Obama Administration approached me about serving
on the CFTC. Now, as a CFTC commissioner, I had tentatively accepted
an invitation to return to SEFCON to address the audience from my
new perspective as a regulator.

"The White House will not grant you a waiver. They consider it
non-essential. You can't speak at the conference."

Swaps Breakdown

Before I continue the story of SEFCON and the Obama White House,
let's step back to answer a preliminary question: What are derivatives
and swaps?

Though unfamiliar and forbidding terms to some, derivatives and
swaps are nothing less than the foundations of a stable and secure financial system. And, as I will explain later in this book, the advent of derivatives on cryptocurrencies has paved the way for a dramatic expansion
and maturation of crypto as an entirely new investment asset class and
subject of innovative financial services.

Derivatives are tools that transfer risk among willing participants.
They allow an individual or institution with risk they don't like or cannot bear to transfer that risk to someone who's capable of bearing it in
return for some payment. We use this idea all the time in our daily lives.
We constantly "hedge our bets" by offsetting our risk. For example, we
might stretch to buy a condo near the seashore, but hedge our investment by renting it out to people all summer long to get some money
back. We lower the risk of our investment in the condo by sharing it
with others.

History of Derivatives

Investors, farmers, and manufacturers have used derivatives for thousands of years to manage commercial and market risk. The classical philosopher Aristotle describes the Greek mathematician Thales making money off options contracts on olive presses as early as the sixth century BCE.[2] Derivatives allow users to guard against gains or declines in the value of underlying physical or financial assets, such as agricultural commodities, interest rates, stocks, bonds, trading indices, or currencies. They do this without requiring the user to buy or sell the underlying assets. In this sense, derivatives are a form of insurance, but one that does not require the insured to incur a loss in order to recover.

American derivatives markets go back at least to the nineteenth century. The first were agricultural commodity futures markets in cities like New York, Philadelphia, Chicago, St. Louis, New Orleans, and Kansas City. These markets allowed farmers, ranchers, and producers to hedge production costs and delivery prices. That, in turn, helped ensure that American consumers could always find plenty of food on grocery store shelves.

Derivatives markets are one reason why American consumers today enjoy stable prices in all manner of consumer finance, from auto loans to home mortgages. Derivatives markets influence the price and availability of the energy used to heat homes and run factories. They also help set the interest rates borrowers pay on home mortgages and the returns workers earn on their retirement savings. Airlines use derivatives, too. The reason carriers are willing to quote us a fare for a ticket on a flight six months from now is that they are hedging their future fuel costs. The same is true for oil producers and refiners.

Agriculture Futures

Say I am a farmer and I own 444 productive acres—the national average for a family farm. Assume further that I rotate between soybeans and corn, which is common. To keep my farm in business and my bills paid, I need to know a lot. I know my soil and the effects of various weather patterns on my crops. I know what my farmhands cost and what my gasoline costs. I know what my seed costs. I know what my fertilizer costs. What I don't know, though, is what the price is going to be for soybeans come November. So, I add up all the costs for the year—the farmhands, the tractor, the gasoline—and that comes to $6.75 a bushel. But when I go to market, I know from experience that soybean prices could range anywhere from $6.00 to $9.50 per bushel. Those varying prices could spell the difference between windfall profits and bankruptcy.

So how do I transfer that risk to somebody who is willing to bear it? Well, what I can do is enter into a contract on the futures market. I lock in $7.75 a bushel for at least half my production. That way I know that if there is too much supply and bushels are selling at less than my $6.75 cost, I'm going to make at least a dollar more and keep my farm solvent. Of course, I'm giving away some of my upside if the price goes up to $9.50 a bushel. But at least I'll make those profits on the other half of my production. I'm trading risk for certainty.

Global trade also depends on derivatives. Without markets to hedge the risk of fluctuating currency exchange rates, manufacturers and growers would be afraid to accept any currency for their exports other than their own. Without markets to hedge the risk of differing interest rates around the globe, banks and borrowers would be reluctant to transact cross-border loans. Without derivatives, goods, services, and capital would not freely flow across national frontiers. In short, there would be no global marketplace.

Fortunately for the world economy, a handful of true visionaries in Chicago—such as Leo Malamed[3] and Richard Sandor[4]—invented financial futures, swaps, and other derivatives. Fortunately for the United States, these products—so essential to global commerce—are priced in US dollars and remain largely traded in New York and Chicago to this day.

While often derided in the tabloid press as "risky," derivatives—when used properly—are economically and socially beneficial. More than 90% of *Fortune* 500 companies use derivatives to manage global risks of varying production costs, such as the price of raw materials, energy, foreign currency, and interest rates.[5] In this way, derivatives serve the needs of society to help moderate price and supply to free up capital for economic growth, job creation, and prosperity. It has been estimated that the use of commercial derivatives added 1.1% to the size of the US economy between 2003 and 2012.[6]

Derivatives make it easier for Americans and American businesses to participate in the growth of our economy. As battered and bedeviled as the American Dream may be these days, it would truly be a myth without swaps. The reason the standard American homeownership tool is a 30-year fixed rate mortgage is because of derivatives. If you think about it, interest rates are not staying flat for 30 years. Interest rates bounce all over the place. But banks are entering into swaps contracts in order to reduce their interest rate risk so they can offer you that fixed rate. Same deal with five-year loans for auto purchases. In Western developed economies, so much of the price and supply stability that we consumers enjoy is provided by these derivative markets.

When you step into your supermarket, do you ever stop and ask: Oh gosh, was it a good harvest this year? Will I have to pick over a few rotten tomatoes? Will there be any bread on the shelves? You do not. You just wander the aisles filling your shopping cart with an abundance of fresh fruit, vegetables, and produce year in and year out. Well, thank derivatives for that.[7]

In many nations around the world, people *do* experience those concerns. When there are bad harvests and undeveloped and insecure trading markets, not only are the shelves bare—but there may be no food next year because the farmers will have gone bankrupt.

Food for the Future

As of 2014,[8] about 800 million people around the world today were undernourished. That's roughly one in nine of the world's 7.2 billion people—a staggering shortfall. Now consider that there will likely be another two billion people on earth in 30 years.[9] Even if those projections are only half accurate, we will have another one billion people on earth by 2048. How will all of these people be fed?

Clearly, the world's agricultural exporting nations, including the United States, will play a big part in feeding the globe in the decades to come. These food exporters can feed an additional billion people because of the critical support of well-functioning financial and derivatives markets. Efficient and well-regulated derivatives markets serve at least two critical roles in helping to feed the world's growing population. First, they allow markets to resolve imbalances dispassionately and efficiently by providing reliable and fair benchmarks for prices. Second, they reduce price volatility in a resource-constrained world by removing the economic incentive to hoard physical supplies. They allow farmers to quantify and transfer risks they want to avoid at a reasonable price to persons willing and able to hold that risk. They help control costs and facilitate return on capital to support essential investment in farming equipment and agricultural technology necessary to meet increased global food demand. Providing farmers this risk protection reduces earnings volatility and thus price volatility, benefiting everyone, including millions of consumers who have never heard of derivatives markets.

The greatest beneficiaries of global derivatives may well be the world's hungriest and most vulnerable. If derivatives trading were ever to suddenly cease, they would certainly suffer the most from the extreme price volatility in basic food and energy commodities that would result.[10] In developed economies like the United States, we rarely have to worry about such things thanks to two main types of derivatives. The first type are traded on organized exchanges, like the Chicago Mercantile Exchange, and are called futures or options. The second type are traded in a more negotiated process called "over the counter." Many of the latter trades are referred to as "swaps," because two parties agree to exchange cash flows and other financial instruments at specified payment dates during the life of the contract.

I have explained how swaps and other derivatives work so that the reader will later understand their importance in the emergence of Bitcoin and other cryptocurrencies. For now, it's swaps that brings us back to our story.

A Good Long Walk

SEFCON V was set to take place in Manhattan on Wednesday, November 12—just six days after I learned that I would not be permitted to speak there. Hundreds of industry executives and regulators were expected to attend and my colleague CFTC Chairman Tim Massad was giving the luncheon keynote address. I was one of the few Republicans in financial leadership roles who had vocally supported the swaps reforms in Dodd–Frank and, in particular, its mandate that swap transactions occur on CFTC registered swaps execution facilities. I had an important contribution to make to the discussion.

Preventing me from attending was an ethics rule adopted by the Obama administration. It bars senior and cabinet-level administration officials from speaking at events sponsored by a former employer unless said official receives a waiver. The idea is to prevent senior officials from using their government office to benefit a former firm by appearing at that firm's events to drive attendance and admission fees.

I thought I would easily qualify for a waiver. First, I was never a paid employee of the WMBAA, only an unpaid, voluntary board member.

Second, the ethics rule in question, by its terms, applied only to executive branch agencies, not independent agencies like the CFTC. Although I had signed a pledge to comply with the rule because Obama personnel staff had asked me to, the underlying order was never intended to reach officials serving in non-executive branch, independent agencies like the CFTC.

Third, at my request, the WMBAA had not announced my attendance at SEFCON V and, therefore, my appearance could not have boosted paid attendance.

Finally, I was both an outspoken supporter of the Dodd–Frank reforms that created the SEF rules and one of the most knowledgeable government officials available to address the industry.

Still, I had signed the waiver, I was relatively new to my post, and once the White House says no, it is exhausting to find the relevant official and make an appeal on short notice. We needed a workaround.

I called my staff together, including my cautious and savvy chief of staff, Jason Goggins; legal counsel, Amir Zaidi; and senior legal counsel, Marcia Blase. Ever meticulous, Marcia explained how several weeks before she had inquired about obtaining a White House waiver with the CFTC's Chief Ethics Officer, a former Obama administration lawyer who had helped craft the pledge itself. That lawyer had seemed optimistic about getting the waiver, according to Marcia, but now, with four business days to go, the White House had surprised us with a "no."

My staff was upset. Jason, especially, was spoiling for a fight. He wanted to challenge the CFTC Ethics Officer by demanding written confirmation of the White House denial. Marcia recounted her conversation with the ethics lawyer. My head hurt. I needed to take my own counsel. I said I would step out, get a sandwich, and that we should reconvene in an hour.

I strode through the hall of the CFTC's ninth-floor executive suite past the black-and-white photos of a dozen former agency chairs and then, further down the hall, past the living color photos of the current commissioners. I rode the elevator down to the red marbled lobby of the CFTC headquarters and walked past the uniformed security guards before the large etched-glass CFTC seal. I exited the building onto 21st Street in Northwest Washington—an area north of Foggy Bottom and south of Dupont Circle.

Returning to a lifelong habit of peripatetic processing of important information, I began to walk fast. I headed north on 21st Street across New Hampshire Avenue. The neighborhood quickly changed from modern rectilinear glass office blocks to hexagonally flared, flower-boxed

Victorian residences. I paced onward toward Massachusetts Avenue and turned left on Embassy Row. I walked past the Cosmos Club,[11] where I had lived for six weeks the summer before while looking for an apartment.

I saw no upside to wasting time trying to reverse the denial of the waiver. The issue was how to deliver my message. The speech was ready. It was good, and it was important. It would be my first major speech on US soil as a CFTC Commissioner. It was an important opportunity to define myself and my agenda to a critical audience of peers in the New York financial community. I intended to reiterate my pro-reform credentials as a supporter of the swaps trading provisions of Title VII of the Dodd–Frank Act. At the same time, I planned to criticize the CFTC's peculiar implementation of certain of those provisions.

As I turned right, past the bright magenta-flowered myrtle trees of the Cosmos Club garden, and walked up Florida Avenue, I reflected on the fact that I may have been one of the most long-standing advocates of swaps market reform from either political party to serve as a CFTC commissioner.[12] In 2000, when I first left New York law practice and entered the swaps industry, I was struck by the fact that, unlike in most overseas trading markets, swaps brokerage was not a regulated activity. This omission hurt the professionalism of US swaps markets compared to overseas markets, in my view.

Not long after, I became a supporter of what's known as "central counterparty clearing" of swaps—that is, the practice in which a central party acts as an intermediary between buyers and sellers. In many derivatives markets, for instance, a clearinghouse serves this role, acting as the buyer to every seller and the seller to every buyer. The clearinghouse also ensures that the parties honor their contractual obligations over time.

I had seen firsthand how the emergence of central clearing in the energy swaps market increased trading liquidity and market participation. Before the financial crisis, I had led an effort at a brokerage called GFI Group to develop a central counterparty clearing facility for credit default swaps. That initiative led to the formation of IceClear Credit, which today is the world's leading clearer of those products.

I also was a supporter of greater swaps transparency. My experience from the 2008 financial crisis was that financial regulators lacked visibility into the risk that large financial institutions could fail due to inability to pay their financial obligations. Undoubtedly, swaps and other derivatives contributed to the financial crisis through the writing of credit default swaps protection by the giant insurance company American International Group, known as AIG. An equal or greater contribution came from the opacity of another complex product—not a derivative—that made its way onto bank balance sheets: collateralized mortgage obligations. While some derivatives transactions had come to be centrally recorded, what was missing was reliable information for both regulators and the marketplace about the true value and risk of these instruments. Government authorities simply did not have sufficient data to accurately assess the implications of the potential failure of a Bear Stearns, Lehman Brothers or AIG on derivatives counterparties throughout the financial system. They had little ability to assess the true danger—short of telephone calls in the middle of the crisis to specialized firms like GFI, where I was working at the time. That was just not good enough.

So, by the time Congress began drafting the bills that would become Title VII of the Dodd–Frank Act, I was already a vocal advocate for its three key pillars of swaps market reform: regulated swaps execution, central counterparty clearing, and enhanced swaps transparency through data reporting. As a Republican, my support for Dodd–Frank's swaps provisions made me a maverick in my party, which had mostly opposed the legislation. Yet, as a businessperson, I believe that intelligently regulated markets are good for the economy and job creation. My support for parts of Dodd–Frank was driven by my professional and commercial experience, not academic theory or political ideology. These particular swaps reforms were organic and not terribly radical.[13] Market participants were already at work on two of them—without government urging—when the crisis hit. Completing all three reforms correctly was the right thing to do. That is why I supported swaps market reform.

Generally, in the American system, after Congress passes a law requiring new regulation by a federal agency, the agency designs and implements the rules. That gives regulators a lot of clout. No matter how good a law sounds on paper, whether it actually improves anything hinges on how the regulations implementing it are drafted. The devil is in the details.

In a remarkably short time after the passage of Dodd–Frank in 2010, the CFTC implemented most of its mandates. By the time I joined the

Commission in 2014, the CFTC under its then chairman, the trenchant Gary Gensler (today chairman of the Securities and Exchange Commission), had already effectuated most of the swaps reforms, far faster than any other regulator in the United States or abroad. In particular, its implementation of the swaps clearing mandate was highly effective, significantly increasing the volume of transactions cleared through clearinghouses.[14] Chairman Gensler and his fellow CFTC commissioners and staff deserve enormous credit for this remarkable achievement.

The CFTC also moved quickly to cause swaps transactions to be reported to swaps data repositories, referred to as SDRs.[15] Yet despite these sound steps, the establishment of global standards for categorizing swaps trades was assigned to intergovernmental bureaucracies, rather than to bodies made up of swaps counterparties themselves. That was a misstep. The process of developing standards took on a life of its own. While important work was done, a decade after the financial crisis SDRs still could not provide regulators with a complete and accurate picture of the true risk of failure of a large swaps dealer in global markets.

The CFTC's least successful implementation of swaps reform, in my view, related to the trading and execution of swaps. In Dodd–Frank, Congress laid out a fairly simple and flexible framework for trading swaps. It required certain swaps to trade on regulated platforms called "swaps execution facilities" (SEFs). Congress defined these SEFs as trading systems or platforms "in which multiple participants (can) execute or trade swaps by accepting bids and offers made by other participants that are open to multiple participants in the facility or system, through any means of interstate commerce." The key phrase is "any means of interstate commerce," a phrase with a rich constitutional history, which US federal courts have interpreted to cover almost an unlimited range of commercial and technological enterprise, including those conducted over the telephone.[16]

As I would explain at length in my upcoming white paper, Congress had expressly permitted SEFs to offer various flexible execution methods for swaps execution. Unfortunately, in carrying out this mandate, the CFTC—improperly in my view—attempted to re-engineer swaps market structure by limiting methods of transacting. It grafted onto its SEF rules a number of market practices borrowed from exchange-traded futures markets. That was the wrong model and resulted in an overly complex and highly prescriptive contraption that was not only bad policy but inconsistent with the language of the law.

In my speech, I intended to say that Congress got much of Title VII of Dodd–Frank right. It had laid out a straightforward and flexible swaps trading regulatory framework well suited to the episodic nature of swaps liquidity and swaps market dynamics. I would also say that, in my view, the CFTC's implementation of the swaps trading rules missed the congressional mark. I planned to explain that over the past two decades the swaps market had grown organically into a global market serving important commercial needs and it needed a set of rules that worked for its unique niche. The speech would announce that I would be issuing a white paper analyzing the mismatch between the CFTC's swaps regulatory framework and the inherent dynamics of global swaps markets. I'd also be describing the adverse consequences that had already resulted.[17] The paper would propose a comprehensive, better-suited approach to regulating swaps trading.[18]

Now, as I turned back south onto Connecticut Avenue and headed for Dupont Circle, I wondered: Was I being denied a waiver to speak at SEFCON V because of my likely criticism of the CFTC and, by implication, the Obama White House? Was I being denied the right to speak, not because of where I was speaking, but because of what I might say?

If so, the denial was wrong. I had a right to speak that the White House should not have denied. I had every right to call it as I saw it. And, after 14 years in the swaps industry and 16 years practicing business and finance law in New York and London, I knew what I was talking about.

Lemons into Lemonade

Cutting across Dupont Circle past its grand marble fountain, I reached a decision. Okay, I could not give a speech at SEFCON. That did not mean I could not give a speech. The First Amendment was still intact. I would give the speech, just not at SEFCON.

I ducked into a deli and grabbed a sandwich and a lemonade. I then turned south onto New Hampshire Avenue and walked 300 more yards to 21st Street and the CFTC offices. I greeted the security detail, tapped my electronic card to open the double turnstiles, and then rode the elevator back to the ninth-floor office suite.

Back at my desk, I called the staff together, unwrapped my sandwich, and laid out my plan.

"I'm going to give the speech . . . just not at SEFCON.

"We'll explain right up front that I intended to give it at the conference, but that the White House denied a waiver to speak. We'll release the speech to the press and post it on the CFTC website on the morning of the conference.

And so we got to work. We revised the speech to address a lay audience and set it to be released the evening before the conference. We also provided an advance copy to a business reporter, Katy Burne of the *Journal*, whom I knew from my years in the industry. I knew that she would cover the substance of my remarks from a business perspective, not from the usual political winners–and–losers viewpoint of the inside-the-beltway media. In the middle of these preparations, the *Financial Times* informed us that they were about to publish an op-ed that I had submitted several weeks before touching on some of the same issues.

With our plan in place, I headed up to Philadelphia for college parents' weekend with our elder son and then to our home in New Jersey. On Monday, I crossed the Hudson River by ferry to the CFTC's office on Broadway in downtown Manhattan. I rode the elevator to the 19th floor and greeted the helpful receptionist. Fishing out my keys, I unlocked the door to a simple but comfortable office, set down my briefcase, sipped a coffee and logged onto a computer. Scrolling through the morning's emails, briefings, and press clippings I was delighted to see that the FT had published my piece. Here are a few key passages:

> "In 2009, world leaders in Pittsburgh pledged to better regulate emergent global swaps markets through the co-ordinated efforts of national and supranational regulators.
>
> "Five years later, global co-ordination is not going well. Instead of collaborating with foreign regulators, the US Commodity Futures Trading Commission (CFTC) developed swaps 'transaction level' rules based on the wrong template of the structure of the US futures markets. . .

"To maintain healthy global markets, we must regulate swaps execution and clearing in a well-crafted and harmonious manner across jurisdictions."[19]

Later that afternoon, I got on the telephone with Katy Burne of the *The Wall Street Journal* and answered several questions she had about my speech. She also asked me about the White House's refusal of the waiver. I told her that I declined to question the White House's decision, but that she was free to make her own inquiries.

The following evening as the organizers of SEFCONV were setting up their podium and exhibition hall at the Grand Hyatt Hotel on 42nd Street and Lexington Avenue, Katy's story ran. She nailed it.

"A top U.S. regulator said new rules governing the multitrillion-dollar derivatives markets are sending swaps trading overseas, threatening Wall Street jobs and potentially destabilizing financial markets.

"In remarks he intended to deliver at an industry conference this week, J. Christopher Giancarlo, the lone Republican among four commissioners at the Commodity Futures Trading Commission, said the agency's rules have split the swaps market into domestic and foreign niches, as non-U.S. firms seek to avoid CFTC oversight.

"Mr. Giancarlo said he had planned to deliver the remarks Wednesday at a conference in New York. He said he withdrew after unsuccessfully seeking a waiver of government ethics rules that view his past work with swaps brokerage firms as a conflict. CFTC Chairman Timothy Massad is scheduled to deliver the keynote speech at the conference Wednesday.

"Mr. Giancarlo has long been a critic of the implementation of CFTC swaps-trading rules, though he backs mandates for overhauling the swaps market in general, including the requirement that many be processed through clearinghouses, which guarantee trades. New clearing and data-reporting rules for swaps were well-crafted and are meeting their objectives, he said."[20]

Meeting in a Tower

The next morning, I was in Manhattan early for a series of meetings with market participants at several trading firms and brokerages.

I intended to understand firsthand how the new swaps trading and bank capital rules were impacting trading markets. My day began with an 8:30 a.m. breakfast meeting at Goldman Sachs. Other meetings at other firms would take me late into the evening.

My chief of staff, Jason Goggins, and I announced ourselves in the lobby of the state-of-the-art, yet deliberately unostentatious office tower of Goldman Sachs on West Street in the World Financial Center. The Goldman name was barely present on the ground floor where we were greeted warmly by one of the firm's understated government relations executives. He led us up to a large conference room filled with an assortment of the firm's derivatives traders, business managers, and regulatory compliance officers. They went around the table, introducing themselves. I asked the group to tell me how the new rules were working and what impact they had, if any, on the firm's ability to serve its clients. The repeated answer was that the rules were causing the firm to cut back service to its smaller customers. I ran through some ideas for proposed rule changes, which they seemed to support. I wondered whether they would continue to support changes once they mastered the complexity of the current rules and built the systems necessary to deal with them.

Following the meeting, Jason and I were escorted up to the serene executive floor with a panoramic view across the Hudson River to New Jersey. There we met Goldman's President, Gary Cohn. I knew Cohn from my time at GFI when Goldman was an important client and he was our primary point of contact. Well informed and voluble, Cohn was a straight shooter in the hard elbows arena of interdealer trading. He was also fair-minded, though never to the detriment of his firm.[21]

Cohn invited me to get comfortable on his low-lying sofa with a cup of fresh coffee. He had read the piece in the *Journal*. He elaborated on the theme that I had just discussed with his managers, that the impact of not only CFTC regulation, but the whole panoply of rules and regulations imposed by Dodd–Frank, the G-20 Financial Stability Board (FSB), the US Federal Reserve Board, and US Financial Stability Oversight Council (FSOC) was to cause Goldman and its competitors to reserve cash rather than putting it to work on behalf of clients. As a result, Goldman would offer its limited resources more selectively to its best and largest clients. It was another incidence of ill-crafted regulation helping big companies over small ones.

I left Cohn's executive suite and headed to meetings with other New York swaps trading firms. I had no way of knowing that in just a few years Gary Cohn would play a key role in my career trajectory.

Meanwhile, I received word from a number of attendees at SEFCON that my speech and the announcement of the white paper were causing quite a stir. Undoubtedly, the White House's waiver denial ensured that the speech that was not given at SEFCON received far more attention than it would have garnered if it had been given from the SEFCON podium.

Thank you, CFTC Office of General Counsel and, maybe, the White House. As a junior commissioner, I could not possibly have received that much attention without your help.

Chapter 2

Starting Grid

I think this is the greatest and best country in all the world, with its great sunlit spaces and its long long roads, and best of all the roads that are not made yet, and the stories that no one has told because they are too busy living them.
—Nellie McClung (author and social activist), *In Times Like These*

Moving on Up

So exactly how did I find myself in November 2014 tangling with the White House for permission to speak at a New York business conference? Well, it came about because five months before in June 2014 I had become the newest of five commissioners of the US Commodity Futures Trading Commission. The faraway journey that brought me there is a unique story in its own right.

There is a road in New Jersey that embodies the American experience and my own. Bloomfield Avenue stretches northwesterly away from Newark's gritty asphalt to the lush Watchung Mountains. Laid out in the early 1800s, Bloomfield Avenue was New Jersey's first county road. It arcs across Essex County, linking a series of towns metamorphosing from urban streets peopled by newly arrived immigrants to manicured lawns gracing mansions housing descendants of the Pilgrims.

Bloomfield Avenue also arcs across my family's history. In the first decade of the twentieth century, my father's maternal grandparents, Loretto Onorio Greco and his wife, Maria Louisa, left the *Valle di Comino* in the central Italian region of *Lazio*. They traveled first to Paris and then across the Atlantic and much of the North American continent to the coal mines of Pictou, west of Walsenberg, Colorado. There they gave birth in 1909 to my grandmother, Fiorina, the second child of nine. Eventually the Greco family made its way to Newark's First Ward—then one of the largest Italian immigrant communities in the United States. There Onorio became prosperous as a property developer before returning to Italy.

While in Newark, the teenage Fiorina met my grandfather, Celestino Fortunato Giancarlo, known as Charlie. He was born in 1903 in Lucca in the Tuscany region of Italy. His parents were itinerant laborers who would journey north each spring to work in northern European cities, mostly as masons and gardeners. Charlie's mother died when he was 12, forcing him to leave school for work. As a result, he never formally learned to read or write. His father remarried an Italian woman living in Paris named D'Agostino and started a new family. In 1921, at age 18, my grandfather and his older brother caught a ship out of Cherbourg for America, where they set to work as laborers in Newark. He never saw his father again.

In America, Grandpa Charlie worked hard and rose to be foreman of one of the Irish run construction crews that built Newark during its heyday in the 1920s. Losing his job in the Depression, he labored by day as a brickmason and by night as a watchman at Newark's Budweiser brewery. He remained in building construction the rest of his life.

Grandpa Charlie's only child, my father, was born in Newark's First Ward in 1931 and baptized at St. Lucy's Catholic Church, the community's spiritual center. The church is but a few hundred yards from the start of Bloomfield Avenue as it departs Newark. In the early 1940s, Grandpa Charlie followed the avenue to its first stop, Bloomfield

Township, where he purchased a newly constructed, two-story, wood-frame house along with the adjoining lot. There he planted tomato plants and fig and cherry trees. He was satisfied in that house and never lived anywhere else.

Grandpa Charlie exemplified hard work, honesty, and no bullshit. He was a bit rough, but straightforward and loving. He was constant and clear where he stood. He didn't say a lot, but what he said was right. In his mind, a person does what he has to do without complaining or expecting a leg up.

My father, born Ettore Giancarlo, was far more ambitious. His gaze was much farther up the road. He and my grandmother spent his first years in the provincial town of Sora, Italy, with her prosperous parents and younger siblings. My father was the first grandchild and enjoyed attentive affection. He returned to New Jersey with my grandmother before the Second World War, when he changed his name to its English translation, Hector. As the war ended, he was a high school cadet at La Salle Military Academy, a boarding school on Long Island. He developed into an excellent rifleman and a concert quality violinist. He had good looks and charm and craved excitement, especially the thrill of fast cars that he hoped to afford one day. His marksmanship made him popular, his musical virtuosity got him a college scholarship, and his smile and vitality enthralled more than a few girls, including my (very attractive) mother.

My mother's sights were also set up the road, much farther along Bloomfield Avenue. She was born Ella Jane Schwarz, the year after my father was born. Like him, her ancestors were immigrants, but of a more educated class. Her paternal grandparents were upright and Germanized Poles, who immigrated to Berlin in the 1800s. Her great-grandfather, Josef Alfons Schwarz, taught pharmacology in the 1850s at the city's renowned Humboldt University. His son Wladyslaw, called Walter, emigrated first to Brooklyn and then Jersey City, where he opened a pharmacy. His first child, Berthold, was born in 1898. Four years later, Walter graduated as a physician from Eclectic Medical College of New York City and saw the birth of his second son, Henry, my grandfather.

Both Schwarz brothers followed their father into medicine. In the case of my grandfather Henry, it was by way of Fordham University and Eclectic Medical College, in Cincinnati, Ohio. There in the 1920s,

Henry met and married my grandmother, Florence Klinkenberg, the daughter of a prosperous Ohio building supplier and his Irish-born wife, Ella. The couple soon returned to New Jersey, living in the apartment above his suburban medical practice on what was then called Hudson Boulevard. There, he and Florence had two children, Henry Jr. and my mother, Ella Jane. Like my grandfather Charlie, Henry was hardworking, modest, and content.

Meanwhile, Henry's older brother Berthold established his office in the center of Journal Square, Jersey City's fashionable downtown. Alongside his medical practice, Berthold served as a part-time health director for Bankers National Life Insurance Company, then one of the largest American health and accident insurers. In time, he rose to be executive vice president. Although somewhat unmindful of his medical practice, Berthold Schwarz turned out to be a brilliant financial investor and portfolio manager. His family became one of New Jersey's most prominent, with a box at New York's Metropolitan Opera House and a sprawling home in tony Upper Montclair that my mother would some-times visit and admire. It was a far distance up Bloomfield Avenue.

While different in means, the Schwarz brothers were alike in patri-otism. After Pearl Harbor, Berthold's two sons left medical school to enlist in the US military. Not long after deployment near Bastogne, Belgium, Berthold's younger son died fighting in the Battle of the Bulge.

My grandfather Henry, just turned 40, enlisted in the US Army Air Corps. He had been a teenager during the First World War and recalled his father treating American doughboys in quarantine for the Spanish Influenza before shipping out of Jersey City. Now, as a new World War began, Henry was an experienced physician, familiar with the infectious diseases that plagued city residents. He was eventually commissioned a captain and appointed medical commandant at a series of North American training bases, overseeing health conditions. He served a year at Daniel Field near Augusta, Georgia, and was then assigned to Fort Thomas, across the Ohio River from Cincinnati. He brought with him his wife and children and installed them in great-grandma Ella's spacious house in the suburb of Hyde Park, where he visited on weekends. As the war ended, Henry returned to New Jersey with his family, having retired from the Corps with the rank of Major, an honor he held with pride the rest of his life.

My mother and father were introduced by high school friends a few years after the war. Hector was young and brash, heading to Manhattan College and thinking about medical school. Ella was determined and set on nursing. She would go on to Columbia Teacher's College to receive her bachelor's degree in nursing. The couple dated throughout college.

Hector took advantage of his language fluency and the post-war strength of the US dollar to enroll in Italy's fine but inexpensive medical school at the University of Padua, one of the world's oldest. In December 1954, while returning home for Christmas, his flight from Rome descended into New York's Idlewild Airport, rammed into a pier, burst into flames, and hurtled into the waters of Jamaica Bay. Twenty-six passengers died. Miraculously, my father escaped the submerging aircraft and swam to shore, one of only six survivors, His carefree days were at an end.

Soon my parents were married, taking up residence in Italy. During school breaks they skied in Cortina, saw the follies in Paris, stood in the stalls at *La Scala,* and visited my father's cousins in Terracina, on the Mediterranean. They acquired a series of European sports cars and survived my father's participation in the famous Italian auto rally, the *Mille Miglia.*

In 1957, their first child was born, Charles Henry, named after our two grandfathers. Hector graduated from medical school the following spring and returned to New Jersey. There, in 1959, I was born.

My father's medical career thrived. He did his residency in general surgery and otolaryngology at the renowned New York Eye and Ear Infirmary. He was inquisitive about everyone and everything, ideal for the halcyon days of the early 1960s in New York, when the city was a global center for medical innovation. He created operating room procedures that had never been done before. He experimented with new medical technologies. He introduced ultrasound, which he had encountered in Italy, into American surgical practice. He was fearless, engrossed, energetic, and brilliant. He relished being a doctor.

On the west side of the Hudson, Hector first joined and then took over Uncle Berthold's Jersey City medical practice. Like his father and father-in-law, he was self-employed and entrepreneurial. His surgical innovations attracted attention, his practice boomed, and, in the late 1960s, he and my mother launched a successful skilled nursing facility in northern New Jersey in a new building constructed by my grandfather, Charlie.

My parents then moved up the metaphorical road—though not literally, west on Bloomfield Avenue this time. That would have taken them too far from the buzz of Manhattan. Instead, they headed north along the Hudson river to a town a lot like Upper Montclair, the East Hill neighborhood of Englewood.

While my father was building his medical practice and with my brother and me as preschoolers, my mother returned to Columbia University to earn a master's degree. After bearing two more sons, Michael and Timothy, she ran the burgeoning private nursing home facility. Still, she always seemed to have time for her four boys. On Monday through Friday, she was up early in pumps and pearls. Yet on Saturdays she'd teach us to punt a football, bodysurf a wave, or even drop a water ski and slalom.

Together, my parents were a force. They were each determined, strong, and stubborn. It was as if their unshakable will, by itself, could make things happen. And it did. In all kinds of ways. They were a force in the minds of their sons. We were expected to lead lives of achievement, self-reliance, and dignity. But each of my parents' willfulness also caused turmoil in their marriage, which began to rupture. First gradually, and then precipitously.

Groovin'

For me, the 1960s began as soon as I could stand on two feet and take a good look around. I liked what I saw. My world seemed colorful, melodic, and good. After school, we played football, stickball, and basketball in the backyards and driveways of our leafy, 10-block neighborhood until my mother's loud whistle called us home for dinner. Most everything we touched or ate was made well and produced domestically, indeed locally. Many of our clothes were sewn in New York's garment district, televisions made in Trenton, furniture crafted in Connecticut, vegetables grown on New Jersey farms, meat butchered in town. My grandfathers, Charlie and Henry, drove cars made in Detroit: Cadillacs and Buicks, respectively. They were solidly built, and just as finely made as the Mercedes that my European-styled father drove. In fact, my dad's Mercedes looked rather pedestrian compared to their cars. Theirs were aspirational. The tail fins on Grandpa Charlie's 1962 Sedan DeVille made it appear as if it could take off and fly. The tiny tail bumps on Dad's Mercedes made you wonder how it ever got across the Atlantic.

I respected the cultivation and the language facility of my European aunts, uncles, and cousins—whom we visited some summers—and the many French, Italian, and Hungarian doctors who attended my parents' dinner parties. Yet, I preferred American things—especially football, rock 'n' roll, the Jersey Shore, the New York World's Fair, the Apollo space program, and muscle cars—all of which seemed to express the future's limitless possibility.

We went to a cheerful Catholic elementary school. We were fortunate to attend junior and senior high at the nondenominational Dwight-Englewood School, a fine private college "prep" school that assiduously set out a broad framework for how to think rather than imposing a narrow worldview of what to think. I respected and somewhat envied my older brother, Charlie, who seemed to win every academic award Dwight-Englewood bestowed. Unlike me, he was kind, easygoing, athletic, and wickedly smart. Like my dad, he loved gadgets, spending days at a time constructing electronic devices, even TVs and early computers. Unlike him, I played electric guitar, wore my hair long, and got into some trouble. A few times, Charlie got me out. I was probably less helpful than he was to our good-natured younger brothers, Mike and Tim.

I attended Skidmore College in picturesque Saratoga Springs, New York. There, under the guidance of some exceptional professors, I experienced a time of personal satisfaction and accomplishment. During my junior year, almost 21, I took an academic leave of absence, got a basement flat in London, and worked as a researcher for Sir Ronald Bell, a member of the House of Commons. It was during Margaret Thatcher's first term as prime minister. I was drawn to her unabashed advocacy for entrepreneurship, civil society, individual initiative, and anti-Communism. I admired her unapologetic rejection of the British welfare state, high taxes, industrial policy, and detente with the Soviet Union.

One evening, I was invited to meet Mrs. Thatcher with a dozen or so other young Americans working in Westminster. We gathered in the magnificent, crystal-chandeliered Pugin Room in the Palace of Westminster overlooking the Thames. As twilight warmed the windows, Mrs. Thatcher engaged us with her quick wit and enthusiasm. She described human liberty and free market capitalism as the essential foundation for achievement of humankind's greatest aspirations. She explained how government control and statism stymied limits on personal growth and societal advancement. Though it lasted less than 40 minutes, the meeting made a lifelong impression.

After graduation, I spent three years in Nashville, Tennessee, mostly living with two buddies in a ramshackle apartment building adjacent to Centennial Park. I studied law at Vanderbilt University during the week and listened to country music in bars on weekends. In September 1984, I began work on Wall Street as a first-year associate lawyer at the prominent law firm of Mudge Rose Alexander and Ferdon, where Richard Nixon had once been a partner. I had accepted the offer to train as a corporate lawyer, but, after nine months, I was still spending six days a week drafting municipal bond indentures. I left for an even more venerable New York City practice, Curtis Mallet-Prevost, Colt & Mosle.

Joining Curtis Mallet proved an important move. And not just for my career. The same week I started, so did a comic and kindhearted woman who caught my eye. Regina Beyel, from Long Island's Suffolk County, worked evenings as a floor secretary at the firm to earn tuition at New York's Hunter College, where she was studying to be a teacher. As a young associate I worked a lot of late nights—even when it wasn't necessary, as I gradually fell in love with Regina. In the fall of 1988, while we were dating, the firm asked me to do an extended stint in London. They pressed me for a quick answer and a start date. So I took courage and proposed, but with the caveat that a "yes" meant moving abroad. Regina said yes to both marriage and what turned out to be a three-year European honeymoon.

Returning to London was wonderful. We rented a one-bedroom flat just off Kensington High Street, made friends, threw dinner parties, traveled throughout the British Isles and on the Continent and, during England's damp winters, lay by the fireplace to stay warm. In its glow, our marriage was forged.

Dot-Com

In London in the early 1990s, I started a new program for the firm. Called "An Entrepreneur's Guide to Doing Business in the U.S.," it was targeted at British tech startups. My law practice grew.

In a few years, Regina and I moved back to the United States. With her encouragement, I stepped down from Curtis Mallet and launched a boutique law practice representing European emerging technology companies. With my good friend Paul Gleiberman—a brilliant lawyer—Giancarlo & Gleiberman grew rapidly to 14 lawyers, with offices in New York and Washington.

Regina and I then started our family. Within a space of four years, Emma, Luke, and Henry were born. At the firm, Regina did the billing and bookkeeping. She'd bring our babies with her and let them sleep in drawers pulled out of file cabinets. Our client numbers increased. We moved on up the road, acquiring a ramshackle, shingle style 1897 Victorian house in a quiet neighborhood in northern Bergen county. The house had no insulation, air conditioning, finished basement or garage, but it had charm. We set about repairing and restoring it room by room. Whatever it lacked, it had an abundance of children's laughter, hearty Sunday suppers, and a warm welcome to every visitor.

The 1997–2000 Internet bubble was then inflating. To handle the enormous workload, I merged my New York practice into Brown Raysman, a trailblazing, tech-focused law firm started by the innovative Peter Brown and Richard Raysman. With their support, I cofounded the first ever legal journal of online financial trading.[1]

Not long afterward, I represented a group of investors led by Michael Adam, a brilliant pioneer of automated market trading.[2] I advised them in acquiring Fenics, then and now, a widely used tool to price and trade currency options. In early 2000, Fenics retained a large investment bank to conduct its initial public offering in London. Again with Regina's encouragement, I took a leave of absence from Brown Raysman to manage the IPO. I found a flat in London and immediately went to work. The stock market was approaching a historic high. It was a frantic period, with weekdays spent in London and weekends in New Jersey.

Suddenly, alas, it was over. On April 14, 2000, US stocks plummeted 9%, capping off five days of stunning losses that handed the Nasdaq composite index a 25% loss, its then worst weekly performance ever. The Dow Jones industrial average also tumbled, trouncing the previous record one-day percentage drop and triggering circuit breakers at the New York Stock Exchange. The dot-com bubble had burst. A few days later, Fenics' IPO was shelved. I returned to the United States to assist the investors in a sale of the company. I had taken a chance and it had failed.

In fact, it turned out for the best. The buyer of Fenics was GFI Group, an "interdealer broker," which is a type of institutional agent that operates marketplaces for wholesale trading by the largest banks and financial institutions. Interdealer brokers, or IDBs, as they are known, were the precursors to SEFs that Congress recognized in Dodd–Frank. GFI Group specialized in brokering a type of derivative financial instrument called a swap. Swaps, as I mentioned earlier, do not trade on recognized exchanges, but rather on private, managed trading networks of the kind operated by GFI Group.

I immediately hit it off with GFI's brilliant founder, Mickey Gooch. He encouraged me to stay on and implement his vision of highly efficient marketplaces for financial institutions melding skilled professional brokers with market data, software analytics, and automated trade execution. I accepted.

As GFI's head of corporate development, I helped raise several rounds of private equity. With the proceeds, we opened additional offices in financial centers around the world and built some of the first electronic platforms for trading swaps. We also invested in the former Chicago Board of Trade Clearing Corporation and helped convert it into the first clearinghouse for credit default swaps, or CDS. In time, GFI grew into the world's largest trading platform for CDS products and other over-the-counter derivatives.

GFI's offices were then at 100 Wall Street. One summer day not long after joining the firm, I was returning from lunch when I came across a crowd in front of our building. At its center was a young man dancing wildly. I chuckled and went up to the office. Coming out of the elevator, I saw many of the brokers looking out the window and laughing at the young dancer. Someone explained to me that he was a GFI trainee serving a half hour's punishment for having screwed up a lunch order. When the dancer returned later, he was teased mightily. Someone shouted, "What a waste of a Wharton education!"

I was surprised at the hazing. I relayed the story to Gooch, who said that, rather than being a random bit of unpleasantness, what took place was an important part of the young man's training. Successful broking—the shorthand term for what brokers do—required individuals to remember for short periods of time discrete sets of random pricing data segmented by individual customers. Because the financial consequence of getting such pricing wrong could be enormous, prospective brokers had to develop memory skills away from the desk. Thus, trainee brokers listened to and recorded transactions for months before actually handling a trade. They also were required to take lunch orders that were made deliberately complicated. They were crazy things, like:

> "I'll have a ham sandwich on whole wheat with two pickles, no lettuce,
> but olive paste on one slice of bread and honey mustard on the other
> and three oranges. No, make that two oranges and hold the
> honey mustard!"

Gooch explained that the trainee would get 12 such orders at once and, if he screwed up just one, the consequence was a half hour dancing on the corner or some other ridiculous embarrassment that they would never forget. Once the trainee could handle a lunch order with tens of dollars at stake, he could begin to undertake more sensitive work with millions of dollars at stake.

In 2005, I directed GFI's highly successful initial public offering (IPO). The next year, we conducted our secondary offering and completed a major acquisition. By 2008, GFI had grown to 18 offices around the world and was generating record revenue. We operated the trading platforms on which most of the world's credit default swaps were traded.

Then the 2008 financial crisis hit. Panic had been building steadily in financial markets since the demise of Bear Stearns that March. A double bubble had burst of housing prices and consumer credit, as lenders became concerned that falling residential and commercial property values would imperil repayment of mortgages. An extraordinary "run on the bank" ensued with rapidly falling asset values preventing US and overseas lenders from meeting their cash obligations. That marked the beginning of a financial crisis that was devastating for far too many businesses and families.[3]

On Wall Street, concern was rife about imminent failure of the world's largest investment and commercial banks. Tension was rising on our broking floor as summer waned and our front office staff worked under greater stress to maintain orderly markets. Mortgage companies Fannie Mae and Freddie Mac were placed under federal conservatorship to the tune of $187 billion and the Fed lent over $180 billion to bail out AIG. The storm was upon us and GFI was at its center.

In early September, a senior official at the New York Federal Reserve Bank called us. He was asking about the CDS trading exposure of several major banks, including Lehman Brothers. By then, trading conditions were deteriorating by the hour. It became clear that the regulator had little means, short of frantic telephone calls to firms like ours, to read all the danger signals that derivatives trading markets, especially CDS markets, were broadcasting.

In late September, Treasury Secretary Henry Paulson and Fed Chair Ben Bernanke submitted a $700 billion bailout package to Congress to stave off almost certain collapse of the global financial system. Yet, the damage had been done. The United States and, indeed, the world were entering the Great Recession, the worse financial calamity since the Great Depression eight decades earlier.

In 2009, the G-20 governments met in Washington and later in Pittsburgh to formulate a collective response to the crisis. Among the many steps proposed were reforms for swaps markets. These included moving bilaterally cleared swaps into central counterparty clearinghouses, increasing counterparty risk transparency, and executing swap transactions on regulated platforms.

As I've said, these were appropriate reforms. Indeed, the first two were innovations toward which the market was already moving on its own, while the third one just made common sense.

Speaking with my GFI colleagues, I argued that these reforms were not only inevitable, but they also would be good for financial swaps markets. I was concerned, however, that clumsy enactment and implementation of these reforms could minimize their benefits. It was essential that the interdealer brokers be heard as the legislation was crafted and implemented.

With the keen support of Gooch and GFI's savvy CEO, Colin Heffron, I organized a government relations effort for the firm in the summer and autumn of 2009. I hired a well-regarded Washington lawyer, Mike Gill, and made several trips to Washington to meet with members of key House and Senate committees on financial services and agriculture. It did not take me long to come to the view that individual action by GFI and each of its interdealer broker competitors would be inefficient or worse. A better course would be collective action by the five largest firms (or "the five families," as we sometimes jokingly called ourselves). We decided to form a US trade association: the Wholesale Markets Brokers Association Americas (WMBAA).[4]

WMBAA launched over lunch in late 2009 at a private dining club in the historic India House on Hanover Square, just off Wall Street. Chris Ferreri, a seasoned executive with natural presence and command, was voted the first president. Serving with Ferreri on the board were Bill Shields, GFI's sharp-eyed chief of compliance; Julian Harding, a smart, cultured and elegant Brit who had founded one of the first electronic foreign-exchange options brokerages; Sean Bernardo, a Jersey boy who was smart to the ways of Wall Street; Steve Merkel, a demanding and brilliant lawyer; and me. Our Washington guide and counselor was Micah Green,[5] whose charm, self-confidence, and determination would open many doors. The WMBAA was thus born.

And not a moment too soon. The Barney Frank–chaired House Financial Services Committee was moving fast with a bill that would eventually make its way into the Dodd–Frank Act. A section of the bill that would become Title VII dealt with swaps products. It contained four operative mandates: registration of swaps dealers and major swap participants, channeling of more bilateral swaps transactions into central counterparty clearinghouses, increasing counterparty risk transparency, and execution of swap transactions on regulated platforms.

Over the winter and spring of 2010, our merry band discussed the draft legislation in countless calls and trips to Washington. I testified before Congress several times as a swaps market expert. In July 2010, Dodd–Frank was passed into law. As the then president of the WMBAA, I issued a public statement commending President Obama and Congress for passage. I believed then and believe now that Congress got the swaps reform provisions of Dodd–Frank right.

Who, Me?

Over the next several years, the CFTC under Chairman Gary Gensler set about rapidly implementing Dodd–Frank's swaps mandates. In January 2013, CFTC Commissioner Jill Sommers, a Republican, announced her intention to leave the agency. Not long after, I was contacted by staff for Senate Minority Leader Mitch McConnell asking if I was interested in being recommended to the Obama administration to replace Sommers. After a lot of thought and discussion with Regina, I said yes.

The 14 years I spent with GFI were some of the most satisfying years of my life. I owed a great deal to Mickey Gooch, Colin Heffron, and so many great GFI colleagues. I also owed a lot to my WMBAA colleagues for the work that got me noticed and considered for service at the CFTC. And, of course, I owed everything to Regina, who once again gave her blessing to a new and unanticipated adventure.

As I said goodbye to GFI, my business colleagues held a rousing going-away party for me at my favorite Wall Street restaurant, Delmonico's.[6] At one point, I left the party to go to the men's room. As I passed through the bar, a young man came up to me to wish me well. He said, "You probably don't remember me, but I was the guy dancing on the corner 14 years ago." I asked what he was doing now. He said he was the number two guy on JPMorgan's fixed income trading desk in North America. Clearly, he had learned his lessons well.

In August 2013, President Obama announced my nomination. The following March, I testified before the Senate Agriculture Committee alongside fellow CFTC nominees Tim Massad and Sharon Bowen. After Senate confirmation, I was sworn in on June 24, 2014, by Supreme Court Justice Clarence Thomas in a moving ceremony in the House Agriculture Committee Hearing Room overlooking the Capitol. In addition to many friends and family members, the attendees included Senator Rob Portman of Ohio, House Agriculture Committee Chairman Frank Lucas, Congressmen Mike Conaway and Scott Garrett, and my new colleagues, CFTC Chairman Massad and Commissioner Bowen.

I began by thanking Justice Thomas and the other distinguished guests. I then thanked my mother and father and three brothers—all gathered for the first time in decades and, as it turned out, for the last time ever. I thanked Regina for her love and support and the gift of our three children, Emma, Luke, and Henry.

I then said:

> "Today is indeed an honor for me and my family. What a thrill for a guy from New Jersey to be nominated by the President of the United States, to be confirmed unanimously by the US Senate, to be welcomed today by leaders of the House of Representatives and to be sworn in by an esteemed member of the US Supreme Court. "Wow! What a country!" And what an honor.
>
> "As I said in my confirmation hearing, I come from a line of doctors, nurses, and business entrepreneurs, simple immigrants almost a century ago. My grandparents and great grandparents would beam with pride if they were here with us.
>
> "And yet, they would not be surprised. Instead, they may have found it thrilling along with all the other amazing aspects of this wonderful country. A country where extraordinary things happen quite ordinarily."

That day the sun was indeed ". . . *shining down . . .*" on a new road. I had been given the opportunity to travel that road on the merits of my knowledge and expertise, not because of party or personal loyalty. I had no other Washington ambitions other than to serve five years for my country and make a good showing of myself. I had no partisan political agenda to fulfill. I owed no one, and no one owned me.

So, here I was, once again, embarking down a new section of highway, *twisting and unwinding*, far from where I started. It passed through that intersection of law, markets, and technology that consistently remained the course of my career. And soon I would feel the powerful tailwinds of the Internet of Value and see the dawning rays of cryptocurrencies.

Chapter 3

Heading Down the Highway

On a straight but undulating road, you don't concentrate on the next brow, but the one after that, and anything in between you will (or should) have taken account of long before you reach it.
—Michael Costin (auto racing engineer), describing the racing state of mind, *Trackrod Motor Club Newsletter,* Dec. 1973

The Layout

The US government formed administrative agencies to regulate commercial activity in the late 1800s, with the creation of the Interstate Commerce Commission. Applying powers delegated by Congress, these agencies publish rules and regulations; determine whether laws, rules, or regulations have been broken in particular cases; and impose fines and other sanctions on transgressors.

To perform these functions, Congress has conferred upon these agencies both quasi-legislative and quasi-judicial powers. They can issue licenses, set rates, and shape or even outlaw business practices.

Some agencies are federal executive departments, like, say, the Department of Transportation or Department of Agriculture. Other agencies exist outside the executive departments. The latter are referred to as independent agencies, because they report to both legislative and executive branches of government and the president's power to dismiss the agency head or its commissioners is limited. This independent structure insulates the agency from the political winds that sweep over Washington. The best-known independent agencies are probably the Federal Reserve Board, the Federal Communications Commission, the Federal Trade Commission, and the CFTC's sister agency, the Securities and Exchange Commission.

The Commodity Futures Trading Commission is another independent agency. Though less well known, it is of critical importance to the stability and prosperity of global financial markets. It was established in 1974 on the initiative of some visionary leaders of the Chicago commodity futures exchanges. The new agency assumed responsibility for regulating commodity futures markets—a role that, from the 1920s[1] until then, had been performed by the Department of Agriculture. The CFTC operates under the statutory framework of the Commodity Exchange Act (CEA),[2] a law that was originally passed in 1936 but has been amended several times since.

The CFTC is composed of five commissioners who serve staggered five-year terms. They are chosen by the president and confirmed by the Senate. No more than three of the five commissioners can be of the same political party. The commission is a creation of Congress, which has delegated power to it. The delegation is necessary because derivatives markets are so large, vast, and ever-changing that close scrutiny is necessary. Congress does not have the time or expertise to exercise daily oversight over them. So it delegated authority to the commission, which the commission is to wield in a fashion shielded from the expediencies of short-sighted politics.

The US derivatives markets—regulated by the CFTC—are the world's largest, most developed, and most influential. They are relatively unmatched in their depth and breadth. They provide deep pools of trading liquidity at low transaction cost and with minimal friction, and facilitate participation by a vast and diverse array of global counterparties. They are also some of the world's fastest growing and technologically innovative markets of any kind.

Price Discovery

US derivatives markets are outstanding at providing efficient and undistorted price discovery. Farmers look at the prices set on agriculture futures exchanges to determine for themselves whether they are getting fair value for the crops they sell to local grain elevators. At the same time, the grain elevators use futures market prices as the basis for what they offer local farmers at harvest. The US Department of Agriculture uses that same information to make price projections, determine volatility measures, and make payouts on crop insurance.

The value of many of the world's most important agricultural, mineral, and energy commodities is reliably established in US futures markets. Importantly, those prices are set in US dollars. Dollar pricing of the world's commodities provides an enormous and unparalleled advantage to American producers in global commerce. Thanks to dollar pricing, neither producers nor consumers in the United States need a currency hedge on top of their commodities hedges.

US derivatives markets are also considered to be some of the world's best regulated. The United States is the only major country in the Organization for Economic Co-operation and Development to have a regulatory agency specifically dedicated to derivatives market regulation: the CFTC. There is a connection between singularly focused federal regulation and having the world's most competitive derivatives markets. For over 40 years, the CFTC has been recognized for its principles-based regulatory framework and econometrically driven analysis. The CFTC is respected around the world for its depth of expertise and breadth of capability. Too often underfunded, at times underestimated, certainly underrecognized, the CFTC is unquestionably the most innovation accommodating market regulator in Washington's alphabet soup of agencies. And, oh yes, unlike almost every other federal financial regulator, markets and institutions overseen by the CFTC did not fail during the 2008 financial crisis.

When I arrived at the CFTC, my focus was still on the recent past—the 2008 financial crisis and the regulatory response to it. I was determined to complete derivatives reform, but I was also resolved to do it in a way that would promote market efficiency and economic growth. I was particularly focused on two outstanding Dodd–Frank implementations: swap execution facilities and position limits.

Within three months of my swearing-in, an important change occurred in the commission's composition. Commissioner Scott O'Malia stepped down to join the International Swaps and Derivatives Association, or ISDA. During his almost five-year tenure, O'Malia had been a minority commissioner, meaning that his political party held no more than two seats on the five-member CFTC Commission. Under the CFTC's authorizing statute, up to three seats and majority voting power were with the other party, the party of the president, Barack Obama. Under that structure, O'Malia had nevertheless mastered the role of a minority commissioner, negotiating rule improvements when he could and issuing vociferous and well-articulated dissents when he could not. Even for CFTC rule proposals he voted against, O'Malia always seemed to be in detailed negotiations to the very end.

I would miss O'Malia's tutelage. His unexpected departure left me as the only Republican alongside three Democrats. Tim Massad, an exacting Wall Street lawyer, was the new chairman, giving him control of the entire agency staff and its agenda. Mark Wetjen, an earnest and approachable former high-ranking Senate staffer, was the most senior commissioner. Sharon Bowen, who had been paired with me during our Senate confirmation hearings, was a principled lawyer and consumer advocate.

In American football terms, I was a defensive free safety covering a capable quarterback and two skilled receivers. In that role, I had no authority to call the plays or direct the staff's rule writing and implementation. I had only a slightly better chance to get their focused attention. I had to use other means to influence it. I chose the written word. With the help of my brilliant staff counsel, Amir Zaidi, who had previously advised O'Malia, I set to work on the promised white paper. Writing it occupied much of the autumn and winter, including the holiday break.

White Paper

On January 29, 2015, we published the 80-page work. It was the first time in CFTC history that a Commissioner's office had ever written such an extensive treatise. The white paper reviewed how swaps worked and examined their social and economic utility. It laid out the structure of the global swaps markets. It explained why swaps did not trade on exchanges like stocks and futures, but in over-the-counter markets like corporate bonds. It also explained the role of swaps dealers and other market participants.

The paper then argued that Congress did not give the CFTC the power to dictate market structure or appropriate business models for swap exchange facilities. The correct regulatory structure, it continued, would be one in which the CFTC registered and oversaw these facilities, but otherwise left them to conduct their business according to broad principles rather than restrictive operational constructs. Despite frequent talk about Dodd–Frank's supposed electronic execution model and its exchange trading "mandate," there is no such requirement in Dodd–Frank. Instead, the law expressly allowed SEFs to operate "by any means of interstate commerce." That meant, the paper concluded, that such facilities were entitled to exercise economic freedom in choosing their trading methods.

The most important audience for the white paper was the CFTC staff itself. I hoped it would dissuade them from applying the commission's ill-conceived rules in a rigid and restrictive fashion. Yet, I also knew the white paper would receive attention from Capitol Hill policy-makers and financial media. I hoped it would convey that one can be in favor of market reform and yet oppose a peculiar implementation of the reform.

The white paper made a huge impact. It got very positive reviews from members of the influential Futures Industry Association, the global association for those who work with exchange-traded futures and options. Together with the ISDA—the association for those who work with derivatives *not* traded on exchanges—these two organizations were the leading resources on these markets for public officials and investors worldwide.

For years, I had known the friendly and fair-haired FIA president, Walt Lukken. We worked in the same building in lower Manhattan following the financial crisis. Lukken and I agree on many things, including love for rhythm and blues. He has done and said more about the issues I care about than anyone I know.

Lukken told me that the white paper was getting compliments for the quality of the writing, its comprehensive analysis of a range of issues, and its formulation of workable alternative proposals. Many market participants said that it addressed concerns that they had raised when the SEF rules were being proposed that had never been addressed. Lukken directed an FIA group to draft a set of specific rule-change proposals to bring to the CFTC.

More important was the paper's impact on the CFTC staff. In conversations, I could tell that they were becoming more conversant with the characteristics of over-the-counter swaps markets distinguishable from the exchange-traded futures markets with which the staff had long-standing expertise. Market participants told me that staff interactions were increasingly substantive and better informed. One long-standing CFTC watcher told me that the white paper encouraged agency staff to have a more open-minded approach to Dodd–Frank implementation.

Some of this change was undoubtedly due to the new collegial approach of Chairman Massad. Still, the white paper played a key role in this awakening with respect to swap exchange facilities.

Lawyer Steven Lofchie had this to say in his blog, the *Cadwalader Cabinet*:

> "The [current] CFTC SEF trading rules did not receive substantial support from either the buy side or the sell side. Whether or not one agrees with the specific recommendations made by Commissioner Giancarlo, it is difficult to see the logic of the CFTC's continuing defense of market structures and trading rules that few participants favor and that do not contribute to market stability in any way. Significant

credit should go to the Commissioner for his persistence in compelling the CFTC to revisit these flawed rules."[3]

In August 2015, the first significant changes occurred. The agency staff agreed to recognize additional methods of swaps trading as acceptable under CFTC rules, as was reported, for instance, by Reuters' Mike Kentz.

> "CFTC staff has deemed auction-style execution protocols for over-the-counter swaps as allowable under the Dodd–Frank regime for trading derivatives on swap execution facilities, putting to rest a controversial issue that had been playing out behind the scenes for over a year . . .
>
> "The decision solidifies the use of another method of execution alongside the existing request-for-quote and central limit order book methods, which so far have not been enough to attract activity to the nascent trading platforms that launched two years ago . . .
>
> "The CFTC had pushed back on approving auctions over the last year for fear of scuppering efforts to increase pre-trade transparency in OTC swaps, a key tenet of the Dodd–Frank Act.
>
> "The argument that Dodd–Frank provides specifically for flexibility in execution methods via language that states SEFs may execute trades "through any means of interstate commerce . . . was first expounded by now-commissioner Christopher Giancarlo at the outset of the rule-making process five years ago, when he was executive vice-president at inter-dealer broker GFI Group . . . Giancarlo has stuck to his point but thinks the agency needs to codify the change publicly with more detail."[4]

This decision was an essential step in allowing swaps trading some of the flexibility that Dodd–Frank authorized.

Action by No Action

A greater breakthrough came the following January 2016, almost a year after the white paper's publication. It was my first day back in Washington after Christmas break at our home in New Jersey. In the office, I met with my staff to hear their analysis of the agency's proposed individual permanent registrations for the first 18 Swap Execution Facilities.

We went through each application. My staff counsel, Amir Zaidi, a rigorous lawyer and former analyst at the Federal Reserve Bank of New York, identified the different business models offered by each firm.

It quickly became apparent that the applications reflected a comprehensive range of business models. These included hybrid electronic and voice-based systems, mechanisms called "request for quote" and "central limit order books," as well as fully electronic auction systems. Some of the applicants sought to serve primarily wholesale—or "sell side"— market participants, while others sought to serve both "sell-side" and "buy-side" players. Some of the SEFs focused on just a few types of swaps, while others planned to handle a wide range. It was clear that the staff had bent over backwards to allow SEFs to operate by "any means of interstate commerce" as Congress had promised in Dodd–Frank.

Though delighted with the result, I was disappointed by the elaborate, administrative procedure that produced it. That result was a fair amount of circumvention of the ill-conceived SEF rules. Those peculiar rules, by their terms, required SEFs to restrict their business models to just two means of interstate commerce: "request for quote" and "central limit order books." CFTC staff were now recommending, however, approval of SEF registrations that allowed a broad set of trading methods. In my view, that was exactly the right outcome, because that was what Congress had always envisioned and specified in the language of the Act. But what a ridiculous, roundabout way to do the right thing.

The guts of the workaround hinged on conditioning SEF approvals on applicants' compliance with five staff letters, called "no-action letters." Each letter effectively waived flawed swaps trading rules that I had identified in my white paper.

This was bad administrative law on several levels. First, rather than the CFTC lifting the inappropriate limits on SEF business models, the CFTC was just ignoring those limits. Second, the opaque mechanisms being used would make it very hard for other market participants to understand what modes of swap execution the CFTC was really permitting. Observers would have to pore over the fine print of each and every SEF registration that was approved and then extrapolate the unstated rules that were quietly being applied. Third, relying on a hodgepodge of "no action" letters would force market participants to jump through pointless hoops of make-work.

I told my staff I intended to issue a blistering public statement. I would declare that the whole thing was a sham and that "the Emperor had no clothes."

Amir's face turned down. I asked why. He told me that market participants were sorely afraid of my doing so. Everyone knew that it was a charade to pretend that SEFs were being restricted in their business models when, in fact, they were being allowed to operate competitively. But the industry also knew that Dodd–Frank advocates needed to maintain the appearance that they were "cracking down" on Wall Street. If I was candid about what the staff had done, then Dodd–Frank proponents might have to profess shock and foist more restrictions on SEFs. In short, everybody was hoping that I would keep my mouth shut. I got the point.

So what had started with a bang was ending with a whimper. The CFTC staff had folded their tent on the flawed SEF rules. My white paper had served its purpose. I could not take credit, however, for a good outcome that no one wanted to admit had taken place. We had arrived at the right outcome but through the wrong means. The right means would have been for the commission to openly acknowledge that economic freedom, never having been abridged by Congress, could not be abridged by an unelected regulatory body like the CFTC.

The situation was not satisfactory in the long term. What the staff permitted today, it might not permit tomorrow. The only right thing to do would be to change CFTC rules. I would keep my mouth shut for now. But I made up my mind to try to change the rules in the unlikely event I ever got the chance.

Position Limits

Buoyed by the success of the white paper, I returned to the fray on another contentious issue: position limits. Position limits are pre-set restrictions on the amount of futures contracts that may be held by traders. They had been put in place and managed by the exchanges and the CFTC for decades. The purpose of position limits is to prevent market participants, especially large traders, or groups of traders, from manipulating large positions to unduly affect market prices or exert control over markets.

The renewed debate on position limits began before I joined the commission and, as it would turn out, continued after my departure. Dodd–Frank required the CFTC to establish a new and broader set of position limits as necessary to prevent "the burdens associated with excessive speculation causing sudden or unreasonable fluctuations or unwarranted changes in price." It was one of the few Dodd–Frank mandates the agency had still not successfully implemented when I arrived.

The CFTC had actually adopted a comprehensive position limits rule back in 2011 amidst a huge behind-the-scenes dogfight. But a year later a federal court struck it down, ruling that the CFTC had not, as required by the language of the Dodd–Frank Act, made a formal finding that the limits it sought to impose were necessary to prevent burdens on interstate commerce.

In December 2013, the agency put out a revised position limits proposal, expressly finding that its limits were "necessary." But market participants—especially agriculture and energy producers—heavily criticized the proposal as overly restrictive, which it was.

Now, in 2015, the commission was getting ready to revise that 2013 proposal. I wanted to make sure we got it right.

Years before, as a practicing lawyer, I always made a point of visiting new clients at their places of business to learn what they did and how they did it. I couldn't really help a client, I felt, until I understood how the client made a living.

When I joined the CFTC, I knew better than most people in Washington how Wall Street banks used swaps and other derivatives to make a living. Still, I knew little about how American farmers, ranchers, oilmen, and manufacturers used derivatives to make *their* livings. Now, as a commissioner, I decided to find out. I would go visit them.

Over my five years at the CFTC, I would travel across well over half the country to meet with thousands of Americans who depended on CFTC-regulated derivatives in their livelihoods. I eventually visited 22 states that depended on CFTC regulated products to hedge the prices of agriculture, mineral, or energy that they produced. In the course of those travels, I descended 900 feet underground in a Kentucky coal mine, climbed 90 feet in the air on a North Dakota natural gas rig and went even higher in an Arkansas crop duster. I walked factory floors in Illinois, oil refineries in Texas, grain elevators in Indiana, and power plants in

Ohio. I milked dairy cows with family farmers in Melrose, Minnesota. I met with grain and livestock producers in New York, Montana, Iowa, and Louisiana. In Kansas, I met Mary and Pat Ross at their feedlot in Lawrence, traveled to Ken McCauley's corn farm in White Cloud, and visited Pat O'Trimble's soybean fields in Perry. In Michigan, I toured the Ford Rouge automobile manufacturing plant, visited a grain mill in Frankenmuth, and met with farmers and agricultural product suppliers at a fertilizer depot in Henderson.

In the first-ever, bipartisan, CFTC agriculture tour, Commissioner Wetjen and I flew to Iowa to visit the John Deere combine factory in Moline, the World Food Prize Foundation in Des Moines, and the corn and soybean fields just north of Clear Lake. (While there, we walked far out into a cornfield to pay homage at the site of the plane crash that killed rock 'n' roll pioneers Buddy Holly, Ritchie Valens, and J. P. "The Big Bopper" Richardson.[5])

While these visits were delightful in their own right, they made me a better-informed regulator of American commodity futures markets. In corn fields and pole barns, I spoke directly with participants in CFTC regulated markets. These conversations gave me essential credibility back in Washington to address the impact of CFTC rules on the everyday people who depended on futures markets to hedge their production risks. They taught me that the number one concern of corn, soybeans, pork, and dairy producers is the fairness of the price they will get paid at harvest. That's what puts food on *their* tables.

I was not opposed to a position limits rule that would curb excessive speculation, especially by large financial traders. At the same time, it was essential that those limits not become so wooden or inflexible that they distorted the markets or harmed American agriculture or energy producers. That's what would happen if the rules interfered with those producers' ability to protect themselves against the vast declines in commodity prices that could occur—and were, in fact, occurring. If the prolonged collapse in commodity prices continued, and the position limits rule was not made workable, we would be burdening hedging activity at precisely the worst time.

My principal qualms regarding earlier position-limits proposals had been just that. I feared they would restrict *bona fide* hedging activity or harm America's farmers and energy producers. Both had been sorely affected by plummeting commodity prices and service provider consolidation. I was not willing to support a poorly designed rule that had to be continually tweaked through no-action letters and other ad hoc staff interpretations and advisories. That approach had become too common at the CFTC in prior years. We had to carefully consider the impact of any new proposal on America's almost 9,000 grain elevators, 2 million family farms, and 147 million electric utility customers.[6]

The position limits proposals that I reviewed during my time as a minority commissioner were very detailed and complex, hundreds of pages in length, with thousands of footnotes. In too many cases, the proposals would have imposed additional paperwork, compliance costs, and burdens that would have done little to limit excessive speculation. I expressed my concern that they would likely result in higher costs for consumers of food and energy, which would be felt most heavily by low-income Americans.

I called for the CFTC to take better account of the costs and benefits of its rulemaking. This was especially urgent given the slow growth of the Obama economy and the administration's philosophy of attacking seemingly every issue with still more regulations.[7] The job participation rate—the percentage of Americans in the workforce—had not been this low in over 35 years.[8] During the Obama years, one in three Americans between the age of 18 and 31 were living with their parents.[9] And in one out of five American families, no one had a job.[10]

Overregulation was not making things any easier. Under President Obama, business regulation cost the United States more than 12% of GDP or $2 trillion annually.[11] The average manufacturing firm spent almost $20,000 per employee per year on complying with federal regulations.[12] For manufacturers with fewer than 50 employees, the cost rose to nearly $35,000 per employee.[13] In a mediocre economy with many out of work and facing dwindling employment opportunities, we should not have saddled American consumers with higher prices for energy, food, and other commodities.

Also, in the aftermath of a period of expansionist rulemaking, it was imperative for the CFTC to base rulemaking on hard data. Far too often, CFTC rulemaking was built upon anecdote and supposition. To the extent the CFTC's 2013 position-limits proposal had been based on data at all, that data had been out of date, unreliable, and riddled with errors. I refused to support a new position-limits rule in the absence of better data justifying it.

In spring 2015, at a Texas energy markets conference at the esteemed Houston Club, I put it this way:

> "Some people love to cite data when it supports their arguments. When it doesn't, they conveniently ignore it. In the case of position limits, there is an entire absence of any data based, quantitative foundation for the proposed regulations. This absence cannot be ignored. It draws into the question the entire efficacy and validity of the CFTC's proposed position limits regulations."

What I didn't know at the time was that there may have been a reason the data was so poor. The CFTC's office of chief economist was evidently being blocked from producing the type of "data-based, quantitative foundation" required for any worthwhile regulatory proposal. This would come to light six months later, when a report of the CFTC's Inspector General revealed:

> CFTC "economists identified position limits as an example of a topic on which economic research is no longer permitted . . . Several other economists confirmed their impression that [The Office of Chief Economist] is now censoring research topics that might conflict with the official positions of the CFTC . . . [The Inspector General] discussed this concern on multiple occasions with the current Chief Economist. He agreed that he had initially rejected a research proposal on position limits on the basis that it was politically controversial."[14]

Both publicly and privately, I denounced the flimsiness of the purported economic basis for the position limits proposal. I made clear to my colleagues and the staff that I would support a well-founded, well-crafted rule, but I would vigorously and vocally oppose a poorly conceived one not based on sound data.

In the summer of 2016, the CFTC released for public comment a supplement to its December 2013 position-limits proposal. It relaxed the procedures for persons seeking exemptions to pursue certain specific, bona fide hedging strategies. It also defined methods for recognizing trading strategies for which exemptions would be available.

I had encouraged and supported this supplement. While not the broad revamping of the position-limits proposal that I preferred, it was a solid step in the right direction. I believe it evidenced the thoughtful attention of Chairman Massad.

Later that year the staff put forward a proposal with still more improvements. It relied on up-to-date commodity and market data, was more practically designed, and would be less costly to comply with. I supported its publication for public notice and comment. This improved proposal came about at least in part, I believe, due to the pressure that I had exerted. My farm and oil patch visits had given me the credibility to insist that American farmers and energy producers not be allowed to become collateral damage of reforms meant to rein in Wall Street.

A few years later, I would direct the CFTC's work on a revised position-limits proposal. We were determined that the rule be responsive to public comments. We would not place regulatory barriers in the way of long-standing hedging practices used by American farmers, ranchers, producers, and manufacturers. While I was not able to present the proposal for a commission vote before I left the agency, my team did leave behind a working draft that served as a foundation for a quite good rule that was adopted by the commission six months after my departure. Progress made.

This commitment to data-driven analysis would drive my interest in blockchain technology (as I will soon discuss) and underlay the CFTC's response to Bitcoin futures soon on the horizon.

Chapter 4

Scanning the Horizon

If you make the mistake of looking back too much, You aren't focused enough on the road in front of you.

—Brad Paisley (singer-songwriter and
guitar virtuoso) *Country AirCheck,* June 2015

Nighttime Driving

When I recount my travels as a public official, I often mention a 2016 trip to Ellis County, Texas, about an hour south of Dallas. In the tiny railroad depot town of Bardwell (population 649), I met an older farmer who grew corn, cotton, sunflowers, and winter wheat on a thousand-acre family farm. It was a bright, gentle, spring afternoon with wheat being harvested and corn stalks and sunflowers in mid-growth. I was there to understand the production of cotton, the basis of an important CFTC regulated commodity future product that set the global price.

I climbed into the farmer's truck and we drove to look at his fields and operations. Many years before, he explained, he had met his wife at church. One of her uncles invited him to farm family land. The farmer had then built it up over many decades. When he first started, he never imagined that it would become his life's work. But it had, and he was proud of what he'd created. He was now gradually handing over responsibilities to his son.

The farmer took me to see the county cooperative cotton gin. It was a large, two-story mechanical contraption occupying a giant tin-sided barn off the county road. The gin operated only at cotton harvesting time each autumn. Nevertheless, it was serviced year-round to be ready to work without interruption when needed. During that four- to six-week period, the gin ran almost continuously.

As we were driving, we passed a field of mown vegetation.

"That field looks like it was just cut," I said.

"Yup. Cut it last night."

"I'm guessing it's winter wheat."

"Yup."

As we drove, I thought over what he had just said. I asked: "You cut it last night? How'd you do that?"

"I'll show you."

He pulled over to the side of the road. He took out his iPhone, gave it a few swipes, and handed it to me, showing me a video. The screen was mostly black, but what looked like two sets of headlights were moving across it.

"What am I looking at?" I asked.

The video was taken the night before, he explained. Two headlights were of his combine harvester; the other two were those of his tractor, which was pulling a chaser bin into which the combine was shooting the harvested wheat. The two vehicles were running side by side.

He had been in the tractor, and his son in the combine. GPS satellite navigation guided the combine through the night. Vehicle telemetry held the tractor in place alongside the combine. His airborne drone took the video.

I was amazed. I had learned about "precision agriculture," as it's called, and farm tractor GPS navigation during a visit to John Deere's Iowa testing grounds the year before. Here, however, was digital-age farming being conducted on an ordinary American family farm. It was real.

Later, after saying goodbye to my host, I drove back to Dallas. On my flight to Washington, I reflected on a father and son reaping a wheat field in the dark of the night, observed closely by their own airborne drone. It struck me that the work of farming—which since the dawn of humanity had been a labor-intensive, daylight activity—could now be conducted by a handful of people around the clock. Digital technology had worked this transformation.

Precision Farming

Precision farming marshals advanced technologies to dramatically increase and optimize productivity. It reduces consumption and waste while boosting land productivity. It reduces the use of water, fertilizer, and herbicide while minimizing emissions and soil compaction—all to the benefit of the environment. Satellite, aerial drones, and terrestrial sensors continually monitor the health of fields. Specialized equipment doses fertilizers and plant protection products in a finely tuned manner. Precision steering and tractor driving systems vastly enhance both farm labor and soil efficiency. Thanks to advances like these, society won't necessarily need more acreage to feed the earth's burgeoning population—just continually improving technology.

Driving Through the Rearview Mirror

If the digital revolution was working such radical transformations in farming, one of humankind's oldest occupations, it should be no surprise that it was also remaking the world's capital, commodity, and futures markets. The electronification of markets and the advent of program trading and artificial intelligence have radically altered the financial landscape, with far-ranging implications for capital formation and risk transfer.

Nevertheless, in my view, market regulation generally and by the CFTC in particular was not keeping pace. The agency was stuck in a twentieth-century time warp, indifferent to the financial technology revolution. Its futures rules, for instance, had been written at the time when "open outcry" traders would use colorful shouts and hand signals to strike deals in the trading pits of Minneapolis, Kansas City, New York, or Chicago. Those trading pits were now dormant, largely supplanted by electronic trade execution run by remote software algorithms and, increasingly, artificial intelligence. The CFTC seemed to be an analog regulator in a digital marketplace.

I was also struck by how backward-looking financial market regulation was. The Dodd–Frank Act was then five years old. As important as it is (and it is important), Dodd–Frank can be seen in time as the last major "patch" of the old analog, account-based financial system. It better addresses problems of the past than it does those of the future. Financial regulators, the press, and market participants still spent too much time focused on its myriad mandates—edicts intended to prevent a recurrence of the 2008 crisis.

Peacetime generals are said to be preoccupied with fighting the last war. Economists over-analyze the last depression. And financial regulators take steps to ban the market abuses that caused the last crisis. But a future crisis is unlikely to duplicate the last one. We were paying too little attention to emerging trends that could lead to the next shock.

It was as if the regulators were all riding together in a car at high speed on an interstate highway. The Dodd–Frank Act was an enormous rearview mirror that stretched across almost the entire windshield. The regulators were continually scouring that mirror, looking backward in time. Meanwhile, financial markets were rapidly evolving. New and unfamiliar vehicles and concerns were approaching at breakneck speed, unseen by the rearward-focused drivers.

In June 2015, I was in London to talk to American and overseas securities regulators at the annual meeting of the International Organization of Securities Commissions, or IOSCO.[1] Four hundred market participants and securities professionals were gathered at the Queen Elizabeth II Center, a conference hall across the street from Westminster Abbey, where sessions were punctuated by the somber tolling of Big Ben.

When my panel was called, we took our chairs in a semicircle. My co-panelists included senior securities regulators from the European Union and Hong Kong, a senior official from the International Monetary Fund, senior executives from JP Morgan and other global banks, and my former CFTC colleague, Scott O'Malia, now representing ISDA. Seated next to me was the moderator, a commanding financial markets journalist.

The discussion began with each participant, in turn, opining on the most significant challenges confronting financial market regulators. Without exception, each panelist referenced the crushing impact of the 2008 financial crisis, the appropriateness of the reforms, and the importance of implementing them promptly. The volume and timbre of their voices settled into a monotone of dull, regulatory-speak. They all talked about the last financial crisis. Not a single one described any new threats or challenges to financial markets.

Peering over the Dashboard

As it turned out, I spoke last. I started by acknowledging that my perspective might be somewhat unique, since I was a new regulator, having spent a career in the private sector operating global swaps trading platforms.

Based on my commercial experience, I said, I saw three key challenges facing contemporary regulators, none of which are addressed by Dodd–Frank.

They were cyber-attacks, the coming digital automation of markets, and the diminution of trading liquidity. None of my co-panelists had mentioned any of these three things, I noted.

I then stressed that the world's financial markets are used as a battlefield by global belligerents, both nation-states and non-nation-states. I had been on Wall Street on September 11, 2001, I recounted, and had personally witnessed the destruction of the World Trade Center. The terrorists targeted those buildings not just for symbolic purposes, I continued. They did so because they wished to destroy America's financial markets, which operated out of those towers. The terrorists had even shorted stocks several days before the attacks because they expected the markets to collapse along with the towers.[2]

Efforts to destroy Western financial markets and economies continued, I said, and regulators could have no illusions about it. It was increasingly being conducted by well-organized and funded organizations, in many cases, with foreign state support. They were using state-of-the-art technology enabling sophisticated system hacking and financial ransomware. I added that, despite the overriding threat of cyber destruction, neither Dodd–Frank nor much of the global reform effort addressed it.

The second challenge was the digital revolution in trading markets. Automation was transforming many industries. Financial services would not be immune from the continuing evolution of the Internet. We had already seen the dramatic rise of computerized trading in the futures and equities markets to the point where algorithms were driving a majority of trading activity. Financial markets would soon be conducted predominately by algorithmic trading, not by humans.

I noted that several panels at the conference were discussing proposed regulations to shape human conduct in financial services. But how much would human behavior and trader conduct count for, I asked, in a world driven mainly by nonhuman, electronic trading. Algorithmic trading—or "algo trading," as it was known—was creating a much different market in critical respects. That led one to ask: What did "culture" mean in a world of robots? Also, how would regulation remain effective when something called distributed ledger technology enabled direct, peer-to-peer market transactions without regulated intermediaries?

At this point, I could tell that I had the audience's attention. They had stopped staring at their mobile phones and were looking at me.

Then I barreled into the third major challenge: regulation itself. I asked a rhetorical question: "Are all these regulations that have come out of the last financial crisis a cure, or are they a new disease?"

Pained looks came over the faces of my fellow panelists. I then continued: "We have now had seven years of unprecedented central bank involvement in global capital markets and five years of relentless regulatory reform. Incidentally, I support most of the reforms having to do with swaps. Yet we have to be honest. It has resulted in an uncoordinated mess of rules and regulations that, while individually justified, are mostly uncoordinated.

"The lack of coordination is having one aggregate impact: constriction of trading liquidity. Everybody here knows what trading liquidity is, right? The ability to buy or sell in a market without causing an enormous change in price. As a principal in a firm that operated trading markets, I am aware that managing trading liquidity is complicated. Yet, I know from talking to traders and market operators that the quality of liquidity in global wholesale markets is changing for the worse. It is not the case in every market, but it is the case in a number of critical markets. We saw diminution of trading liquidity (in October 2014) in the US Treasury Market, we see it now in the German Bund market, and we fear we may see it in Treasury repo markets (which, in fact, we would see in a few years' time). There is a good chance that the deterioration of trading liquidity is a product of the hodgepodge of regulations constraining bank capital as well as the impact of accommodative monetary policy and quantitative easing.

"Whatever is causing the deterioration in liquidity, we regulators need to understand it, and deal with it. It's not good enough to just keep saying 'let's get these regulations done and then we'll figure out the impact.' We need to understand the impact regulation-by-regulation and do a much better job of fine-tuning the regulations themselves. Let's not lower the risk of bank insolvency from the last crisis, while increasing the risk of market illiquidity in a future crisis. *Let's not turn the cure into the disease.*"

When I finished, you could hear a pin drop. After a beat, the other panelists seized on my points and started arguing with gusto. The moderator was now delighted to have some conflict she could work with. I just sat back and enjoyed it.

The experience confirmed in my mind the herd mentality—"groupthink"—that exists just as much in government as in any other occupation.[3] In 2015, the regulatory herd was grazing together in a familiar patch: post-crisis reform implementation. Most were still looking at the past to define the present. I was determined to prod the herd to lift their heads out of the grass and look to the horizon.

So what did I see ahead in the summer of 2015? I saw the increasing dominance of automated, computerized trading executing millions of orders per second known as "high-frequency trading" (HFT). That had exciting potential upsides: enhanced trading liquidity, increased market access, and lower transaction costs. It could also increase trader productivity through greater transaction speed, precision, and sophistication. At the same time, automated trading presented some new challenges. These included the risk of flawed algorithms or data misinterpretation by computerized analysis and mathematical models that increasingly replaced human thought and deliberation.

High-Frequency Trading

A 2018 CFTC study dispels the narrative that the growing presence of high-frequency trading has in some way made markets less stable.[4] The study looked at large intra-day price movements, known as "sharp price moves." It analyzed 2.2 billion market transactions in 16 different futures contracts from all four major commodity market sectors: agricultural, energy, financial, and metals products. The analysis covered a five-year period from 2012 through 2017 through both Obama and Trump administrations.

Among other things, the study found that neither the frequency nor intensity of sharp price movements increased demonstrably during the five-year period, the same time period that saw a large increase in HFT trading activity. Rather, the study found that sharp price movements are linked to market fundamentals and reaction to new and changing market information. The CFTC research shows that, not only had there not been any trend toward more frequent short-term price swings, but many of the biggest price swings could be explained, not by the activities of HFTs, but by longer-term, heightened market volatility and by the direct revelation of information and news events. The study disproves an oft-stated argument that financial transaction taxes are necessary to reduce volatility caused by high-frequency trading, since HFT activity is not a particular source of sharp volatility episodes in the first place. Rather, a transaction tax would limit trading liquidity, the diminishment of which in key markets and at critical times caused in part by mis-calibrated bank capital rules is far more responsible for flash crashes than the activities of HFT trading.

There were still other digital innovations that presented regulatory opportunities and challenges. They included "big data analysis" to enable more sophisticated data review and interpretation; artificial intelligence to read market signals and adjust trading strategies; and "smart" contracts that could value themselves and calculate payments in real time. They also included distributed ledger technologies, including something called the "blockchain" that underlay Bitcoin and other cryptocurrency.

Blockchain Briefing

If you're not familiar with distributed ledger technology, or DLT, I'll explain the basic idea. In a nutshell, it's a shared and tamperproof ledger for recording transactions, tracking assets, and building trust. It removes intermediaries and replaces them with a system open to all users and operated on a consensus basis on vast networks of computers operated anonymously.

Now let's unpack that.

We're all familiar with grocery receipts, retirement account statements, and corporate earnings reports. These are all types of ledgers. The forms that ledgers can take have evolved over the course of recorded history from Sumerian clay cuneiform tablets to Medieval vellum land records to paper savings bank passbooks to—with the rise of computers and the Internet—today's online bank statements.

The security of financial ledgers has always been taken *very* seriously. Think back to, say, the shipping office of a merchant freighting concern at the Port of Philadelphia in the 1870s. The office manager had a ledger where he and his staff would record and sign every arriving shipment. Entries were made in ink, something hard to alter at that time. The ledger was then locked in a safe. If a client had a question about a shipment received, the ledger was the authority. An unscrupulous freighter captain tampering with a ledger might get himself keelhauled.

Whatever form ledgers took over the centuries, until now they all needed to have the information they contained confirmed by an intermediary or central authority of some kind: for instance, a bank, a clearinghouse, a trading counterparty, or a merchant records clerk.

Today, however, the Internet is obviating the need for that central authority and replacing it with consensus-based authentication protocols.

What is a consensus-based authentication protocol? One example is the one that makes Wikipedia possible. So let's recap what Wikipedia does.

Not too long ago, if you wanted to know the history of, say, Edinburgh Castle, you might go to an encyclopedia. The encyclopedia's publisher commissioned experts to write entries on various topics and then charged for access to that information. A retained historian might write the entry that would define Edinburgh Castle for generations of readers.

Wikipedia has supplanted most proprietary encyclopedias by offering a massive online reference library. It does not hire any expert to validate the truth about Edinburgh Castle. Instead, it calls upon a vast, disparate, and decentralized group of contributors—scattered across the globe but connecting online—to volunteer information and arrive at the true history of Edinburgh Castle determined by a consensus reached by all of the contributors. No longer is truth what one expert says it is, but what a broad consensus of persons responsible for the outcome determine it to be.

Similarly, distributed ledgers like blockchain allow people who have no particular confidence in one another to collaborate without having to rely on a neutral central authority. If the truth of the history of Edinburgh Castle can be established online through decentralized consensus, so too can the origin and ownership of things of value, such as ship cargoes, agricultural and mineral commodities, contracts, stock certificates, property titles, cultural assets like music, votes in an election, and even personal identities.

In fact, distributed ledgers are actually far more reliable at recording financial transactions than Wikipedia is at recording historical information. Though the reasons get technical, here's a rough idea of why.

The best known distributed ledger is "the blockchain." It became famous in 2008, when the inventors of Bitcoin proposed it to record Bitcoin transactions. Blockchain is, as the name suggests, a chain of conceptual blocks. Each block is a digital vault that contains information. That information could be, for instance, an amount of money and who it belongs to; a "check-marked" compliance notation that's part of an automated reporting system; or a receipt for a shipment of fresh salmon arriving at the Fulton Fish Market.

When entering a new transaction, the user waits for a sophisticated automated algorithm to verify the entry. Then a new block is created and coded with a hashtag—a digital fingerprint—that is associated with the unique information contained within. Importantly, every block in the chain is marked not only with its own hashtag, but with that of the block immediately preceding it.

Blockchain Security

The blockchain is protected by several layers of security. To begin with, each block is protected cryptographically. But even if a hacker does manage to break into and tamper with a certain block, any changes will alter the block's hashtag. That anomaly, in turn, will be detected by every subsequent block in the chain. While it's theoretically possible for hackers using very high powered computers to try to conceal their having hacked into the first block by also hacking into all subsequent blocks (to alter their hashtags), still another blockchain technology—called a proof-of-work test—renders this almost impossible. The proof-of-work test requires that new computers accessing a chain must solve a time-consuming computational problem that, in effect, slows down "bots" and automated hacking tools, crippling their efficacy. But the crowning layer of security is a form of consensus-based authentication protocol—analogous to Wikipedia's. Due to the distributed nature of the blockchain, every participating computer has a copy of the complete chain. So any attempt to alter that chain will be evaluated by thousands of computers. An outlier chain—the one that was tampered with—will be rejected because it contradicts the network's consensus about what the chain should look like.

The potential applications of digital ledger technologies are legion—and quite breathtaking. DLT could facilitate transfer of anything from hockey tickets to magazine subscriptions, to auto repair warranties, to airline loyalty rewards, to apartment leases directly from you to your intended recipient without going through middlemen. One day it might even bring us more secure and verifiable voting systems, whether for corporate proxy contests, customer satisfaction surveys, or presidential elections. Voters would know with computer certainty that their ballots were counted properly, and that every other voter's ballots were counted only once.

In the financial industry, digital ledgers offer the prospect of faster, cheaper, and more accurate transactions, because they can be effectuated without third-party intermediaries. They can also be used to create so-called smart securities or derivatives—financial instruments that can value themselves in real time, calculate and pay interest, and even terminate themselves at the end of the contract term. Today, a growing number of banks are experimenting with issuing corporate bonds on digital ledgers, leading to substantial savings in cost, mistakes, and time.[5] Even more important than the foreseeable uses of DLT are those that cannot now be fully envisioned that cross organizational, regulatory, and mental boundaries.[6]

First, Do No Harm

I came early to believe that regulators should encourage and not hamper innovation involving digital ledger technologies. Among the speeches I gave on the subject was one in March 2016, at the Depository Trust & Clearing Corp. in New York, which was excerpted the next day in *The Wall Street Journal*:

> "The emergence of distributed ledger technology. . . may revolutionize the world of finance. In fact, the Bank of England has called DLT the "first attempt at an 'Internet of finance.'" DLT has the potential to link networks of legal recordkeeping the same way the Internet connects networks of data and information. It will have profound implications for global financial markets by increasing settlement efficiency and speed, linking recordkeeping networks, reducing transaction costs and increasing market access. It will broadly impact financial markets in payments, banking, securities settlement, title recording, cyber security and trade reporting and analysis . . .
>
> "Yet, . . . investment [in DLT] faces the danger that when regulation does come, it will come from a dozen different directions with different restrictions stifling crucial technological development before it reaches fruition . . . I believe that innovators and investors should not have to seek government's permission, only its forbearance, to develop DLT so they can do the work necessary to address the increased operational complexity and capital consumption of modern financial market regulation.
>
> "Regulators have a choice in this regard. I believe we can either follow a regulatory path that burdens the industry with multiple onerous regulatory frameworks or one where we come together and set forth uniform principles in an effort to encourage DLT investment and innovation. I favor the latter approach."[7]

The world was changing. Our parents' financial markets were disappearing. It was time for the CFTC to become a twenty-first-century digital regulator by embracing new technologies like blockchain.

Round Up the Usual Suspects

During my first two years at the CFTC, I settled into a pleasant and productive working relationship with my fellow commissioners—Sharon Bowen, Mark Wetjen, and Tim Massad—notwithstanding our varied perspectives. I respected that Massad, as chairman, had the power to put forward regulatory initiatives to which I could only react. As the lone Republican, I saw my role as similar to what, in the UK Parliament, is known as "the Loyal Opposition." I offered constructive and responsible input without betraying my fundamental principles. On international matters, I provided Massad with especially close support in his sometimes difficult negotiations with the CFTC's regulatory counterparts.

In November 2015, the CFTC published for comment Regulation Automated Trading, or "Reg AT." It was the agency's first large-scale attempt to catch up to the digital revolution occurring in futures markets. I applauded Reg AT to the extent that it drew on industry best practices, provided flexible risk-control parameters, and refrained from requiring regulatory pre-approval or pre-testing of computer algorithms. My early positive take was shared by many market participants.

Less positive were Reg AT's broad scope, hazy objectives, and inconsistencies regarding the activities it covered. It compelled a broad swath of market participants to register with the CFTC for the first time, subjecting them to rules, reporting requirements, and costs. It struck me as an instance of regulatory empire building—a classic Washington maneuver: recognize a new innovation in order to force ever more businesses into the regulatory framework.

Reg AT was also intellectually suspect, in my view. It was driven by a few anecdotes of bad behavior, rather than by any quantitative evidence that automated trading caused market harm. Its objectives were more political than market driven. It was being put in place so that when the next market crisis hit—and bad rules like this one helped guarantee that one would—government officials could claim they had been prepared.

Yet registration alone is not particularly effective public policy. The blunt act of forcing thousands of automated traders to register did not begin to address the complex issues that were arising from the digital revolution in modern markets.

Worse still, Reg AT contained a notorious provision that weakened intellectual property rights. It required that the proprietary source code for trading algorithms be made available to the CFTC or the US Justice Department at any time without a subpoena.

This was very troubling. In our innovative free market economy, intellectual property is "holy"[8] and should not be easily compromised. As I anticipated, the source code provision of Reg AT provoked vehement opposition from trading firms. They loathed the prospect of forking over invaluable trade secrets—the crown jewels of their operations—to government officials with a checkered record at best as guardians of confidential information. The threat of losing sensitive intellectual property in a hack of a government agency could have a chilling effect on financial technology innovation in the United States.

I shared my concerns with Chairman Massad. It was a matter of principle, I said. I recognized that exigent circumstances might warrant requiring a firm to turn over source code to regulators in a particular case. But the government should at least be required to obtain a subpoena from a judge in those instances, I argued. The subpoena process would provide property owners—traders, in this case—an opportunity to at least challenge the scope, timing, or necessity of the government's inquiry and to assert any legal privileges that might apply.

The Subpoena

The subpoena process protects property owners against the government's exercise of arbitrary and tyrannical power. Woven into the Bill of Rights, the subpoena process is a bulwark of liberty that predates the American Republic, going back to English common law. Protecting the due process and intellectual property rights of market participants was hugely important to me as a lawyer, a regulator, but most importantly, as a citizen.

"Things would be like in the movie *Casablanca*," I told one audience, in describing the impact of the Reg AT proposal. "You know the scene, when a crime has been committed, and Captain Renault says, 'Round up the usual suspects!' Well, the next time we have a market crisis, the regulators will say, 'Go round up all those newly registered automated traders, check their source codes, and charge somebody with a crime!'"

Feel the Road

In July 2016, I went to Michigan to meet with farmers. In the tiny town of Henderson, I met with 20 local growers and agricultural service providers. Many of them said they were concerned about the impact of electronic trading on futures markets. Some were reluctant to enter into futures contracts at all, they said, for fear of being "run over" by the algorithmic traders. Markets had become so volatile, with trades made at such lightning speeds and in such massive quantities that they were fearful to even get involved.

I was of two minds about what they were telling me. On the one hand, they were not wrong. The market was changing. It did have a different "feel" to it—less human, and more robotic.

On the other, I saw no clear basis for CFTC involvement. Market change in itself is not a predicate for regulatory action. It is not the job of regulators to stall change simply for the sake of keeping things as they are.

The nub of it was that, in 2016, the CFTC lacked sufficient understanding of the effect automated trading was having on markets. It could not yet identify a demonstrable problem, come up with a targeted solution, and measure its success.

The problem was not that the CFTC was not gathering good market information. To its credit, the agency had improved its quantitative data-gathering in recent years. With respect to the swaps markets, it had established swap data repositories (as mandated under Dodd–Frank). As for futures markets, the CFTC was monitoring high-quality transaction and counterparty data—though it still had limited access to order book (message) data, which was necessary to thoroughly analyze the impact of algorithmic trading on markets.

The problem was priorities. The agency simply was not set up to analyze and understand changing market dynamics. It was using its data mainly to prosecute fraud and manipulation, indeed an important and worthwhile task. But that work could not provide answers to the important questions of the farmers of Henderson, Michigan. Further, the CFTC's ongoing focus on the 2008 crash meant the agency remained somewhat inattentive to the overall condition of America's fast-changing markets, aside from robust prosecution of fraud and manipulation. In my view, the CFTC was devoting insufficient human capital, technology, and data analysis to understanding how futures markets were evolving. The agency needed to do a better job of addressing qualms about the changing "feel" of the market.

And it wasn't just farmers who were concerned about these frighteningly rapid changes. Market professionals had growing concerns about the concentration of trading power in a few mammoth market participants, about the increasing incidence of volatility spikes, and about diminution in trading liquidity.

Improving Signal to Noise Ratio

In October 2016, with the presidential election now just a few weeks away and the Obama administration in the home stretch, I was invited to the DuPont Circle headquarters of Washington's prestigious American Enterprise Institute (AEI) to outline a forward-looking approach for US market regulators to keep pace with twenty-first-century digital markets.[9]

Obviously, I had no idea who the next president would be or what type of CFTC leadership he or she would appoint, but I wanted to make some recommendations for the next administration. Before a large audience of Washington policymakers, I urged the CFTC and other US market regulators to follow five principles when regulating digital markets: embrace innovation, protect intellectual property, repurpose old rules for an emerging digital age, unburden the economy for growth, and champion US markets.

My first point was that regulators must embrace technological change. This was especially so when it came to the promising wave of innovations in financial technology, collectively referred to as "FinTech." Thanks to these new technologies, we could now use our smartphones to deposit checks, apply for credit, raise money for a business start-up, or manage investments—perhaps with the assistance of a "robo" adviser. At a more revolutionary level, FinTech also included distributed ledger technologies and blockchain technology, the foundation of cryptocurrency like Bitcoin.

I argued that the regulator's credo should be the same as a doctor's: "First, do no harm." This approach would benefit not only US financial markets but regulators, too. It was time to open regulatory doors and minds to the great promise that blockchain held for analyzing trading data, overseeing healthy markets, and mitigating financial and operational risk.

Regulators needed to engage in a real dialogue with innovators and understand the impact technology was having on the marketplaces they oversaw. They needed to partner with innovators, experiment with them, learn from them, and innovate alongside them if they were ever to keep pace with the digitization of modern markets.

My next point was about the primacy of protecting intellectual property. For US financial markets to remain the world's most attractive for technological innovation and capital investment, intellectual property rights had to be well protected by law. Referencing Reg AT, I urged that the source code of market participants remain private—accessible to the CFTC only by subpoena. Any other approach would damage both the commission's integrity and its positive working relationship with market participants.

Moreover, regulators needed to do more to protect intellectual property than simply reaffirm the subpoena process. They had to ensure that whenever market participants did provide proprietary data or intellectual property to regulators—under subpoena or otherwise—that property would be protected from cybertheft, breach, and misappropriation. Cyber risk was undeniably a major threat to twenty-first-century financial markets. In the past, the federal government had been a poor guardian of private, confidential information against that risk. That had to improve. Regulators' system security had to be no less robust and effective than that of the businesses under its jurisdiction. If market regulators were to effectively oversee digital markets, they could not become a weak link in the financial system's defenses against cyberattack. To attract digital innovators to American shores, regulators had to afford more intellectual property protection—not less—than competing jurisdictions.

I then said that regulators had to revamp analog rules to keep pace with digital transformation. Step one was to recognize that most regulatory legislation was written with the previous generation's markets in mind. Regulators had to rethink and repurpose analog rules and regulations for digital markets. At the CFTC, this had to be done with fidelity to its traditional approach: regulation based on principles.

Repurposing rules for the digital age also meant getting past antiquated "command-and-control" government solutions. Regulators had to work more cooperatively with trading firms, exchanges, clearinghouses, and self-regulatory organizations. They had to eschew regulatory empire building. Requiring more firms to get licenses before doing business did nothing to help regulators keep pace with digital transformation of financial markets. In addition, regulators had to avoid tunnel vision. With respect to the US derivatives markets, success could not be measured solely by whether large institutional traders and modern algorithmic "prop shops"—firms that utilize their market knowledge and experience to create proprietary strategies to trade their own capital for profit—could operate without disrupting markets. It had to be measured also by whether end users—like the farmers I just met in Michigan—could still safely and successfully hedge their costs of production.

I added that regulators needed to do their part to unshackle the American economy. I observed that Americans during the Obama years were living through the weakest economic recovery since the Great Depression.[10] US gross domestic product (GDP) had not grown more than 2.5% in any of the past half-dozen years—the slowest rate of growth since the United States began compiling reliable statistics a century before.[11]

Regulation was costing 11% of GDP, or almost $2 trillion annually.[12] That amounted to nearly $15,000 per household per year.[13] That burden was falling particularly hard on small employers. Overregulation was a barrier to the capital investment that would otherwise be stimulating job creation and wage growth. Regulators had to evaluate carefully the costs and benefits of each new rule: Would it advance or restrain economic progress?

Finally, I said that we had to champion American markets. The major capital and risk-transfer markets—in cities like New York, London, and Hong Kong—were in daily competition to attract the world's investment and trading. Every global financial center wanted to attract FinTech businesses and the jobs and investment they would bring. The United States seemed to be falling behind in this contest. In 2016, the British FinTech sector was employing more people than New York's.[14] American regulatory frameworks, including those managed by the CFTC, were widely seen as complex, conservative, and, in some respects, hard to navigate without a phalanx of expensive Washington lawyers and lobbyists.[15]

If America hoped to protect its vital national interest in maintaining robust financial markets, then regulators had to oversee markets holistically. We had to focus more on troubling systemic challenges like diminution of liquidity, volatility spikes, participant concentration, and market fragmentation. We needed a regulatory culture that was in tune with the needs and concerns of American markets, and not just narrowly focused on enforcing rules against market manipulation. We needed then (and still need today) a regulatory culture that fosters and enthusiastically encourages US-based financial innovation and value creation.

With this 2016 speech, I had laid out what I thought were the key steps for financial market regulation in the twenty-first century. It seemed to be well received by the audience at the American Enterprise Institute.

It would be a few months before I would know if any of those steps would be considered beyond that room.

Chapter 5

Meeting the Locals

When all's said and done, all roads lead to the same end. So it's not so much which road you take, as how you take it.
        —Charles de Lint (writer, poet, and musician), *Greenmantle*

Summer Breeze

Ordinarily, September in Washington is marked by warm sunshine, dry air, and a returning breeze. The lightening languor signals the passage to fall.

Every four years, though, autumn on the Potomac is marked by a dense, frenzied cloud of politics. You can't escape it. It's omnipresent. Politics blares from radios and TVs in apartments, airport lounges, and barbershops and dominates the chatter in swank restaurants and loud Irish bars.

As fall arrived in 2016, presidential politics was particularly feverish. Constitutional term limits were guaranteeing an end to the Obama era, and one of the two candidates vying to succeed him was totally unprecedented: Donald J. Trump.

I had spent most of August giving but a sideways glance toward the presidential race. I knew from my farm travels that Trump was winning over rural voters, while Hillary Clinton had a lock on urbanites. The race would be won or lost in the suburbs. There, Trump was behind. Yet nothing Clinton said or did seemed to engender strong passion as far as I could tell. The race was still up for grabs.

I had been raised to believe that politics and religion were matters best kept to oneself. Although I was a registered Republican and had served as president of my small town's Republican club, I had supported—and continue to support—both Republicans and Democrats. Much of American business did the same. I am less interested in party than policy. To me, politics is not a religion; it does not define morality. Party does not signal virtue or reveal what is in a candidate's head or heart.

I generally support candidates and policies that respect personal and economic freedom. That drives much of my support for technological innovation and entrepreneurship. You can't have the prosperity we love without free enterprise, the cradle of innovation, the spirit of America. The Declaration of Independence proclaims that "life, liberty, and the pursuit of happiness" are "unalienable rights." I believe this means that Americans have the right to enjoy not just political liberty but economic liberty as well. Pursuing "happiness," an unalienable right, can be done as readily in one's vocation as it can be done on one's vacation. To the extent their choices are not unlawful, free people have the right to choose how to make their living, unfettered by the preferences of politicians.

That fall, Thomas Peterffy, an immigrant from Communist Hungary who had founded a trading firm called Interactive Brokers, had been running a weekly ad in *The Wall Street Journal*. It captured well my views about this and every election:

> "Politicians come and go, but the judges they appoint and the laws and regulations they create remain. This election is about whether our

personal liberty and freedom to succeed is better protected in a free-
market economy or one under government control."

At the time, I had also been reading a remarkable book I'd picked up
in August at the well-stocked North Shire Bookstore in Saratoga Springs.
It is about the University of Washington's eight-oared crew team that
represented the United States in the 1938 Berlin Olympic games and
narrowly edged out Italy and Germany to take the gold medal.[1] It's also
the story of the tenacity and teamwork that led the oarsmen far beyond
their plain social circumstances to the highest levels of achievement and
world recognition.

In reading the book, I reflected on my desire to compete in a different forum. I wanted to wage the good fight to modernize financial
markets and regulation in service of economic liberty. As a minority of
one in the Obama years—with other oars sometimes pulling against
mine—it had been a struggle. How great it would be to have a team
pulling together.

Yet I knew that such a world could only come about through seis-
mic shifts beyond my control. All I could control was my own oar. If I
did that well and consistently, the rest would take care of itself. If I was
meant to help modernize US financial markets, it would happen. If not,
then I would have no regrets that I had given it my all these past few
years and left nothing behind. I had signed up for a five-year hitch—in
or out of the majority—and would serve it out.

Politics or Policy

In Washington, everyone understands that policy success requires a
degree of political skill. At the same time, political success requires some
mastery of public policy. As I got to know many leading public officials,
I sensed that they fell into one of two categories. They either had strong
political skills or a deep mastery of policy. Few excelled at both.

I had been appointed to the CFTC because of my policy chops.
Politics was my weaker suit, as I soon found out. Not that I was completely

inept. But now I was playing with the big dogs. The Washington political class are pros—serious players who can demolish amateurs without breaking a sweat. I missed having beside me on the commission the political mentoring of experienced Capitol Hill veterans like Republican Scott O'Malia and Democrat Mark Wetjen, who departed in August 2015, not long after our bipartisan Midwest farm tour.)

Earlier in 2016, I had stumbled in the political sphere. I had noticed certain drafting flaws in Dodd–Frank's establishment of the CFTC's Energy and Environmental Markets Advisory Committee. I clumsily tried to exploit those in a committee report that—quite rightly— criticized the weak economic analysis then underpinning the CFTC's position-limits proposal. It was one of the few maneuvers I tried at the CFTC that was driven more by politics than policy.

It was a mistake. The report was immediately attacked on procedural grounds, and those criticisms were amplified in the press. The resulting hullabaloo must have been vexing to my committee members—private citizens who wished to avoid political exposure. More important, my strategic misstep undermined the goal of improving the rule proposal.

I had goofed up the politics, but I was not going to lose the policy argument. So I publicly withdrew the report. I had learned a lesson about not presuming to play politics, where my talents were limited.

That August, however, I was able to draw upon my policy back-ground—my forte—to good effect. I had been closely following the upcoming implementation by the CFTC and US bank regulators of new global rules adopted the year before for mandatory margin pay-ments by large banks on certain swaps transactions. The rules were set to come into effect worldwide on September 1, 2016. Although the rules had been globally agreed upon, already, 21 of 24 overseas regulators— recognizing the delicate financial climate—had declared a pause in the rules for their national firms. Yet the CFTC and other US regulators were still barreling ahead demanding that US firms meet the deadline on their own.

For several weeks in August, I had worked the phones with traders and brokers—not CEOs, but actual front-line traders—to gauge the likelihood of market disruption. It was clear that a disaster was in the works. On August 31, I issued a public statement warning of the trading liquidity crunch that would occur when US dealers suddenly would not be able to trade with their non-US counterparts that were excused from the new rules.[2] I said the decision would put US industrial and other companies that sensibly sought to hedge commercial risk at a disadvantage compared to their overseas counterparts. American businesses would either face higher costs or choose not to hedge their risks—undermining the whole ostensible purpose of Dodd–Frank: reducing systemic risk.

Sure enough, within just 24 hours of my public statement, Asian swaps markets—the first to open each global trading day—froze up in chaos and confusion over application of the new margin rules. US banks could trade only with each other, while being shunned by non-US banks that sought to avoid being subject to the higher margin levels. With the major US banks sidelined from their customary role handling large trading orders across the market, and the smaller non-US banks lacking adequate capacity, the Asian trading markets almost ground to a halt. It took days to recover market equilibrium at the cost of billions.

This disruption easily could have been avoided if the CFTC and its sister agencies had been less concerned with sticking to an arbitrary deadline and more concerned about causing unnecessary market shock. Worse, it demonstrated some regulators' indifference to the health and welfare of US firms. Rather than putting US firms first, they were putting them last.

It also showed that, when it came to global swaps markets, I knew what I was talking about.

Your Money or Your Life

As a minority commissioner, one of the more difficult policy choices I faced concerned my state's former governor, Jon Corzine. In late September 2016, my chief of staff, Jason Goggins, got a call from Andrew Ackerman, an even-handed journalist at *The Wall Street Journal*. The call was about a $5 million settlement then under consideration that would have ended the CFTC's enforcement action against Corzine. It had to do with the 2011 collapse of the commodities brokerage firm, MF Global Holdings Ltd., where Corzine had been CEO at the time. Ackerman asked us to confirm that the settlement was being held up because I was demanding a higher financial penalty and that Chairman Massad and Commissioner Bowen were unwilling to overrule me and risk being embarrassed by a dissenting statement I might make.

Wow. Ackerman was close, but not quite on the money. The truth was far more interesting.

The enforcement action predated my arrival at the agency. Corzine was the former CEO of Goldman Sachs who made $400 million from the firm's initial public offering in 2000. The following year, Corzine, a Democrat, spent $62 million of that money running for—and winning— one of New Jersey's US Senate seats. In 2005, before finishing his Senate term, Corzine was elected governor of the state.

After losing reelection to Chris Christie, Corzine became CEO and chairman of MF Global, a venerable financial firm whose roots went back to the eighteenth-century Atlantic sugar trade. When Corzine joined, MF Global was an essential commission merchant for many American hedgers and traders of agricultural commodities. However, Corzine quickly set out to reorient the firm toward hedge-fund style trading, making large bets on European sovereign debt. It was a bad idea.

By 2011, MF Global was suffering huge quarterly losses on its trading bets, which was hammering its share price and dropping its credit rating. On October 31, 2011, trading in MF Global stock was halted, and soon thereafter, the firm declared Chapter 11 bankruptcy. It was one of the 10 biggest bankruptcies in US history. Shortly thereafter, the CFTC and Justice Department began investigations into hundreds of millions of dollars in missing customer funds. Corzine quickly resigned as CEO.

The CFTC does not have the legal authority to bring criminal charges. Instead, it refers potential crimes to the Justice Department for possible prosecution. For reasons of which I am not aware, the Obama DOJ declined to charge Corzine criminally. In 2013, the CFTC filed civil charges against Corzine for using funds from MF Global customer accounts for its own proprietary purposes, alleging one count of "misuse of customer funds" and one count of "failure to supervise diligently."[3]

The complaint drew extensively upon email and recorded phone conversations.

In June 2016, my team and I were briefed on the status of the case. The CFTC's gritty director of enforcement, Aitan Goelman, and his veteran deputy, Gretchen Lowe, walked us through the details of a tentative settlement that would require Corzine to pay a $5 million penalty. They took pains to show me that the amount was in line with comparable agency settlements. After three years of litigation, they explained, Corzine wanted to settle as soon as possible so he could start a new business advising wealthy clients.

The final details of the settlement would have to be approved by the full commission. Goelman asked if I was comfortable with it. I said I'd think it over.

I thought about it all night long.

I thought about the American farmers and ranchers I had met who wanted to know why the CFTC had allowed Corzine to hijack and destroy MF Global. I thought about the regional agricultural co-ops that hadn't been able to pay dividends to their members because their money was tied up for years in the MF Global bankruptcy. I thought about all the US senators I had heard bewail that no Wall Street executives had gone to jail after the financial crisis. Yet those same senators never once asked why the Obama Justice Department failed to bring criminal charges against their former Senate colleague. I wondered how I would explain to American taxpayers letting Corzine return to proprietary trading in CFTC markets after paying a penalty that was a measly fraction of his princely compensation as MF Global's CEO.

The next morning, I attended the regular Wednesday meeting of the CFTC senior staff. Afterwards, I took Goelman aside and told him the proposed settlement did not sit well with me. I said I was disappointed that the agency was not permanently banning Corzine from trading in CFTC-regulated markets. The omission would subject the agency to ridicule. I asked what further restrictions could be obtained in the settlement. I later laid out my concerns in a written memo to the division of enforcement.

I heard nothing further about the matter until that September call from *The Wall Street Journal* reporter, Ackerman, asking if I was the one holding things up. Jason, Marcia, and I discussed how to respond.

Ackerman's information was inaccurate. It wasn't about the money; it was about the paltry restrictions. I told Jason to tell Ackerman that we could not confirm his information and, furthermore, pursuant to office policy, we would have no comment on pending litigation. I then immediately went to have another serious talk with the CFTC's enforcement director.

On January 5, 2017, Corzine and the CFTC executed a settlement order requiring him to pay a $5 million penalty for his role in MF Global's collapse.[4] More importantly, the CFTC imposed a lifetime ban on Corzine from registering with the agency in any capacity whatsoever or working for a futures commission merchant registered with the agency.[5] It was the right outcome at last.

Making Introductions

In October 2016, Regina and I hosted a small dinner party at our Washington home. We had the privilege of living in a suite at the Kennedy Warren Apartments, a grand and historic building in the elegant Woodley Heights neighborhood. Among our guests were Brian Quintenz, whom President Obama had nominated in March 2016 to serve as a CFTC Commissioner, though he had not yet been confirmed. (He would take office in 2017.) Quintenz had my full support, as did his co-nominee, Chris Brummer, a dynamic and forward-thinking professor at Georgetown Law School.

Also present was the truly brilliant Hester Peirce. She was a former aide to Sen. Richard Shelby, chairman of the Senate Banking Committee, and now an adjunct professor at George Mason Law School. I had recently contributed a chapter to a book she coedited on financial regulation.[6]

We were also joined by Neil Chatterjee, a savvy aide to Senate Majority Leader Mitch McConnell. Chatterjee had help shepherd my nomination through Senate confirmation, as he had those of many others.

Rounding out the group was my old Washington "Sherpa Guide," Mike Gill, who had recently joined my Commission staff. His assignment on this particular evening was to keep the conversation flowing while Regina and I served the meal and beverages.

I had looked forward to the dinner with excitement. Our apartment had once been the residence of Lyndon Baines Johnson when he was a Congressman. No doubt he had hosted dinner parties with prominent political leaders of the time. Now, 80 years later, the same suite was the setting for a gathering of rising financial regulators. Quintenz, Peirce, and Chatterjee would each go on to serve with distinction at the CFTC, SEC, and Federal Energy Regulatory Commission, respectively.

Among other things, we discussed the importance of strong civil law enforcement in financial market regulation. We agreed that regulatory direction in a Republican administration would have to be robust and determined.

We talked about the raging battle of the Obama years between Washington regulators on the one hand and Wall Street banks on the other. The politicians promised to diminish the influence of Wall Street by increasing the power of regulators. In reality, however, Wall Street had worked behind the scenes to protect its power by influencing the work of legislators and regulators.

As a consequence, we agreed, both the political class and a handful of Wall Street banks and large financial institutions had emerged the winners. The politicians had succeeded in deflecting onto Wall Street Washington's share of blame for the 2008 financial crisis, while the surviving Wall Street banks had just grown bigger and more powerful. The losers had been everyday small businesses, local banks, job creators, innovators—which, although the drivers of the real economy, lacked able protectors in Washington.

Given the chance, we agreed that evening, we would focus on the concerns of Main Street rather than those of Wall Street. Given a chance, we would pursue a market-intelligent, pro-innovation agenda.

Finger Food

Earlier that election year, I had a very long, rough day—but one that ended with an epiphany about Washington, DC.

The morning began very inauspiciously with an incident that cast a pall on the remainder of the day. The incident stemmed from my long-standing love of driving, inherited from my father. At the age of 13, I began driving up and down our long driveway in Englewood in a 1929 Model A Ford, with an unsynchronized, three-speed manual transmission, that my father had picked up at a car auction. In high school, I worked weekends to buy a used 1972 Citroën DS. Since then, I had owned Chevy Camaros, Saab Turbos, and Mercedes Kompressors, and had found opportunities to drive Ferraris, Alfas, and Jaguars. I passed driving tests in New Jersey, Tennessee, and England. I've driven in New York City, London, Miami, Los Angeles, Rome, Paris, Hong Kong, and Bogota, Columbia—driving on either the left- or right-hand side of the road as appropriate. I drove a Saab 900 across Switzerland, a borrowed Aston Martin through London's West End, a Chevy Tahoe along South Dakota's Iron Mountain Road,[7] and a 14-seat Mercedes minivan on Italy's Strada Statale 163, which runs along the coast between Sorrento and Amalfi.[8]

I also drive too fast. That morning, I was rushing to make an early staff meeting. I pulled into the underground parking garage, whipped around the turn to my spot and then—BAM! I had slammed my Volvo's right rear fender against a foundation pillar. I'd just done about $2,000 damage.

Muttering to myself, I grabbed my briefcase and found the elevator to the ninth floor. The day was hectic. I dashed from one meeting to the next while still steaming about my fender.

In the early afternoon, I wanted to step out for a sandwich, but kept getting distracted. By 3:30 p.m. I was starving, but my secretary told me I had to leave soon for a cocktail reception.

I called Jason Goggins into my office and tried to beg off. He said I shouldn't. The reception was sponsored by a large multinational corporation that produced trading market information. I had accepted the invitation several months before and was expected. Moreover, he said that he had arranged with the chief of staff to Senator Bob Corker of Tennessee for the senator and me to speak together at the event about promoting blockchain innovation. Sensing that I was still resistant, Jason said, "Beside, there will be lots of food at the reception."

Jason won. We exited the agency headquarters and got into a waiting big black car. A few blocks later, we came to a standstill in traffic. The car radio was blaring excepts from a Congressional hearing that morning in which some booming politician was in high dudgeon. She was dressing down someone in the private sector for using an apparently legal strategy to reduce his business's income taxes. She was saying something to the effect of, "The people elected Congress to set this country's tax policies and I'm sick and tired of corporations finding ways to get around the laws we write!"

The rant exacerbated my hypoglycemic headache. I had the driver turn off the radio. The congestion cleared at last and we arrived at a modern building near the Capitol. We rode a designated elevator to the 11th floor and strode out onto a boxwood lined, wood-planked roof terrace. The sun had broken through a passing cloud, and there was a warm scent in the air.

The view of the Capitol building was inspiring—its glorious dome having just recently emerged after years enveloped in scaffolding. It lifted my spirits.

Now, I had to find food.

Gathered on the terrace was a classic collection of Washingtonians. Just in front of me: a former senior market regulator and his merry band of lobbyists. He was, as ever, crisply and professionally dressed in navy blue and white. His business partner was nattily attired in a coat and tie in tones of French blue and mauve. A junior partner wore bold pinks and mint greens. The young associate of the troupe, only recently recruited out of government, was sporting off-white linen trousers, a blue blazer, a coral pink silk tie, and a matching pocket square. I teased the new associate good-naturedly about his sartorial amalgamation of the firm's dress code.

In Washington, firms like this one are as ubiquitous as the leaves on the trees. They are the trusted confidants of both those holding office and those who seek to influence them. Poorly understood and often denigrated, these folks lubricate the wheels of government. They help the political class understand the impact—often unintended—of proposed and existing legislation and regulations. In this respect, they are exercising free speech and helping petition government for redress of grievances, two freedoms guaranteed by the First Amendment of the Constitution. In any case, they sure knew how to dress.

The senior lobbyist was relishing a full plate of food that intensified my hankerings. Just as I spied the *hors d'oeuvres* table behind us, along came the host firm's CEO. The lobbyist graciously introduced us. The CEO knew his stuff when it came to the CFTC. We talked about the regulation of financial benchmarks and indexes, like the S&P 500 stock index. The lobbyist opined that pending EU benchmark regulation was less about market safety and soundness than about industrial protectionism for European competitors in global trade. I agreed and expressed my view that Congress was unlikely to emulate EU benchmark regulation.

When the conversation ended, I set off in a now desperate search for nourishment. I was shouldering my way through the crowd when I noticed the arrival of Sen. Corker, who was, alas, headed in my direction. He cut me off before I could reach the *hors d'oeuvres*.

One of the dapper lobbyists miraculously appeared out of nowhere, introduced us and just as quickly faded away, leaving us to chat—just a few feet from trays of enticing appetizers. Their aroma further excited my cravings. I would make the conversation short.

Corker motioned me to follow him to a shady spot—far from the food. But I realized that this was an important opportunity for me, if I could control my appetite. He was an important member of the Senate Banking Committee, as well as a successful former businessman. I began touting the enormous commercial and economic promise of the blockchain. I told him that the United States should lead its development just as it had that of the Internet. It was an opportunity to show leadership in financial services and economic growth.

The word "blockchain" seemed to grab Corker's attention. I bored in for at least three minutes and then promised to brief his staff.

Mission accomplished, I could now eat. I found a long table spilling over with *charcuterie,* grilled vegetables, couscous, artichoke salad, cheese, crackers, and baskets of sliced pita bread. I hurriedly loaded my plate, grabbed a napkin, and looked for a fork—but found none. I circled the table twice. There were no utensils anywhere.

"Pardon me," I asked a passing server. "Where can I find a fork?"

"Oh, no," she said. "There are no forks."

Puzzled, I asked the same question of a well-dressed woman who was carefully placing slices of cheese and smoked meats on her plate.

"There are no forks at these events," she said.

She then questioned, "Are you new to Washington?"

"Almost two years."

Then she unraveled the mystery.

"Look," she explained, "if forks and knives were on the table, this event would be a 'dinner.' And if this were a 'dinner,' then all these Senators and Congress people would have to pay out of their own pockets to be here. But so long as there are no forks and knives—no 'cutlery'—then this is a 'reception' and, under Congressional ethics rules, they can attend free of charge."

"So how are we supposed to eat couscous and artichoke salad?"

"Crackers and toothpicks and pita bread," she answered. "It's a bit awkward, but it saves the politicians having to spend their own money."

I thanked her, and found a place to sit. Now ravenous, I chowed down, rather ill-manneredly.

Finally satiated, my mind regained its balance. The setting sun cast an orange light on the well-patronized tables, with their bounteous offerings being regularly replenished. Three crowded bars were stocked with premium brands. A piano player tinkled away in a corner.

I saw many well-known senators and members of Congress. I watched their interactions with the invited guests, with whom they were obviously quite familiar. I witnessed none of the hostility between legislators and business people voiced at the Congressional hearing I had heard over the radio on the way here in the car.

It then struck me: The only people at this party circumventing laws written by Congress were the members of Congress themselves. No cutlery meant no need to pay for this sumptuous meal nor the generous open bar.

Clearly, American politicians were just as adept at finding legal loopholes as that unfortunate, castigated businessperson who had found a legal way to reduce taxes. In fact, the politicians were more clever. Congress had written a rule that signaled restraint and probity, while undermining it with a subtle—but gaping—loophole. The politicos could mount high horses and denounce people in the private sector for doing just what they were getting away with here tonight.

You have to hand it to the political class: They are pros.

They also know how to enjoy a good spread.

PART II

READING
THE DASHBOARD

Chapter 6

Taking Hold of the Wheel

Take care of your car in the garage, and the car will take care of you on the road.
—*Amit Kalantri* (author, mentalist, and magician), *Wealth of Words*

Consequences

On Tuesday, November 8, 2016—Election Day—I arrived early as usual at the CFTC headquarters. I greeted Cicero, the cheery security guard at the ground-floor reception desk. Then, gripping my morning copies of *The Wall Street Journal* and *Financial Times*, I headed to the elevator.

Once inside, I immediately turned to the *Journal's* lead editorial. It concerned the CFTC's decision the previous Friday, in which I had been outvoted 2–1, to put out Reg AT for public review and comment.[1]

"Most Americans probably think the ability to issue a subpoena, which compels the production of information, is an awesome power. It is especially awesome for CFTC commissioners who can vote to issue them without seeking a judge's approval or finding probable cause. Mere suspicion of wrongdoing or even puzzling market activity is sufficient. But commission Democrats . . . think the subpoena power is not enough.

"So [they] voted to propose a new rule that will—without the need for a subpoena—force regulated companies to hand over the algorithms they use to automate financial trades. Few people care what happens to electronic trading firms. But Americans should understand the power about to be transferred to one agency, and consider how quickly others will want the same power.

"The subpoena process provides property owners with due process of law before the government can seize their property," noted Commissioner Chris Giancarlo in his Friday dissent. "As a legal principle, it was woven into the Bill of Rights. As a bulwark of modern civil society, it protects the liberty of the governed from the tyranny of the government."

Wow, this was gratifying: a strong Election Day endorsement of my position. Appearing in the country's largest circulation financial newspaper, this article put my dissent into the broader context of the feverish growth of the federal state and the erosion of Americans' economic liberties—factors I felt were at the heart of that day's presidential election. I was chuffed.

Tonight would be fascinating. It would be the first and, I hope, the only presidential election that would have a direct bearing on the future course of my life and that of my family. It would likely determine my day job for the next several years. Never had my career path been so dependent on an event so beyond my control.

As states' polls closed that evening in staggered intervals and results began rolling in—at 7:00 p.m., 7:30 p.m., 8:00 p.m., and 9 p.m. Eastern Time—Trump was winning the states that he was expected to win and nosing slightly ahead in battleground states. His surprising performance continued as he was declared the winner of Florida and North Carolina, while running strong in Pennsylvania, Wisconsin, Michigan, and Iowa. As his lead held up, I kept an eye on overseas equity and commodity futures markets. They were selling off sharply—presumably due to the unexpected outcome and uncertainties surrounding Trump's unconventional personality, raising my professional concern. Around 11 p.m., when Trump took Wisconsin, the networks' talking heads were projecting that the trend would lead him to victory. It was an amazing four hours.

Twenty or so minutes after midnight, after checking overseas markets again, I said goodnight to Regina, who wanted to stay up longer. I climbed into bed, less to sleep than to reflect on what had happened—and what to do. As the only Republican at the CFTC, I would be the agency's point person for the president-elect. I ran through my mind the priorities for the following day.

I awoke sharply at 3:30 a.m. I slipped out of bed and turned on the television. Trump had indeed won and would be the 45th president of the United States. The United States had once again marked a peaceful transition of power.

The next morning, I was at my office desk by 5:45 a.m. I was reviewing Asian market conditions, which seemed to have settled. I emailed Chairman Massad, requesting an early meeting. At 8 a.m., I spoke to my office staff, explaining that our day's priorities were to monitor any adverse market reactions and address concerns of agency staff.

A half hour later, my team and I entered the CFTC's ninth-floor boardroom for the senior staff meeting. Division directors, deputies, and senior managers filled the chairs. Senior personnel in New York, Chicago, and Kansas City attended by videoconference. The air was charged. I strove to maintain a relaxed manner but felt under the gaze of many eyes—some soft, some hard, some fearful, and almost all weary.

Chairman Massad arrived late, welcomed everyone, and said he would make a few comments before turning to regular business. Hesitantly, he started describing his first adolescent memory of electoral disappointment. It had been Richard Nixon's election in 1968. Despite Hubert Humphrey's loss, he said, the world did not come to an end. The country went on and the sun rose the next day.

"As Americans," Massad continued, "we must accept the will of the people and do what is necessary to help the country move forward." I noticed a tremor in his usually steady voice.

I thanked Massad for his poignant words. I said that the evening's results were a surprise to many on both sides of the aisle, including myself. The situation that morning was new for all of us. I understood that the change in Executive Branch control had potential impact on some of their careers and livelihoods, I said. I promised to speak with them individually in the coming weeks as the president-elect formulated policy for the agency. I did not know what the election meant for me, I continued, but I was determined to do my part to make the transition as smooth and successful as possible. I asked for their cooperation. I closed by saying that I remained a staunch supporter of the agency and its fine staff. Whether I had the honor to chair the agency in the new adminis-tration or merely advise a future chairman, I would do everything I could to make sure that both the agency and its mission were preserved and supported.

This seemed to sooth some of the agitation. The regular meeting began with a few division reports, including a report on volatile market conditions. The surveillance team said it would continue to monitor markets for spoofing and manipulation to see if anyone was taking improper advantage.

These struck me as the wrong priorities. The agency's first priority should be watching the markets for adequacy of liquidity and other trad-ing conditions that could cause margin breaches and cascading systemic failure. Identifying market manipulation was important but should be a second-order concern.

A short while later, I began to notice subtle upgrades in the way that my staff and I were being treated—so subtle that I couldn't tell if they were just coincidences. First, Amir, my staff counsel, came into my office to report a curious experience. An office facility manager had called him to ask if he wanted the heat turned on in his office on Friday, when the agency would be closed for Veterans Day. The offer surprised him, Amir said, because he'd never been asked that before. In fact, he'd been denied HVAC during service on previous holidays even when he had specifi-cally requested it.

I said that I, too, had been surprised by something similar. That morning, someone finally came to repair the broken toilet in my suite after I'd been complaining about it for months. Well, I guessed it was true: Elections have consequences.

A few days later, I stood waiting for the elevator on the 11th floor of the Kennedy Warren Apartments. A professionally dressed, middle-aged woman walked slowly in my direction with her head downcast.

We greeted each other as the elevator arrived. I stood outside and held the door as she entered.

SHE: Another day and I still feel like I have been hit by a car. It is going to take a long time to get over this.

ME: Well, you know, this is the way of American life. In other countries, power does not change at all, except at the point of a gun.

SHE: I know. I just hadn't expected it. I'll adjust.

ME: Actually, it is pretty remarkable. Eight years ago, our country, despite its history of slavery, elected an African American as president. That could never have happened in most other countries. It is something I am proud of. Now, after 30 years of government by professional politicians and two ruling families, America has elected a non-politician. That would also rarely happen elsewhere.

SHE: Maybe that is also something to be proud of. . .

ME: Let's hope so.

Taking Charge

Over the next few weeks, I met with the heads of each division to find out who wished to stay and who wished to go. Enforcement Director Goelman and the agency's general counsel, Jonathan Marcus, said they would leave for the private sector. Two capable CFTC veterans, Vince McGonagle and Rob Schwartz, stepped in superbly to serve as their acting replacements, ensuring a smooth transition.

In December, President-Elect Trump tapped Goldman Sachs President Gary Cohn as director of the National Economic Council. Cohn and I spoke not long afterwards. He told me that he had responsibility to recommend the new heads of the SEC and CFTC. Trump wanted to interview potential SEC chairs, Cohn explained, but I would be the pick for the CFTC. He told me to get ready to hit the ground running on Inauguration Day. Cohn added that the new administration planned to prioritize economic growth and job creation, something I should keep in mind as I developed the agency's new agenda.

As I thought about Cohn's admonition to "hit the ground running," I was determined to avoid a case of "the slows," as President Abraham Lincoln put it.[2] I had effectively just ended a 30-month training period for my new role, so I had excuses to avoid taking action. We had a great staff waiting to be assured of my good intentions. I wanted to run the agency in an inspired and uplifting manner. I decided to make a series of changes.

My approach to management had been honed by 30 years in the private sector. I had run a large law practice and served on the executive committee of a publicly traded company. I believed in active leadership. The tone set at the top permeates down through the organization over time.

My leadership approach had three key elements. The first would be to articulate a clear ethos and mission and then state it every chance I had, every place I went, and to everyone I met. At the CFTC, the ethos would be professionalism, care, and market intelligence. The mission would be to become a highly competent, twenty-first-century regulator for twenty-first-century financial markets.

The second element would be to recognize, promote, and develop hard-working and talented staff, but not micromanage them. I would use both individual and group settings to do this. I would meet individually and regularly with members of the senior staff for brown bag lunches at the small conference table tucked in a corner of my office. I would inquire about their unit's problems and how they were being dealt with, and about the unit's best performers and how they were being developed. I would offer suggestions and take note of the manager's progress and satisfaction level. I would make a mental note to check back with the manager in a few weeks to see how things were progressing. I would use these meetings to encourage the development of management skills and leadership down through the chain of command.

I would also use scheduled Monday and Wednesday group meetings with the senior staff to review progress of agency matters. I would make sure that division directors and mid-level staff were talking to each other, sharing both operational and policy developments. The agency had too many silos. It also did not easily interact with other agencies. All of that had to end.

Finally, I would take advantage of frequent regional and agency-wide town hall meetings to articulate our ethos and mission, but also learn what was of concern to the staff at large. Some chairmen were said to have dreaded these events. I looked forward to them.

The last element of my management style was something I call: Don't Be a Jerk. It was a warning my mother would give me whenever I was selfish and rude as a boy. It meant: be modest, mind your business, and treat people with respect. I would strive to comport with that standard myself and, by setting an example, convey that I expected it of every CFTC employee in every interaction with each other, with contractors, with market participants, with business petitioners, and with the staff of other agencies. The goal was that whenever members of our staff introduced themselves as being from the CFTC, the other people would immediately recognize that they were smart, collegial, and competent.

When I first arrived at the CFTC from the business world in 2014, I admit I had some of that smug, private-sector bias against government workers. I saw them as "entitled." I was wrong about that. There's no question there's waste in government, and there's no question that the 80/20 rule[3] applies in government as it does in the private sector. But many Americans simply don't realize how intelligent, motivated, and informed most of their public servants are. It was my honor now to lead them while showing them the dignity and respect they deserved.

That is not to say that I did have some strong disagreements with agency rules and policies. But it was never about the people.

That was how I felt about Tim Massad, too. Though we sometimes disagreed on policy, it was never disagreeable to work together.

A week before Inauguration Day, I spoke at a conference at the Roosevelt Hotel in New York. As outgoing chairman, Massad spoke before me and took a few questions. One commenter referred to the past few years at the CFTC as a "a rocky road." When it was my turn at the podium, I said:

> "Before giving my prepared remarks, I want to say a few words about
> my colleague, Tim Massad. There have indeed been various rocky roads
> in the history of the CFTC, but the last few years have not been so.
> Rather, Chairman Massad has brought a thoroughness, a thoughtfulness,
> and a proper pacing to the agency that had been sacrificed in the effort

to implement Dodd–Frank on the rushed timetable that Congress imposed following the financial crisis. Chairman Massad is a man of integrity, conscientiousness, and intelligence and the CFTC has benefitted from his able leadership, as I have."

Priority: Leaders

Inauguration Day—January 20—was a chaotic affair. Mike Gill had been administratively authorized to swear me in as Acting Chairman, which only required presidential designation, not Senate confirmation. The plan was that—within an hour of Trump's swearing in—I would recite the oath in front of the US Navy Memorial on Pennsylvania Ave. Unfortunately, that spot, which was along the inaugural parade route, was thronged with brawling anti-Trump protestors who had drawn a large police presence. We found refuge on the rooftop of a bank nearby. There, against the backdrop of the Capitol, I took the oath in front of former CFTC Acting Chairman, Walt Lukken, as well as my mother, wife, and children.

It was time to assemble the team. In the course of a 30-year career, I had boiled down my hiring criteria to three: subject matter mastery, team play, and leadership. My new division heads needed to be recognized and respected experts in their fields. They also had to commit to actively managing their units and working cooperatively, internally and externally. They had to be ready to lead.

The first and most important choice was chief of staff. Early that fall, Jason Goggins—with two young children and another on the way—had departed the agency for the private sector. For more than two years, Goggins had served me exceptionally well. He tempered my impulses and helped me avoid many rookie mistakes. I would not have made it through those years without him.

Fortunately, to fill this crucial post I was able to recruit my old counselor, Mike Gill. Gill is smooth, likable, and well informed. But beneath his quick wit and easy Irish charm, he is a shrewd and perceptive manager.

I explained to Mike that the role would be different from the one Goggins performed while I was a minority commissioner. Now that I would be chairman, my chief of staff would be the agency's chief administrative officer. He would oversee not just the chairman's office but all agency functions upon which the entire commission relied. It would be a significant position. Happily, Mike took the job and filled it masterfully.

One project Mike took on had a memorable name: Project KISS. That stood for "Keep It Simple, Stupid." It was a general review of existing CFTC regulations to minimize burdens and costs, while still ensuring the achievement of statutory objectives.[4] Over the 40-year course of the agency's life, it would be extraordinary if some of its rules hadn't fallen out of date or become obsolete. Some had been designed for marketplaces that no longer existed. My friend and former SEC senior director Norm Champ wrote in his book, *Going Public*,[5] about how out-of-date rules and policies can bury commonsense practices like barnacles on a ship's hull.

With Commissioner Bowen's support, we adopted Project KISS on a bipartisan basis. Agency staff identified dozens of antiquated rules suitable for review. At the same time, we invited market participants to identify out-of-date practices, too. Basically, the agency was just doing the same thing you do when you periodically clean out your closets and throw away what you don't use anymore.

That summer, veteran commodities and energy writer John Sodergreen wrote in *Risk Desk*, a trade magazine he publishes:

> For nearly eight months, the Giancarlo team has been hard at work KISS-ing and reviewing a multitude of stuff his two predecessors took pains in ramming down the market's (and staff's) throats . . . 'There's a plan and a list and a schedule,' one insider told us. Judging from the level of chaos we see daily at the White House and on a similar level at the Hill at times, we reckon agencies like the CFTC may indeed be soon operating with a level of independence they may not have enjoyed in many, many years.[6]

One unfortunate challenge I faced during the transition period was the imminent departure of my senior counsel, Marcia Blase. She was one of the most knowledgeable and longest-serving lawyers at the agency, and had served as a trusted adviser to many commissioners and chairs. In late 2015 I had convinced her to stay on an extra year, but now she was determined to retire. As her replacement, she wisely recommended a younger lawyer with equal legal skill and judgment, Maggie Sklar.

I missed Marcia's thoughtfulness and good nature, but with Maggie I suffered no loss in quality of regulatory analysis or integrity.

I then turned to finding a new director of enforcement. I was determined to transition the agency from a "coercive" enforcement approach, which focused on imposing harsh sanctions, to an approach that sought to induce compliance through more measured responses. Just before Inauguration Day, I found the right person for this task when Gill and I interviewed Jamie McDonald. He was a tough Oklahoman who had graduated from Harvard, clerked for Chief Justice John Roberts Jr., and was now prosecuting crooked New York politicians as an Assistant US Attorney in the renowned Southern District. Jamie accepted the post and, over the next several years, emerged as one of the agency's most respected leaders.

Next, I recruited a new general counsel. I was looking for someone who could help me resolve a tense, ongoing labor dispute, establish better labor relations, and enkindle *esprit de corps* in the counsel's office.

I hired Dan Davis, an assiduous and full-hearted lawyer with expertise in government agency processes and procedures, including labor negotiations. With Dan's acumen, we settled an ongoing dispute with the National Treasury Employees Union, which represents staff employees, other than political appointees. In fact, the first phone call I placed after being sworn in was to the union's chapter president, Mary Connelly, one of the most conscientious employees I have ever known. It was a first step in trying to effect a course change in agency–union relations.

I also needed to choose a director of international affairs. I was not very familiar with the work of the existing director, Eric Pan, whom Massad had recruited from the SEC. Pan's background was impressive—an A.B. in Economics from Harvard College; M.Sc. in European and International Politics from the University of Edinburgh; and J.D. from Harvard Law School. Since Pan was a Democrat, I assumed he would step down. Party loyalists wanted me to replace him with a card-carrying Republican. Right now, however, I needed his help.

Early on the first Monday after the Inauguration, I received two important, congratulatory phone calls. One was from Jerome Powell, the then governor (now chairman) of the Federal Reserve Board, while the other was from Andrew Bailey, CEO of the United Kingdom's

Financial Conduct Authority (now governor of the Bank of England). Each wanted to discuss an upcoming globally agreed-upon deadline—March 1, 2017—for swaps trading firms to start posting daily margin. There was credible information suggesting that as many as 90% of market participants were not ready for the change and would be forced out of the market. The situation looked similar to—but even worse than—the circumstances the previous September that had briefly triggered an Asian liquidity crisis. Powell and Bailey wanted to know if I would act.

In fact, I had already received requests for relief from the deadline from American life insurers and asset managers who warned they'd be unable to fully hedge risk if the deadline held. I told Bailey that I was preparing to issue a broad "no action" letter that would permit them to phase into compliance over a six-month extension.

Over the next several weeks—and with the help of Pan's tactical expertise—we worked to overcome institutional resistance at key central banks and international bodies and build a global coalition in favor of replacing the fixed March 1 deadline with a six-month phase-in that everybody would adhere to. Pan arranged for a series of late-night and early-morning calls to regulators across the globe, from Tokyo to Hong Kong to Singapore to London to Paris to Bern to Toronto. We convinced some Obama holdovers at the FDIC, the Office of the Controller of the Currency, and the Fed to join the effort. Our efforts were assisted by some compelling data about the magnitude of the problem provided by ISDA.

Our efforts were gaining momentum. In mid-February, barely three weeks into the job, Pan and I set off for Europe for face-to-face meetings with regulatory leaders. We traveled from London to Brussels and then on to Milan for an executive board meeting of IOSCO, the International Organization of Securities Commissions. At Pan's smart suggestion, I had spoken to IOSCO's chairman, the respected Ashley Alder. I convinced him to place on the agenda a statement of support for my six-month phase-in of the deadline.

On the Sunday evening before a morning meeting at the Bank of England, I met Pan in the rosewood-paneled dining room of fabled Durrants Hotel,[7] my regular London digs for three decades. The room was dark and intimate. The meal, as always, was delicious. Over a fine bottle of claret, we had a good talk and reviewed our upcoming four-day schedule.

I complimented Pan on the support he was providing me. I told him that, if I were to continue leading the CFTC, I would not pull away from America's commitment to the swaps reforms set out in the 2009 Pittsburgh Accords, nor would I relinquish US influence on international bodies like the G-20's Financial Stability Board (FSB) and IOSCO. Instead, I would act to reverse the ill-crafted and overly prescriptive implementation of those reforms. I would use American participation on international bodies to steer them toward principle setting rather than one-size-fits-all regulatory standards.

I asked Pan if he could wholeheartedly support this approach. He said he would because it accorded with his thinking. He added that he did not see his role as policy setting but as policy execution—supporting the commission, whoever was chair, and whatever the policy. That was my expectation, I told him, and the only loyalty I wanted was loyalty to the agency's mission. I looked for him to serve as best he could and, if he couldn't, to come to me directly and not go to the press or Capitol Hill. Pan agreed, and I offered him the job. We shook hands on a decision I was never to regret.

By the end of the week European, Asian, and North American regulators unanimously accepted our proposal. IOSCO issued our statement, and the March 1 deadline became the start of a six-month phase-in period that achieved the goals of swaps reform without roiling world markets. We'd gotten it done.

Building the Brand

Back at the office, I needed to fill the role of communications director. Its then director, Steve Adamske, a veteran Washington "flak" whose fair-mindedness I had come to respect, was moving on. Yet, he graciously agreed to stay while I found his replacement. Here I was looking for a "two-fer": someone who could both communicate the agency's underlying purpose and mission and protect it from the continual press battering it had endured for years.

In short, I wanted someone to take ownership of the agency's image, enhance it, and safeguard it from all detractors. My first choice was the great political strategist Tony Sayegh, but he had already been recruited to head communications for US Treasury Secretary Steven Mnuchin. So instead, with Sayegh's help, I recruited Erica Elliott Richardson, who had been running communications for the House Majority leadership. Richardson would revitalize our communications team, while convincing the press that there was only one way to deal with the CFTC: through the front door, honestly and fairly.

While awaiting Richardson's arrival, I asked why the CFTC's Office of Public Affairs did not oversee the Office of Consumer Outreach, a unit set up in 2011 to direct public education but which seemed to operate on its own without coordination with the rest of the agency. Steve Adamske explained that my predecessors had not wanted to disturb the degree of bureaucratic inertia necessary to reposition the consumer unit. I asked Adamske to discuss the matter with Commissioner Bowen. With her support, we soon had the paperwork drawn up that Adamske personally walked around for signature in one of his final acts as public affairs director. By the time Erica arrived, the steps were taken to reposition the office to better support the agency's overall mission.

In just a short time, Richardson made the CFTC both more transparent and responsive to citizens and investors, issuing robust and accurate communications. I was pleased when energy writer Sodergreen covered our efforts later that year:[8]

> "Unlike the past 15 years we've been covering the CFTC, you'd be hard-pressed to find an issue or rule before the Commission that you couldn't discover its exact status. The current agency leadership has made clear its top priority is to keep the markets it oversees fully engaged and informed. Or, at the very least, at a higher level than we've seen in the past decade. . . Transparency was seemingly never a priority at the agency during the Obama administration. No irony lost on that. We note that Chairman Chris Giancarlo foreshadowed much of this new agency strategy for keeping markets informed well before he was confirmed as Chairman earlier this year.

"We recall that nine months ago he mentioned the future production of regular blogs and podcasts, and they've been running weekly since August. . . We've seen the hiring of Hill veteran Erica Richardson as new head of the public affairs office. And, as we saw this past week, formal press conferences are held."

Picking Captains

The CFTC's division of swap dealer and intermediary oversight (DSIO) is responsible for supervising the derivatives trading firms, commission merchants, and swaps dealers that trade in CFTC markets. To direct it, I recruited lawyer Matt Kulkin, a young Steptoe & Johnson partner with whom I worked closely before joining the commission. Fresh and forward-looking, Kulkin had keen people management skills that were acutely needed at DSIO.

The office of chief economist (OCE) had been headed by Sayee Srinivasan, an astute industry veteran. Sayee accepted my invitation to join the chairman's office to work on several key projects. One of these involved working with the Federal Reserve and the UK Financial Conduct Authority to transition US markets away from the scandal-plagued LIBOR interest rate benchmark.

For chief economist, I welcomed Bruce Tuckman, a professor at New York University's Stern Business School. With a PhD from the Massachusetts Institute of Technology, Tuckman is a world-renowned expert in swaps markets. A true polymath with the rare ability to convey complex subjects in simple terms, Tuckman would help bring the agency's swaps expertise up to the level of its long-standing mastery in futures. Under Tuckman, OCE research would increasingly be published in scholarly journals—which, in turn, happened to attract even more prominent economists to the agency. In 2018, Bruce Tuckman and I published a written response to a public discussion of modern finance by the Vatican's Holy See that had criticized some use of derivatives products.[9]

To direct the Office of Legislative and Intergovernmental Affairs, I poached from Senator Pat Roberts—a Republican from Kansas who chaired the Senate Agriculture Committee—a polished Louisianan named N. Charles "Charlie" Thornton III. Assisted by the poised Ann

Wright, Charlie would serve as lead liaison to members of Congress and key executive branch agencies. I credit Charlie with successfully slicing through the Gordian knot that for years had clenched shut the purse strings of CFTC Congressional funding.

One of the harder CFTC posts to fill was the division of clearing and risk (DCR). This unit supervises firms involved in clearing derivatives transactions—a truly critical function in achieving global systemic risk management. The division had not had a permanent director since 2014, when a respected, 12-year agency veteran departed. Three acting directors had succeeded him, but none had changed the division's silo-like nature. Over that period, the division's élan had also faded. I was determined to revitalize it.

Eric Pan recommended Brian Bussey of the SEC. I liked him as soon as I met him. Bussey knew the subject, knew the bureaucracy, and knew how to get things done. Brian went on to do a fantastic job for the CFTC before retiring from government in 2019.

Street Smarts

The most complicated personnel moves concerned the Division of Market Oversight (DMO). It oversees futures exchanges, swaps execution facilities, and swap data repositories. The moves were challenging because of a big gap I saw in the CFTC's operations.

I had become conscious of the gap about a year earlier. In February 2016, an industry contact in London called me around dawn. The spread between the price to buy or sell professionally-traded instruments based on something called the European bank CDS index was rapidly "gapping out," he said. That meant that the cost of insuring against the default of European banks using the credit derivative market was quickly becoming very expensive. The increased expense was a sign that the market was growing concerned about the possibility of widespread failure of European banks. There was growing concern that it could trigger systemic risk, the possibility of severe instability that could cause the collapse of the broader economy. His warning was confirmed by press reports later that morning. Having lived through this exact scenario back in September 2008, in the days before Lehman Brothers collapsed, I was alarmed.

The CFTC's Market Surveillance Branch was housed in DMO. I sent the following email to the division head:

> "I trust we are keeping a close eye on trading conditions in CDS indices, especially in European bank stocks. I am concerned that the loss in liquidity in the single name bank CDS market over the past eighteen months is now exacerbating the widening of spreads in the European bank CDS index market. This may harm the efforts of European banks to raise capital to fund current operations. The effect could be quite serious. I am concerned that trading in US bank and broader CDS indices may come under increasing pressure as a result. Please keep us apprised of any adverse developments. Thanks."

Not long after, Goggins was told by a senior staff member that the job of the Division of Market Oversight (DMO) was to look for manipulation and misconduct in the markets and not to analyze market conditions for systemic problems that might impact overall market health. DMO referred my inquiry instead to the Office of Chief Economist.

Good grief! By the time economic studies were completed, a crisis could occur. The looming situation was a matter for immediate market intelligence and assessment, not one for after-the-fact quantitative economic analysis. Wasn't that was the whole point of Dodd–Frank—to prevent financial crises before they happened?

The situation reminded me of September 2008 when, still in the private sector, I was trying to get the Federal Reserve Bank of New York to better understand the immediate relevance of what we were seeing in the CDS markets. One of the reasons I had joined the CFTC in the first place was to bring that experience to bear. The agency needed to be able to interpret market data signals and take preemptive action as the next crisis was brewing—not after it was too late.

The February 2016 episode had been troubling. It was clear that DMO did not see monitoring overall market conditions as within its bailiwick unless the conditions were caused by rule infractions or trader misconduct that could be referred to the enforcement division. The agency clearly didn't appreciate that general swaps market dynamics could signal dangerous tectonic shifts in the broader financial markets even without specific misconduct.

With Massad's departure approaching, I met with Sharon Bowen to discuss my concerns. I noted that the CFTC's then stated mission was to foster "open, transparent, competitive, and *financially sound markets to avoid systemic risk* [italics mine]"[10] and to protect market users and their funds, consumers, and the public from "fraud, manipulation, or abusive practices." In that construction, fostering "financially sound markets" came before policing them for "fraud" or "manipulation." Yet, no one had ever set up a CFTC unit dedicated to monitoring markets for current financial soundness. It was a gaping omission.

With Bowen's support, I intended to close that gap by assigning to DMO the responsibility for monitoring derivatives markets for systemic risk. As I told one audience at the time, "The CFTC must get smarter by focusing on current and emerging market structure and dynamics and not just on participant behavior."[11] If Dodd–Frank was about enhancing the government's ability to detect the approach of systemic storms, then the CFTC's lifeguards needed to be not only punishing rowdy beachgoers but scanning the horizons for looming dangers far out at sea.

I designated Amir Zaidi, who had been my senior counsel, to become head of DMO. I knew he could execute this critical mission. We moved the Market Surveillance Branch into the Division of Enforcement, where it was better situated. Then we created a new unit in DMO, the Market Intelligence Branch. This new branch would analyze data and information from multiple sources to evaluate current derivatives market conditions and identify emerging market dynamics, developments, and trends. We also charged it with conducting critical market studies and providing advice on policy, risk management, and oversight to the commission, Congress, other federal agencies, and the general public.

Under Amir's direction, the new Market Intelligence Branch was soon producing valuable analysis and intelligence. To assist him, I brought on Andrew Busch, a crisp and irrepressible communicator of market economics, as the CFTC's first Market Intelligence Officer. His brief was to help the outside world make sense of derivative markets. Within 18 months, Amir managed to recruit Mel Gunewardena to head the new branch. Gunewardena was an adroit former managing director at Goldman Sachs and Deutsche Bank, with decades of experience in global derivatives markets and clearing. With Amir's support, Mel had direct dialogue not just with me as chairman, but with all the commissioners and senior officers. The idea was that if any commissioner wanted to understand a matter of current market dynamics, there would now be a designated executive to turn to without layers of bureaucracy.

I would often call Mel on my way into the office to ask about market developments that I had read about or heard mentioned on the morning business broadcasts. He always either had the answer or was quickly able to get it from his team or contacts in the industry. Sometimes, just after Mel finished walking me through some current global market development, I would get a call from the US Treasury or a Congressional committee asking the same question. I would explain the situation with the information I'd just gotten from Mel and sound like a genius!

With the market analysis gap now being closed, I focused on getting the market intelligence branch's output into the hands of the people who needed it most: the commissioners and their staffs. For decades at the agency, the Market Surveillance team had made presentations to the commissioners at a brief Friday morning meeting. These meetings had been poorly attended and had been discontinued altogether before I arrived in 2014.

Upon becoming acting chairman, I reinstituted that Friday morning meeting and assigned Andy Busch and the Market Intelligence Branch to lead it. It was designed as a tight, 15-minute market review focused on current movements in commodities in five areas: agriculture, metals, energy, foreign exchange, and interest rates. In 2017, we added Bitcoin as a sixth asset class subject to weekly review (versing the CFTC's senior staff in the instrument before most of official Washington had even heard of it). Questions from staff and commissioners followed each presentation. All four CFTC offices—Washington, New York, Chicago, and Kansas City—would participate by teleconference or mobile phone. At least one Friday each month, the market review would be extended for a deeper dive into specific markets or trading conditions.[12] (At one of these monthly reviews, Daniel Gorfine instructed CFTC commissioners and senior staff in the intricacies of Bitcoin mining.) I encouraged broad participation in these meetings to raise agency-wide understanding of current market conditions, while honing the presentation skills of the Market Intelligence team.

Working with Zaidi to stand up the market intelligence branch was a great experience. In the course of recruiting its staff, one candidate, who did not wind up with an offer, asked me if my approach would be more "business-friendly." I bristled. I said that a regulator's role was not to be business-friendly or business-unfriendly. Neither was conducive to good regulation. Our goal was to be market-focused and exceptionally market intelligent, I said. Market regulators must be thoroughly informed about market conditions, structure, participants, products, trading activities, and regulatory impact. That was the right way to fulfill our mission to foster open, transparent, competitive, and financially sound markets free of fraud and manipulation.

Teamwork

The week after my swearing-in, I had lunch in Washington with Jay Clayton. He'd been nominated as SEC chairman the week before. I wanted to use this opportunity to get to know him, rather than to delve into the many open issues between our two agencies. Like me, Clayton was a New York corporate lawyer. We had traveled in some of the same Manhattan business and legal circles.

We chatted over some warm appetizers. I felt comfortable with Clayton and sensed his decency and integrity. He had grown up in a family of competitive brothers, as I had. Clayton is affable, but not gregarious; forthright, but thoughtful.

We talked about the nomination process, the laborious background checks, and horrendous financial disclosures. We talked about the intrusive press attention. Clayton noted that some SEC watchers had remarked that he did not know what he was in for. I said:

> "Hey, none of us know what we're in for. But you and I are M&A
> lawyers. We know how to get things done. We know that a good deal has
> to be a win/win for everyone. For the past few years, there has been a
> litigator running the SEC. It is hard to make that work. Litigators see the
> world in binary terms—they either prove their case and win or don't
> prove it and lose. It's not like making a deal where interests are compro-
> mised to satisfy the whole. We've got this."

We had a good laugh. I felt that if Clayton and I wound up heading our agencies, we would have a great working relationship.

The Senate confirmed Clayton in May, and he was sworn in shortly afterward. He and I started a practice of getting together for dinner every six weeks or so, occasionally with our senior teams, but mostly by ourselves. We'd meet at quiet clubs and restaurants in downtown Washington. We'd each have a few open issues scribbled on the backs of envelopes that we used to compare notes and build cooperation between our agencies. We got along well, and our friendship would turn out to be critical during the cryptocurrency firestorm soon to come.

By early summer, the CFTC's Friday market review meetings were up and running. We had invited National Economic Council staff to listen in, and I invited Clayton and his SEC staff to participate, too.

A few days later Clayton called. He said:

> "Chris, I like what you are doing with your weekly market reviews.
> We're doing something similar over here at the SEC. Why don't we do
> this briefing across all the financial market regulators?"

I thought it was a great idea. Having now served as chairman for several months, I was flabbergasted to find out that there was no regularly scheduled conversation among the heads of US financial agencies to share data and analysis about ongoing market conditions.

Just like that, Clayton's idea was adopted. Every Friday morning we held a brief phone call among senior staff of the CFTC, the SEC, Treasury, the Federal Reserve, and the NEC. Often the leaders attended. At least once a month the agency heads themselves would present and discuss market issues and concerns. These briefings became truly indispensable during instances of market stress. We were able to all get on the phone and sort through what was happening. Jay Clayton deserves a lot of credit for initiating this first-ever, regular synch-up of US financial market regulators. I hope these weekly briefings are being maintained by the Biden administration.

Benefiting greatly from my cordial working relationship with Clayton, I set out to establish positive links with fellow leaders of all the agencies that interacted with the CFTC, especially the Federal Reserve Board and the New York and Chicago Federal Reserve Banks. I built good working relationships with Joe Otting at the Office of the Comptroller of the Currency and with both Marty Gruenberg and his successor, the accomplished and cheeky Jelena McWilliams at the Federal Deposit Insurance Corporation. I also conducted active dialogues with overseas authorities, including senior officials at the Bank of England, the UK Financial Conduct Authority, the European Securities Markets Authority, the Japanese Financial Services Authority, the Monetary Authority of Singapore, the Hong Kong Futures and Securities Commission, and the various Canadian provincial securities regulators.

Taste Test

I especially enjoyed working with the incoming treasury secretary, Steve Mnuchin. Mnuchin is razor-sharp, homing in on the most efficient path to a policy goal. He goes straight to the crux of any issue—at times almost too quickly for those who may wish to ponder nuances. He has unbridled self-confidence and presence, and is personally competitive. But he's not politically partisan.

He's also quite friendly and affable. I saw him deploy a deft personal touch one hot and humid summer afternoon in 2017, when Washington was raging with partisan rancor. An acrimonious Senate debate the night before over repealing Obamacare had left many Washingtonians—even those of us not directly involved—with raw nerves and drained spirits.

That afternoon I hurried through a thundershower to the Treasury Building for a meeting of the Financial Stability Oversight Council (FSOC). "F-Sock," as it was known, was established by the Dodd–Frank Act to identify and respond to risks to the financial system and promote market discipline. It is responsible for breaking down silos between regulators in order to "identify and respond to the risks to the financial system and promote market discipline."[13] FSOC is chaired by the treasury secretary and has nine other voting members: the Federal Reserve chairman, the comptroller of the currency, the directors of the Federal Housing Finance Agency and the Consumer Financial Protection Bureau, the chairs of the SEC, the CFTC, the FDIC, the National Credit

Union Administration Board, and one independent member with insurance expertise. FSOC is today the one statutorily required gathering point for America's economic and financial regulators.

FSOC meetings were held in the treasury secretary's conference room, a grand American Empire–styled chamber with a 20-foot, vaulted and painted ceiling and tall, draped windows facing an internal courtyard. On the opposite wall are oil portraits of Washington and Lincoln. At one end is a magnificent carved oak clock case. At the other is a table beside which a waiter often served beverages.

As one of the first Trump appointees to take a seat on FSOC, I watched the council's tone gradually relax from scripted to casual as Mnuchin encouraged collegiality in often unexpected ways.

On this particular day, summer storm clouds outside cast a gloomy light. The room filled gradually with agency principals and deputies. On the conference table were tent name cards for Steve Mnuchin, Janet Yellen, Marty Gruenberg, Jay Powell, Roy Woodall, Richard Cordray, Mel Watt, Keith Noreika, Mark Watters, Mike Piwowar (appearing in place of Jay Clayton, who was recused due to a conflict of interest), and me. It was a mix of Obama and Trump appointees. The deputies sat behind us in armless chairs against the wall. Bill Dudley, of the New York Fed, was participating by phone.

Mnuchin entered last and, as usual, kicked things off quickly and affably. Despite his breeziness, the tone of the meeting was as glum as the weather. Sensing the mopery, Mnuchin said that he wanted to interrupt the discussion with an observation. The room tensed up.

In a serious voice and just the hint of a smile, he said:

> "We are all aware of the ongoing political polarization of Washington, especially after last night's Senate debate. These are difficult times. No doubt, most of us fall on one side of that divide or the other."

With this, I could sense the anxiety in the room over what Mnuchin would say next.

> "When I look around the table, I see . . . (pause) . . . an almost perfect divide . . . (pause) . . . between members drinking water and those drinking Diet Coke. I am happy to say it looks like we are perfectly balanced!"

Everyone did a double take and then exploded with laughter as we all glanced around to see that he was right. The chuckling went on for minutes. The ice had been broken, and the meeting now proceeded with gusto. It was a master stroke of personal leadership.

Battle Ready

I remember the day like it was yesterday. It was a bright, sunny, late summer morning in Manhattan. It was September 11, 2001. I was at work at 100 Wall Street, the offices of GFI Group. I felt a thud, heard a bang, and then, through my office window, saw smoke coming from the side of the North Tower of the World Trade Center. I joined other colleagues in the lobby before a large-screen TV where we saw the second plane hit the South Tower. After some hurried decision making, we dismissed non-essential office staff. Not long after, I boarded an East River ferry and made my way to the packed roof deck. The ferry slowly rounded Manhattan's Battery in full view of the burning towers. The captain announced over the loud speaker that we would attempt to evacuate office workers crowding the World Financial Center pier at the foot of the towering infernos. As the ferryboat drew closer to the frenzied shoreline, I witnessed with my naked eye bodies leaping from the blazing buildings. Then, I watched each tower, in turn, shudder and slowly collapse floor by floor into a cloud of smoke and devastation.

I mourned that day and ever after the deaths of friends, neighbors, and financial industry colleagues. I have not forgotten.

I also recall the extraordinary efforts our firm and Wall Street colleagues took to get markets back up and running in the weeks after.

To some degree, my interest in serving on the CFTC derives from my experience on 9/11. I wanted to play some role in defending US financial markets from further destruction. The victims of 9/11 died at the hands of determined plotters who sought not just human slaughter and destruction of a symbol of Western financial markets, but annihilation of the markets themselves, an unending war. They failed to crash the stock market in 2001, but that attack was just an opening salvo.

Within weeks of becoming CFTC chairman, I called into my office Tony Thompson and David Taylor. They were, respectively, the agency's executive director and the associate director of the division of market oversight. I'd heard them speak authoritatively on cybersecurity two years earlier at an agency roundtable. I asked them:

ME: When was the last agency-wide simulated disaster exercise?
THEY: Never.
ME: What?
THEY: Never. We have never done one.
ME: I'm shocked. We did them routinely in New York after 9/11 and Hurricane Sandy.
THEY: They are not too common in the federal government.
ME: What is required by the agency's disaster recovery and business continuity plan?
THEY: Our plan was never finalized; it is still in draft.
ME: Okay. We've got a problem. I want you to begin a process of recurring, agency-wide, simulated disaster exercises. Starting immediately, we will do an exercise at least every six months. Use different scenarios: cyber-attack, computer system failure, financial meltdown—everything we can think of. Also, get me a copy of the draft plan. We're going to test it in the drills and then finalize it before something bad happens. By the way, things happen in threes. Having lived through 9/11 and Hurricane Sandy, I'm expecting the third one to follow me here to Washington.

Over the next two and a half years we conducted five agency-wide disaster-recovery drills—the first in the agency's history. All commissioners and senior managers participated. For several drills, we brought in an expert moderator from the Department of Homeland Security. At others, we had observers from Treasury and the Federal Reserve Board. One was conducted jointly with CME Group, which operates the Chicago Mercantile Exchange. For the first four we provided notice. The last one, a week before Christmas holiday, was unannounced. That was done to add even greater realism. Real emergencies never come with advance warning.

Thompson told me there was a saying in the military: "You fight as you drill." Through this new program, we tested and retested our ability to respond to various possible crises. It allowed us to review and revise the disaster recovery and business continuity plan, and to see it approved by the full commission shortly before I left.

Happily, it turned out that I was wrong: a crisis did not follow me to Washington. But one did arrive after my departure: COVID-19. I know our regular disaster training helped the CFTC cope with the challenges of the pandemic with greater confidence and certainty.

During my first week on the job, I also had a briefing by the agency's hardworking chief information security officer, Naeem Musa. He presented me with a scorecard of cyber defenses, reviewed each category with me, and said that the agency either met or exceeded government standards.

After a few minutes, I pushed the briefing paper away from me. I said:

"Naeem, I've heard you give this presentation a few times at the Senior Staff meeting. I take you at your word that we meet government standards in these categories. With respect, I am not too impressed by those standards.

"Your job is to tell me what are our vulnerabilities and what we need to do to fix them? My job is to get you the resources to do it.

"From now on, I will meet with you and your team every month. You and I are going to make this place bulletproof."

Fostering Innovation

Tim Massad's departure after Trump's election left Sharon Bowen and me as the only commissioners. No nominations were pending.

Bowen is one of a rare breed in professional life. Fun-loving, but hardworking. Affable, but penetrating. Easygoing, yet principled. Her commitment to the disenfranchised and less fortunate is unwavering. So is her interest in how technology can lessen human inequality.

I approached Bowen with an idea of creating a new group within the agency focused on FinTech and crypto. I called the project "LabCFTC." Earlier, I had asked Jeff Bandman, a former member of Massad's staff, to advise on how best to promote US FinTech innovation while making the agency a more effective regulator for twenty-first-century digital markets. Bandman's report had furnished some great suggestions that I drew upon.

LabCFTC launched on May 17, 2017. We held an evening ceremony at the New York Stock Exchange, at an event hosted by the New York FinTech Innovation Lab. In the audience that night was Commissioner Bowen, without whose support LabCFTC would never have come to be.

A few months later, I recruited Daniel Gorfine to head up LabCFTC and serve as the CFTC's first chief innovation officer. He was the perfect choice. Smart, cheerful, and curious, he was a Brown University grad and an adjunct professor at Georgetown Law School. He would, indeed, go on to establish LabCFTC as the focal point of the agency's FinTech and crypto policy analysis and development and of its engagement with innovators. During the next two years, LabCFTC conducted "office hours" with more than 250 FinTech and crypto-engaged entities in Manhattan, Chicago, San Francisco, Silicon Valley, Austin (Texas), London, Singapore, and elsewhere. It published several primers on virtual currencies and smart contracts[14] and staged the first-ever CFTC FinTech conference.[15] It served as an agency-wide resource to better inform Commissioners and staff on Fintech and crypto-related developments. Externally, LabCFTC acted as a hub the Commission could use to collaborate and share best practices with other US and international regulatory authorities. Through it, the agency entered into FinTech cooperation arrangements with market regulators in the United Kingdom, Singapore, and Australia.[16] Under Gorfine's mantle, LabCFTC became the benchmark for federal agencies in FinTech and crypto engagement, testing, experimentation, education, and policy consideration.

Fortuitously, LabCFTC's 2017 launch came just in time to help inform the Commission on the topic of crypto assets—especially Bitcoin—as we shall soon see.

Unanimous Confirmation

In March 2017, the White House nominated me to serve as full chairman (i.e. no longer "acting").[17] At my request, the nomination would not extend my original five-year term, ending in April 2019.

In June, at my confirmation hearing, I testified before the Senate Agriculture Committee, the CFTC's oversight committee.[18] The committee recommended me for a vote of the full Senate, and, on August 3, 2017 I was unanimously confirmed.

To me, the vote proved two things: first, that many Senators didn't know what the CFTC did and, second, that I hadn't pissed off enough of them during my first two and a half years on the job!

Two new commissioners were confirmed alongside me: Republican Brian Quintenz and Democrat Rostin Behnam. The commission now had four of its five seats filled: two Republicans and two Democrats. However, Commissioner Bowen had previously announced that she intended to step down as soon as possible. Since Massad's departure, shortly after Inauguration Day, Bowen and I—Republican and Democrat, respectively—had together authorized creation of the Market Intelligence Branch, LabCFTC, Project KISS, and a host of new employment practices to improve agency labor relations. I would miss Sharon's smarts, principled stands, and bipartisan goodwill.

I liked and respected Brian Quintenz and Rostin Behnam. Physically handsome, with intensity and intellectual rigor, Quintenz would develop into a principled and strongly supportive commission colleague. Polished and politically astute to the ways of Washington, Russ Behnam was not only a fellow New Jerseyan, but also from my same county, Bergen, in the northeastern quadrant of the state. With two of three commissioners from the Garden State, the CFTC—long known for its closeness to the agricultural South and Midwest—was being briefly dominated by two Jersey boys! Take that, Kansas!

Seal of Office

The week of my Senate confirmation, I was working in the agency's lower Manhattan offices. On Thursday—the day of the Senate vote—I got a call from our legislative affairs chief, Charlie Thornton in Washington. He told me the president had signed my formal commission papers and the White House wanted me sworn in immediately as full chairman.

I had decided to take the oath in front of a large, battered, metal agency seal that sat on a pedestal of honor in the lobby of the CFTC's New York office. There, in front of about 35 staff, I was sworn in as 13th chairman of the US Commodity Futures Trading Commission. I made a solemn undertaking "to support and defend the Constitution of the United States against all enemies, foreign and domestic" and to "well and faithfully discharge the duties" of the commission.

After receiving a kind round of applause, I said a few heartfelt words thanking the staff for their service. It seemed that each attendee stayed a few extra minutes to shake my hand and genuinely wish me well.

As I think back on the moment, it seems quite fitting for me to have been sworn in New York, rather than Washington, for it was largely there, during my long career in the private sector, that I had gained the skills and experience that I would draw upon to lead the agency.

I had consciously chosen to take the oath before that seal for a second reason. It had once marked the agency's entryway on the 37th floor of the World Trade Center. It had fallen into the rubble during that horrible day when foreign terrorists killed Americans on a mass scale, halted our free markets, and hobbled our economy. Yet, their victory was momentary. Our markets rebounded and our agency recovered. Miraculously, that metal seal had been found during the cleanup months after the attack. So, at the entry of the CFTC's New York office, that seal now hangs again—bent and battered, but a powerful emblem of the resiliency of American financial markets and of our agency's enduring vigilance in overseeing them. For me, it was a reminder that there are indeed enemies, foreign and domestic, against whom we must still defend our markets.

Sign of Peace

Back in Washington the next week, I learned something else about the CFTC's seal. I was Ubering back to the office from a meeting on Capitol Hill with the associate director of the market intelligence branch. He asked me if I knew the significance of the images in the CFTC seal. I well knew that the seal featured the American eagle holding the scales of justice while balancing a plow and a mechanic's wheel. Its elements signified the agency's responsibility to balance the interests of agriculture and commerce in financial markets, I added.

The associate director further asked if I had noticed which way the eagle was facing. I admitted that I hadn't. He said that the CFTC eagle looks to its right side, the side of peace. He said it was similar to the Great Seal of the United States, in which the eagle also looks to its right. That eagle holds a bundle of arrows and an olive branch in its right talon, symbolizing that America has "the strong desire for peace, but will always be ready for war."

The associate director, a long-serving agency official, then told me that when the CFTC's Washington office was expanded earlier in the decade, the large, cut-glass seal overlooking its lobby was inadvertently turned the wrong way when it was installed, so that the eagle appeared to be looking over its left shoulder—the side of war. The official felt the flawed installation marred the agency's feng shui—the ancient Chinese system of balancing objects in places to promote harmony and a sense of well-being. The cut-glass eagle was then repositioned in 2014, he continued, so that it became, once again, a conduit of good fortune for the CFTC. I was fascinated by his story.

Indeed, I hoped he was right, especially with Bitcoin futures now just around the bend.

Chapter 7

Bitcoin Approaches the Beltway

Thank goodness she was in a car.
She had always heard it was safe to be in a car in a storm like this. Just keep
driving, her mind encouraged as she rolled her window up and pressed her foot
down on the accelerator. She gripped the plastic steering wheel with both hands
and glanced into the rearview mirror. She could see a car was approaching and
noticed the sky was lighter behind her. Great, she was driving into the storm, not
outrunning it. She took a deep breath and turned on the radio for some news,
maybe a weather report, but all she heard was static and some garbled words.
        —*Constance O'Day-Flannery (author),* Heaven on Earth

Bits and Bytes

Just as I was settling in as Chairman, the first major market rally in
Bitcoin was gathering steam. With the help of fledgling LabCFTC, the

agency began carefully analyzing this new asset class, reflecting my commitment to data-driven analysis.

Within nine months of my becoming CFTC Chairman, the agency published a "Primer on Virtual Currencies," the first of its kind by any major market regulator.[1] We were determined to understand the topic well.

So, what is cryptocurrency?

Generally speaking, cryptocurrency is a digital representation of value built upon a decentralized computer network in which transactions are verified and records maintained using cryptography to avoid forfeiture and consensus mechanisms in place of centralized authorities. As I will explain in Chapter 15, cryptocurrency solves the four shortcomings of existing forms of money: localism, exclusivity, latency, and cost. In doing so, cryptocurrency is a historic and revolutionary remaking of money and finance.

Cryptocurrency, or crypto, is a digital asset that can be used for at least one of the three traditional functions of money. Those three functions are a store of value, a unit of account, and a means of payment. Let's take them in turn.

A store of value is what it sounds like. Although we can store value in tangible property—like a house, say, or jewelry—for the most part we store our wealth in cash, bank accounts, or retirement plans denominated in some major sovereign currency, like US dollars, British Pounds, or Euros.

A currency is also a unit of account in that we measure the worth of things in it. In America, the prices of groceries, gas, or a new car are priced in dollars. We also measure the value of our bank and retirement accounts in dollars. Similarly, many corporate earnings and the US gross domestic product are measured in dollars.

Finally, currency is a means of payment. For instance, we can use it to pay for groceries, gas, or the purchase of a car. We can also pay our taxes with it. Corporations use currency to pay dividends.

Today, there are thousands of different cryptocurrencies with an aggregate value of over $1.5 trillion dollars.[2] They each perform at least one of these functions—to a greater or lesser extent. The most widely held cryptocurrency is Bitcoin. Some consider it a good store of value—possibly even better than gold—because it is limited in quantity, portable, hard to counterfeit, and easy to authenticate.

As a unit of account, on the other hand, Bitcoin is not yet widely used. Not many commodities, for instance, are denominated in Bitcoin. Even Bitcoin itself is mostly accounted for in dollars.

As a means of payment, Bitcoin is gradually becoming more common, though it is hardly ubiquitous. Some online retailers, like Overstock.com, accept Bitcoin for payment, as do some service providers, like Expedia.com.[3]

Each cryptocurrency exists on a distributed ledger of some kind. These ledgers use cryptography (as well as other technologies) to protect the security of transactions, the integrity of supply, and other aspects of the system—hence the name, crypto.

Unlike dollars or euros or British pounds, most cryptocurrencies today are not issued by sovereign governments. They circulate, instead, in a decentralized ecosystem outside of the global banking system. Cryptocurrencies also generally exist in digital token form, which is something that I will explain later when I discuss a sovereign form of cryptocurrency called central bank digital currency.

So what is Bitcoin, then?

Bitcoin is the founding father of all cryptocurrency. It was invented in late 2008 by an unknown person or group of people using the name Satoshi Nakamoto. The idea was set out in a paper published online, entitled: *Bitcoin: A Peer-to-Peer Electronic Cash System.*[4]

Whether coincidental or not, the timing of the paper's release—just a few weeks after the 2008 collapse of Lehman Brothers—was certainly propitious for Bitcoin's adoption. Confidence in the financial system and the institutions that administered and regulated it had sharply diminished. A currency that held out the promise of circumventing and obviating all those authorities was alluring.

Software for the Bitcoin system—in an open-source format—was then released in January 2009.

Bitcoin transaction activity grew slowly over the next few years. For a while it flew under the radar of much of the public and, indeed, of financial regulators (except for law enforcement). Until 2017. Then it suddenly became front-page news and has remained so.

Bitcoin, you will remember (from Chapter 4), is transacted on the blockchain—a form of digital ledger technology. Basically, transactions are confirmed not by a central intermediary—like a bank—but by the consensus of participants in the system.

Given this structure, how would participants be incentivized to do all those crucial confirmations? They would need to be paid to do so. But if the payment was in sovereign money, then a central authority or institution would need to be found to do so. Yet, putting in place a central authority to pay members of the participating community would defeat the whole point of the distributed ledger—the blockchain—to avoid dependence on controlling and, potentially, vulnerable intermediaries and instead use the consensus of all network participants to run the system.

The solution that "Satoshi Nakamoto" hit upon was to reward members of the participating community with the opportunity to receive valuable Bitcoin itself.

Bitcoin Mining

The specific methodology used to do that is called "Bitcoin mining," which is unique to Bitcoin. (Not all cryptocurrencies operate this way.) Mining is a way of both verifying transactions and, at the same time, minting new Bitcoin—units of value.

And that is the purpose of Bitcoin: to incentivize parties, known as "miners," to add to an existing blockchain as transactions occur on the network. The system pays miners Bitcoin that can then be saved or used in exchange for services or goods, including other cryptocurrencies and traditional money. Bitcoin mining, of course, has nothing to do with picks or shovels. It has to do with computer power. Miners update the ever-growing Bitcoin blockchain by verifying each new transaction, as we discussed earlier.

To verify a new block, a miner must solve a fairly complex mathematical equation, or "proof of work." The equation is readily solvable with computing power, but time-consuming to generate. The first participant to solve the equation is rewarded with newly created Bitcoins.

The Bitcoin protocol specifies that the payment for adding a block will be halved every four years or so. When the total limit of 21 million Bitcoins is reached by the year 2040, miners will no longer be rewarded with new Bitcoin, but by some other payment. That means that there is a mathematically limited worldwide supply of Bitcoin.

Many people find this feature of Bitcoin—that the total quantity of tokens is capped—very attractive. By contrast, the US Federal Reserve has unlimited power to put new US dollars into circulation. Other sovereigns can do the same to their currencies. Bitcoin cannot be diluted in the same way.

Bitcoin's unique proof-of-work mechanism has some positive and negative effects. As we mentioned in Chapter 4, the mechanism makes it almost impossible for a hacker to tamper with the Bitcoin blockchain. Indeed, more than a decade since inception, no hack is known to have succeeded in doing so in any large-scale way.

On the other hand, the proof-of-work system consumes an extraordinary amount of electricity (because high-performance computers are used for mining). This energy usage may be seen, in part, as a feature of the blockchain architecture, not a flaw, in that it makes the distributed ledger resistant to a type of hack called a "Sybil" attack.[5]

Yet, energy-intensive proof-of-work mining of Bitcoin and some other cryptocurrencies have engendered environmental concerns. According to some calculations, Bitcoin mining consumes more electricity than the entire country of Norway.[6] On the other hand, compared to overall energy consumption in countries like the United States and China, Bitcoin's energy consumption is relatively light and comparable to energy utilized in the current distribution of cash through bank branches and ATMs.[7] It is also comparable to the energy used in physical mining of earth metals for coins.[8] Moreover, the energy consumed in Bitcoin proof-of-work mining may be mitigated by so-called "green energy" sources and use of carbon offsets.[9]

Other cryptocurrencies do not share this environmental drawback—at least not to the same degree. Some use a decentralized transaction confirmation protocol called "proof of stake" that is far less energy intensive.[10] The reader will recall from Chapter Four the basics of distributed ledger technology, such as blockchain. I explained how it allowed people who have no particular confidence in one another to collaborate without having to rely on a neutral central authority to make sure that nobody spends the same money twice. I said that it replaced central authorities with a "consensus-based authentication protocol" to determine which transactions are legitimate.

There are two major consensus mechanisms used by most crypto-currencies. There is the "proof of work" protocol used by Bitcoin and others, including the initial form of another cryptocurrency, Ethereum, known as Ethereum 1.0. There is another major consensus mechanism called "proof of stake" that is often used in newer cryptocurrencies. Ethereum, the second most widely utilized cryptocurrency, is transitioning to such a "proof of stake" validation process.[11]

The "proof of stake" mechanism performs the same function as "proof of work" to select which network participant will complete the next series of transactions in the blockchain and earn a corresponding amount of crypto. While each crypto protocol is different, generally the participants in "proof of stake" protocols are required to post or "stake" amounts of their own crypto and become a network validator. Generally, a "proof of stake" algorithm randomly and anonymously selects a valida-tor to complete the next series of blocks which work is then attested by the other validators. Those validators with the most and longest standing amount of staked crypto generally have a higher chance of being selected. Once the set number of attestations are complete, the network updates the blockchain and the process starts again.

From Silk Road to Main Street

When I joined the CFTC in 2014, few policymakers, regulators, or money managers were paying attention to Bitcoin and crypto assets. Though many young people were fascinated by it, the few older people who had heard of it dismissed it as a fad—or worse.

Indeed, Bitcoin unquestionably had a dark side. Though that side likely accounted for a small percentage of Bitcoin's use, whatever that percentage was—it was really dark. Bitcoin became linked to anarchism, the Dark Web, and even to financing terrorism. In 2011 a notorious darknet marketplace called Silk Road had sprung up where illicit trans-actions were paid for in Bitcoin. During its two and a half years in opera-tion, thousands of illicit drug dealers, weapons dealers, human traffickers, and other criminals used Silk Road to sell illegal goods and services to well over 100,000 buyers and to launder hundreds of millions of dollars.[12] The FBI shut it down in fall 2013.[13]

Mainstream Bitcoin users—the good guys, so to speak—were lucky that cryptocurrencies weren't banned altogether. The Southern District of New York is still sending people to jail from the Silk Road network as this book is being written![14]

Bitcoin wasn't much in the dialogue during my first few years at the commission. Yet, I was intrigued early on. In February 2015, I met with a group of cryptocurrency developers who were making the rounds, talking to federal and state regulators. Their objective was to establish a more predictable regulatory environment for digital assets in the United States. The group was led by a former CFTC chairman, Jim Newsome, and by Perianne Boring, head of the Chamber of Digital Commerce—a group founded the summer before.

Also involved were Cameron and Tyler Winklevoss, a famous pair of identical twin brothers. Six and a half feet tall, mid-30s, and handsome, they were former Olympic rowers and, now, Bitcoin entrepreneurs (and authors of the preface to this book).

A few years earlier, the Winklevoss brothers had been portrayed negatively in *The Social Network*, a film about the founding of Facebook. In 2004, they had sued Facebook CEO Mark Zuckerberg for allegedly stealing their ConnectU idea. The suit was settled in 2008 for about $65 million. The brothers had then invested a fair bit of that sum in Bitcoin, at one point owning nearly 1% of all Bitcoin in existence. When the cryptocurrency group met with me in the CFTC's boardroom, the twins had recently launched their cryptocurrency exchange, aptly named Gemini.[15]

The group's members stressed that, unlike some in the emerging cryptocurrency industry, they were pro-regulation. They pitched me on providing leadership in establishing a coordinated US regulatory structure that would foster innovation and investment in cryptocurrency.

I saw that their goals were honest. But I also felt they were naïve in believing regulators or legislators could come up with a smart and uniform regulatory structure at this early stage in crypto asset development.

I told them to be careful. With the stench of Silk Road still in the air, there were still significant calls to suppress Bitcoin. They didn't want to encourage a major US regulator to jump in and throw together some highly restrictive or overly complicated regulatory scheme that other regulators—here and abroad—might then emulate.

Instead, I suggested, they should show thought leadership by formulating basic principles for a sensible regulatory framework. I suggested they search out some legal scholars in the field and work with them to develop a set of core principles for cryptocurrency regulation. Then they should find kindred spirits on Capitol Hill who—with support from regulators like me—would champion rules built upon those principles.

My thinking at the time was that Bitcoin was virtual currency 1.0. It would not be long, I believed, before crypto would be huge. After the meeting, I wrote in my journal:

> For decades, parts of Africa were held back developmentally by underinvestment in telecommunications infrastructure. Then mobile telecommunications technology came along and bypassed the need for terrestrial telephone infrastructure. Now, everyone in Africa communicates by cell phone.
>
> It is the same thing with currencies. Many parts of the developing world lack a global means of exchange because their sovereign currencies are pretty worthless outside [each particular nation's] borders. Bitcoin could allow them to bypass that deficiency.
>
> However, there is more to this technology than just a medium of exchange. It is also a store of value. Things of value that are hard to physically possess—like a software license or music or ownership of a car or a piece of land or a share of stock—will become much more accessible with this technology. [Crypto assets and digital ledgers] will allow us to program money and tie it to these things of value. The "chain" will become the storehouse recording office of who owns what and who has access to what. This is an amazing nascent technology that I need to understand better.

Into the Fray

I began to read everything about cryptocurrency that I could get my hands on.[16] In late summer 2015, I confronted my first Bitcoin-related challenge as a commissioner. The agency's Division of Enforcement had been studying a Bitcoin options trading platform called Coinflip, which had come into operation in 2014. The division was now seeking commission approval to bring and, simultaneously, settle a civil action against the platform. The settlement forced Coinflip to cease trading because it had not registered with the CFTC and was not complying with the agency's regulations.

I joined with my fellow commissioners in approving the settlement. With prescient leadership by Chairman Massad, the commission stated on September 17, 2015, "The CFTC holds that Bitcoin and other virtual currencies are a commodity covered by the Commodity Exchange Act."[17] Although the order received little attention at the time, it turned out to be a landmark announcement. It signaled that the CFTC's regulatory authority extended to US trading of derivatives on Bitcoin and possibly other virtual currencies. It also extended CFTC enforcement authority over fraud or manipulation involving Bitcoin derivatives and Bitcoin itself.

It is important for the reader to understand that the CFTC does *not* have regulatory authority over markets or platforms conducting cash or "spot" transactions in commodities. Spot markets involve transactions where the parties take immediate delivery of the underlying commodities as compared to future delivery. If the CFTC did have direct authority over spot transactions, then not only would the CFTC oversee wheat, cattle, and heating oil futures, but it would also regulate farmers' grain sales, cattle auctions, and sales of home heating fuel.

The same applied to crypto. By declaring Bitcoin to be a commodity, the CFTC asserted its full regulatory authority over Bitcoin futures and other derivatives, but only limited enforcement authority over spot Bitcoin transactions.

In contrast to the spot markets, the CFTC does have both regulatory and enforcement authority under its governing statute over derivatives on commodity-type virtual currencies traded in the United States. This means that for derivatives on commodity-based virtual currencies traded in US markets, the CFTC conducts comprehensive regulatory oversight, including imposing registration requirements and compliance with a full range of requirements for trade practice and market surveillance, reporting and monitoring and standards for conduct, capital requirements, and platform and system safeguards. In addition, the CFTC has enforcement jurisdiction to investigate through subpoena and other investigative powers and, as appropriate, conduct civil enforcement action against fraud and manipulation in commodity-type, virtual currency derivatives markets and in underlying virtual currency spot markets.

Professionally, my attention was being increasingly drawn to Bitcoin-related developments. In June 2016, an unusual, investor-directed species of venture capital fund called the DAO (decentralized autonomous organization) lost one-third of its funds to hackers due to a vulnerability in its software code written on a distributed ledger underpinning a crypto asset called Ethereum.[18] That November, CME Group—which operates the Chicago Mercantile Exchange—formed a joint venture with another firm to calculate and publish the Bitcoin Reference Rate (BRR), an aggregation of Bitcoin spot prices.[19]

In June 2016, the commission was engaged in an enforcement action involving another cryptocurrency exchange—the Hong Kong–based Bitfinex.[20] I supported the commission's approval of a settlement. Our order confirmed the CFTC's authority over Bitcoin and other cryptocurrency trading platforms that allowed trading on a leveraged or margined basis, or financed by the platform. These trades were known as "financed retail transactions."[21] In 2010, the Dodd–Frank Act had given the CFTC general authority over financed retail transactions, but this was the first time the agency was applying it to a cryptocurrency.

The Silk Road stink still lingered over Bitcoin well into 2016. Most US regulators weren't saying it was good or bad; they were just silent. Concern about Bitcoin was far greater outside the United States. European and some Asian regulators were very skeptical.

As Bitcoin became too big to ignore, the international community became engaged. In early 2017, participants in IOSCO meetings, especially Europeans, pushed to create an international task force that would take a critical look at Bitcoin. Europeans generally try to establish regulatory frameworks earlier in the lifecycle of new technologies than other jurisdictions.

The early US response to Bitcoin and cryptocurrency was different. It reflected a traditionally more open-minded approach to technological innovation. The American approach generally lets new innovation progress further to see if it can be accommodated within existing regulatory frameworks or if new specific regulations are appropriate. While there are advantages and disadvantages of both the European and American approaches, I favor the American approach over the European one, which too often results in innovation that solves for regulatory needs over commercial ones. In contrast, the American regulatory approach has many times been to follow the Hippocratic Oath of "First, do no harm" to early innovation while its core value proposition is established and public policy is identified.

"First, do not harm" had been the successful strategy that American regulators adopted toward innovations relating to the early Internet. The approach arose in the mid-1990s when Newt Gingrich's Republican Congress and Bill Clinton's Democratic administration encouraged the private sector to lead development of the Internet.[22] They directed US regulators to avoid undue restrictions; support a predictable, consistent, and simple legal environment; and to respect the "bottom-up" nature of the technology and its cultivation.[23] It worked spectacularly well.

US regulators' early approach to Bitcoin was informed by the experience of the first wave of the Internet. It was not long, however, before a big distinction became clear. The difference was that the first wave of the Internet was about making *data and information* broadly available on worldwide computer networks. Historically, information had enjoyed constitutional protection—the rights of free speech and expression—in both the United States and other Western democracies. Accordingly, the decentralization of control over information during the first wave of the Internet took place in a regulatory "light" zone. No federal agencies were directly overseeing the exchange of data—so none had to be overcome.

Today's new Internet wave is different. It is not about information, but about things of value, like personal identity, property titles, and money. Unlike private information, governments have long presumed broad authority to oversee banks, trading exchanges, and other servicers of things of value and their interaction with consumers. The decentralization of things of value is taking place in a regulatory "heavy" zone, including an alphabet soup of federal and state regulatory agencies from bank and insurance regulators to consumer protection bureaus to securities and derivatives regulators. It was only a matter of time before all these regulators discerned their appropriate authority in this new wave and sought to exercise it. So far, all eyes were on the CFTC, which saw the surge early.

Bitcoin Rally 1.0

The year 2017 turned out to be a turning point for Bitcoin. Early in that year, the value of a Bitcoin token surpassed the $1,000 mark for the first time ever. By June, it had climbed above $3,000. The Bitcoin buzz was building.

Meanwhile, I was taking hold of the CFTC steering wheel as agency chairman and sorting out my priorities. As soon as Daniel Gorfine came on board in July 2017 as the CFTC's first-ever Chief Innovation Officer, the agency launched a deep-dive into virtual currencies. LabCFTC began conducting research and working on a draft analysis to increase the agency's understanding of this growing phenomenon.

It was just in time. That summer, the Chicago Board Options Exchange (CBOE)[24] notified the CFTC that it intended to self-certify a new product: Bitcoin futures.

It is worth taking a moment to understand what self-certification is. The Commodity Exchange Act and CFTC regulations permit futures exchanges, in their role as self-regulatory organizations, to quickly bring new products to the marketplace by certifying that they meet the CFTC's core principles. Licensed exchanges may do this on as little as 24-hour notice before trading. Congress deliberately authorized the self-certification process to give futures exchanges the liberty to originate innovative derivatives products. They did not want cautious regulators—overly concerned with the political risks of being blamed for product failures—hampering the pioneering of new financial markets. Thus, the CFTC does not need to "approve" new products. If it simply fails to block a new product before the clock runs out, the product can be released.

Self-certification has long been thought to function well. It's consistent with public policy that encourages the market-driven innovation that has made America's listed futures markets the envy of the world. Since self-certification first went into effect in 2000 through the year 2017, more than 12,000 new futures products were self-certified[25]— more new futures products than any other marketplace on the globe.

When the CBOE informed the CFTC that it planned to self-certify a Bitcoin futures product, the division of market oversight began studying it. Fortunately, the LabCFTC research helped the entire agency get up to speed. At weekly meetings over the summer months and into September, the DMO staff apprised all the commissioners of CBOE's progress.

Meanwhile, Bitcoin's popularity was continuing to grow exponentially. Its price crossed the $5,000 threshold for the first time in September 2017. With the news of the pending launch of regulated Bitcoin futures, the price continued upward. In Internet chatrooms and on Twitter and Facebook, observers discussed their FOMO ("fear of missing out") as Bitcoin's value rose to the moon (a phenomenon shorthanded simply as "moon"), further driving up the cryptocurrency's price.

To better keep up with the fast-moving developments, I instructed the CFTC's new Market Intelligence Branch to monitor and report on Bitcoin as an additional asset class during its market review presentations to the full Commission on Friday mornings. Staff of the new branch also made themselves available for regular briefings to my fellow commissioners. I also instructed Erica Richardson to deploy the resources of the Office of Consumer Outreach, now under her remit, to generate targeted educational materials and programs for the public on investing in Bitcoin and virtual currency.

At about the same time, we got a surprise from the CME Group.[26] A few months earlier, a senior CME executive had told the agency that it was not presently contemplating the launch of a Bitcoin futures product. On October 31, CME abruptly announced that it would launch a cash-settled Bitcoin future product by the end of the year.[27] I viewed the launch of Bitcoin futures by CME and CBOE as the latest moves in their esteemed tradition of world-leading product innovation. It also was an important indicator of the seriousness of Bitcoin as a financial instrument.

Preparing for Launch

A few days later, Mike Gill and I spent an afternoon with market oversight chief Zaidi and his staff to go over the self-certification process for CBOE and to anticipate what we might receive from CME. Zaidi believed that the CFTC had an opportunity to play a more meaningful role in shaping these self-certified products rather than just acting as a rubber stamp. He said:

> "Look, the CFTC has more expertise on cryptocurrency than any of the other agencies because of our enforcement work going back to 2015. But this is our first analysis of a cryptocurrency derivative as a trading instrument. The agency is in a good position to promote innovation in a smart way while making sure these offerings are safe and sound. This is our chance to give entrepreneurs the ability to work in a safe, regulated market."

Among other things, Zaidi laid out how his staff would be able to gather information from the Bitcoin futures exchanges to check for anomalies and disproportionate moves. They would be in regular discussions with CFTC surveillance staff and would provide trade data to them when requested. He felt that in gaining such visibility, the CFTC could better look out for Bitcoin consumers and other market participants. This visibility would also enhance the agency's ability to prosecute fraud and manipulation in both the new Bitcoin futures markets and (to some extent) in underlying Bitcoin spot markets.

We were joined by Brian Bussey (from the clearing and risk division) and Matt Kulkin (from the swap dealer and intermediary oversight unit). They wanted to be sure that Bitcoin futures were sufficiently margined. In futures markets, initial margin is the amount of money that a trading party must deposit and keep on hand with a broker when opening a futures position. Initial margin generally represents a small percentage of the notional value of the futures contract, typically 3–12% for well-established contracts. Then there is maintenance margin, which is the amount of money trading parties need to post at any given time to cover losses. When markets are changing rapidly, and daily prices are volatile, margin requirements are often bumped up to cover the increased market risk. If the funds in a trader's account drop below the required margin level, they may receive a margin call requiring the deposit of more funds or a reduction in—or even liquidation of—the position. The CFTC staff were already pondering what would be appropriate margin levels for the new Bitcoin futures products.

I came away from the meeting satisfied that the CFTC staff was on top of the issue.

Foreign Correspondence

On November 9, I left Washington for a long-scheduled trip to Asia to build stronger personal and institutional relations with regulatory leaders in Japan, Singapore, and Hong Kong. Mike Gill had gone ahead to the meetings in Tokyo, and we met up in Singapore. At the time I departed the United States, I still hadn't heard anything directly from CME about their new Bitcoin product. I suggested to Zaidi that he call CME and inquire about their latest plans.

After fruitful meetings in Singapore, I arrived in Hong Kong on the evening of November 15. Upon landing, I learned that Thomas Peterffy had taken out a full-page ad in *The Wall Street Journal*. Peterffy was the Hungarian-born founder of Interactive Brokers, one of the largest providers of clearing services for brokers. I admired Peterffy's entrepreneurial achievements, as well as his staunch anti-Communism. Rendered in big, bold type, Peterffy's letter was addressed to me:

> "This letter is to request [the CFTC] require any clearing organization that wishes to clear any cryptocurrency or derivative do so in a separate clearing system isolated from other products.
>
> "Margining such a product in a reasonable manner is impossible. While the buyer (the long side) of a cryptocurrency futures contract or a call option could be required to put up 100 percent of the value to ensure safety, determining the margin requirement for the seller (the short seller) is impossible."

Peterffy feared that exchanges would offer low margins to entice buyers to do business on their platforms. If they did so, he worried that the wild trading swings that Bitcoin was known for could imperil both the trading platform and its traders.

Peterffy advocated isolating Bitcoin clearing or trading in an exchange that only cleared cryptocurrency transactions in order to mitigate systemic risk. He continued:

> "Unless the risk of clearing cryptocurrency is isolated and segregated from other products, a catastrophe in the cryptocurrency market that destabilizes a clearing organization will destabilize the real economy, as critical equity index and commodity markets cleared in the same clearing organization become infected."

My first reaction to the Peterffy letter was that the great man's concern was misplaced. Notwithstanding explosive growth, the total Bitcoin futures market was still minuscule compared to mature markets. At the time of his letter, the total value of all the world's Bitcoins was less than $300 billion dollars, while the value of all outstanding cryptocurrencies combined was in the $600 billion range. Even the larger figure was less than the market capitalization of, say, one large publicly traded US company like Berkshire Hathaway (around $650 billion)—a highly valued enterprise, but a tiny part of America's over $22 trillion economy. To put it in another context, the value of all the world's gold was estimated to be about $8 trillion, dwarfing the size of the total cryptocurrency market at the time.

I understood that Peterffy was objecting not to Bitcoin itself but to the trading and margining of Bitcoin futures on the same trading platform as other derivative products. But, again, some perspective was needed. Our agency staff estimated that, even though numbers were increasing, the value of all outstanding Bitcoin futures contracts at any one time (known as "open interest") for the first few years would only be less than $200 million. In comparison, the notional amount of the open interest in CME's WTI crude oil futures was more than a thousand times greater—a sum in the hundreds of billions of dollars. Similarly, the open interest of Comex gold futures was about $75 *billion*. It would be almost impossible for any margining failure of Bitcoin futures to bring down a clearinghouse and "destabilize the real economy"—which was Peterffy's stated concern.

My other reaction to the Peterffy letter was its irony. Here was a paragon of daring entrepreneurialism that I so greatly admired, who had escaped from European socialist central planning to arrive penniless in America. He had succeeded in its free market economy by challenging legacy financial systems with new innovations, like the handheld computers he introduced onto traditional stock exchange trading floors. And yet he was objecting to this new wave of crypto innovation that must have seemed so foreign to the more traditional asset classes handled by his highly successful trading firm, Interactive Brokers.

Yet it was neither the substance nor the irony of Peterffy's letter that concerned me. It was the public impression it would leave. Suddenly, the

CFTC's handling of Bitcoin futures self-certifications would become part of a much larger conversation going on worldwide about crypto. The letter dramatically raised the stakes with respect to the CFTC's engagement with virtual currencies. The media was hungry for anything blockchain or Bitcoin. Reporters and editors were going to jump on it. Peterffy's letter helped put the CFTC in the middle of a global controversy with enormous stakes for politicians, investors, citizens, and free markets.

Task Force Crypto

In Hong Kong, I met with Ashley Alder at the Securities and Futures Commission, and with ministers of the Hong Kong Treasury and central bank, known as the Monetary Authority. As with so many discussions with my Asian counterparts, the topic was financial innovation.

One evening in Hong Kong I was given a reception by business leaders at the US Consul General's residence, known as The Peak. It is a beautiful home set in a dramatic location on a ridge high above the city. Some guests and I stepped onto the balcony in the moonlight and viewed the city lights below, stretching north to the harbor and, in the other direction, to the South China Sea. Hong Kong appeared so very peaceful. There was no hint of the turmoil that would soon accompany China's crackdown on civil liberties.

I flew back to Washington over the weekend with Peterffy's letter still on my mind. Thus far, the analysis of Bitcoin futures had been conducted largely by the CFTC's Division of Market Oversight, although the Division of Clearing and Risk was also on board analyzing a range of clearing margins. I decided it was time to take a broader, more policy-focused view of the Bitcoin self-certifications.

Back in the office on Monday morning, I formed an ad hoc cryptocurrency task force. It was composed of the heads of each key policy division: Jamie McDonald (enforcement); Amir Zaidi (market oversight); Matt Kulkin (swap dealer and intermediary oversight); and Brian Bussey (clearing and risk). In addition, I called in Dan Davis, the agency's general counsel; Maggie Sklar, my senior counsel; Daniel Gorfine (head of LabCFTC); Erica Richardson (communications director); Charlie Thornton, to brief Congress; and Mike Gill, chief of staff, to handle just about everything else. I wanted to consider every angle. I asked each participant to weigh the impact of the pending self-certifications on their areas of responsibility and assess any market or other risk. I requested that everyone talk to each other openly and candidly. I asked Gill to make sure that the other commissioners were updated and able to voice any concerns.

The group discussed the self-certification process throughout the day and long into the evening. No major market risks were identified. No flaws in the draft certifications were recognized. The only regulatory grounds the agency had to block the launch of Bitcoin futures was to find that the certifications contained a false statement, were inconsistent with the Commodity Exchange Act, or that the products themselves (and not the underlying spot markets) were "readily susceptible to fraud and manipulation."

The market oversight staff reported that the CME Group had recently given it a presentation on its Bitcoin futures product. In addition, both exchanges—CME Group and the Chicago Board of Options Exchange—had duly responded to staff inquiries by taking appropriate steps. Zaidi said that, on a fair analysis, there was little basis for blocking either self-certification.

From my perspective, the only remaining bases for rejection involved subjective value judgments, political inertia, or fear of ridicule. Those were not sufficient. The job of a market regulator was not to make value judgments about products like Bitcoin but to make sure that markets worked fairly, soundly, transparently and efficiently free of fraud and manipulation.

I further thought that straining CFTC rules to conjure a way to block Bitcoin futures and avoid political risk would depart from the approach that had allowed hundreds of other unconventional futures products to come to market over the past decade and a half. It would betray the CFTC's history of encouraging market innovation and set a troubling precedent for the future.

At a deeper level, I sensed that blocking these new futures products would not, in any case, stop the rise of Bitcoin or other virtual currencies.

It would be like England's ancient King Canute setting his throne by the seashore and commanding the incoming tide to not wet the soles of his feet. The crypto tide would continue to rise and wash over regulators' ankles and legs.

It was a strange challenge we were facing. If we concocted a way to block the self-certifications, trading in Bitcoin and other crypto would still continue, but far away from the well-regulated markets that the CFTC supervised. We would be abandoning Bitcoin trading to a wild, unregulated fate. Yet, by not blocking, we would be almost certainly fostering the growth of a legitimate, institutional Bitcoin futures market, a market that the CFTC would need to police effectively.

The decision was indeed momentous.

Chapter 8

Go Time

Nothing is, as it was.
Each day is a clean slate. You have to create
A whole new path instead, Find another gear;
Or a different vehicle To get there. Many roads lie ahead, Limited only by
imagination
And determination. Keep moving, You'll find another way.
          —Carolyn Brunelle (poet and painter), "Shifting Gears"

Taking Action

My beloved mentor, Henry Galant, professor of government at Skidmore College, was fond of the aphorism, "To govern is to choose." It was a *bon mot* of Galant's own mentor, Pierre Mendès-France.[1] It meant that good government means making decisions, even hard ones.

As chairman of the agency, I had the authority and the duty to over-see the staff's response to the self-certifications of Bitcoin futures. I was increasingly coming to the view that I would not seek ways to block them. Instead, I was inclined to let them proceed and, in so doing, establish the world's first regulated market in which investors could conduct crypto price discovery, transact in transparent and orderly markets, and establish fair market value.

Nevertheless, with the support of the new crypto task force, Amir Zaidi and his team in the Division of Market Oversight were putting the self-certifications through a process of unprecedented scrutiny he called "heightened review." The futures exchanges were by and large cooperating, and we were wresting valuable concessions. We'd be obtaining trading data that would enable us to better protect consumers and Bitcoin market participants and to better detect fraud and manipulation. We were also negotiating to seek higher trading margins to ensure adequate collateral given the underlying volatility of Bitcoin.

I did notice one anomaly about the self-certification process, however. Though I thought it was generally smart, pro-innovation public policy, I realized it had a flaw. When a regulated exchange chose to self-certify a new product, it obligated the CFTC to study that product and to police it for its susceptibility to fraud and manipulation. Indeed, the fact that the product went through CFTC vetting tended to increase public confidence in it when it launched, increasing its value to the exchange. But while all the benefits of a successful product launch would go to the exchange, the agency's costs of studying and policing it fell entirely on the US taxpayer. This is called a "free rider" problem. It is why when you remodel your kitchen, town building inspectors charge you a fee to review your plans and your construction. Otherwise, those costs would effectively be borne by your neighbors in the form of tax assessments while you enjoyed the increased value of your home.

The CFTC should be able to charge appropriate fees to registered exchanges for the reasonable costs of reviewing new self-certified products and Congress should allow the CFTC to use such fees to defray the costs of new product reviews. In most cases of routine self-certifications, these fees would be nominal.

Covering Bases

At the end of my first full day back in Washington—and still fighting jet lag from the prior week's journey through Asia—Mike Gill and I cabbed over to *Fiola Mare*, an elegant Italian restaurant beside the Potomac River in Georgetown. There we sat down with NEC Director Gary Cohn; his unflappable second, Andrew Olmem; Jay Clayton; and Clayton's close lieutenant, Alan Cohen. Although we were in a quiet nook, the conversation was fun and rollicking with tales of Manhattan life and business deals of old.

Of course, we also discussed government. We talked about the progress toward tax reform, which Cohn believed had the votes to pass Congress. The NEC's goal, he said, was accelerating the US economy to exceed 3% economic growth and the job creation that would follow. Cohn also complimented Clayton and me on how fast we had gotten up to speed in our jobs and on the fact that we were working together. He said having chairs of the SEC and CFTC that worked together rather than against each other was, in itself, a "Washington miracle." He encouraged Clayton and me to appear together on more New York business media and at more Congressional hearings.

I asked Cohn what else we could do to help.

"Just do smart, impactful regulation," he said. "No radical stuff, just smart stuff that will make the economy grow and create jobs."

"Okay," I responded, "since you mention 'radical,' let me tell you about Bitcoin futures. Did you see Peterffy's letter in the *Journal*?"

"Yeah, what was that about?" Cohn replied.

I then reviewed the two self-certifications coming to the CFTC and how we were handling them. We were inclined to move forward, I said, but would appreciate a gut check from him.

Cohn agreed with our approach. He liked our strategy of going forward to gain better futures trading data and data from the spot markets that set the price for Bitcoin futures.

As a former commodities trader, Cohn understood that although professional traders were unwilling to trade on unregulated spot cryptocurrency platforms, they would trade actively on CFTC regulated futures markets—including on the rise or fall of Bitcoin prices if a Bitcoin futures product was launched.

Jay Clayton was listening carefully during this conversation. He asked a few probing questions about how the CFTC self-certification process worked. I knew Clayton had his issues with the explosion in ICOs, or initial coin offerings—a type of crowdsourced corporate fundraising by a company seeking to launch a new venture or product by selling a cryptocurrency "token." I was sympathetic to Clayton's cautiousness. He had to protect the integrity of 90 years of US securities law and practice. Yet I was glad he never suggested blocking Bitcoin futures, which would have made things quite awkward. Instead, he asked me to join him in an op-ed discussing the benefits of technological innovation and warning market participants about the dangers in crypto investing, to which I readily agreed. It would turn out, however, to be another six weeks before we settled on the final language.

The next morning, I made a series of calls to critical futures clearing members, including senior executives at Goldman Sachs, JP Morgan, and Morgan Stanley. I also spoke to Tom Sexton, the head of the National Futures Association (NFA), the industry's self-regulatory organization; and to Walt Lukken at its trade association, the Futures Industry Association (FIA). Walt said he had heard a few concerns from some FIA members, but nothing significant.

From these conversations, I discerned several substantive issues. One was the level of initial margin that was going to be required to trade the new product. CBOE was proposing a 40% initial margin to discourage fast money retail participation. CME, in contrast, had initially wanted to use a 20% margin and had, during the self-certification review process, bumped that up to 27%. As a result, some clearing members were concerned about margin arbitrage.

These were well-regulated exchanges open primarily to institutional participation. I wasn't worried about somebody's grandma betting her retirement savings on Bitcoin futures. She would not have met the legal qualifications to trade the futures product. But since this was such a volatile market, we needed to set appropriate margins so that even seasoned traders did not end up blowing through the reserves at the clearinghouse. So we wanted the CME to raise the bar still further on its margins.

I also spoke to Thomas Peterffy at Interactive Brokers. I told him that the total Bitcoin futures open interest would be tiny compared to the open interest of mature futures products. I said that CFTC staff felt that it would be impossible for any margining failure of Bitcoin futures to bring down the clearinghouse and harm the real economy. Peterffy acknowledged the points but still urged me to require CME to segregate the clearing margin of Bitcoin futures from the clearing margin of other products. I countered that the agency experts said such segregation would itself destabilize the clearinghouse and that it was better to pool all the margin together. He politely disagreed. I explained that the CFTC's product self-certification process did not give the agency discretion to direct clearinghouse margin segregation. For that reason, I said my hands were tied.

By late Tuesday, the ramifications of the pending Bitcoin futures self-certifications were much more evident to me. So was my jet lag from my trip to Asia. I left the CFTC at 5 p.m., went to my apartment, and fell asleep. I awoke four hours later. Then I drove to New Jersey.

On the Wednesday before Thanksgiving, I had a long conversation with CME's forceful chairman, Terry Duffy, who was his characteristic self, a combination of charming, incisive, and blunt. I wanted to establish common ground. I outlined several concerns. But I also let him know that I was not inclined to try to block CME's self-certification, provided that the CFTC staff got more comfortable with how our concerns were addressed.

Duffy was willing to work with us on higher margins. But he was resistant to our interest in obtaining trading data from the spot futures exchanges that were providing prices for the new Bitcoin futures. Duffy said that CME's lawyers were telling him that they could force the self-certification on us. I replied that, in that event, the CFTC would surely state publicly that its concerns had not been satisfied. The moment was suddenly tense, but then resolved when we both laughed and agreed that neither of us wanted a public scrape. I encouraged patience and collaboration to address staff concerns. He agreed.

I was buying time.

Physical Delivery

Meanwhile, a curious new issue had arisen. We were wrestling with the concept of what constitutes "physical delivery" in the virtual currency context. It is a legal standard that delineates CFTC jurisdiction that, ironically, has little meaning in the virtual world of the Internet of Value.

Let's step back from cryptocurrencies, and talk about conventional commodities. The CFTC generally does not have jurisdiction over "spot" markets for commodities. Remember, a spot market is a market in which one takes immediate delivery, as opposed to future delivery. As I explained before, if the CFTC had direct authority over spot markets, then it would regulate everyday sales of commodities like beef, grain, petroleum and gold at cattle markets, grain elevators, gas stations, and jewelry stores—not exactly what Congress intended. Unless there is fraud or manipulation in those spot markets that impacts trading in derivatives, then the CFTC stays out of them.

Instead, the CFTC primarily regulates derivatives markets, like futures and swaps, based on those underlying commodities. When a commodity is sold for cash, Congress has decreed if the seller delivers the commodity to the buyer within 28 days, then it is a spot market and the CFTC does not have primary jurisdiction. If the delivery takes longer, then the CFTC has jurisdiction. (Why 28 days? There is a tremendous amount of folklore around that, but suffice to say that 28 days is the delivery window Congress wrote into law for all commodities except foreign currency.)

Now let's return to cryptocurrency markets. In 2016, as I mentioned, the CFTC had brought and settled an enforcement action against Bitfinex, a Hong Kong–based cryptocurrency platform. The agency had found that Bitfinex was engaged in certain of the special practices that would trigger the need for CFTC registration, and that it had not complied with that rule. But a side issue that had arisen there—and had not been definitively addressed in the CFTC order—was whether Bitfinex was also violating the 28-day delivery rule with respect to the cryptocurrencies being sold on it. Since then, we'd begun to see other cases raising similar questions. Cryptocurrency market participants who wanted to comply with the law weren't sure what the law was.

The problem was this: Many spot platforms were selling virtual currencies to purchasers without registering those sales on the digital ledger of the currency in question. These were known as "off-chain" transactions (i.e. off blockchain). Market participants liked off-chain transactions because they avoided incurring mining fees to record the transaction on the blockchain. But these sales also seemed to undermine the integrity of digital assets themselves. The public digital ledger, after all, was what was supposed to make transactions secure without the intervention of trusted intermediaries. Because of these off-chain transactions, the public ledger no longer provided an immutable record of all transactions.

To our knowledge, none of the platforms we were investigating were acting fraudulently. They were not, for instance, selling more currency than they had title to. But a case could be made that off-chain sales were not spot transactions at all, because settlement was not final at point of sale. That might make them swaps transactions. That would mean that the platforms would need to register with the CFTC.

I wanted there to be clarity on these questions. I also wanted the agency to provide that clarity forthrightly. I didn't want to force market participants to have to guess at what the law was by studying a series of disparate court orders. If they got it right, they proceeded without hindrance. If they got it wrong, they would be subject to an enforcement action by the CFTC. It was legal Russian roulette. When I was in the private sector, that sort of "policy by enforcement" used to drive me crazy.

I told our Division of Market Oversight—specifically, assistant chief counsel Phil Raimondi—to begin the process of drafting guidance. Then, I directed our enforcement chief, Jamie McDonald, to pause the enforcement actions stemming from the 28-day delivery rule until the guidance was provided to the market.

Jumping forward, the commission did eventually publish for comment—in December 2017—a proposed interpretation of "actual delivery" in the context of virtual currencies.[2] Final guidance came out in March 2020[3] after I had left the agency. It has not been universally welcomed by the crypto community. Nevertheless, I continue to believe that transparent policymaking is preferable to asking market participants to infer a rule from a series of opaque enforcement actions.

Checking In

On a drizzly Tuesday after Thanksgiving 2017, I left my house in New Jersey a bit before 7 a.m., drove to Weehawken, and took the ferry across the Hudson to Wall Street. I walked up Maiden Lane to the Federal Reserve Bank of New York and made my way to the conference center for the Third Annual Conference on Treasury Market Liquidity. At noon, I gave a keynote speech about the importance of ample trade size liquidity in US financial markets.[4] I drew on some superb new research by the CFTC's Office of Chief Economist. I also used the speech to commend Bill Dudley, the retiring president of the Federal Reserve Bank of New York, for his public service.

I then made my way to the Reserve Bank's President's Suite and a comfortable private conference room that Dudley had kindly provided. A short while later, I was joined by Treasury Secretary Steve Mnuchin and his chief of staff, Eli Miller. I had asked for this meeting to outline the issues involved in the self-certification of Bitcoin futures.

Mnuchin greeted me warmly and I thanked him for his time. I explained that there were three issues of note in the launch of Bitcoin futures that I wished to discuss. The first was the objection raised by Peterffy concerning the segregation of client collateral in the guarantee fund. The second issue was setting the right level of initial margin. The third issue was whether the price of Bitcoin futures would be readily susceptible to manipulation.

I told Mnuchin that Peterffy's concern did not seem to be widely shared by other clearing members or CFTC professional staff. There was virtually no systemic risk in what would be a small open interest in Bitcoin futures compared to the overall clearinghouse guarantee fund. In fact, the major clearing members seemed opposed to Peterffy's position because they wanted to be able to further margin their trading of Bitcoin futures with the excess collateral they had at the clearinghouse, an efficient use of capital—but something they could not do if margins were segregated. Besides, the self-certification process gave the CFTC no specific power to require segregated margining.

Items two and three, however, were more significant, I said. Issue two was about protecting small market participants, and issue three was about giving the CFTC better data to help police Bitcoin futures and spot markets for fraud and manipulation.

Mnuchin asked good questions. He was especially interested in the self-certification process. I explained the free-rider aspects of the exchange being able to self-certify a new product and then advertise that they are operating a regulated market while the CFTC is left to bear the cost of reviewing the application at taxpayer expense.

Mnuchin was interested in this concern. Ultimately, he said that he agreed with my approach of focusing on issues two and three. He asked me to keep him updated on my progress.

I had now briefed my top three financial market counterparts about the Bitcoin futures launches: Treasury Secretary Mnuchin, NEC Director Cohn, and SEC Chairman Clayton. So far, I had encountered no opposition, and even discerned tacit support. In the coming weeks, I would also apprise counterparts at the Federal Reserve. Nevertheless, as an independent agency, the responsibility was the CFTC's alone. Everything else was courtesy.

Counting Down

Back in the DC office on Wednesday, November 29, I spent the day occupied with Bitcoin futures. I reviewed where things stood: commission staff held rigorous discussions with CBOE over the past four months, CME over the previous six weeks and, over the past few days, with a new entrant, Cantor Exchange, which was now preparing to self-certify a Bitcoin binary option. The three exchanges had agreed to significant enhancements to contract design and settlement.

I told Bussey to require CME to raise the initial margin requirement to not less than 35%. He came back an hour later and said that they agreed.

I then instructed Zaidi to require CME to amend its contracts with Bitcoin spot market operators (who supplied prices for their index) to make available underlying market data and trading positions. CME pushed back vigorously. They said that it would be difficult to do in time for the scheduled launches. There were a few tense phone calls between staffs. At some point, an executive at CME's clearinghouse threatened to go ahead and self-certify its Bitcoin futures products. We ignored the challenge.

The meeting with the staff virtual currency team went late into the evening. The team worked out what we would require to enhance information sharing with the underlying cash Bitcoin exchanges to assist CME, CBOE, and Cantor in conducting satisfactory surveillance. Zaidi emailed out our requirements.

On Thursday morning, he got a satisfactory reply to our requirements from the three exchanges just before I was scheduled to speak again by telephone with Terry Duffy, CME's chairman. On the call, I thanked Duffy for CME's cooperation. All in all, considering the amount of discretion afforded to futures exchanges under the law, CME, CBOE, and Cantor had been remarkably cooperative with the unprecedented requests we made of them.[5]

I also called Clayton at the SEC with a heads-up on our decision. He said he readily understood the unique character of CFTC self-certification and voiced no concern.

Out of respect to my international regulatory peers, I also placed calls to Andrew Bailey, head of the UK's Financial Conduct Authority (FCA), Steven Maijoor, chair of the European Securities and Markets Authority (ESMA), and other EU financial regulators. Several continental European regulators expressed disapproval saying that the CFTC was "legitimizing" Bitcoin, though none asked me to stop.

Eric Pan, who was out in Hong Kong at the time, briefed Ashley Alder, Jun Mizuguchi, Lee Boon Ngap, and Oliver Harvey, the heads or senior executives, respectively, of the market regulators for Hong Kong, Japan, Singapore, and Australia. Pan reported that they were quite interested in understanding the CFTC's self-certification process. Alder, in particular, said he understood the CFTC's self-certification process, and appreciated the conditions we had been able to negotiate.

Good to Go

On December 1, the CFTC announced publicly that it would not try to block launch of CME's and CBOE's new Bitcoin futures products. In our press statement, I said:

"Bitcoin, a virtual currency, is a commodity unlike any the Commission has dealt with in the past. As a result, we have had extensive discussions with the exchanges regarding the proposed contracts, and CME, CFE [i.e. the CBOE Futures Exchange] and Cantor have agreed to significant enhancements to protect customers and maintain orderly markets. In working with the Commission, CME, CFE and Cantor have set an appropriate standard for oversight over these Bitcoin contracts given the CFTC's limited statutory ability to oversee the cash market for Bitcoin. . .

"Market participants should take note that the relatively nascent underlying cash markets and exchanges for Bitcoin remain largely unregulated markets over which the CFTC has limited statutory authority. There are concerns about the price volatility and trading practices of participants in these markets. We expect that the futures exchanges, through information sharing agreements, will be monitoring the trading activity on the relevant cash platforms for potential impacts on the futures contracts' price discovery process, including potential market manipulation and market dislocations due to flash rallies and crashes and trading outages. Nevertheless, investors should be aware of the potentially high level of volatility and risk in trading these contracts. . .

"As with all contracts offered through Commission-regulated exchanges and cleared through Commission-regulated clearing-houses, the completion of the processes described above is not a Commission approval. It does not constitute a Commission endorsement of the use or value of virtual currency products or derivatives. It is incumbent on market participants to conduct appropriate due diligence to determine the particular appropriateness of these products, which at times have exhibited extreme volatility and unique risks."[6]

In covering the news, *Wall Street Journal* reporter Alexander Osipovich pointed out:

Bitcoin futures would allow traders to bet the price of the digital currency will rise or fall, as they can with commodities such as oil, corn and gold.

Market proponents argue that this could reduce volatility in the underlying market, by allowing an easy way to "short" Bitcoin—that is, bet its price will fall. Futures would also allow Wall Street banks and other big financial players to hedge against a price collapse.

Invented less than a decade ago, Bitcoin has attracted intense investor interest this year, largely because of an extraordinary price surge.

It cracked the $10,000 mark Tuesday, after having started the year at $968.23, according to CoinDesk.

But skeptics call it a bubble, and Bitcoin remains tarnished by its lingering association with money laundering and other illicit activity.[7]

Band on the Run

That evening, I boarded a flight for Minneapolis with Minnesota Representative Collin Peterson, a gruff but good-natured, "Blue Dog" Democrat who was his party's leader (and later chairman) of the CFTC's oversight committee, the House Agriculture Committee. We visited with Minneapolis Federal Reserve Bank President Neel Kashkari and, among other things, discussed Bitcoin futures.

Then, at last, it was time to kick back and have some fun. Peterson and I drove to the Double Tree Hotel in Bloomington, Minnesota. There I would be joining members of Peterson's music group, the 2nd Amendments, in performing at the annual ball of the Minnesota State Cattlemen's Association. The band derived from an earlier Peterson band, the Amendments, that had included former congressman Joe Scarborough, the cohost of *Morning Joe* on MSNBC.

The setting was an enormous indoor space, half the size of a football field, in a large convention hotel. There was an indoor swimming pool in one corner and bars and seating areas spaced all around. The band was set up on risers in the other corner.

We took our places. My Deering banjo and a borrowed Gretsch guitar were waiting for me. So was a cold can of beer. On keyboards was former Missouri congressman and gubernatorial candidate, Kenny Hulshof. In front was Hulshof's former Congressional chief of staff and lead guitarist, Manning Falachi. Behind us was Congressman Peterson's aide and drummer, Zach Martin, and to the side was Library of Congress researcher and bassist, Dan Wolf.

With Peterson singing and me on guitar and banjo, the band performed a mixture of country, blues, and—unusual for me—polka music. I looked out over an audience of several hundred couples in jeans and cowboy boots. Many got up to dance. Meanwhile, kids from the swimming pool occasionally ran over in their wet bathing suits, danced wildly with their parents, and then ran back to jump in the pool. I laughed, lost myself in the moment, and relaxed for the first time in days—maybe weeks.

One young couple danced close to the bandstand. During a short break between songs, the wife thanked us for performing. She explained that for her ranching family the annual cattlemen's meeting was their only yearly vacation and they were making the most of it. She asked us to play a slow ballad. When we started up again, we played Eric Clapton's "Wonderful Tonight." The couple danced slowly back into the throng holding each other a little bit closer.

On Saturday, I flew to central Missouri and then took an Uber to Jefferson City, the state capital. Sometime after 6 p.m., the band arrived in a white minivan driven by Kenny Hulshof and pulling a two-wheeled, U-Haul trailer. I hopped in and we drove away to a funky downtown district of restaurants and bars. We pulled up in front of the Mission, a storefront blues lounge. We set up our equipment and—after a dinner of fried chicken, rice, and turnip greens washed down with draft beer—we performed late into the night in front of a good-sized crowd.

Much too early the next morning, we met in the hotel parking lot. Then we drove several hours south to Lake of the Ozarks, a large reservoir in south central Missouri created in the 1920s by damming the Osage River. You may know this area from the hit Netflix series *Ozark*.

We pulled up in front of the Tan-Tar-A resort, a dated 1960s conference center. It was packed with Missouri farmers. We were greeted in the lobby by representatives of the Missouri Farm Bureau, who ushered me to a first-floor guest room that had been converted into a recording studio. There I taped an interview with Missouri farm radio. That night, with Collin Peterson singing lead and playing Telecaster, we performed for about 800 farm couples. They danced until 2 a.m. and we played our hearts out. It was marvelous.

Friendly Fire

On Monday, back in a business suit in Washington, I met with the new Federal Reserve Board vice chairman for Bank Supervision, Randy Quarles. I knew Quarles from his private equity career at The Carlyle Group and the Cynosure Group, as well as his previous postings in the George W. Bush administration. With his steel-wool flecked hair and chiseled profile, Quarles presents as the archetypal Wall Street banker. He is a serious and thoughtful man. We discussed, among other matters, Bitcoin futures.

"I saw the announcement the other day," Quarles said. "I thought, 'Wow, that looks risky. I'm glad that Giancarlo knows what he is doing!'"

When Mike Gill and I left Quarles's office, Mike said, "You know, you earned a lot of goodwill. If you were another chairman, there would be a lot of second-guessing of this decision. Instead, you are getting the benefit of the doubt from Quarles—as well as from the NEC and the Treasury."

"Yeah, I have the benefit of the doubt until we screw it up. Then we'll lose the benefit and just have the doubt!"

We laughed, but the point was clear. Ready or not, we owned the Bitcoin futures decision and, inevitably, we now owned crypto as well. There was no turning back.

We did take some flak. On December 6, Walt Lukken, head of the Futures Industry Association, called me with a heads-up that the FIA would be publishing an open letter outlining various complaints about the launch of Bitcoin futures. The letter suggested that the CFTC could have done more to solicit public input and delay launch of the products. Rhetorically, the arguments had some resonance. But as a practical matter, they were not realistic. Neither statute nor rule authorized the CFTC to prevent CME or CBOE from launching their products until public hearings could be held. And even if the CFTC could have rushed hearings or requested other public input, it is unlikely that the outcome would have changed. The agency staff had already determined that the Bitcoin futures applications complied with applicable laws and regulations. And more importantly, the exchanges had the legal right to force the issue.

I suspect the letter was prompted by some large banks who were the exchanges' principal clearing members. They were not really opposed to Bitcoin futures *per se*, but they were annoyed about the way CME Group launched the new product. They said they had not been adequately consulted. They felt that CME's self-certification process had moved too fast for them to get ready to serve their clients and make money.

The fracas was a commercial matter between big, publicly traded banks and a big, publicly traded futures exchange—not something that could be addressed at the discretion of the CFTC chairman. Congress had purposefully designed the self-certification process to be expeditious for the exchanges, not necessarily for their members. It could only be hoped that commercial logic would drive adequate consultation between exchanges and their members. In this particular case, consultation may well have been inadequate.

Still, I instructed the CFTC examinations team to look into how the exchanges went about engaging their clearing members in the process of introducing new products. In any case—and as I expected—the FIA letter was catnip for some members of the Washington political press.

Sounding the "All Clear"

A few days later, on a cold December morning, I caught the Acela for New York City's Penn Station.

I had not slept well. The launch of CBOE's Bitcoin futures product would take place in a few days. CME's product would then launch a week later. The day before, the price of Bitcoin had jumped 40% to around $16,000. It was a sharp reminder of the volatility in the underlying spot market on which the new futures would be settled.

The two exchanges had better be ready.

As the Acela hummed along, I reviewed in my mind the concessions we had extracted from the exchanges, including the margin hike and the access to new data that would enable us to better oversee markets. Yet, I knew the CFTC's credibility was on the line.

I called Ed Tilly, CBOE's earnest CEO. I asked if he was ready for the launch of the new Bitcoin futures product. I told him CFTC staff would be carefully monitoring the kickoff. I asked him to take seriously any market disruptions or other problems and to let us know earlier rather than later what they were seeing in the trading data. The earlier we knew, the more we could help. He agreed to stay in close contact.

But my Bitcoin stress wasn't going to ease that day. After arriving at New York's Penn Station, I caught the number 2 train to 42nd Street. There, I crossed the platform and waited for the local to 50th Street. I checked my email and saw that Treasury Secretary Mnuchin wanted to speak by telephone in the next half hour. I thought, "Mmm, guess I know why he's calling."

Alighting at 50th Street and 7th Avenue, I called my old friend Jeff Poss, a partner at Willkie Farr & Gallagher. I asked if I could use a conference room at Willkie's nearby offices to take the call. Thirty minutes later, alone in Willkie's 48th floor conference room overlooking Central Park, my cell phone rang. I was greeted by the Treasury Secretary's upbeat, "How ya doin'?"

I joked that I was "Doing fine, under the circumstances of Bitcoin!"

"That's what I wanted to talk to you about," he said.

I had guessed right. Mnuchin had some Bitcoin bile of his own.

He referenced our conversation the week before.

"I never expected that Bitcoin would double in value in just a few days!" he said.

He didn't ask, but I surmised that he wanted assurance that we were prepared for the two upcoming launches of Bitcoin futures. I reviewed our preparations, including the monitoring that would be done by our Division of Market Oversight and Market Intelligence Branch. I also briefed him on my recent conversations with the chief executives of CME and CBOE.

Mnuchin asked if I was comfortable with the margin levels. I explained that we had pushed the exchanges to raise them and were prepared to require further boosts if needed. I reiterated that, although we inherited the self-certification process, we had used it to obtain various concessions from the exchanges.

Mnuchin acknowledged the point. He told me that he was putting together a virtual currency working group, composed of bank and market regulators, that would meet the following week after a scheduled FSOC meeting. I volunteered to have the CFTC's virtual currency team give a presentation on the first few days of Bitcoin futures trading. He readily accepted.

As the call was winding down, I made a point of asking Mnuchin, "So, you're good with everything, right?" As the head of an independent agency, I did not need sign-off from the Treasury Department. But I was a good team player and I wanted to know if there was any institutional opposition.

"Yeah, I just wanted to check you got what you needed," Mnuchin said, "and your team is good to go."

"Yes, we got what we wanted, and we're good to go."

Then, I tried once more: "So, we're good, right?"

He half-laughed and said, "Yeah, we're good."

I immediately took it. "Thank you, Mr. Secretary."

Back in Washington that evening, I was confident we were ready for CBOE's Bitcoin futures launch that weekend. We had shifted into overdrive. We'd briefed members of Congress and the other regulators. We briefed the other two Commissioners, Behnam and Quintenz, who were remarkably conversant with the pending new product. Additionally, Erica Richardson, our communications director, had arranged a background briefing for reporters. She wanted to make sure the media understood that the CFTC's *declining to block* self-certifications was not the equivalent of Uncle Sam giving his seal of approval to Bitcoin.

We had also increased our consumer education efforts releasing a podcast on Bitcoin investing and Bitcoin futures, a consumer advisory on virtual currency investing, and a brochure on Bitcoin basics. We even created a dedicated CFTC Bitcoin webpage. We were also actively engaged in bilateral consumer education efforts with the American Association of Retired Persons and the Consumer Finance Protection Bureau. No other regulatory agency, in the US or abroad, had done as much Bitcoin consumer education as the CFTC.

The CBOE launch went off without a hitch. Staff of our market oversight and enforcement divisions had stayed up all Sunday night and were in constant contact with CBOE's professional team. Everything went according to plan.

After a full day on Monday catching up on matters and reviewing trading data, I was in my office early on Tuesday for a meeting with Bill Dudley, outgoing President of the Federal Reserve Bank of New York.

Dudley and I had a good working relationship. I had arranged for the CFTC to provide the New York Federal Reserve Bank with various CFTC swaps trading data sets concerning derivatives markets that had not been forthcoming under my predecessors. I think such interagency cooperation is what American citizens expect of their public officials. We would continue it with Dudley's very able successor, John C. Williams.

This morning Dudley wanted to discuss our decision not to try to block Bitcoin futures. In anticipation, I brought in our full virtual currency team: Gorfine, Zaidi, McDonald, Bussey and Kulkin. We gave a run-down of what we were seeing in the early days of trading. Dudley initially voiced skepticism. We carefully went over the data we were collecting. We explained that the product launches were going well and collateral margins were appropriately set. He could see that we had thought carefully about the matter. When we were through and saying goodbye, Dudley said, "You made the right decision." This was enormously satisfying from a regulatory peer whom I respected.

In a very interesting side story, a senior Treasury official had called Mike Gill about self-certification a few days before. As Mike explained to me later:

> "He called me and suggested we were grandstanding by allowing Bitcoin futures to go forward. Further, he was concerned we had 'mainstreamed Bitcoin.'
>
> "As he's throwing me this curveball, undoubtedly to see how I would react, I knew I had a moment to use a tidbit I'd been saving if I needed it. After the Silk Road arrests, the FBI seized the assets involved including 52 million dollars of Bitcoin. Then the feds auctioned off the Bitcoin—as they always do with *legal assets*.
>
> "So I told the official that the U.S. government had already 'mainstreamed' Bitcoin. They did it by holding auctions and selling off Bitcoin to the public. The feds wouldn't auction off heroin, would they? These were official actions that recognized that this commodity was legally held and the owners had price exposure. As such, the futures exchanges were the safest most transparent way to hedge that exposure.
>
> "That shut him up."

Later that morning, I went over to Capitol Hill to meet with Senator Debbie Stabenow, a Democrat from Michigan. The senator and I discussed the CFTC's budget, cyber protection, and Bitcoin futures. She voiced no concerns. She was complimentary about my administration of the agency and my work with her former senior staffer, Rostin Behnam. I thanked her for her consistent support for the agency and her continuing kindness to me. It was a very warm chat. Yes, a Republican agency chair and a Democratic senator getting on very well. No big deal, America. It can happen when you cultivate relationships, keep your word, carefully pick your battles, and perhaps most importantly, plan to stick to your departure date.

Before the Council

In mid-December, I hosted our management team for a half-day offsite to discuss restructuring the agency for greater operational efficiency. All the CFTC division and office directors attended, as well as members of the planning team. Each director presented restructuring plans. We enjoyed excellent give and take, and the group discussed matters from an agency-wide strategic perspective—not like owners of silos. The spirit of cooperation was what I had sought to instill.

Then I got into a large black Ford Expedition and headed over to the Treasury Building with Mike Gill, Dan Gorfine, and Rich Danker, an astute aide who coordinated my work on the Financial Stability Oversight Council. Today's FSOC agenda included a discussion of our self-certification of Bitcoin Futures.

Clearing Treasury Building security, I ran into Jay Clayton. He took me aside and asked if I would do a joint television appearance to discuss Bitcoin. I agreed. We walked together into the Treasury conference room that was buzzing with conversation. I was relaxed as I said hello to Federal Reserve Chair Janet Yellen, Vice Chairman Randy Quarles, Mel Watt of the Federal Housing Finance Agency, Marty Gruenberg of the FDIC, members of the Treasury team, and others.

I took my assigned seat, laid out my papers, and quickly glanced through my presentation slides. I made some notes and got ready to go.

Secretary Mnuchin arrived, sat down across from me, and called the meeting to order. He first addressed an important court ruling on everyone's minds. MetLife had won a US District Court ruling rejecting FSOC's designation of it as a "systemically important financial institution" under Dodd–Frank. He said that FSOC would now consider whether to appeal that ruling.

Item two on the agenda was, yes, Bitcoin futures. Mnuchin began with some extemporaneous remarks. He talked about Bitcoin's use in illicit finance and tax evasion. He said that he had a lot of concerns, especially the use of Bitcoin by ordinary consumers.[8] His tone was fairly negative. Then he asked me to give my presentation.

I discussed the recent self-certification process for the CBOE and CME products. I dove deep into my prepared materials, explained statutory limitations on CFTC discretion, and described our "heightened review" process. I detailed the concessions we were able to wrest from the exchanges, including higher margins and the provision of data to monitor the underlying spot market trading. I was pleased that Mnuchin did not rush me.

Afterward, there were some straightforward questions—especially from Mick Mulvaney, the acting head of the Consumer Finance Protection Bureau. It was a good conversation and I felt comfortable leading it. Toward the end, Jay Clayton also expressed his views about the serious dangers of Bitcoin as a means of making illicit payments and as a speculative asset, but did not express any disagreement with the CFTC actions. Mnuchin wrapped up by saying that he was forming a Bitcoin task force at Treasury and would invite the CFTC, SEC, OCC, and Fed to participate.

We later adjourned and walked down to the historic Cash Room on the second floor. In the nineteenth century, the US treasury had once used this room to provide banking services to area commercial banks, including the disbursement of coins and currency from government vaults. The marble-clad, two-story room had been the site of many press conferences, receptions, and bill-signing ceremonies. It had even hosted President Grant's Inaugural Reception in 1869. Gathered there today were—in addition to us—some members of the press and the general public. The scene was being aired live on C-Span. After a staff presentation of the 2017 FSOC Annual Report, Mnuchin called upon me to talk about Project KISS. I summarized the program and described some of its accomplishments. I was pretty animated in my presentation. Throughout, both Mick Mulvaney and Janet Yellen nodded their heads in agreement.

On the way back to the office, one of my colleagues commented that Mnuchin had subtly "sandbagged" my presentation on Bitcoin futures with his negative opening remarks. I replied that I wasn't too bothered by it since the Treasury secretary had confirmed his broad support in our recent phone call. Still, I wondered how others had interpreted Mnuchin's somewhat dour remarks before my presentation.

Meanwhile, the price of Bitcoin continued to skyrocket. From $7,500 in early December, it had risen to $10,000 within days.

The launch of CBOE Bitcoin futures on December 10 had no noticeable impact on the price run-up. By December 17, Bitcoin had reached its then all-time high of $19,783.21. That evening, CME opened trading in its Bitcoin futures product. Everything went smoothly. As with the CBOE launch, CFTC staff monitored activity and stayed in close contact with the exchange. There were no hiccups, and trading picked up. Yet within days, Bitcoin's "spot" price dropped 30% in value, one of the bigger Bitcoin market corrections ever. The price bounced back to $16,000 the following week. On December 28, it was still over $15,000 at opening, but then dropped to the mid-$13,000s by the end of the trading day.

Clear Mountain Air

As 2017 closed, my three brothers and our families, friends, and cousins gathered for a fun-filled post-Christmas week in Colorado. We were there to celebrate my brother Charlie's 60th birthday. With us were my kids, nieces, and nephews—all Millennials and Gen-Zers. On several evenings, as we gathered for dinner after skiing, they would ask about the CFTC's entry into the world of Bitcoin.

I was surprised by the depth and intelligence of their interest. One of my nieces had purchased Bitcoin several years before and was especially well informed. Talking to her and listening to the cousins talk to each other, it struck me that the energy and momentum behind virtual currencies were not just driven by technological efficiencies and benefits. There was something else going on—something generational and cultural.

My generation became familiar with branch banking services in our teens with the deposit of our first paychecks from summer or after-school jobs. Today, most kids form institutional relationships with mobile phone providers, video game and social media platforms and online retailers well by the age of 14. Yet, by age 16 most kids today still do not have bank accounts. It is unlikely their generation will ever have the loyalty to traditional banking practices that they have for online and mobile service providers. Convincing them that Bitcoin and cryptocurrency is dangerous, while traditional banking is fun and safe, is as about as effective as bidding them to lean to use a manual transmission, if they are interested in driving a car at all.

It was clear that behind the skyrocketing interest in Bitcoin was something more fundamental—a community that views technology as an agent of social change. Many members of it, like my children, nieces, and nephews, had come of age during the 2008 financial crisis from which Bitcoin had emerged.[9] They had lost faith in a faltering financial system and the leadership and institutions that presided over that mess. They had lost faith in traditional financial news media that more often lampooned their perspective than sought to understand it. They had lost faith in their parent's economic stewardship, in the same way that, 50 years earlier, Baby Boomers had lost faith in their parents' leadership during the Civil Rights Era and the Vietnam War.

Skiing each day in the fresh mountain air, I reflected on the past few months' journey down the Bitcoin "rabbit hole." I thought a lot about the potential impact of Bitcoin futures and the underlying asset itself, Bitcoin. I wondered if it was more than simply a new tradable commodity. Was it bigger than that? I wondered if Bitcoin was a fundamental change in the nature of money, something that could, for the first time in human history, allow money to transcend time, space and social class. Was money being changed by a technological breakthrough or by a new generation's expectations for money? Or, was it both? These questions continued to occupy my mind in the following years. In time, I came to see that Bitcoin was truly remarkable, a fundamental breakthrough in the concept of value that I will discuss later in this book.

On the flight back East I read an article by Sheila Bair, a former CFTC Chair whom I respect, in which she wrote:

> Value—like beauty—is in the eye of the beholder. Instead of making value judgments about Bitcoin, what government should do is first make

sure our policies don't feed the frenzy. . . Government should also take steps to help ensure that the Bitcoin price—whatever the market assigns it—is reflective of investors making informed decisions, free of fraud and manipulation.[10]

I retraced in my mind every facet of the self-certification process. Our approach had been a balanced one. Doing nothing would have been irresponsible. Ignoring virtual currency trading would not make it go away. Nor would it have been a prudent regulatory strategy.

Blocking self-certification would have also been a mistake. It would have meant virtually no federal regulatory oversight of Bitcoin markets for fraud and manipulation. It would have ensured that Bitcoin spot markets would continue to operate as a one-way retail bet—always trending upward in price until the momentum died. Futures markets would act as a moderating and maturing force for Bitcoin as they have for most every other investment commodity. They would provide a way for both retail and professional traders to effectively take both long and short positions in Bitcoin—betting on its price to go up or down—in transparent and well-regulated markets. Between upward bets and downward bets, Bitcoin's true market value would be discovered.

I agree with Sheila Bair that a market regulator should not be empowered to make value judgments about the wisdom of tradable instruments that are otherwise legal. Our task was to make sure that the price that the market assigned to those tradable instruments accurately reflected investor sentiment free of fraud and manipulation. Without a forum for short interest, Bitcoin's inexorable 2017 price rise suggested a bubble. If it indeed was a bubble, then the risk was that when it inevitably burst, it would burst at $200,000—rather than, say, $20,000. Such a catastrophic collapse would cause losses of life savings and livelihoods and, as likely, a Congressional overreaction, possibly outlawing cryptocurrencies altogether.

Better "a stitch in time to save nine," as the adage goes. In this case, the "stitch" was to allow commercial forces and the CFTC's own regulatory processes to proceed as designed and intended, without "moralistic" interference.

All in all, we had done the right thing.

Circumstances, however, would soon prove the truth of another old adage: "No good deed goes unpunished."

PART III

SLIPSTREAM

Chapter 9

Facing Resistance

"A critic is a man who knows the way but can't drive the car."
—Kenneth Tynan (theater critic), as quoted by
Godfrey Smith, *New York Times*, 1966

Battling Narratives

Many contemporary observers take it as a given that the media is an accessory to one political party or the other to bring down opponents. And that is actually true of some reporters, I believe. At the same time, most reporters are conscientious professionals. They may not always write the story I want them to write, but they are careful and accurate. There is also no doubt that Donald Trump liked to generate controversy. The media covered those controversies because those stories sold. Both sides were implicated when it came to the fire and fury of the media's relationship with the Trump administration.

To encourage fair coverage, we worked hard to be open and to make available crucial information for market participants, policymakers, the press, and the general public. Most press coverage of the CFTC and its welcoming approach to new technology was fair and impartial. That was due in some part, I think, to our own fair treatment of the press. I believe democratic values demand that agencies and leaders be transparent, open, and informative. Some leaders attempt to control the media by keeping news strictly controlled. Many times in our history, business and political leaders have lied and misled the public about critical events. It happened with weapons of mass destruction before the Second Iraq War. It happened during the Obama administration with, "If you like your doctor, you can keep your doctor." It's happened with corporate scandals, like Volkswagen's "Clean Diesel" scandal, involving cheating on emissions technology.

When you're the head of a federal agency, you are a newsmaker. You soon learn that certain editors and reporters are angling for clicks and controversy, no matter the facts or the cost to the public's understanding. It doesn't take long to know who they are.

Other journalists use news and events to support an invariable, simplified moral fable, complete with a cast of familiar villains and heroes. For journalists writing for left-wing readers, the villains could be Wall Street banks, oil and drug companies, CEOs, and gun owners. Those writing for right-wing readers feature villains who are college professors, Hollywood activists, Antifa rioters, and Democratic city mayors. Not surprisingly, the heroes in one side's narratives are often the villains of the other's.

In January 2018, upon returning to the office after our family trip to Colorado, I did a scheduled telephone media interview on the subject of Bitcoin futures. When it was over, I felt as if I had been in a roadside ambush. I patted my pants pocket to be sure my wallet was still there.

My staff had initially scheduled the call with a junior reporter. I was surprised to find that, during the interview itself, the junior reporter was accompanied by a second, more senior journalist. The senior reporter specialized in longer articles that targeted public officials with clouds of vague allegations. They were often punctuated with damning commentary from academics and other policy experts. During my time at the CFTC, I was twice able to present policy experts cited by this reporter with information that the reporter had not provided to them prior to the article appearing. In both cases, the experts went so far as to issue public statements revising the viewpoints they had expressed in the articles based on the supplemental information.

This senior reporter now tried to keep me off balance with aggressive questioning, including about things I had said during internal meetings that he had learned from inside sources. After a while, his snarky tone and condescension annoyed me, and I started coming back at him.

The two journalists seemed of the view that the launch of Bitcoin futures was wrong and that I had been irresponsible in permitting it. They implied that I had ignored concerns whispered by fellow regulators, recklessly overtaxed the agency's limited resources, and, worse, jeopardized the US economy. They implied that I had not prepared the agency to handle Bitcoin futures. They also suggested that I had allowed the self-certifications to monopolize too much of the agency's attention and become a distraction from other agency business. I responded that the CFTC was well prepared—having been acting in the virtual currency space since 2014—and that we remained on course with respect to a broad range of agency action.

They charged that the CFTC was too far out in front of other federal regulators on Bitcoin and had little administration support. They said that unidentified persons at the Fed and the SEC were critical of my actions. I said I would not respond to unnamed sources. They queried what I said at a recent FSOC meeting concerning Bitcoin.

They asked whether we had the resources to monitor the newly self-certified products. I pointed out that, as an executive, I had to find the funds. There was nothing in the Commodity Exchange Act that authorized the CFTC to block a self-certification on the basis of scarce resources. In any event, because we had anticipated the constant evolution of technology—whether Bitcoin, blockchain, or otherwise—we had requested additional resources in our recent budget.

As I became less defensive, the senior journalist's tone changed. He began to try to flatter me, citing my efforts to advance the agency's technological capability. He suggested the CFTC had been a sleepy agency. Now, by moving out in front on Bitcoin, the agency had gained the spotlight and, by implication, so had I. I rejected that this was any kind of grab for glory. It was just a matter of doing our job. We had a responsibility to be prepared for technological innovation, of whatever kind. Being prepared for Bitcoin was no different than being prepared for cyberattacks. We had to be forward-looking and ready for whatever was coming down the pike.

That is where the interview ended—for now.

S.P.E.C.T.R.E.

On Tuesday, January 9, Eric Pan and I took the overnight flight from Washington to Zurich. There we caught the train to Basel. Arriving later that morning, we checked into the picturesque Schweizerhof Hotel on Centralbahnplatz, or Central Train Plaza. We got some rest, had some lunch, and walked a short distance to an incongruously futuristic, circular tower. It was the offices of the Bank for International Settlements. The "BIS," as it was known, is considered the central bank to the world's central banks.

We announced ourselves to a heavily armed guard, presented our passports, and passed through high-security, bulletproof-glass turnstiles. Once inside, we went up one floor to a large white lobby full of white chairs and white sofas and equipped with a couple of pod espresso makers.

We were there to attend a regular meeting of the Steering Committee of the Financial Stability Board. The FSB is an international body created following the 2008 financial crisis by the G-20 (or Group of Twenty) nations. It is an international forum for the governments and central banks of 19 economically significant countries[1] and the European Union (EU). The FSB is funded by the BIS—which, in turn, is funded by the world's central banks—and operates out of the BIS's headquarters.

The Financial Stability Board (FSB)

The FSB plays an essential role in monitoring risk in the global financial system and recommending actions to mitigate it. It coordinates the work of financial regulatory agencies, like national bank regulators, and international standard-setting bodies, like global associations of securities regulators, toward the goal of assessing vulnerabilities and increasing the resilience and durability of the global financial system. It recommends actions to be taken at the national governmental level and encourages coherent adoption and implementation. Following the 2008 Financial Crisis, the FSB played a key role in recommending and coordinating implementation of global market reforms.

The FSB serves at the international level much of the same monitoring and coordinating function that the US Financial Stability Oversight Council (FSOC) serves for the US economy. However, there is an important difference between the bodies. Whereas FSOC is composed of regulators covering a wide range of US economic activity from life insurance to housing finance and securities issuance, the FSB is dominated by national central banks and finance ministries (overseas counterparts of the US Treasury Department). This membership structure leads to an organizational bias in favor of economic systems primarily driven by traditional bank lending rather than market-based finance based on securities and derivatives markets. This bias suits continental Europe and Japan, with economies that are primarily financed by traditional lending by large incumbent banks. It presents challenges, however, for the United States, the United Kingdom and some advanced Asian economies that are more dynamically balanced between bank-based and market-based finance.

Notably, neither the CFTC nor the FDIC are voting members of the FSB. That is so even though those agencies are, respectively, the market regulator and bankruptcy authority of the world's preeminent trading markets and clearinghouses for global derivatives. My understanding is that it was the Obama administration—not the G-20—that decided to exclude these US agencies—a peculiar decision that limits US influence in the FSB and leaves market regulators underrepresented. As a consequence, the FSB lacks leadership and expertise regarding policies for global swaps markets and derivatives clearinghouses. The exclusion also means that the United States has a weak voice in the FSB relative to the numerous European countries which share a single regulatory perspective through the EU.

In 2016, in an effort to partially rectify this imbalance, Eric Pan was able to arrange for then Chairman Massad to participate in FSB meetings as a guest. At my request, when I became CFTC chair, FSB Chairman Mark Carney graciously continued the practice—allowing me to participate in FSB discussions, though not to vote.

As Eric and I sipped *demitasses* of Nespresso coffee in the second floor lobby area, large doors swung open, ushering the group into a large, white meeting room. A large circular band of a conference table sat in the center, like a ring of Saturn, topped by a tangle of video screens and audio equipment. The guests greeted each other while circumnavigating the table to find their assigned seats demarked by large printed place cards. As Chairman Carney's discretionary guest, I was seated next to him.

Around the table were three dozen or so treasury secretaries, finance ministers, heads of financial standard-setting bodies, and central bank governors. These were the top dogs of the global technocratic elite, unaccountable not only to voters but, for the most part, to national legislatures. I had met many of them before in numerous settings, including this one. Each one was impressively credentialed, highly erudite, and self-possessed.

The US delegation was led by Treasury Under Secretary for International Affairs David Malpass, Fed Reserve Governor Lael Brainard, and SEC Chairman Clayton. Behind the delegates was another ring of tables for the attendees' senior deputies, known as "plus-ones" in government jargon. As a nonmember, I was not permitted a plus-one, so Eric Pan had to remain outside in the lobby. Behind the plus-ones were walls of black-tinted glass through which I could make out red and blue lights of audio equipment and ghostly figures translating and recording the discussions.

Carney called the meeting to order and then deftly went through the agenda. I was primarily interested in two items. The first was the work of the FSB's "Derivatives Assessment Team" analyzing global derivatives trading data, most of which had been compiled by the CFTC.

The other was cryptocurrency. After an intro from Carney, I painstakingly detailed the recent launch of Bitcoin futures. I explained how the CFTC's self-certification process had led to the launch of the world's only regulated and transparent market for Bitcoin futures that would provide a moderating and maturing force for this new digital asset class.

The follow-on conversation was predictable. The reactions of central bankers and finance ministers from major continental economies ranged from uncomfortable to antagonistic. On the other hand, financial market regulators, of which there were only a few of us in the room, were more positive. Ashley Alder on behalf of regulators of the world's major securities and derivatives markets spoke approvingly of the CFTC's action, on which he had been fully briefed in December.

So far, the conversation had proceeded as I expected. I was, therefore, startled when Jay Clayton jumped in with a somewhat dire warning. He said that voters and politicians would hold regulators accountable if things blew up and retail savers and investors were hurt. Clayton's remarks riled the room. Several central bankers interjected with similar warnings. The governors of the two most powerful continental EU members retreated to their own animated private conversation about the horrors of Bitcoin, ignoring the other speakers. The discussion eventually turned to proposals for the FSB to study and make recommendations on cryptocurrency risk. US Treasury Under Secretary Malpass gave me a look that let me know that yet another new FSB project was exactly what he wanted to avoid.

As the discussion drew to an end, Chairman Carney graciously allowed me a closing word. I said that the group needed to keep things in perspective. All the Bitcoin in the world added up to less than the market capitalization of a single national bank. It was hardly a threat to the world economy. I then said:

> "Look, crypto is not going away. We can't ignore it or try to suppress it. Better to bring it into effective regulation, encourage transparency, and let market forces work out its true value. That is what the CFTC has done. Technology like this is like a roaring wind. You can take shelter

from it, get blown away by it, or hitch a sail and ride it. In the U.S., we prefer to harness technology, not hide from it. You're all going to have to choose."

I was worked up and was sure it showed. It took me a while to relax. The meeting moved on to other items of little relevance to derivatives market supervision. My mind wandered. My eyes took in the extraordinary room. It was painted entirely in white. The floor plan was in the shape of a logarithmic spiral or nautilus shell. The ceiling bore a detailed plaster replica of the rifled gun barrel template from the opening scene of every James Bond movie—when agent 007 walks from right to left before shooting a pistol at the viewer. It struck me that the room—with its blinking lights and moving shadows behind black glass—could have served as a movie set for a meeting of SPECTRE's global crime syndicate.

As one FSB delegate monotonously went on about some highly technical topic, I envisioned him to be one of Ernst Blofeld's henchmen. I imagined myself petting a white cat while pulling a lever beside my chair that opened a trap door, plunging him into a pool of hungry sharks.

Drinks for Two

When the meeting ended, we adjourned to the top of the BIS tower for dinner. In addition to the FSB delegates, invitees included members of the Group of Central Bank Governors and Heads of Supervision (known as the GHOS) of The Basel Committee on Banking Supervision, the primary global standard-setter for the prudential regulation of banks. Outgoing Federal Reserve Board Chair Janet Yellen was the guest of honor. She was effusively praised in remarks by Jens Wiedmann, then BIS board chairman and president of the German central bank. While he was speaking, current Italian Prime Minister Mario Draghi, the former chairman of the European Central Bank and previous FSB chairman, incessantly texted away on his phone. Yellen spoke warmly about the excellent work and collegiality of the Basel Committee, which she said she would miss when she soon stepped down. I was touched by her simple graciousness.

I met up with Jay Clayton later that night at the Schweizerhof bar. He ordered a beer. I had Scotch. Clayton and I had become true comrades over the past few months. We were Washington outsiders coming in to do one job and one job only—run our agencies as best we could. When we were done, we planned to go home—not hang around for another Washington job. That gave us a lot of freedom to call it as we saw it and to do what we thought was right.

I knew Clayton's policy objectives, and he knew mine. We would do what we could to support each other. We knew there was a long history of noxious rivalry between our agencies. We had agreed that we would not allow ourselves or our agencies to be pitted against each other by the press, politicians, or other regulators—in the United States or abroad.

Our drinks arrived. Clayton toasted my FSB presentation on Bitcoin futures. He seemed to be concerned that I might have been annoyed by his comments. If I was, it was in large part due to jet lag.

Clayton asked me: "What would you say if it turned out that tomorrow's front pages said that Boko Haram was using Bitcoin to buy weapons to shoot kids?"

"Jay, if that's the concern, then we had better first suppress the US dollar because illicit drugs and weapons are most often paid with hundred-dollar bills stuffed in briefcases. Look, crime is crime, whether it is rewarded with diamonds, dollars, or crypto. Is the Federal Reserve to blame if Boko Haram uses US dollars to buy weapons? Is Tiffany to blame if they use diamonds? Is the CFTC to blame if they use Bitcoin? If we are afraid that an innovation like Crypto will be used for crime, then we had better shut down all new technologies, because at some point, they'll all be exploited by criminals. Our goals as regulators is to steer innovation towards it's good use, away from the bad."

Clayton backed off. I knew he was right about public perception. Silk Road, cybercrime, and Bitcoin ransomware did nothing to help the image of Bitcoin or the CFTC's greenlighting of Bitcoin futures. Yet, I was beyond any squeamishness about the self-certification. I was done taking crap about it. It was the right decision.

Clayton admitted that his perspective was shaped by the SEC's colossal battle against unregistered initial coin offerings. When he had first stepped into his role the previous spring, Clayton had embarked on a positive, forward-leaning agenda to open the securities private placement markets to greater retail participation. But since then, he had been buffeted by an explosion in initial coin offerings (ICOs)—a variation on an initial public offering (IPO) of securities. He was seeing too many businesses and individuals publish simple white papers outlining some new cryptocurrency, throw together a website or app describing how it works, and then raise millions of dollars in funding through advertising. The problem was that many of the ICOs amounted to offerings of securities that required fulsome disclosure of material information and registration of the offering with the SEC.

Securities Offerings

Under US law, offerings of securities must be accompanied by registration with the SEC and the full panoply of disclosures, processes, and investor protections that the securities laws require. The SEC—formed by President Franklin D. Roosevelt and Congress after the Great Depression—was built upon two pretty basic concepts. First, if you are going to sell people an interest in a venture—be it stocks or bonds—you are going to disclose every piece of information that's important or material to their decision. Second, you are going to register that securities offering with the SEC so they can hold you accountable. Ninety years later, those two pillars still support the core of what the SEC does.

In Clayton's mind, there was little difference between selling a traditional interest in a corporation (in the form of a stock certificate recorded on a central ledger) and selling an interest in an enterprise built around a cryptocurrency (recorded through a blockchain entry on a distributed ledger). Attempts to distinguish the two exalted form over substance. In each case a security was being offered, and securities laws had to be followed.

Clayton was rightly determined to uphold the SEC's regulatory framework. Left unchecked, unregistered ICOs would undermine the institution he had been sworn to uphold, he believed. He would not let it happen on his watch. He was marshaling every tool at his disposal—including the bully pulpit—to keep the ICO locomotive on the rails of US securities laws.

I sympathized, both as a friend and a regulatory peer. Despite superficial contrasts—many saw Clayton as discouraging Bitcoin while they saw me as encouraging it—we were actually motivated by the same impulses. I had also been striving to uphold the integrity of *my* institution's regulatory and procedural foundations—by **not** blocking Bitcoin futures self-certification. If I had concocted a way to block Bitcoin futures, I would have called into question previous self-certifications of many unconventional futures products. That would have set a precedent for blocking future exchange-traded derivatives simply on the basis of the unfamiliarity of the underlying technology. *That* wouldn't happen on *my* watch.

I told Clayton, "This is great. You've got to protect the mission of the SEC by gunning down a swarm of unregistered cryptocurrency ICOs. I've got to protect the mission of the CFTC by ignoring full-page newspaper ads demanding I stop the self-certification of Bitcoin futures. You and I are each fighting to protect our agency's legal frameworks when it comes to cryptocurrency. You have to do it in the negative, and I have to do it in the affirmative. I guess the good news is each of us is either a goat or a jackass depending on one's point of view."

That was good for a laugh. I asked the bartender for another Scotch and bought Jay another beer.

"The press will try to pit us against each other," I continued. "So will some of the politicians, and the technocrats. Let's not let that happen."

"You bet," Jay replied.

Then he turned to a related topic.

"I don't think your draft of our joint op-ed on virtual currency is strong enough," he said. "I want to rewrite it. You mind?"

We had agreed to do the op-ed during the dinner with Gary Cohn in November. We knew that the optics of us working together would be powerful. My draft had emphasized openness to technological innovation, but vigilance against crypto fraud and manipulation. I suspected that Clayton would rework it with a greater emphasis on investor protection. I told Jay to go ahead and redraft the piece.

Then I brought up the Senate Banking Committee hearing at which he and I would be testifying in early February. I asked what he wanted to achieve there.

"Let's make sure they know we are on the job, focused, and taking action," Jay said.

Agreed.

Two weeks later, *The Wall Street Journal* published our joint op-ed.

Distributed ledger technology, or DLT, is the advancement that underpins an array of new financial products, including cryptocurrencies and digital payment services. Many have identified DLT as the next great driver of economic efficiency. Some have even compared it to productivity-driving innovations such as the steam engine and personal computer.

Our task, as market regulators, is to set and enforce rules that foster innovation while promoting market integrity and confidence. In recent months, we have seen a wide range of market participants, including retail investors, seeking to invest in DLT initiatives, including through cryptocurrencies and so-called ICOs—initial coin offerings. Experience tells us that while some market participants may make fortunes, the risks to all investors are high. Caution is merited.

A key issue before market regulators is whether our historic approach to the regulation of currency transactions is appropriate for the cryptocurrency markets. Check-cashing and money-transmission services that operate in the US are primarily state-regulated. Many of the internet-based cryptocurrency trading platforms have registered as payment services and are not subject to direct oversight by the SEC or the CFTC. We would support policy efforts to revisit these frameworks and ensure they are effective and efficient for the digital era.

The CFTC and SEC, along with other federal and state regulators and criminal authorities, will continue to work together to bring transparency and integrity to these markets and, importantly, to deter and prosecute fraud and abuse. These markets are new, evolving and international. As such they require us to be nimble and forward-looking; coordinated with our state, federal and international colleagues; and engaged with important stakeholders, including Congress.[2]

Seeing Red

The next day, Eric Pan and I flew back to Washington via London. Waiting for my bags at Dulles airport, I started answering emails. I called Erica Richardson to sign off on a public statement she had sent me.

"While I have you," Erica said, "one of the two reporters who interviewed you recently says he spoke to the SEC. He plans to report that both Chairman Clayton and Treasury Secretary Mnuchin directly told you to stay the self-certifications of Bitcoin futures, and you went ahead anyway."

Seeing red, I said, "That's a load of crap! I met with Mnuchin and Cohn and discussed it with them before I decided. Neither of them objected. Mnuchin told me he was good with our approach. I didn't need to get Clayton's sign-off, but I did give him a heads-up the day before—as I did with a half dozen other regulators. No one asked me to stop."

I told Erica about the November dinner with Cohn; the December meeting at the New York Fed with Mnuchin; and Mnuchin's call a week later—all positive. I instructed her to tell the journalist that his information was incorrect, and we would challenge him.

As my taxi made its way up Washington's Rock Creek Parkway, I wondered about the origin of this misleading story. I recalled that during my telephone interview the week before, the reporters had mentioned the December FSOC meeting, where I had discussed Bitcoin. I then remembered Mnuchin's and Clayton's cautious remarks about Bitcoin at that meeting.

I called Erica back. "I think I know where this got started. Some 'deep state' person at the December FSOC meeting must be saying that Mnuchin's and Clayton's remarks at FSOC were a rebuke of my position. That's rubbish. Mnuchin and Clayton only expressed their general concerns with Bitcoin. They did not say that I should stop self-certification of Bitcoin futures. No one did. Someone in the room is talking out of school to cause trouble. Please call Treasury and let them know what is going on."

A few hours later, Erica emailed me: "Just had (separate) conversations with SEC and Treasury. Both agencies have denied the reporter's contention, which seems to have sent him into a bit of tailspin. I think that this anecdote was a cornerstone of his article."

The next morning Erica and Mike had a call with the junior reporter. He admitted he was unable to confirm his information. He said that he would still report that both Mnuchin and Clayton had expressed to others that they were dissatisfied with my actions. Mike asked to whom

Mnuchin and Clayton had confided their misgivings. He declined to name them. He also said that he had one former regulatory official who said on the record that my actions were misguided.

Later, the junior reporter called the chairman of the House Agriculture Committee. His chief of staff provided the reporter with a written quote that the committee chairman was fully satisfied with the CFTC's efforts. The Ag Committee was the CFTC's oversight body. An incredibly important committee, right? Yet somehow a statement of the Chairman of a key Congressional committee supporting the agency's action never made it into the reporter's story.

When the story finally ran, our work to correct the record had had some impact:

> Giancarlo, a former executive at a swaps brokerage firm who became an agency commissioner in 2014 and chairman last year, is fond of referring to the CFTC as a "21st century regulator." In December he took the agency headlong into the cryptocurrency fray when he allowed two exchanges to offer futures contracts based on Bitcoin—which will allow investors to bet on the price rising or falling without buying the cryptocurrency itself. This could clear the way for new investment products and make it easier for large institutional investors to get involved. "Ignoring Bitcoin trading doesn't make it go away," Giancarlo says. "Technology is a given, and the agency needs to keep pace."
>
> The fast-tracking of Bitcoin futures provoked a storm of criticism, including from the biggest banks, which are responsible for settling the trades, as well as some Democratic lawmakers. Both Mnuchin and Securities and Exchange Commission Chairman Jay Clayton privately questioned why the process was moving so quickly, according to people familiar with the discussions.[3]

Then the story included an admission: "SEC spokesman John Nester says 'the characterization is inaccurate.' A Treasury spokeswoman who asked not to be named disputed that Mnuchin questioned the speed of the futures roll-out."[4]

While quoting critics, the story also acknowledged:

> The Chairman's embrace of new technology has been praised by some lawmakers and former CFTC members as necessary and forward-thinking. "It's actually pretty gutsy of the CFTC to have taken this on in a full-throated way," says Bart Chilton, a former Democratic commissioner

who also has an interest in digital currency. Chilton is helping launch one backed by oil reserves.[5]

The story quoted some previous negative comments by Mnuchin, but admitted that the Secretary had recently softened his stance. The reporters must have been highly annoyed to report official contradictions of their reporting about Mnuchin and Clayton's opposition.

Feeling like I was coming down with the flu, I caught Amtrak's Acela express train at 4 p.m. to Newark and took a taxi home. I collapsed into sleep early that night, both mentally and physically exhausted.

Clear as a Bell

On Tuesday afternoon, January 16, I went back to the Treasury Building to participate in a meeting of the Financial and Banking Information Infrastructure Committee of the President's Working Group on Financial Markets. The Committee's membership consists of 18 member organizations from across the US financial regulatory community, both federal and state. The Treasury Department's Assistant Secretary for Financial Institutions chairs the committee.

For this meeting, I was seated to the left of Janet Yellen. As we awaited Mnuchin's arrival, she and I chatted cheerfully. I complimented her on the hearty reception she received in Basel. She told me how much she had enjoyed attending BIS meetings over the years and the *bonhomie* she had experienced. She confirmed that she would be stepping down as Fed Chair in early February and wished me well in my work at the CFTC. I complimented her for her service and hoped she would enjoy her retirement. She said that she "wasn't going anywhere." (It turns out that she meant it.)

After Mnuchin arrived, the meeting kicked off with presentations by the FBI and Treasury on cyber threats to the US financial system. Then Mnuchin turned to the state of cyberattack preparedness of each agency. He went around the room inviting comment, beginning with the Fed. Vice Chairman Quarles gave a brief rundown of the Fed's cyber preparedness. I was next to speak.

As I should have expected, Mnuchin again ad-libbed, "Before you go, update us on where you are on Bitcoin futures."

Mnuchin had a wry smile on his face that was hard to read. Was it mockery or sympathy? I couldn't tell, but I was determined to speak unabashedly. I knew there was a leaker here who might well call the press when the meeting ended.

I said the launches went as smoothly as I expected. The higher margins we insisted upon seemed appropriate. The price of Bitcoin had reset in an active two-way market. It was trading in the $12,000 range—down from more than $19,000 in December. CFTC staff had gathered some limited data and was beginning to analyze it.

I then turned to cyber preparedness. I talked about the CFTC's two focuses—internal and external—and the steps we were taking on both fronts, including our regular disaster recovery and business continuity exercises and drills.

The comments then continued around the room. When Clayton spoke, he could not resist voicing his resoluteness against ICOs. Still, he reiterated the close cooperation between our two agencies and our commitment to our different statutory frameworks. His message of support was clear to everyone listening.

Setting Things Straight

A few days later, I flew down to Naples, Florida, for the annual January conference of the derivatives section of the American Bar Association (ABA). I likened the gathering to the Fed's Jackson Hole conference for derivatives lawyers. My Chairman's address was a comprehensive review of the recent self-certifications.

This speech provided a detailed road map to the CFTC's short, medium-, and long-term approach to Bitcoin and blockchain as the agency moved past self-certification. (The full speech is included in the Appendix.) I closed with these thoughts:

"History has placed us in this moment in time. The digitization of communications and commerce expands our horizons and introduces new ways of thinking, new temptations, new risks, and new opportunities.
  "But, as with all new ideas, there may be—*indeed, there will be*—surprises and challenges . . .

"We are being propelled into a future that is unknown, a future that requires more expertise, more thoughtfulness, more creativity, and more commitment."[6]

On Friday evening, Mike Gill and I flew back to Washington alongside Commissioner Quintenz and his canny and unflappable chief of staff, Kevin Webb. We had dinner together during a layover at the Charlotte airport. I felt good about the ABA speech but exhausted from all the *Sturm und Drang* that preceded it.

Back at the Kennedy Warren that evening, Regina and I plopped on the couch and caught up on family and friends. I told her about the speech and how it was received. I told her that my mind was at peace about the decision not to try to block self-certification.

I also told her how a few journalists had tried to turn the complicated self-certification narrative into a simplistic morality tale. Of course they were entitled to their view that the CFTC was irresponsible in greenlighting Bitcoin futures, but it would have been better to style it as an op-ed—and not present it as news story.

The truth is rarely a morality tale in black-and-white. It is often far more complicated than risk versus safety, truth versus lies, science versus ignorance, good guys versus bad guys, or us versus them. Morality tales are too often the press story that facts are screened to support.

The essayist and philosopher Alain de Botton had it right when he explained,

> "The news knows how to render its own mechanics almost invisible and therefore hard to question. It speaks to us in a natural unaccented voice, without reference to its own assumption-laden perspective. It fails to disclose that it does not merely report on the world, but is instead constantly at work crafting a new planet in our minds in line with its own often highly distinctive priorities."[7]

Yet, for public servants, the complexity of the truth doesn't lend itself to morality tales. With the "assumption-laden perspective" of Bitcoin futures self-certification now on display, I would start tomorrow to prepare for a high-profile hearing with Jay Clayton before the Senate Banking Committee. The hearing was meant to review our respective approaches to cryptocurrency. I could only imagine what simplistic narratives would be aired in that high-pressured political arena.

Chapter 10

"CryptoDad"

Sometimes the best journeys are those, that start when we do not plan, continue how we do not expect and are taking us places we do not know.
—Aisha Mirza (writer, DJ, and crisis counselor), as quoted in *More Wisdom in Failure* by Chimgaemezu Morrison

Kopper Kettle

Tuesday, February 6, 2018, was the date scheduled for a hearing of the US Senate Committee on Banking, Housing and Urban Affairs. It was entitled, "Virtual Currencies: The Oversight Role of the U.S. Securities and Exchange Commission and the U.S. Commodity Futures Trading Commission." SEC Chairman Clayton and I would be the only witnesses.

Senate Banking, as the committee was known, has broad jurisdiction over banking, price controls, deposit insurance, export promotion and controls, monetary policy, financial aid to commerce and industry, and issuance of currency and coinage. Its members included such well-known senators as Richard Shelby of Alabama and Elizabeth Warren of Massachusetts.

The committee was chaired by Republican Mike Crapo of Idaho and its Democratic Ranking Member was Ohio's Sherrod Brown. Brown also served on the CFTC's Senate oversight body, the Agriculture Committee. Unlike the Senate Ag Committee, which held hearings around a long, level table similar to that of a ranch house kitchen, Senate Banking presided from a highly raised rostrum in an august, wood-paneled room two stories in height. The room was designed so that the powerful Senators could look down upon the hapless witnesses gazing up at them. I much preferred the Senate Ag hearing room.

After a week of drafting and redrafting, I submitted my formal written testimony to the Committee on Friday evening, February 2. I met Regina and some friends that night at the Kennedy Warren's cocktail lounge. Friday night regular Derek engaged us with soft jazz on the piano while I enjoyed a Kopper Kettle Virginia Whiskey, my current favorite. I hoped it would help ease me into a good night's sleep.

It did not work. At 3:00 a.m., as Regina lay sleeping beside me, I stared at the dark ceiling of our bedroom with the realization that there was nothing but danger in the upcoming Senate Banking hearing. There was every chance some committee members would pit Clayton and me against each other for our seemingly different approaches to cryptocurrency. Yet, we were both fighting to protect our agency's core regulatory frameworks. For Clayton, that meant shutting down unregistered ICOs. For me, that meant not blocking self-certification of Bitcoin futures. Our goals were similar, but the outcomes were different: SEC disapproval and CFTC approval (or, technically, non-disapproval). The situation was ideally set up for us to be portrayed as clueless and unaligned.

I could hear it:

"Mr. Giancarlo, how could you, as CFTC Chairman, have allowed Bitcoin futures to go forward? Do you have no concern for the innocent American whose retirements will be devastated by irresponsible Wall Street banks investing their 401K money in these dodgy products?"

I worried that the banking committee members would tear into the self-certification process and challenge the decision not to stymie it.

I hoped to deflect attacks with facts and counterarguments, including our Bitcoin consumer education efforts, aggressive enforcement actions, and greater surveillance of underlying spot cryptocurrency markets through the access provided by our heightened review.

My fears had been compounded the week before. Clayton and I had met with our staffs at the SEC's offices for a "murder board" session, where we were asked tough questions by our senior staff to prepare us. It did not go well. Some of our responses had been ragged and contradictory. We had to do better.

On Saturday, I was in the office early and back at the writing table, working on my oral statement for the hearing. I took out the 40-page written testimony submitted the night before and read through it. Frankly, it was boring. It was regulator-speak. I wanted something that would grab the senators' attention and help them understand this new innovation.

I thought back to the conversations about Bitcoin that took place during our family's New Year's ski vacation with my kids, nieces, and nephews—all Millennials and GenZ-ers. I also remembered the earnestness of the cryptocurrency developers who met with LabCFTC and how badly they wanted to be taken seriously. I recalled the extensive blogs and videos I had seen about virtual currencies trying hard to explain this technology. I thought about the energy and momentum that were driving this innovation. Something was going on that was more than technological. It was social; it was cultural; it was human.

Sure, I had no doubt that the cryptocurrency universe contained its share of get-rich-quick schemers, shady entrepreneurs, and even criminals. But it also had a growing contingent of professional and institutional users and real everyday believers, including advocates for the poor and the unbanked, libertarians, pacifists, Occupy Wall Streeters,[1] earnest tech geeks, mathematicians, sound-money aficionados, long-term investors, and many idealistic young people.[2] Whatever their interests, they deserved to be taken seriously, not dismissed or disparaged as fools or idiots.

Thinking about this new generation's interest in cryptocurrency, I knew I had my angle on how to approach the hearing. I took out a sheet of paper and wrote an entirely new opening for my oral remarks.

"We Owe It to This Generation"

On the morning of the hearing, I felt trepidation as I made my way to the fifth floor of the Dirksen Senate Office Building. Jay Clayton and I met in a small waiting room and chatted. We were determined that we were not going to let our agencies be pitted against each other.

I found a spare room where I closed my eyes, said a prayer and relaxed. A little before 10 a.m., Clayton and I entered the austere hearing room and took our places. It was packed with spectators, reporters, and government officials. Every seat was filled and many were standing along the back and side walls. I turned my mobile phone to mute.

Senator Crapo gaveled the meeting to order. He gave his opening statement, followed by Senator Brown. They each expressed concern about parallels between virtual currency and the dotcom bubble. They also mentioned the potential funding of illicit activities. Brown hammered Wall Street.

Jay Clayton delivered his statement first. He emphasized that ICOs were securities offerings under federal securities laws and that the SEC would continue to work with the DOJ and other entities to enforce the law.

When my moment came, I made a subtle gesture of pushing my written remarks to the side and looked directly at the assembled senators:

> "With your permission, I'd like to begin briefly with a slightly different perspective, and that is, as a dad. I'm the father of three college-age children: a senior, a junior, and a freshman. During their high school years, we tried to interest them in financial markets. My wife and I set up small brokerage accounts with a few hundred dollars that they could use to buy stocks. Yet other than my youngest son, who owns shares in a videogame company, we have not been able to pique their interest in the stock market. I guess they're not much different than most kids that age.
>
> "Well, something changed in the last year. Suddenly, they're all talking about Bitcoin. They are asking me what I think and should they buy it. One of their older cousins who owns Bitcoin has been talking about it and has got everyone excited. I imagine that maybe members of this committee may have had similar conversations in your own families of late."[3]

A few senators nodded their heads and I knew that I had their attention. I hit my main chord:

"It strikes me that we owe it to this new generation to respect their enthusiasm about virtual currencies with a thoughtful and balanced response, not a dismissive one. And yet we must crack down hard on those who try to abuse their enthusiasm with fraud and manipulation."[4]

I went on to explain that this meant learning everything we could about virtual currencies. It required keeping things in perspective and bearing in mind the relatively small size of virtual currency markets. We should be wary of voices that were sowing unwarranted fear, uncertainty, and doubt (known as FUD). We needed to educate consumers and coordinate a collective regulatory response. No one agency had exclusive authority, so we needed to work together. Though the CFTC didn't regulate the dozens of trading platforms here or abroad, it did have full authority over derivatives markets for crypto assets that were not under SEC jurisdiction. The CFTC also had limited authority to police underlying spot crypto markets for fraud and manipulation. We would continue with robust enforcement, including recent civil actions cracking down on fraudsters and manipulators. More such suits would follow.

I closed with an excerpt from Clayton's and my recent op-ed in *The Wall Street Journal*: "These markets are new, evolving, and international. They require us to be nimble and forward-looking, and coordinated with state, federal, and international colleagues, and engaged with important stakeholders including Congress."[5]

From that point on, I relaxed and just went with the flow of the conversation. I felt in command and confident. I intended to use my time to do some FUD busting.

Several senators asked good questions. Chairman Crapo wanted to make sure we had sufficient jurisdiction. Clayton responded by calling for regulatory coordination among the federal banking regulators, the SEC, CFTC, and the FTC. He reiterated the importance of a coordinated plan for dealing with virtual currency trading markets. Consumers assumed that they were regulated like a stock exchange, but they're not. We needed to clear up the confusion, and that might require additional legislative authority.

I followed up with a couple of points. Our first step was to recognize where the gap is. The spot markets for cryptocurrencies are not regulated.

The CFTC doesn't have direct regulatory supervision over any spot markets underlying derivatives trading, I explained. The CFTC does not regulate gas stations or grocery stores, for example, but it does regulate futures on oil, wheat, and corn. So while the agency could take enforcement action against fraud in underlying markets, the CFTC cannot set rules and regulations for how those markets operate. I said that other agencies may have a role to play. There's a patchwork of state regulation in this area. Some states have been assertive, others less so. I told the committee this was a policy consideration.

Senator David Perdue, from Georgia, then asked us to address pump-and-dump schemes in Bitcoin or other virtual currency trading. (A pump-and-dump scheme is when promoters of a stock or, in this case, cryptocurrency, make false statements about it in order to sell their supply of it at an artificially inflated price.)

I reiterated that the CFTC had formed a virtual currency enforcement task force, and that more enforcement actions were in the pipeline. We were working the beat hard.

A number of fun colloquies followed. South Dakota Senator Rounds asked whether Bitcoin was a security under SEC jurisdiction or a commodity under CFTC authority. I responded:

> "What's so challenging about Bitcoin is it has characteristics of multiple different things. One of the phrases that's often used is that Bitcoin is a medium of exchange, a store of value, or a [unit] of account. Well those three things have different connotations. . . . If it's a means of—medium of exchange, then it's . . . a currency-like instrument. And yet, as we've seen, . . . Bitcoin [has not been such an effective medium of exchange].
>
> "What we hear is a lot of is people buying and holding. If you—if you go on to the Twitter universe, you'll see a phrase HODL, which means hold on for dear life . . . . In fact, I mentioned in my opening remarks, my 30-year-old niece who bought Bitcoin years ago, and she's a HODL.
>
> "She says I'm going to own it, I don't know what's going to come of it but I want to hang onto it. And she's not a fraudster or a manipulator, she . . . just believes in it . . . . And I think she represents a lot of folks that think there's something in this, I want to hold onto it."[6]

Senator Tom Cotton of Arkansas asked about the potential that Bitcoin's underlying distributed ledger technology held for enterprises, consumers, and, perhaps, government agencies.

I pointed out that if there were no blockchain, there would be no Bitcoin, because they were part of the same technology initiative. I explained that blockchain applications held enormous potential—not only in the financial services and banking industries, but also for, say, recording how charity dollars are spent or refugees are accounted for across the globe. There had been an article just that morning, I noted, about the use of distributed ledger technology to serve billions of people around the world who lacked access to banking services. I also mentioned that, in the CFTC's domain—agriculture futures—66 million tons of American soybeans were recently sold to China through a block-chain transaction, in which all contractual aspects of the shipment from bills of lading and receipt of shipment were conducted on one universal, fully accessible ledger.[7] It was a sign of the enormous efficiencies in global operations and capital that was to come with universal adoption of distributed ledger and blockchain technology.

Distributed ledger technology also held out great promise for regulators, I continued, in that it could help them to conduct very sophisticated market surveillance. If the technology had been widely available in 2008, I said, we may have been able to see the full credit exposure of Wall Street banks to each other in real time. That, in turn, would have enabled much more precisely tailored policy responses to the financial crisis than were possible at the time.

The hearing lasted two hours. I was exhausted when it finished. Clayton and I shook hands warmly and smiled. Throughout the hearing, we had each referenced the other's leadership and our agency's coordination. There was no daylight between us. The respect we had for each other and the roles of our respective agencies was clear.

I felt buoyant. I looked in the faces of my staff for confirmation. I owed them enormous gratitude—especially the ad hoc cryptocurrency working group. It was their work that I described at the hearing. It was their work that was under review and found satisfactory.

Erica Richardson was the first to congratulate me. "You nailed it," She whispered. Later, she emailed me as follows:

Great, great work. When you get some time, take a look at the Twitter traffic about you. You are a hero. Your HODL comments just about broke the crypto corner of the internet, people were so excited. You're being called "CryptoDad," "Batman." And "Crypto OG" (meaning "original gangster").

In fact, my Twitter account was exploding, gaining thousands of followers by the minute. My remarks were celebrated by virtual currency fans around the globe who Photoshopped my likeness into dozens of online images and videos.

The specialty Bitcoin press was pleasantly surprised. Trustnodes.com reported:

> This is probably the first senate hearing many in this space have listened to in full, and in that imposing surrounding, Giancarlo seemed nervous at times while speaking, as if he was to do something brave.
>
> He was, in a way. His leadership took courage for he was going against a seemingly established grain where politicians and regulators only focus on the negatives. He, instead, struck a reasonable balance. Go against the criminals, but respect the ordinary, hardworking, honest people and their enthusiasm.[8]

Joon Ian Wong wrote a ridiculously nice recap story at Quartz.com:

> The enthusiasts who populate "crypto Twitter," an endless stream of gossip, memes, and financial speculation, have a new hero: top American commodities regulator J. Christopher Giancarlo.
>
> The chairman of the Commodity Futures Trading Commission had his star-making turn when he testified to the US Senate banking committee on Feb. 6. He gave the senators an education on crypto slang, and was largely positive about the promise of cryptocurrencies. He had a paltry 1,500 followers before the hearing, which rocketed to nearly 30,000 the following day and around 50,000 today.
>
> Giancarlo has been called "Captain Crypto," the slayer of "FUD," and #cryptodad. Images of him at the hearing have been turned into memes.[9]

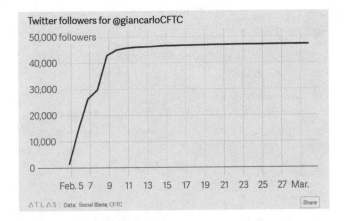

My newfound Twitter fan base was having fun with creative memes and emojis.

Arianna Simpson
@AriannaSimpson

I present to you the Chairman of the CFTC. This is really happening, people.

> 🔵 **Chris Giancarlo** @giancarloMKTS · Mar 2, 2018
> Is #crypto #FOMO your #FridayFeeling? #DYOR at cftc.gov/Bitcoin/index....
> #CryptoDad

2:26 PM · Mar 2, 2018 · Twitter for iPhone

48 Retweets   **239** Likes

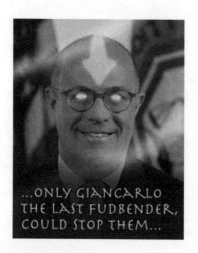

Pomp 🏆 ✅ @APompliano · Mar 2, 2018

You worried the regulators are going to stop crypto in its tracks?

The Chairman of the CFTC (@giancarloCFTC) has "**#cryptodad**" in his Twitter bio.

The regulators are onboard.

Current status: 🚀

💬 28   ↻ 159   ♡ 523   ↑

Sergio Rodriguera Jr @SergioRJr · Feb 12, 2018
CFTC Chairman **Giancarlo** becoming a rock star in **crypto** community
bloomberg.com/news/articles/... **@business** #cryptodad #cryptocurrency
#cftc

CryptoBit 🗣 @bitcoin_whales · Feb 6, 2018
SEC Chairman used #HODL in his explanation to Senate. He's onboard! J.
Christopher **Giancarlo** describes #HODL in the U.S. Senate Committee on

youtu.be/HSPywOS9DWU - Watch video

#Bitcoin ₿ #cryptonews #Retweet #followME #Cryptocurrency #news
#media #CNN **#Bloomberg #Crypto**

↻ 1   ♡ 3

Bloomberg ✔ @business · Feb 9, 2018
Crypto fanboys celebrate a surprising new hero: a D.C. regulator
bloom.bg/2EuKqsr

♡ 6   ↻ 16   ♡ 21

Giuseppe Stuto
@gstuto

Ok, that's it, the Chairman of the US Commodity Futures
Trading Commission just described "HODL" and how it
fascinates him. If that isn't an indicator that crypto is here to
stay, then I don't know what is. youtube.com/watch?
v=HSPywO…

2:17 PM - Feb 6, 2018

♡ 35   ◯ 24 people are talking about this

Tommaso pellizzari
@Tommypellizzari

Quote my words: this will be remembered as an historical
speech. Mr. Giancarlo touched the real point of
#cryptocurrencies i.e. economy, technology and self
sovereignty that so much are catching our imagination
youtu.be/aD8YJ7Nm3Cc via @YouTube

3:49 PM - Feb 6, 2018

♡ 5   ⧍ See Tommaso pellizzari's other Tweets

Forty-eight hours later, I tweeted back:

Coin fans: Thx 4 ur enormous response 2 my recent US Senate remarks. Lol. As you invest remember: caution, balance & DYOR.

In Twitter speak, DYOR meant "do your own research." The tweet was liked more than 21,000 times.

What struck me most about the reaction to the Senate hearing is how little I had anticipated the result. I went into the hearing in an entirely defensive posture. I had assumed that the possible outcomes were entirely binary—either I would survive and make it out alive or my reputation would be trashed. I never expected to emerge as a crypto hero.

One columnist picked up on the point that led me to reframe my oral remarks to the committee—the cultural and generational factors that were driving enthusiasm about cryptocurrencies:

Realization of generational factor in virtual currency: Chairman of the CFTC Made Surprisingly Thoughtful Comments About Bitcoin Today

It's not often you'll hear me say positive things about a U.S. government regulator, but I nearly fell out of my seat when I heard what [CFTC Chairman] Giancarlo, said at today's hearing . . .

[It's] just about as good as you're gonna get from a government regulator. Beyond the fact that he's advocating an entirely reasonable approach, I was shocked to see how well he had his finger on the pulse of one of the most significant and often overlooked aspects fueling Bitcoin and crypto assets overall, the generational factor . . .

I didn't expect a U.S. regulator to get this, and for that I am thankful. So thank you Mr. Giancarlo, for having an open mind and listening to your children. After all, they're the ones who will have to live on this earth a lot longer than us.[10]

By recognizing and dignifying the interests and efforts of young cryptocurrency innovators in their garages and basements around the world, I had struck a chord with them. And, as Treasury Secretary Janet Yellen discovered when pop artist Dessa recorded "Who's Yellen Now?," recognition means Twitter meme status.[11] I was now "CryptoDad."

Now the challenge lay in how to use it to do some good. I had a few ideas I wanted to try right away.

Chapter 11

The Oval Office

"When I'm driving, the fewer distractions there are, the better it is to focus on the job in hand."

—Lewis Hamilton (Grand Prix racer), quoted in
Interview with the BBC

Come on Down

In January 2018, I had called Gary Cohn at the White House. I told him that the European Commission was proposing legislation that would assert regulatory jurisdiction over large US derivatives clearinghouses under CFTC supervision. I explained that this move was in part a strategic response by the EU to Brexit and in part tit-for-tat for an extraterritorial overreach by the CFTC five years before.[1] If adopted, the EU legislation would cause US firms to have to comply with two very different regulatory frameworks. The overlapping and uncoordinated oversight would be disruptive, expensive, and detrimental to the US economy. Not surprisingly, the EU's attempt was opposed by all CFTC commissioners, Republicans and Democrats and on both sides of the Congressional aisle.

I explained that I had been invited to testify before the EU Parliament about their legislation. I planned to say that any assertion of regulatory jurisdiction over US derivatives clearinghouses was unacceptable to the CFTC.

Cohn was supportive and asked how he could help. I said that my argument would be strengthened considerably if I could speak, not just on behalf of the CFTC (for which I had the authority), but on behalf of the United States of America (for which I did not). Cohn said he would let me know. He called back a few days later and asked me to come to the White House to speak to the president of the United States (POTUS).

On Wednesday, February 7, 2018, the day after my testimony at the Senate Banking Committee's "Crypto Hearing," Mike Gill and I headed over to the White House to meet the president of the United States.

A Marine guard opened the door for us to the West Wing reception room that seemed unusually quiet and empty. Gary Cohn came down, greeted us warmly, and took us up to his office. Several young assistants sat at the ready. After settling in at his conference table, Cohn asked me what I wanted to cover with the president.

"I want to explain why our US financial futures exchanges and clearinghouses are vital national interests," I replied.

Cohn asked me to stress the importance of a strong dollar. He warned me that if I mentioned China, President Trump was likely to go off on a 10-minute rant. Duly noted.

I complimented Cohn on the tax bill, that day's budget deal, and for managing to stay out of the limelight.

"Strip away the tweets and other craziness, and this is a very effective administration," he replied. He added that he was enjoying the work and would stay as long as he could to "get shit done."

Cohn also said he'd just been at lunch with the president, who had asked what Cohn would do in a financial crisis. "I told him I would get you, Clayton and Randy [Quarles] in a room and we'd figure it out and manage the problem."

When I asked Gary whether he was enjoying the Washington social scene, he said that his wife liked Washington, but not the discomfort of not knowing which place was her home: New York City or DC.

I understood entirely.

Then we talked about the past 48 hours in the markets, which had been stormy. I said it appeared from CFTC market intelligence that, in the face of fast-moving market conditions, some folks had to quickly unwind positions based on an index known as the VIX that represents general expectations for future market volatility. Cohn agreed.

"We're working carefully with Clayton and the Fed to stay on top of market events," I reassured him.

"Tell that to POTUS," he replied.

Then we were instructed to go into the Oval Office. On the way, we ran into Defense Secretary Jim Mattis and chatted briefly. He was heading down to the press briefing room, where they would discuss the need for defense appropriations. When Cohn and I reached the entry to the Oval Office, we encountered two men talking. Cohn introduced one as Ambassador Lighthizer, the US trade representative. The other was White House counsel Don McGahn, whom I knew. We spoke briefly. Ivanka Trump passed by and entered the secretary's office without saying anything. She was taller than I'd anticipated, having seen her only on television.

We were called into the Oval Office. As directed by Cohn, I entered first and strode in purposefully. POTUS sat at his desk. Beside him was General John Kelly, chief of staff, who stepped back several steps and withdrew. POTUS rose and greeted me warmly.

"It's a great honor to meet you, Mr. President!" I said and gave him a firm handshake.

"I'm pleased to meet you, finally," he replied. "Let's get some pictures! Where is the photographer?"

A second later, a photographer appeared and snapped POTUS and me, standing side by side and smiling for the camera. The president directed me to a chair directly in front of him, with Cohn sitting to my left and McGahn to my right. Between POTUS and me was the famous Resolute desk—the large, nineteenth-century desk used by seven presidents. It was smaller than I expected.

Trump began the conversation in a soft and gentle voice. He thanked me for coming to see him and said that he heard I was doing good work.

I thanked him for the compliment and told him the honor of the visit was mine.

"Not bad, huh?" he asked, indicating with a quick gesture the grandeur of our surroundings—and also, likely, the overall accomplishment of making it there.

"Incredible," I replied. "And incredible to be here. Thank you, Mr. President. The administration is doing great work. The markets are becoming robust. Employment is picking up. I support you in growing the economy."

He smiled and asked where I was from.

"New Jersey." I nodded at McGahn. "Don and I are from the same state."

"I met Chris during the campaign," McGahn said. "He was already at the agency, so he couldn't contribute, but he supported you from the beginning."

"Oh, I love guys that supported me from the beginning," Trump said with a smile. Then he leaned in conspiratorially and, in a slight whisper, said, "You know that Steve Wynn? He says he supported me, but the night before the election he was on TV saying, 'I like Trump, but I'm not opposed to Hillary.' They asked him who would win, and he said, 'Umm, Hillary.' So, Steve says he was with me from the start, but he wasn't really."

Then POTUS changed tack: "Where in New Jersey?"

"Bergen County, but I made my career in New York. I helped build a business on Wall Street that launched some of the first electronic trading platforms for swaps and derivatives."

Cohn piped in. "Chairman Giancarlo knows the markets. He and I go way back. We did business together. He built a great company and is doing a great job."

My credibility now reinforced by McGahn and Cohn, I got to the point.

"Mr. President, I support your instruction to put American interests first. I know your priorities are economic growth and job creation. And that's why I want to talk to you about America's futures exchanges and clearinghouses."

I explained the efforts by the EU to assert regulatory jurisdiction over US derivatives clearinghouses. I said it challenged fundamental American sovereignty, to which POTUS vigorously nodded his head. I explained that it would subject key US financial institutions to peculiarities of European law and regulation—even in serving US customers. In a crisis, it could cause enormous confusion and breakdown. That was especially so with respect to how the clearinghouses valued collateral held against trades. EU regulators were inclined to insert themselves into collateral management decisions by clearinghouses if they thought it necessary to prop up the Euro by preventing undervaluation—or "haircuts," as they are called—of EU government securities. It would be a mess.

Fearing that I might be losing POTUS's attention, I concluded by saying, "We just cannot have two drivers holding the steering wheel. The EU should drive their car and regulate their clearinghouses, and we should drive our car and regulate our clearinghouses. It's as simple as that."

POTUS sat back and said, "I totally agree."

Then, he asked, "What about China?"

I tried to steer around the question by saying, generically, "Well, one of the strengths of the US dollar is that it is the currency used to price most of the world's global ag commodities, like wheat, corn, soybeans, and cotton; most of its key precious and industrial metals, like gold and steel; most of its energy commodities, like oil and natural gas; and most of its key contracts, like foreign exchange. Other countries would love to see the price of crucial food, energy, and industrial commodities denominated in their currencies. It is one of the reasons why we have to maintain our exchanges in the US, under our regulations without political micro-management. It's a matter of vital national interest."

"But what about China?" insisted POTUS. He was determined to pull that cat out of the bag. "Do you think we should have tariffs on Chinese steel?"

I replied that he had already sent a message to the Chinese with tariffs on refrigerators and should wait and see the results. I said, "You have shown strength; now let's see how they respond."

POTUS said, "Gary does not agree with me on steel tariffs."

Gary sat there and said, "No, I don't."

POTUS then asked me about NAFTA.

"Give them 18 months," I replied, "and say we'll pull out if there's no resolution by then."

"Good idea," he said, looking pleased. "You and I see eye to eye."

Next on the quiz: Europe. "They're sneaky, aren't they?" he asked.

I said, "The Chinese want to supplant US commodity markets with their own; the Europeans want to indirectly regulate US markets. There is a professor in New York who has studied how the EU operates and calls it the 'Brussels Effect.'[2] It is similar to what California does. The EU passes very strict and expensive regulations for multinational companies that sell to people inside their borders. These regulations are so extensive that the big companies find it easier to adopt them for their entire world-wide operations and not just for Europe. That way, the EU ends up exporting its regulations all over the world. But here's the catch: Often the EU exempts smaller EU companies from the requirements, or just doesn't go after them if they avoid the rules. So it is basically a way to protect Europe's smaller national industries while placing costs and expense on more successful global competitors that are often American companies."

"What would you do?" asked POTUS.

"Well, knowing that I have your support would strengthen my hand with the EU in defending our jurisdiction over US clearinghouses," I replied.

"You have my support," he said.

"Saying to the European Parliament that I am speaking on behalf of the United States is a lot stronger than saying that I am speaking on behalf of the CFTC."

"You can say that."

"Thank you, Mr. President."

I went on, "More broadly, I don't think that pulling out of international standard setting bodies is the right course for the United States. We need to insert ourselves firmly in these international committees and assert leadership just as our economic competitors do."

I turned to the G-20 Financial Stability Board. It had three and a half dozen members on its governing committee I explained, with only four from the United States. So there were many more members from Europe, with its smaller and less globally significant financial markets, plus the EU itself and the European Central Bank.

"You should be on it," POTUS declared. Turning to Cohn, he said, "Gary, get him on that committee.

"I know Mark Carney very well," continued POTUS. "Tell Mark to get Chris on that committee."

The next question was what I thought of "Randall" and "Steven." I complimented them both and said that the administration had put together a great financial services team.

"Clayton?" he asked. "You know he'd be managing partner at Sullivan & Cromwell if he wasn't here."

I said that Clayton and I were working very well together. We were ramping up work on better harmonization of our two agencies' regulations. That would unlock trapped capital, which would be better invested in economic growth.

POTUS said: "More than three percent economic growth! That's the target. They say it can't be done. It can! Let's focus on that and do it. Three percent plus economic growth and huge job creation. That's your job. That's what we're going to do. It will be great for the country."

"I got it," I said.

We talked about market conditions, and whether the recent run-up in asset prices posed any risk of a crisis like the last one. I told him about the CFTC's new emphasis on market intelligence to better understand market structure, dynamics, and trading conditions. This was the direction the agency needed to move in. Putting in a plug for our recent budget request, I said we would be investing in market analysts, economists, and artificial intelligence to do an even better job of seeing market developments before they turned into problems.

Answering POTUS' question, I said that, "Right now, from what I see, US markets are working just as they should be."

POTUS then turned the conversation back to one of his favorite subjects: tariffs on Chinese steel. I told him about a visit I had made to the Williston Basin in North Dakota a few months before. Democratic Senator Heidi Heitkamp and I had spoken to a driller on a Bakken oil rig who was using drill shafts made from Chinese steel. He told us that Chinese drill shafts broke three times as often as American ones, but they were still cheaper to use—even with the lost time and effort to pull them out of the ground and replace them.

"Maybe that makes better business sense," POTUS posited.

"Not if they're using unfair labor practices and hurting our workers," I replied.

"You're right. You and I see eye to eye," POTUS said again.

General Kelly came through the door. "Mr. President, two-minute warning." He was letting POTUS know that several Senate Finance Committee members were waiting outside.

"Okay," said POTUS, "but we still need a few more minutes here." Kelly departed.

"What do we need to do to keep from getting shafted by our trading partners?" he asked. "I've stopped going to countries that we have a trade deficit with."

Once again, I gave him my straight opinion. "We need to stay strong," I said. "The agency and department heads should follow your lead and get tough. It's going to take a little time for them to figure out that things have changed. But they will. We just have to stay determined and be willing to say no. That is what I intend to do next week in Brussels," I added.

"I like the way you think," was POTUS's response. "You and I need to meet once a month." Turning to Cohn, "I want to meet with this guy once a month."

Once again, Kelly's head appeared in the doorway. I knew my time was up, so I pushed my chair back and thanked POTUS for his time. Cohn and McGahn got up and departed.

"This is a fantastic room," I added as I stood up, admitting that I had never visited it before.

POTUS: "Well, let me show you around."

"That's Thomas Jefferson," he said pointing to an oil portrait by the American painter Gilbert Stuart.

"That's Abraham Lincoln," he said pointing to a bronze bust on a table below the Jefferson portrait. "It was sculpted by a guy from New York. The same guy who designed the double eagle gold coin."

Kelly interrupted again with the slightest intonation of urgency: "Mr. President, the senators are waiting."

"Okay, I'm coming." Then, turning me, he said, "Let's get another photo." He called for the photographer as I wondered what had become of the photos we took at the beginning of the meeting. This time POTUS seated himself at the Resolute desk and put on his "bulldog" face, with me standing beside him. Snap, snap, snap.

As we shook hands goodbye, POTUS grabbed my shoulder and added warmly, "I enjoyed meeting you. Keep up the good work."

General Kelly led me out of the Oval Office.

Standing in the doorway with his hand outstretched to me was someone I recognized.

Child of the Seventies. Me, my mother Ella Jane, younger brothers Mike and Tim, father Hector and older brother Charlie. Double breasted jackets were in vogue that year. (Giancarlo family photo)

Honchos of Wall Street. 2010 Launch of GFI Group on the New York Stock Exchange. Me, Ron Levi, Chief Operating Officer; Scott Pintoff, General Counsel; Colin Heffron, President; Mickey Gooch, Founder and Executive Chairman; Jim Peers, Chief Financial Officer. (Giancarlo personal photo)

Swearing in as a CFTC Commissioner, June 2014 by Supreme Court Justice Clarence Thomas with sons Luke and Henry, daughter Emma and wife Regina. (Giancarlo personal photo)

Meeting CFTC stakeholders 900 feet underground in the Cardinal coal mine near Madisonville, Kentucky. (Giancarlo personal photo)

Meeting CFTC stakeholders on the ground at scores of family farms in more than two dozen states visited during my five-year term at the CFTC. (Giancarlo personal photo)

Meeting with Senator Chris Dodd and President Barack Obama in 2010 upon passage of the Dodd-Frank Wall Street Reform and Consumer Protection Act. (Rights and image being obtained from Steve Schwartz)

Meeting in the Oval Office with President Donald J. Trump in 2018 to discuss oversight of US derivatives markets. (Official White House Photo)

Joint Interview with Federal Reserve Board Chairman Jerome Powell in October 2017. (Rights being obtained from Alamy)

Sharing a few thoughts with SEC Chairman Jay Clayton while Senators take their seats for hearing of Senate Banking Committee in February 2018. (Giancarlo personal photo)

Announcing the 2019 "Bridge over Brexit" between the CFTC, Her Majesty's Treasury, the Bank of England and the UK Financial Conduct Authority with Mark Carney and Andrew Bailey, former and current Governors of the Bank of England. (Rights being obtained from Financial Times)

With fellow CFTC Commissioners Brian Quintenz, Dan Berkovitz, Dawn Stump and Rostin Behnam in 2018. (Official CFTC Photo)

My CFTC leadership team. Brian Bussey, Matt Daigler, Mike Gill, Eric Pan, Maggie Sklar, Bruce Tuckman, me, Dan Davis, Sarah Summerville, John Rogers, Jamie McDonald, Matt Kulkin, Erica Richardson and Amir Zaidi. (Official CFTC Photo)

With my bride of 30 years in front of the Kennedy Warren Apartments on our way to the White House Correspondents Dinner in 2016. (Giancarlo personal photo)

Receiving the Freedom of the City of London, an honor stretching back to the 14th Century with Catherine McGuinness, Chair of the Policy and Resources Committee, City of London Corporation and Erica Richardson, liveryman of the Worshipful Company of Painter-Stainers and CFTC Director of External Affairs. (Giancarlo personal photo)

The first and likely last time any CFTC Chairman takes to the musical stage in the CFTC hearing room to say farewell with the 2ⁿᵈ Amendments band: Manning Falachi, lead guitar; Kenny Hulshof, former Missouri Congressman, keyboards; Collin Peterson, Ranking Member of the House Agriculture Committee, guitar and lead vocals, me, Dan Wolf, bass guitar, and Zach Martin, drums. (Giancarlo personal photo)

On stage before a large and live audience at Bitcoin 2021 with Brian Brooks, former Acting Comptroller of the Currency (Giancarlo personal photo).

"Hello, Chairman," he said. "I'm Jared Kushner," shaking my hand with a warm smile. Standing just behind him was his wife, Ivanka.

"Nice to meet you," I replied.

"I hear you are the 'CryptoDad.'"

"Well, I don't know about that, but I guess I like the title better than some of the others I've been called." He and Ivanka both smiled.

"Let's meet again," said Kushner. "I want to understand Bitcoin."

I said, "That would be a pleasure."

McGahn walked me back to the West Wing reception area. He commented: "That went very well. The president took a shine to you."

"Do you think he really wants to do those monthly meetings?" I asked.

Without much conviction, he said, "We'll see."

Mission Accomplished

Thinking back about the meeting, I feel that it could not have been more effective. I went to the Oval Office with one purpose: obtaining authorization to speak on behalf of the US government in opposition to the EU's attempt to infringe upon the CFTC's jurisdiction. I received it. Over the remainder of my term as CFTC Chairman, I would fight a running battle with the EU over this issue. The express support of the president of the United States allowed me and the CFTC to be resolute on the matter. Our bipartisan determination (continued under my successor), frequent public calls for regulatory deference,[3] and, perhaps most importantly, the CFTC's later withdrawal[4] of its 2013 assertion of extraterritorial jurisdiction caused the EU to grudgingly concede much of the issue sometime after my departure.

President Trump was attentive and responsive to the issue I came to discuss. He also could not have been more personally gracious and generous with his time. I was not "starstruck," as I had been when I met Margaret Thatcher as a student intern. Trump did not have the cool poise of Barack Obama, when I had met him a decade before. But in that one meeting, Donald Trump was presidential in his own, very unique way.

A month later, Gary Cohn resigned from the administration. Apparently, President Trump demanded his allegiance on the imposition of steel tariffs, and Cohn said that he could not provide it. I thought back to my conversation with President Trump when he said, "Gary does not agree with me on steel tariffs." Gary did not hesitate to say, "No, I don't."

Trump's breezy tweets after Cohn's resignation—to the effect that there were plenty of people to replace Cohn—were undignified. Yes, senior government positions may be easy to fill. But there are not plenty of candidates with Cohn's credibility across the spectrum of business and finance. Closer to the truth was that the administration was struggling to attract highly qualified people to staff federal agencies—and go through the grueling confirmation process. The challenge of recruitment was not helped by the prospect that hard-working and accomplished professionals might meet a quick and unceremonious departure if they ever disagreed with the president on a matter of principle—or even for lesser reasons.

I had made up my mind. I'd stick to my plan to leave Washington when my term ended the following year. I would not accept another appointment, even if one was offered to me.

I was never called back to the Oval Office. I never met or spoke again to President Trump. The CFTC was not made a voting member of the G-20 Financial Stability Board. But none of those things were the purpose of the meeting.

I got what I came for, which helped support the mission and authority of the CFTC that I was sworn to protect.

I also got my picture taken in the Oval Office.

Chapter 12

The Road Goes On

Speed has never killed anyone.
Suddenly becoming stationary, that's what gets you.
 —Jeremy Clarkson (motoring writer and broadcaster), *Top Gear*

What Next?

A few days after the Senate Banking Committee Hearing in February 2018, I called a meeting of our virtual currency task force. I reviewed the issues raised in the Senate hearing and complimented them for their work. Following the launch of Bitcoin futures, I wanted an update on three ongoing work streams: improving our own knowledge of virtual currency, educating consumers, and enhancing enforcement.

All three were proceeding apace. LabCFTC was continuing its public engagement, with an upcoming visit to Silicon Valley and numerous scheduled meetings with virtual currency trading platforms. Meanwhile, our Office of Consumer Education Outreach was producing advisories and pamphlets and partnering with the US Consumer Financial Protection Bureau and the American Association of Retired Persons for a series of education initiatives. Finally, our Division of Enforcement's Market Surveillance Branch was analyzing new Bitcoin trading data. In January alone, it had filed three virtual currency enforcement cases against fraudsters.

That evening, I slipped out of the office, strode through the back alley, headed south on 20th street to the corner with "Eye" Street. There I entered Aperto Restaurant and took a table in the back. A few minutes later, Clayton joined me. We greeted each other warmly. He complimented me on my performance at the hearing that was now being widely touted as one of the more notable recent Senate events. I offered similar compliments. I called him "Batman." He said, "No. You're Batman. I'm Robin." We laughed. He was aware of a current Twitter meme.

We covered a lot of ground, including the momentum of the weekly market intelligence call that Clayton had initiated. Clayton suggested putting Hester Peirce—now a Trump-appointed SEC Commissioner—and CFTC Commissioner Quintenz together to resuscitate several initiatives to harmonize the two agencies' rules. Knowing that they had first met 18 months earlier in my Washington apartment, I thought it was a great idea. We agreed to make it happen. Our dinner was productive and pleasant as always.

Up in the Ether

In the months to come, I directed my internal crypto team to begin working on digital asset issues in a focused manner alongside our colleagues at the SEC. Mike Gill, Daniel Gorfine, Amir Zaidi, and Jamie McDonald began a bimonthly informal meeting with the SEC's Bill Hinman, director of the Division of Corporation Finance, the agency's astute senior adviser for Digital Assets, Valeri Szczepanik, and others.

Though there were now literally thousands of virtual currencies circulating, it was becoming clear that two key ones were likely commodities: Bitcoin and Ether. While Bitcoin had already been formally recognized by the CFTC in 2015 as a commodity, Ether had not yet.

Ether is the digital currency built on a so-called smart contract platform called Ethereum.[1] Ethereum is sort of like a computer operating system for crypto and decentralized computer systems for financial services known as "DeFi" that I will discuss in Chapter 15. Ethereum enables developers to build decentralized applications and smart contracts on its blockchain. A smart contract behaves like a self-operating computer program that automatically executes when specific conditions are met. The platform allows the smart contract's code to be run exactly as programmed, without any possibility of downtime, censorship, fraud, or third-party interference. Like Bitcoin, Ether is decentralized, meaning there is no managing authority through whose actions Ether derives its value.

Following the success of Bitcoin futures, CFTC-regulated exchanges were beginning to consider offering Ether futures contracts. Although I could not control the timing of an Ether futures self-certification, I wanted to be ready.

During the first few months of 2018, our CFTC team discussed with the SEC their views of how Ether was similar to Bitcoin in being a commodity and how it lacked the characteristics of a "security" under the SEC's jurisdiction. That authority was delineated by something called the "Howey Test," named after a 1946 Supreme Court case determining whether a transaction qualifies as an "investment contract," and is therefore considered a "security" subjecting it to disclosure and registration requirements under the SEC's authorizing statutes, the 1933 Securities Act and the 1934 Securities Exchange Act.

Staffs of the CFTC and SEC cannot speak with authority on behalf of either commission; only those matters voted upon by the respective commissions are authoritative. Still, staff divisions can issue "no-action" letters and "staff guidance" without formal action of the full commission. The opinion of a division director can be forceful, even if couched as spoken not on behalf of the commission.

On June 14, 2018, the respected head of the SEC's division of corporation finance, Bill Hinman, flexed some of that muscle. At a finance conference, he stated: "Based on my understanding of the present state of Ether, the Ethereum network, [and] its decentralized structure, we believe current offers and sales of Ether are not securities transactions."[2]

Hinman's statement was a milestone in the crypto evolution in confirming Ether alongside Bitcoin as two important crypto assets under CFTC jurisdiction. While it would still take time for CFTC staff to get comfortable with some quirky aspects of Ether—like its thinly traded spot market—it seemed increasingly clear that Ether futures were coming. The growing crypto industry began to rely on Hinman's statement and the similar subsequent statements by my successor at the CFTC.

Grand Tour

Within a week of the crypto Senate hearing I was back at Durrants Hotel in the Marylebone neighborhood of London. I arose at 6:45 a.m. to meet Mike Gill and Eric Pan for breakfast in the dining room. We were joined by Tracy Wingate, a CFTC associate director with international verve and sophistication.

Afterward, we cabbed to the Canary Wharf offices of the Financial Conduct Authority (FCA), the UK body that operates somewhat like a combination of the SEC and CFTC. There, we had coffee with its then CEO, Andrew Bailey. Sage and serious, Bailey is the consummate financial market maestro. His 30 years' experience in key roles at the Bank of England before becoming head of the FCA gives him enormous authority and familiarity with the workings of London's financial markets and their irreplaceable role in the global economy. Going into Britain's 2016 Brexit referendum, Bailey realized more quickly than most UK officials that maintaining London's preeminence as Europe's premier financial services hub had become a matter of existential importance.

Bailey and I had made good progress over the past year on a number of issues of importance to global markets for financial derivatives. That was especially the case with efforts to transition away from LIBOR, the decades-old benchmark used to calculate the rate of interest charged on more than half of US home mortgages. The London Inter-bank Offered Rate is an average of the interest rates on uncollateralized loans made between London banks for a set term—ranging from overnight to a year—for 10 different currencies. LIBOR, however, was no longer drawn from active market activity, like benchmarks for most markets, but rather from daily polls of a small panel of banks. As a result, LIBOR suffered from two shortcomings: shallowness of liquidity because of thin trading volume, and narrowness of liquidity because of its reliance on too few primary dealers.[3] When it comes to potential for manipulation, the second shortcoming may be worse than the first.

Bailey and I both thought that LIBOR had outlived its economic relevance as a benchmark. (So did Fed Chairman Powell, as I knew from our many conversations.) Problems had arisen after a prolonged period of low interest rates, during which some banks had earned an unsatisfactory return on investment on their lending activities. In order to boost that return, they grossly manipulated LIBOR to benefit their loan and bond portfolios.[4] The CFTC, alongside British authorities, aggressively pursued and prosecuted many of these cases. The scandal drew headlines in the international financial press that were a global embarrassment to "the City," the UK's critical financial service industry. LIBOR's disrepute could not be undone.

Bailey had been growing increasingly vocal that the underlying weakness of LIBOR could not be remedied, that its discontinuation was imminent, and that market participants needed to prepare accordingly. We agreed on a series of complementary statements to be made in the weeks ahead. Bailey knew he had my full cooperation and support.

We also discussed European Union efforts to assert legal authority to supervise important US-based derivatives clearinghouses. I made clear that any such assertion would be unacceptable to the United States.

We then signed an agreement between the FCA and the CFTC to collaborate on financial technology innovation and regulation through our in-house FinTech initiatives, the FCA's Project Innovate and our

LabCFTC. It was the first ever formal FinTech collaboration between a US regulatory agency and an overseas counterpart. In a few weeks, our two initiatives would host a joint program in London for the FinTech industry. The arrangement was an enormous accomplishment for our burgeoning LabCFTC and its leader, Daniel Gorfine.

Gill, Pan, and I then cabbed back to the Bank of England in the City. There, I was escorted by a friendly footman in salmon colored livery to meet privately with then Governor Mark Carney. He had in front of him a copy of my written testimony to the Senate Banking Committee.

"This is excellent," Carney said. "I like your recognition of the generational aspect of crypto." We discussed an upcoming FSB call on virtual currencies. He described himself as "crypto agnostic." I felt that a consensus was emerging in the Trump administration against suppression of crypto, I told him, but in favor of a balance of strict law enforcement and openness to technological evolution. I said this approach was consistent with America's traditional embrace of technological advancement.

I shared with Carney my view that the emergence of cryptocurrency was driven by the continued evolution of the Internet into a decentralized transfer mechanism for things of value, especially money. I explained to Carney (as I will explain later in this book), that the Internet of Value made it possible to solve the primary shortcoming of the existing forms of money: the local limitation of cash and the exclusivity, latency, and cost of bank account money. Transferring value would no longer be limited by space and time or the friction of third-party intermediaries.

Carney seemed interested in this point of view, though I could not tell whether he accepted it. Outwardly Carney is poised, affable, and polished, belying enormous inner drive and determination. He does not suffer fools lightly and I suspect he has little patience for pedestrian and unoriginal views. New perspectives, however, like the one I was expressing, he absorbed readily.

Back again in a taxi, Gill, Pan, and I went to Paddington Station and boarded the EuroStar train to Brussels for my testimony to the EU Parliament. Early the next morning, we set out for the US Embassy to the European Union for a breakfast with the financial attachés of various European countries and coffee with the American Chief of Mission.

Incredibly, the cabbie asked us if we wished to pay in "Crypto." I asked, "What type?" He said he preferred "Ethereum or XRP," but would take Bitcoin, "even though the service fees [were] too high."

"How about Euros?" I asked.

"No, I prefer dollars."

Done.

Later we went to the complex of buildings known as the *Espace Léopold,* which is the seat of the European Parliament. We entered the Altiero Spinelli building, a cramped and dreary interior that had the appearance that Carney aptly ascribed to it: "impermanent."

We found our way to the hearing room of the ECON Committee of the European parliament. The committee members arrived slowly and the meeting got off to a late start. Neither the chairman nor anyone else gave an opening statement, as was customary in the US Congress. In my testimony I stressed that any assertion by the EU of regulatory authority over US derivatives clearinghouses would be strenuously resisted not just by the CFTC, but by the entire government of the United States. My remarks were brief but to the point. There would only be one set of hands on the steering wheel overseeing US clearinghouses. They would be US hands.

The following day, we traveled on to Frankfurt for meetings with the European Central Bank, several German commercial banks, and the Deutsche Börse—the major German stock and derivatives exchange. Late that evening, I participated by secure telephone line in a FSOC meeting. I gave an update on work being done by the CFTC's new market intelligence branch. It was an analysis of recent sharp moves in CBOE's Volatility Index, known as the VIX—a tradable instrument that measured the stock market's expectation of volatility based on the S&P 500 index options. Once again, Mnuchin asked me to update the council on Bitcoin futures. I matter-of-factly noted that trading in the products was now quite routine, without adverse incident, with margins appropriately set and no margin breaches.

We next flew to Spain for a two-day meeting of the executive board of IOSCO, the association of global market regulators. In the enormous boardroom of IOSCO's Madrid headquarters, seating was by alphabetical order of country around a ribbon of tabletops arranged in a giant rectangle. That meant that the US and the UK were side by side, placing me again beside Andrew Bailey. As we often did, we found common cause on most of the three dozen or so matters of discussion.

At Chairman Ashley Alder's request, I reviewed the launch of Bitcoin futures—a matter that appeared to be of great interest to the group. I noted some initial research that had been shared with us by the San Francisco Federal Reserve Bank concerning the market impact of Bitcoin futures.[5] The analysis showed that the rapid run-up and subsequent fall in the spot price after the introduction of Bitcoin futures was consistent with trading behavior that typically accompanies the introduction of futures markets for an underlying asset.

The three dozen or so market regulators around the table asked good questions. Those overseeing the more advanced, international markets (Singapore, Hong Kong, UK, and Australia) appeared far more open-minded than those overseeing mainly domestic markets.

F.U.D.

Back in Washington a week later, I participated in a Financial Stability Board call concerning cryptocurrencies. More specifically, the call related to a committee report (which Mark Carney had been discussing in London) that was going to be presented at a G-20 meeting in Argentina in March. Jay Clayton, Federal Reserve Board Vice Chair Quarles, Treasury Under Secretary Malpass, and I joined on the call.

A considerable amount of crypto loathing was palpable through the phone line. The majority of the participants—mostly central bankers from around the world—overwhelmingly expressed fear, uncertainty, and doubt. Many central bankers obviously saw crypto currency as a threat to their national currencies. This FSB call and the earlier IOSCO meeting in Madrid each confirmed my pocket theory of what I call "Fair, Fund, and FUD." First, the market regulators of open and well-developed financial markets can get comfortable with overseeing the trading of crypto currency because they are confident in the ability of market fundamentals to fairly set cryptocurrency prices.

Second, the central bankers of offshore or island economies that host investment funds and protect the assets of sophisticated, offshore customers can get comfortable with holding virtual currency as just another valuable asset.

Third, the central bankers of large domestic, onshore economies concerned with defending sovereign reserve currencies will mostly eye virtual currencies with FUD (fear, uncertainty, doubt). As the saying goes, "where you stand depends on where you sit."

Later that spring, Treasury Secretary Mnuchin kicked off the FSOC Cryptocurrency Working Group that he had promised to form. Principals from the CFTC, SEC, the Federal Reserve Board, the OCC, the FDIC, and the CFPB were all present. At the first meeting, Sigal Madelker, Treasury's brainy Under Secretary for Terrorism and Financial Intelligence, reviewed Treasury's cooperation with the Department of Justice and the Financial Crimes Enforcement Network, known as FinCEN.

Mnuchin made clear the administration's support for financial innovation, but also its determination to proceed against the illicit use of cryptocurrencies by terrorist groups and nations that support them. He rightfully vowed to crack down on the use of cryptocurrency in connection with ransomware, darknet, and drug and arms trafficking.

He had the balance just about right.

Peaceful Waters

I had gotten to know Jerome Powell over the past few years. "Jay"—as he is known to family and friends—and I had formed a relaxed friendship during the Obama administration, when each of us was the sole Republican principal at our institutions. We soon discovered that we were both avid guitarists, and enjoyed discussing the playing styles we were mastering and the instruments we were playing.

Before becoming Fed chairman, Powell oversaw the Fed's work with the CFTC in overseeing systemically important derivatives clearinghouses. This institutional partnership—created by Dodd–Frank—had been quite rocky until Powell and I insisted that our respective agency staffs work together and better coordinate their work. It was a break-through in the institutional relationship between our agencies. That institutional link led to a more active personal rapport, sometimes over lunch and a glass of wine.

One late spring morning a few months after Powell's 2018 swearing in as chairman, Mike Gill and I and another CFTC colleague left the office and walked south on 21st Street across Pennsylvania Avenue toward the Mall. At Constitution Avenue, we turned east and made our way through security into the Eccles Building, the headquarters of the Board of Governors of the Federal Reserve.

The Eccles Building is designed in a mid-twentieth-century archi-tecture known as "starved classical," a formal style stripped of ornamen-tation that was utilized in government buildings by both American New Dealers and European dictators.[6] The building is named after Marriner S. Eccles, chairman of the Federal Reserve Board under President Franklin Roosevelt and a great uncle by marriage of current Federal Reserve Vice Chairman Randy Quarles.

We made our way through the two-story atrium in the center of the building. The walls and floor of the grand room are made of cream-colored travertine marble. We climbed one of the dual staircases that lined each of the long sides of the rectangular room to the broad gallery around the perimeter. I looked up to the center skylight etched with the outline of an eagle.

We first visited with Governor Lael Brainard, who had taken over some of Powell's portfolio, including the Federal Reserve Board's sup-porting role to the CFTC in supervising systemically important deriva-tives clearinghouses.

Brainard is someone to be taken seriously. Keenly intelligent and determined, she sees the world through the lens of the world's most important central bank. Yet she listens well and responds thoughtfully. She has charm and a kind smile that is not too hard to prompt. I found it easy to work with Brainard.

I stressed to Brainard the commitment that Powell and I had made that our institutions would strongly cooperate and collaborate, especially in the area of clearinghouse supervision. I likened the situation to par-enting. We had to stick together as a couple, so that the children we supervised could never play us off each other. She readily agreed. We then undertook to set up ad hoc meetings to discuss and further harmonize our supervision.

Next, we paid a call on Chairman Powell. His secretary went into his office to let him know we had arrived, and he came right out and greeted us in the reception area. He extended warm handshakes and a bright smile and ushered us into his office. We settled into several simply upholstered chairs around a small, round conference table. Powell spread wide his arms and said, "Welcome to my humble abode."

I took in the scene. The Fed chairman's office was, indeed, a modest room—embarrassingly so compared to the chairman's spacious suite at the CFTC. Powell's office was long and rectangular in shape, but less than 16 feet wide. At the opposite end from the one we entered was a polished brown door. It led into the larger and far more august boardroom where meetings of the Federal Open Market Committee[7] were held. Lining one long side of the office were built-in cabinets, shelves, and a countertop upon which sat Powell's computer monitor and keyboard. On the opposite wall were large windows that looked out to the Mall and beyond, to the Washington Monument and Jefferson and Lincoln Memorials.

Other than the brown door, most of the room was a shade of colonial white and appeared freshly painted. This warm hue was lit by bright sunlight streaming through the windows, giving the room a pleasant softness.

"I have a small house in a great neighborhood," Powell quipped. "It is all about location, location, location!" We laughed and I said, "Yeah, location and an unlimited budget!" We laughed again.

I asked Powell if he was finding any time for sailing, now that spring had arrived. He said no, and asked me if I was playing music with any local bands. I told him about the fun I had in December touring Minnesota and Missouri with Collin Peterson's 2nd Amendments. His listened excitedly and said, "I'm jealous!" He meant it and asked for an invitation to a future performance. I promised him one, if he would sit in on guitar.

We discussed a number of things: the CFTC budget, cooperation between the CFTC and the Fed, and the impending demise of LIBOR.

We also discussed his view on the current economy and the Fed's recent rate increases.

"The economy is in a good place right now," he said. "Unemployment is low, inflation is at the right place, earnings are strong, and economic growth is above three percent. It's my honeymoon!"

We ended our meeting with the same warmth and goodwill, wishing each other continued success.

As my two colleagues and I left the building and found a taxi, we talked about the job of Fed chairman. I joked that it probably was the best job in Washington when the economy was good—and the worst job when times were bad.

The following weekend, I reflected on the meeting with Powell in my journal:

It is interesting to compare Jay Powell and his predecessor, Janet Yellen. Both have great interpersonal skills. Yellen is like a wise and well-mannered senior stateswoman, but with a streak of irreverent autonomy. Jay is similarly dignified and well mannered, but easier going and a bit more earthy, demonstrated by the occasional curse word. Yellen enjoys fine dining and good wine. Powell is an accomplished sailor and avid musician.

Yellen spent her career in academic institutions. Powell in law firms, banks, and investment firms. She is most comfortable around scholars. Powell is most comfortable around business professionals.

As an academic and economist, Yellen strikes me as someone who has built an intellectual model of the global economy that seeks to incorporate economic events and anticipate eventualities. She has confidence in that model. Like a mechanic tuning an engine, she readily adjusts it to accommodate foreseeable economic variables.

Powell, on the other hand, strikes me as having a less formalized intellectual framework. Instead, he has greater comfort with the inevitability of unexpected market events. Like a businessman, he has courage and carefully calculated risk tolerance. His mind takes into account the constant risk of unanticipated market events without believing he has all the answers in advance, but believing he has the tools and intelligence to navigate through it when it does.

Powell's skills are those of a sailor. I suspect that he does not expect to know how and when the wind will blow, the tide will run, or the seas will chop, but he will set a course for the far shore and trim the sails to bring the vessel across. I think Powell's defining characteristic is expectation of economic variability and the courage to adjust for it while holding a steady course.

When I wrote this, I had no idea how severely Powell's ability to navigate stormy seas would be tested within two years of moving into that nice, peaceful office.

New Measurements

As bad as the 2008 financial crisis was, its impact had been exacerbated by the lack of clearer, more precise measures of risk, value, and markets. This was particularly the case in the over-the-counter derivatives markets, where the size of the market was measured in something called "outstanding notional amount."

According to this conventional method of measurement, the size of global derivatives markets were in the hundreds of trillions of dollars—far, far greater than any other marketplace on the face of the earth. The problem with this method of measurement was that it did not account for offsetting positions. Imagine if your bank statement only listed deposits you made but did not show any checks you wrote or cash you took out. You would think that you were rolling in dough, when in fact you may well be overdrawn.

Ten years after the financial crisis, the financial service industry and regulators were still using this misleading calculation of swaps markets. It generated astronomical numbers without any real meaning. It beclouded media coverage, policy discussions in Congress, and regulatory rule writing. It hindered dispassionate analysis and sound policymaking. The only ones to benefit were politicians who wished to rail about the dangerous magnitude of the derivatives market or those who wanted large Congressional appropriations to oversee it.

In 2012, Congressman Jack Kingston, then a member of the House Committee on Appropriations, wrote to the CFTC, asserting that "notional value" was not an accurate measurement of systemic risk.[8] He warned that "innocent farmers, ranchers, and producers" would "pay the price" for appropriations that were based upon such misleading numbers. He asked for new measurements that would, in his words, "set the record straight." Yet, nothing was done.

As chairman, I was determined to do something. Upon his appointment as chief economist, I asked Dr. Bruce Tuckman to develop a more accurate measurement of the risk profile of the swaps markets. He and his staff did so in a paper published in early 2018. It introduced the concept of entity-netted notionals (ENNs) as an accurate measure of risk transfer in swaps markets. The ENNs method basically netted related long and short positions, much as debits and credits are recorded in a check book. The result was a much more accurate and realistic assessment of the size of risk mitigation in markets.[9]

Using Tuckman's analysis, $179 trillion of outstanding notional amount in US interest rate swaps dropped to a net amount of $15 trillion. At that size, the interest rate swap market was of the same order of magnitude as other debt markets—such as the US Treasury market, at $16 trillion, or the US mortgage market, at $15 trillion. Suddenly, the market for interest rate swaps regulated by the CFTC could be seen as a normalized, intelligible part of the global economy.

The ENNs methodology provides us today with a far more accurate way to gauge the risk mitigation capacity of global swaps markets. So, the next time you hear frightening references to over-the-counter swaps markets cast in the hundreds of trillions of dollars, don't be fooled. Think to yourself, "Beware, politicians at work!"

Building a Math House

Within a year of taking the reins, our team was pushing engagement with the digitization of modern financial markets through three approaches. The first was through the CFTC's Technology Advisory Committee (TAC), a body that had become moribund since Scott O'Malia's departure, but which Brian Quintenz had shook back into life. The TAC formed subcommittees on digital ledger technology and virtual currency and began meeting regularly to examine virtual currencies, DLT market infrastructure, and custody of digital assets. Once again, the CFTC's TAC Committee did some fine forward-leaning work.

Second, our new market intelligence branch was soon conducting keen market data analysis not just for the commissioners, staff, and other federal agencies, but also for the marketplace. Among other fine work, it published a study of the impact of technological change on the entering of trade orders in US futures markets.[10]

The third avenue was LabCFTC. In its first two years, LabCFTC broke new ground by holding CFTC office hours across the United States and overseas, publishing primers on virtual currencies and smart contracts, analyzing and seeking public feedback on crypto-asset markets and mechanics, holding the CFTC's first FinTech conference, and planning a tech accelerator competition for regulatory innovation.

The CFTC was exploring the digitalization of futures and derivatives markets head-on. Yet at the agency itself, we needed to replace a lot of old regulatory infrastructure with new digital architecture. This was especially so in the field of big data analytics, a rapidly evolving field in which technological proficiency was central to the agency's mission.

Indeed, as management consultant and author Ram Charan has put it, "Any organization that is not a math house now or is unable to become one soon is already a legacy [organization]."[11] This truth clearly applied to market regulators, too. The CFTC needed to adopt up-to-date, "big data," quantitative analytics capabilities. It had to move to the next phase of regulatory data collection and automated analysis using machine learning and artificial intelligence tools. We had to pioneer a new frontier of quantitative regulation that I termed "QuantReg."

There were two important caveats, though. The first was that regulators have to respect confidentiality rights. Market participants are rightly concerned about the handling of confidential data. That is why regulators generally should only gather the data they are prepared to analyze. The centrality of data does not justify regulatory fishing expeditions. Regulators must be vigilant against overreach beyond what the law requires. In addition, regulators must handle all market data in a confidential manner with the highest level of security and protection and be candid and transparent in all data collection practices and uses.

The second caveat is that regulators always needed to retain the fundamentally human dimension of regulating. As we think about market regulation powered by data and machines, it is natural to fear what this may mean for agency staff. And, to be sure, automating traditionally human processes presents real challenges. Yet being a quantitative regulator does not mean replacing human judgment, it means reinforcing it. In fact, the objective of QuantReg is to more firmly support the skilled teams that carry out the agency's ongoing activities in market surveillance, enforcement, regulatory compliance and rule examinations, market intelligence, policy development, and market reform. It means freeing agency staff from repetitive and low-value tasks to focus on high-value activities that require expert judgment and domain knowledge. The point is to marshal quality data—and efficiently and, perhaps, algorithmically analyze it—so that human judgments can be better informed and deployed. Quantitative regulation means melding machines and humans, not separating them.

My belief in the compatibility of humanity and quantitative regulation was reinforced one weekday evening in Washington. I was getting into my car around 8 p.m. in the CFTC's underground parking lot, when I ran into one of the agency's veteran commodity analysts. I said hello and asked why she was leaving so late.

She said "Well, I just started using this new AI tool on some trade data in the cattle futures market and it's showing a whole bunch of trading patterns that I was never able to see before. It's really amazing!"

We said goodnight. As I drove home along Connecticut Avenue, I thought: "How interesting. The fear is that AI will displace people from their work. But here was a bright and talented person not doing less work—she was leaving at 8 p.m.—but obviously more work, and more insightful work, because of AI technology."

Ultimately, our deepening dive into digital technology led me to the clear realization that the CFTC and, indeed, all market regulators, have no choice in the coming decade but to evolve alongside modern digital markets. Regulatory agencies need to become quant-driven bureaus conducting robust data collection, automated data analysis, and state-of-the-art artificial intelligence. The world's preeminent derivatives markets required the world's most advanced regulatory and technological competency. It was time for the CFTC to match its growing market intelligence capability with automated data analysis capability. We had to become a leader in "Quantitative Regulation." This was especially so in the new asset class of crypto.

Here to Stay

In October 2018, I was interviewed by Bob Pisani on CNBC's *Fast Money* program. Pisani asked me what the agency did to protect retail investors. I said:

> "We're very focused on the fraud and manipulation aspects of crypto-currency markets right now. In fact, last week, we just won a big victory in the Boston federal court that certified our authority to prosecute fraud and manipulation in the crypto space and we've been very active at it."[12]

Pisani asked whether the United States was taking a heavy-handed regulatory approach that would entice US-based start-ups to move overseas. I think I surprised him by pointing out that the United States was now actually ahead of the world in offering regulated Bitcoin derivatives trading and clearing.

Then Pisani baited a hook that I declined to bite. He invited me to criticize the SEC for hampering the development of the cryptocurrency industry. Instead, I said, "We're old agencies. Our statutes were written in the 1930s, so we are operating off a 90-year-old piece of 'software,' which we are trying to repurpose for a new innovation that didn't exist earlier."

Sticking to the classic *Fast Money* formula of soliciting a prediction, Pisani asked where the Bitcoin market was headed in the next two years. I said:

> "I think that cryptocurrencies are here to stay. I think that there is a future for them. . . There is a whole section of the world that is hungry for functioning currencies. There is a hundred and forty countries in the world and every one of them has a currency. Probably two-thirds of them are not worth the paper or polymer they are printed on. Those parts of the world rely on hard currencies for large transactions. Bitcoin could solve some of those problems. . ."[13]

Later, I reflected on my last remarks. My estimation of the number of world currencies was 20% below the actual number: about 180. But of much greater concern was my statement that two-thirds of them were not worth the paper they were printed on. I had Mike Gill alert the State

Department to my loose statement to see if they thought it demeaning to our global trade partners and wished me to issue a retraction. We never heard back. Nevertheless, I pledged to myself to be more discreet and avoid such blanket condemnations in the future.

Breaking Records

A few days after my August 2017 Senate confirmation, *The Wall Street Journal* published an unfortunate feature story. It was entitled, "Regulators' Penalties Against Wall Street Are Down Sharply in 2017."[14] The story claimed that the CFTC and the SEC had imposed far lower penalties in the first six months of Donald Trump's presidency than they had during the first six months of 2016, during the Obama administration.[15] It cited unidentified "lawyers who defend financial cases" to the effect that "a business-friendly stance at regulatory agencies in the Trump administration is one of several reasons for the decrease."[16] The article mostly discussed the SEC's enforcement efforts.

Toward the end, the article did acknowledge that "the drop in the CFTC's half-year penalties, to $154 million from $603 million, was mostly the result of two big benchmark-rigging cases it had resolved in May 2016."[17]

The story was way off base. Its lead-in was the narrative that the writers wanted to advance about the "business-friendly" decline in enforcement. Most of the rest of the article contained quotes from random academics and unidentified lawyers voicing opinions that a hypothetical Trump pro-business agenda would reduce enforcement actions. None of them had spoken to me or had any specific knowledge about my enforcement agenda or priorities. As for their statistics, the writers randomly chose the year of 2016 as their benchmark for measurement, a year that had seen a spike in enforcement fines due to resolutions of specific large cases at both the CFTC and the SEC. By using the last year of President Obama's second term (2016) as the benchmark, instead of the first year of his first term (2009), it compared apples to oranges.

I suspected this story might come up in a CNBC television interview scheduled for the following day, and I was determined to be ready for it.

My alarm rang at 5:15 a.m. the next morning at my New Jersey home. Not long after, I walked out my front door, hopped in a black SUV, and crossed into Manhattan on the George Washington Bridge as the rising sun reflected off its steel spans. Forty minutes later, I was sipping a street vendor coffee outside the CNBC studios in the Nasdaq media tower in Times Square. The streetscape bore the material and human vestiges of the prior evening's usual pedestrian throng: trash on the ground and bodies sleeping in doorways. Such sights were relatively uncommon during the last two decades of my career in New York City, but have sadly now become the trade dress of Mayor de Blasio's administration. I was glad that I would be well away from Times Square before the morning's arrival of the numerous grifters and con artists, the painted nudists, and cartoon characters who hound gullible tourists for their cash in return for "selfies."

I went to the studio door, where I was greeted by name and led to the makeup studio, and then upstairs to await the interview. The green room was decorated with large color photos of opening buzzer ceremonies of well-known Nasdaq-listed companies. I placed my briefcase down on a couch, above which hung a photo of a Nasdaq buzzer ceremony for Cisco Systems. In the center of the photo was my brother Charlie, along with other senior Cisco executives and former Nasdaq CEO Bob Griefeld. It gave me a lift for my upcoming live interview.

I checked my talking points once again, as well as the CFTC's morning media summaries. I was ready. I wandered out to the studio and watched as the panel wrapped up a segment. During the commercial break, I was seated at the panel table next to Andrew Ross Sorkin, author of *Too Big to Fail* and editor of *The New York Times* DealBook column. To his right was Becky Quick and to her right was Kevin O'Leary. I greeted them and listened to a departing guest talk about the importance of greater transparency in swaps markets. The countdown began at 15 seconds, and then we were live:

Sorkin: Welcome back to Squawk Box. The Commodities Futures Trading Commission has a newly confirmed chairman joining us. . .: Chris Giancarlo. He was unanimously confirmed by the Senate but he has been working as acting chairman since January. . . Welcome aboard.

ME: It's a pleasure.

SORKIN: What's your first priority? What's the thing you're trying to get done right now?

ME: What we're trying to do right now is focus on market intelligence. Our markets are changing dramatically—these are not our fathers' commodity markets anymore. The famous market that you saw in the movie *Trading Places*—with hooting and hollering, shouting—those markets are now closed. Our markets are trading algorithmically; they're traded virtually. We've got to become a twenty-first-century regulator for the new twenty-first-century digital markets.

QUICK: Mr. Chairman, there was a story in *The Wall Street Journal* that said enforcement under the first six months of the Trump administration had been down significantly. They tie this to the administration's thoughts on business. The CFTC spokesperson has pushed back pretty strongly against this. What are your thoughts on that?

ME: Okay, it was actually flawed logic. In examining how enforcement works, one would understand that in our markets, very complicated markets, enforcement actions take years in development. The actions that we've announced in the first six months of my work at the CFTC are actions that were started under the prior administration. To compare the first six months of this administration with a dollar amount of enforcement actions is a commentary on the priorities [of] the final years of the Obama administration. If one wants to look at [my] priorities. . ., one will need to look a year from now—

O'LEARY: It takes two years to bring an action and collect on it?

ME: No. But it will take at least a year to formulate a case and reach a point where there's actually a court decision, or there may be a settlement—certainly not within six months. The analysis of *The Wall Street Journal* did of the first six months really reflected cases that were begun during the prior administration.

SORKIN: Mr. Chairman, do you believe that you personally and perhaps the administration, in terms of disposition, towards the industry, will ultimately be more friendly? Will you agree that banks will have to hold less in reserves for legal cases, and things like that?

ME: So I really want to push back against the notion of industry friendly. My focus is not to be a friend to any industry. My job as a regulator is to be market intelligent. If I have a bias, it's towards markets. If I have a focus, it's making sure that our regulation is as intelligent, as well formulated for the markets that we oversee. . . , whether it's farmers, ranchers, oil producers, [or] homeowners. . .

SORKIN: Chairman, thank you for coming in.

Sorkin then looked to the camera and teed up the next segment before the director closed the broadcast for the commercial break. He turned to me with a smile and said, "That was really good. We'll have you back on."

A little over a year later, I flew to Minnesota to speak at the Economic Club of Minneapolis[18] about the effectiveness of the CFTC's enforcement program, now a full year under my direction. I announced that the number of CFTC enforcement actions jumped 25% over each of the last three years of the Obama administration and that the total amount of civil monetary penalties imposed by the agency was around $900 million, higher than five of the eight years under Obama.[19] By almost every measure, the first year of my watch had been among the most vigorous in terms of enforcement as any in the history of the CFTC—with more enforcement actions, more penalties, more large-scale matters, more accountability, more partnering with criminal law enforcement at home and abroad, and more whistleblower awards than ever before.[20] Most measures would increase again the following year.

I told the Minneapolis audience, "There will be no pause, no let up, and no relaxation in the CFTC's efforts to enforce the law and punish wrongdoing. We must keep the markets safe and fair for consumers."

Yet, our strong fist of enforcement was also wrapped in a velvet glove—the offer of cooperation and transparency. We offered reduced penalties to firms and individuals that self-reported lapses and cooperated in probes. That was meant to encourage a "culture of compliance." The program was modeled on those of other national law enforcement agencies.

I explained also how a robust enforcement program was compatible with strong economic growth and American prosperity. For the economy to grow, businesses and individuals need to know they're competing on a level playing field. Unlawful activity puts honest businesses at a disadvantage. It impedes free and fair competition. It dampens economic growth. And it undermines democratic values, public accountability, and the rule of law. That's why I was committed to ensuring all companies and individuals play by the rules.

The announcement of our extraordinary enforcement record received modest news coverage. It contradicted the prevailing media narrative of the Trump administration relaxing penalties against Wall Street. Yet it was precisely my experience working on Wall Street that reinforced my commitment to robust regulatory enforcement. I have enormous respect for the good men and women of America's financial service industry who conduct themselves each and every day with integrity and honesty. On or off Wall Street, they are the ones who are betrayed by the very few who engage in wrongful behavior.

We also strove to be transparent in our work. We published the Enforcement Division's *Annual Report*[21] and set out the priorities of our various examination branches. The following spring, we published—for the first time in the CFTC's 40-year history—an *Enforcement Manual*,[22] providing market participants with one-stop guidance to the Commission's enforcement procedures in conducting investigations, pre-enforcement proceedings, and full-blown administrative actions and litigation.

After the speech, I was joined on the dais for an interview by Neel Kashkari, the thoughtful president of the Minneapolis Federal Reserve Bank. At one point in the interview, Kashkari asked my views on the future development of Bitcoin and other virtual currencies. I explained that, while I did not see Bitcoin as a domestic replacement for the dollar, I did think it was a harbinger of extraordinary change in society's conception of money. I said that it would be silly of us to think that the Internet, in its continuing evolution, will not transform money in the same way it has transformed information, social networking, retail shopping, local transportation, travel and leisure, photography, music, and entertainment. I said it was going to happen, and it may well happen at first far away from advanced economies like the United States.

Determined to avoid repeating my earlier, unfortunate slight on CNBC of "two-thirds" of the world's sovereign currencies, I carefully gave a real-world example. I explained that the Sierra Leone currency, the "Leone," was adequate to purchase food in the market in Freetown but not to buy a Toyota, which required hard currency like Euros or dollars. In such economies—where there were many young people equipped with mobile technology—we might begin to see the use of Bitcoin and other virtual currencies as a viable means of exchange.

A few minutes later, Kashkari took questions from the audience. A large black man stood up and in accented English said, "I am from Sierra Leone and I just wanted to say—" My stomach took a slight dive that I had insulted this man's country and national currency and risked another international tiff.

Fortunately, the audience member continued, "—I agree with you. Crypto is taking off in the part of Africa where I am from." I was relieved I would not have to direct another call to the State Department.

It was a good reminder that nothing you say and nothing you do as a government official goes unnoticed by someone. Even if not reported in the press.

PART IV

FINISH LINE

Chapter 13

Last Laps

The engine screamed as he kicked it into third.
He put the right wheel six inches from the grass and kept it there, to a hair, as the
car cornered in an insanely fast four-wheel slide.
He flicked it straight and roared at the hill ahead.
— Ken W. Purdy, "Change of Plan," originally appeared in *The Atlantic*
Monthly, July 1952, reprinted in *Ken Purdy's Book of Automobiles*, 1972,
Cassell & Company, London

Domestic Affairs

CME's Bitcoin futures steadily gained an institutional following. By the anniversary of the product's launch, it had gone mainstream. The gross number of newspaper column inches devoted to Bitcoin fell back into alignment with its underlying price and the clear absence of any threat posed to the global economy. The steady increase in trading had erased most of the controversy around our decision not block self-certification. Even Interactive Brokers, the company run by Thomas Peterffy—who had written the full-page letter upbraiding me in *The Wall Street Journal*, had become one of the biggest dealers in Bitcoin Futures. The product's success belied all the interagency tension and press lampooning directed at us the year before. I was proud that we had remained resolute under the pressure.

The CFTC was now considered the "go to" federal agency for forward-looking cryptocurrency innovation. That recognition drove a lot of creative initiatives in our direction, including various cryptocurrency derivatives products as well as new exchanges and clearing services designed for them. In May 2018, we publicly issued guidance to market participants that sought to launch new virtual currency derivative products.[1] LabCFTC met with hundreds of virtual currency and FinTech innovators in the United States and abroad. Behind closed doors on Capitol Hill and within the Trump administration, my team continued to advocate for a coordinated US government approach to FinTech, generally, and crypto, specifically.

Our internal virtual currency task force worked actively with the SEC to address jurisdictional issues between our agencies. We began to look at other virtual currencies, as we had with Ethereum, to anticipate which might appropriately be considered "commodities" under CFTC jurisdiction. We also coordinated with the Department of Justice and the SEC on virtual currency enforcement matters. Several of those matters led to federal court decisions confirming the CFTC's statutory jurisdiction and legal authority over virtual currency.

In a spring 2019 meeting with Congressman Patrick McHenry, the then leader of the minority Republicans on the House Financial Services Committee, I was asked how Congress could be helpful in furthering sensible crypto regulation. I said that an initial step would be to have the CFTC and SEC formalize and fund the ad hoc virtual currency, joint agency task force that Clayton and I had started. The task force could then begin a process of regularly informing Congress about regulatory challenges and make recommendations for a practical legal framework well suited to crypto and virtual assets. McHenry immediately embraced the idea and developed it. I was delighed to see that idea germinate over the next eighteen months and form the basis of the "Eliminate Barriers to Innovation Act," H.R. 1602, passed by the House in April 2021 that is still awaiting Senate passage as this book is going to press.

Meanwhile, the CFTC further developed its regulatory response to crypto and the rapid maturation of this innovation that I will turn to again in Chapter 15. But first, I want to talk about a few of things other than Bitcoin, FinTech, and quantitative regulation that occupied my time during my two and a half years as CFTC chairman.

Hand on the Wheel

In August 2018, the Senate confirmed two new CFTC commissioners to join the existing three. It had been four years since the agency had had a full complement.

Smart and composed, Republican Dawn Stump brought decades of experience. She had first come to Washington from her native Texas to analyze grain prices for US export market development. Dawn had spent time on key Senate committees, including Agriculture. That's where I had first met her, when she was a key point person on Dodd–Frank. She also had held senior roles at the New York Stock Exchange and the Futures Industry Association.

Democrat Dan Berkovitz was also remarkably experienced. I first met him when had been the agency's general counsel during its early implementation of Dodd–Frank. Before that, he had served on a key Senate committee and as a partner in a prominent national law firm. Principled and high-minded, Dan Berkovitz personifies the phrase "stand-up guy."

With the agency's ninth-floor executive suites now filled with commissioners and their staffs, our work gained momentum. There was a lot going on.

The title of CFTC Chairman is something of a misnomer. It conjures the image of someone presiding over meetings of the commissioners to adopt ongoing rules and procedures. That is an important—but only occasional—part of the job. Far more often the chairman acts in the role of CEO,[2] the agency's primary decision maker with oversight over its daily operations and logistics.

I certainly had not anticipated the amount of ordinary decisions that flowed up to the CFTC chairman's office. Running the agency occupied a third or more of my time and could easily have occupied more. To avoid that, I drew on my business experience to clearly articulate policy direction, set work priorities, and act decisively. But I insisted that decisions I did not have to make were pushed down to executives who were closest to, and most conversant with the issue. I selected division and deputy directors largely based on their efficiency and decisiveness.

I was helped enormously by Sarah Summerville, who I promoted to be director of the CFTC's Office of Diversity and Inclusion. She oversaw its civil rights, equal employment opportunity, diversity, and inclusion programs. Sarah is the personification of the French phrase *savoir faire*, knowing how to handle any situation with grace and discretion. Together, we leveraged diversity to help us do a better job as a market regulator working across a complex global economy. We implemented targeted outreach to minority institutions—such as historically black colleges and universities—to identify potential student candidates for our internship program, which we made a paid program for the first time. We also partnered with Gallaudet University, a federally chartered school for the deaf and hard of hearing, to look for internship opportunities for students.

Staff morale was low when I stepped into the chairman's office. The agency was locked in a dispute with its labor union with a list of grievances and demands before a federal impasse panel. I was determined to turn things around. Few policy objectives could be achieved without the goodwill of the agency's staff supported by a positive work environment. I met with Mary Connelly and her colleagues in the National Treasury Employees Union (NTEU) Chapter 337, as well as with the CFTC's ever-poised Chief Negotiator Shannon Schmidt, and her colleagues. Not only was I determined to resolve the current labor dispute, I would devote the full resources of my office to negotiating a long-term collective bargaining agreement.

Again, I tasked Mike Gill, a master at resolving complex agency personnel and interagency tangles, to manage the process and keep me and the other commissioners regularly briefed. We sponsored a staff-led pay and benefits panel that volunteered hundreds of hours and came up with a series of thoughtful ways to address decades of agency compensation and promotion practices that derived more from management expediency than sound human resource development.

The dispute before the Federal Impasse Panel was soon resolved. and the work of labor negotiations began. Both sides bargained hard on more than 50 specific issues, such as grievance procedures, telework and work schedules, merit promotions, and performance management. There were tense moments, but Mike and I made sure that there was never a reason to question management's goodwill or that of its labor negotiators.

In June 2019, NTEU President Tony Reardon and I signed the Master Collective Bargaining Agreement at a ceremony in the CFTC hearing room. It was the first agency-wide collective bargaining agreement in CFTC history[3] and it came under Republican control, not Democratic. It came 29 months after my call to Mary Connelly on Inauguration Day pledging to get it done. I would not have happened without her, Dan Davis, Shannon Schmidt, and so many other selfless public servants.

I had to tackle many other vexing, administrative challenges. Chief among them was resolving the agency's perennial flat funding. This situation had resulted in part from pockets of Congressional frustration with past agency budget shenanigans. The CFTC lacked some credibility in Congress due to auditors having repeatedly taken exception to the agency's annual financial statements.

As a businessman, I found this unacceptable. Some of the auditors' qualms concerned certain lease obligations for the agency's four offices in Washington, New York, Chicago, and Kansas City that had been incorrectly contracted by a predecessor. Over the next two years, we worked out new leaseholds for all four offices. Thanks to these and other efforts, in 2018 the CFTC managed to receive its first "clean" audit opinion in many years.

In producing our agency budget, we eschewed the usual government practice of taking the prior year's budget and applying a percentage increase. Rather, working with the CFTC's finance team and a fresh sheet of paper, we built a new budget from a baseline of zero, ensuring that each requested dollar served a legitimate purpose. We identified several areas where we could save taxpayer dollars. But we also identified several in which we needed greater investment: market intelligence, clearinghouse examinations, cybersecurity, and financial technology.

Bucking the Trump Administration's call for agencies to keep their budgets flat, I submitted to Congress a modest increase in CFTC funding.[4] The decision was not made lightly. The agency had not had an increase in years, while it continued to lose highly skilled staff to higher pay in the private sector. The agency simply could not recruit the talent needed to effectively fulfill its mission. Over the next two years, I had to summon all of my personal suasiveness, business acumen, and plain doggedness to get it passed. With Charlie Thornton as my *consigliere*, we traversed the mysterious back alleys of Congressional appropriations. We faced down numerous challenges and serious setbacks, including double-dealing by some Wall Street banks that sought to use the CFTC's budget request as a negotiating tool for other legislative concessions—a tactic I would not tolerate.

At last, in February 2019, key House and Senate appropriations and agriculture committees voted to approve increased funding for the CFTC. I was thankful for the funds, but even more pleased by the support it signaled for our mission.

Back to Our Roots

During my five years at the commission, the agency refocused its attention on its traditional foundation: agricultural commodity futures. I've already mentioned the site visits to farmers and agricultural suppliers across the beautiful American heartland. With the support of Kansas Senators Pat Roberts and Jerry Moran, we conceived and convened the CFTC's first-ever annual agricultural futures conference in Overland Park, Kansas.[5] Partnering with Kansas State University, the two-day conference reviewed macro-economic trends and issues affecting our markets, including market speculation, high-frequency trading, trade data transparency, novel hedging practices, and market manipulation. It also covered advances in distributed ledger technology, algorithmic trading, and other emerging digital technologies, such as precision agriculture. Attendance at the Kansas conference sold out two weeks before it opened.

Not long after becoming chairman, I was in the CFTC's Kansas City office with its administrator Chuck Marvine, whose fine work as chief trial attorney was already well known to me. As our conversation concluded, Chuck walked me through the office foyer. We paused in front of the CFTC emblem with its depiction of a farm plow.

I explained that the CFTC was committed to maintaining its presence in Kansas City and that we needed a tangible sign of that commitment. I then asked Chuck to obtain an actual field plow to be put on display in the office lobby. After just a second's hesitation, Chuck said he would get it done.

About four months later, Chuck asked me to schedule another visit to Kansas City. When I arrived at the office, there in the lobby was a true field plow similar to the one in the CFTC emblem. But it was not just any plow. This plow had come from a long-standing Kansas family farm. Chuck personally had bought it at a Sunday farm auction, cleaned it, polished it, and put it on prominent display in the CFTC lobby.

That Kansas farm plow stands today in the CFTC lobby as a commitment of the federal government to oversee trading and pricing markets for agriculture commodities and the family farmers who produce them.

Missing the Mark

Overly restrictive CFTC regulations remained a concern of mine. The CFTC regulations for Swap Exchange Facilities continued to constrain innovation in swaps trading methodology. The underlying framework remained inconsistent with Dodd–Frank, in my view, by being too prescriptive, too burdensome, and too modeled on futures markets. It was also highly subjective, with its administration overly relying upon no-action letters, staff discretion, interpretation, and temporary regulatory forbearance. All that could change under any future administration.

At my request, Amir Zaidi led a comprehensive redraft of the SEF rules. He consulted with market participants. Some firms wanted us to do something more limited, and not a comprehensive rewrite. I chalked that up to regulatory fatigue. I spoke frequently to Amir during the drafting and personally approved the package of proposed changes that was submitted for a vote of the commission in November 2018.[6] The changes received the cautious support of three of my fellow commissioners. It was not supported, however, by Commissioner Berkovitz, who had participated in producing the rules I sought to replace and vehemently opposed my proposal. I respected Berkovitz's position, but was grateful for support from the three other commissioners.

The reaction of market participants was mixed. Over the next several months, in New York and Washington, I met personally with dozens of banks, asset managers, and trading firms. I realized that my proposal had missed the mark. We had attempted to address the fragmentation of swaps trading caused by the existing rules by fostering a market structure of competing and transparent platforms, on which the entire process of liquidity formation, price discovery, and trade execution could take place seamlessly. I had not anticipated, however, the adverse impact our proposal might have on direct relationships between swaps dealers and their customers. The miss was entirely mine.

In early 2019, during a government funding shutdown, I delivered a logistically challenged presentation to an American Bar Association (ABA) convention. I went to the ABA's Washington offices on Connecticut Avenue. I stood at a podium in a small conference room and spoke to a laptop computer placed on a cardboard box a few feet in front of me. My image was then broadcast to hundreds of delegates gathered in the ballroom of the La Playa Conference center in Naples, Florida, for the annual Convention of the ABA Derivatives Law section. But for the shutdown, I would have been there in person.

Among other topics, I discussed the SEF proposal.[7] I spoke about its objectives and was candid about its shortcomings. The goal was not to adopt the proposal at any cost or on any timetable, I said, but to get it right. I admitted that more work needed to be done. I thanked them for their well-considered comments and concerns. I then said:

> "Okay, now let's get down to the real issue . . . the issue that is surely on many of your minds: With billions already having been spent to come into compliance with the existing SEF regime, and with everybody used to it, and with so much other work to do, why do this? Why change the current SEF rules?
> "Let me tell you why. It is about risk and opportunity."

The impermanence of the current SEF rule framework posed risk for market participants, I continued. Staff in a future administration—

perhaps one less sympathetic to free markets—might well change or withdraw the interpretations, guidance, and compliance expectations that have underpinned it. Moreover, the current restrictions on methods of execution may turn out to be, by themselves, a source of trading risk during a liquidity crisis—when swaps counterparties need to be found through less prescriptive and more flexible means of execution.

Improving the SEF rules also presented opportunity, I continued. It was an opportunity to align the rules to the inherent trading dynamics and episodic liquidity of swaps trading and to enhance markets as mechanisms for price discovery and risk mitigation. New rules could also offer existing and new market entrants an opportunity to pursue market innovation, which had waned under the current framework.

Unfortunately, there was not enough time before the end of my term to revise the SEF proposal and fix its flaws—for which I am responsible. I regret not having been able to create a SEF regulatory framework that more expressly fosters economic activity, innovation, and competition than what exists today.

International Affairs

From the first to last day of my service as chairman, I was particularly engaged with international matters. As I had told President Trump, I believe that the US needs to fully involve itself in international standard-setting bodies, just as its economic competitors do. For one thing, it is a way to promote the American values of private enterprise and open, well-regulated markets free from partisan political interference. For another, international regulatory engagement in an increasingly interconnected world increases market intelligence and cooperation by learning from others.

The day after the White House announced my nomination, I told a large audience at FIA Boca that in all of the CFTC's international engagements, the CFTC would act in a forthright and candid manner, displaying leadership when appropriate and respect and due consideration at all times. The CFTC would strive to be considered a trusted and worthy counterparty by its overseas regulatory associates.

During my watch, the CFTC participated in more international work streams than ever before in its history. Confounding critics' warnings of a Trump administration pull back from international engagement, the CFTC increased its engagement in the International Organization of Securities Commissions (IOSCO), the Financial Stability Board, and in IOSCO's joint work with the international Committee on Payments and Market Infrastructures and Basel Committee on Banking Supervision. More importantly, the CFTC chaired or cochaired international working groups on market fragmentation, efficient resiliency of over-the-counter derivatives reforms, commodity principles, cybersecurity, regulation of financial market infrastructures, international data standards, and implementation monitoring and assessment. I am proud that CFTC leadership made it possible to have IOSCO, the FSB, and other groups produce international standards, guidance, and reports. These have substantially advanced the goal of having a resilient global financial system while maintaining robust markets.

I personally attended every IOSCO board meeting I could. I came to know many fine regulatory colleagues from around the world. I was impressed with the high quality of their work and the thoughtfulness of their contributions. I admired the superb chairmanship of IOSCO by Ashley Alder and vice-chairman Jean-Paul Servais, and enjoyed cochairing two global regulatory working groups with Ryozo Himino, the well-respected commissioner of the Japanese Financial Services Agency.

International matters certainly occupied far more of my time than I anticipated. I should not have been surprised, however. When it came to wholesale trading and market activities among large financial services institutions, US markets and firms play a global role that is an order of magnitude greater than that of any other world economy. US banks and trading firms—regulated by the CFTC—dominate derivatives market-making and liquidity provision on most derivatives exchanges around the world, including those in Europe and Asia, which would mostly go dark without the market making provided by US firms. The CFTC is a primary regulator of a number of key overseas derivatives clearinghouses—such as the London Clearing House (LCH Ltd.), which clears the overwhelming majority of the global interest-rate swaps.[8] At the same time many key global commodities and benchmarks are priced and hedged primarily on US markets like the Chicago Mercantile Exchange (owned by CME Group) and ICE Futures (owned by the Intercontinental Exchange).[9] Finally, the CFTC has trained many overseas securities regulators in derivatives oversight through its weeklong training program in derivatives regulation that takes place every year in Washington.

Bridge over Brexit

Second only to New York as a global financial center, London enjoys extraordinary financial prominence in Europe. Of other EU cities, only one was regularly in the global top 20. Of the three most economically developed global regions—North America, Europe, and Asian Pacific Rim—only Europe was so dominated by a single city. (North America's six largest financial centers are all in the global top 20, while Asia's six largest are in the top 11.)

Accordingly, when British voters decided to leave the European Union in 2016 ("Brexit"), a mad grab took place as other EU cities tried to seize pieces of London's wholesale financial services industry. By itself, the clash of European industrial policies was not of concern to the United States. What did engage the United States was the possibility that abrupt or punitive measures imposed by the EU or the UK against one another could put financial and operational strain on US firms that provided most of the financial infrastructure, services, capital, and trading liquidity on both sides of the English Channel. That risk necessarily implicated the CFTC as the regulator of those firms.

In October 2017, Treasury Secretary Mnuchin asked me to present US concerns about Brexit to a group of central bankers and market regulators at a meeting of key US allies in the Washington headquarters of the International Monetary Fund. I quipped:

> "Sometimes we non-European regulators look at Brexit and feel as if we are the innocent children of divorcing parents. We keep getting dragged into a painful separation that we want nothing to do with."

"The painful separation" triggered, among other things, an ongoing tug of war between Brussels and London over London's systemically important and lucrative clearing of Interest Rate Swaps. We could not allow this European tussle to become a threat to the global economy.

From beginning to end, I worked hard to safeguard US interests while not taking sides in the Brexit split. That became increasingly difficult as the failure of Britain and the EU to negotiate an amicable separation caused growing market uncertainty. A "hard Brexit," as it was called—that is, an exit without negotiated terms—would have had little initial impact on financial trading between the United States and the EU, which were established trading partners. But it could have been very disruptive for trading between the United States and the UK, because those two parties could not begin negotiating a bilateral trading arrangement until after Brexit took place. Toward the middle of February 2019, when a "hard Brexit" was becoming a real possibility, trading uncertainty became acute.

I decided to act to avoid market turmoil. With the bipartisan support of my fellow commissioners and a "heads-up" to the US Treasury and the White House, I reached out to Her Majesty's Treasury, the Bank of England, and the UK Financial Conduct Authority (FCA). I proposed a series of bilateral regulatory measures that, in the event of a hard Brexit, would assure market participants of the continuity of derivatives trading and clearing activities between the UK and the United States. The proposals triggered several weeks of around-the-clock consultations and document drafting amongst the four agencies.

In London on February 25, 2019 we announced an agreement. The four-way statement was jointly issued by British chancellor of the Exchequer, Philip Hammond; governor of the Bank of England, Mark Carney; chief executive of the FCA, Andrew Bailey; and me on behalf of the CFTC. Speaking to the international press, I called the deal a "bridge over Brexit."

As soon as my team and I left the press conference, we grabbed the EuroStar train to Brussels, arriving a few hours later. There we reviewed the measures with EU officials, and also managed any ramifications on the EU's continuing efforts to assert oversight over American derivatives clearinghouses. But those maneuverings are a story in their own right—suitable for another book someday.

Ministry of Silly Walks

Toward the end of my public service, I received one of the most pleasant honors of my career: the Freedom of the City of London. A very ancient tradition, it is believed to have been first bestowed in 1237. It was conferred on me in a charming ceremony at the twelfth-century Guildhall in the center of the City of London. The honor arises from the medieval practice of granting worthy persons freedom from serfdom.[10] Among the current privileges that accompany the honor are the right to carry an unsheathed sword in the City and drive sheep across London Bridge. A third privilege is the comfort of a silken rope around the Freedom holder's neck should he or she end up on the gallows. That is one privilege that I intend to put off for as long as I can!

A few days later, with the still lingering memory of that endearing event, I made my way to London's Heathrow Airport for my return flight to Washington. As I proceeded through the check-in process, everything seemed far more professional than in US airports. I expected to see similar professionalism at the security line.

Instead, I was disappointed to experience the same insulting officiousness that is commonplace at too many US airports. I heard the same discourteous bawling at passengers. I saw the same hostile reactions of passengers to the harsh treatment. The only difference was the accent.

Then, I heard an official in charge of herding passengers through the metal screener cut through the unpleasantness with trademark British humor. "Proceed normally," she said. "No goose steps and NO silly walks. I repeat: proceed normally, NO silly walks."

I was glad to know that Monty Python's "Ministry of Silly Walks"[11] was still in operation, encouraging Her Majesty's subjects to enjoy a bit of a laugh as they endured the inconvenience of modern transportation.

Chapter 14

Checkered Flag

Life is never a straight line It's a circle never ending To get to where you're going Take another road that's bending.

—Roger Turner (poet), "Take Another Road"

Turning in My Chips

I do not often visit gambling casinos. When I do, I use a "double or nothing" method. I go in with a set amount, say $500, and then I walk out the door when that amount of money is either doubled or gone.

So it is with public service. If you think you will go in and stay until you win every battle you wish to fight, you will never leave. That is because few political battles are ever fully won. Most just evolve and get fought at another level, get subsumed into other issues, or get forgotten about as the world moves on.

On the other hand, if you enter the political arena and say you will fight hard and then retire after a set number of seasons, you will lose some battles but win your fair share and still leave on your own terms. That approach frees you to focus on the mission without always keeping an eye out for the next political job up the ladder. The problem in Washington is not that people leave too *soon*, it is that they stay too *long*.

From the beginning of my service on the commission, I knew I would leave Washington in 2019, at the end of my five-year enlistment. Not only did I know it, but I made sure that everyone I recruited to work for me knew it as well. That fact allowed us to be fully attentive to the job at hand.

It was not that I was unhappy at the CFTC. On the contrary, I enjoyed every minute of it. I had come to love the rank-and-file staff and respect their dedication and commitment. I was proud to be their captain and wished to earn their trust. I enjoyed running the agency and was indefatigable in asserting its authority and mission. I also keenly understood global markets and institutional trading. I brought that insight to bear as those markets returned to robust health. I was also proud of any contributions that our work at the CFTC provided to the accelerating US economy and increased employment. More importantly, I was proud of the steady hand—and market intelligent oversight—that my team brought to the CFTC's work regulating US derivatives markets.

On the other hand, Washington politics and politicians bored me. The endless twaddle about phony things and phony causes was wearying. Washington seemed so juvenile, like high school for grown-ups without the lighthearted humor. I much preferred the honesty of business.

Naïve illusions to the contrary, politics is ultimately about gaining and wielding power over people and society. In politics, the scorecard of success is measured in power. Political success leads to more power. Political failure leads to less power.

Furthermore, appearances are crucial to exercising power. Political success comes from appearing to possess the virtues and character needed to draw a sufficient number of votes to stay in power. It is form over substance. The appearance of virtue may be divorced from actual possession of it. Some have it and some don't. Periodic elections every two, four and six years are the few opportunities in the US for an objective assessment of gaps between virtue and the appearance of it.

Business operates on a different principle: substance over form. One either adds value to the lives or investment accounts of customers or one does not. Some do and some don't. If one does, they prosper. If one does not, they struggle. There is an objective scorecard for adding value. It is called a financial statement. That statement shows in a relatively standardized and mathematical way whether value has been added. And it is rendered regularly, as frequently as every ninety days, if not more often.

In one of his soliloquies, the fictional *House of Cards* politician, Frank Underwood, muses about a former Congressional staffer:

> "Such a waste of talent. He chose money over power. In this town, a mistake nearly everyone makes. Money is the McMansion in Sarasota that starts falling apart after 10 years. Power is the old stone building that stands for centuries. I cannot respect someone who doesn't see the difference."[1]

Frank Underwood was wrong. I have worked in senior roles on both Wall Street and in Washington. Both have elements of hypocrisy and self-dealing. Yet both are occupied by mostly good and virtuous people. In the wrong hands, politics is just as much a McMansion as any sleazy financial bucket shop. And in the right hands, business can build beautiful stone buildings that care for the sick, house the poor, entertain the weary, and support well-earned retirements. Both politics and business must serve the public. Their practitioners should have more humility in performing that service.

Like Frank Underwood, some public officials come to believe theirs is a nobler calling than the private sector. Yet, no politician that I met during my time in Washington has any reason to look down their nose at American businesspeople. The same is true in the other direction. Most of our federal and state employees work hard and are not corruptible. After five years, I saw that there is no greater morality in politics than in finance. Ultimately, America's prospects derive from the goodness and values of its citizens with whom sovereignty resides. They must ever remain a check on the prerogatives of the politicians and the business-executives who are there to serve them.

Meet the New Boss

My time in Washington was almost up. It was time to prepare to leave the casino.

In the summer of 2018, I met with the White House Office of Presidential Personnel and confirmed that the next year would be my last. I preferred to step down when my commission expired in April 2019, I told them, but would stay slightly longer at the request of the president to assure a smooth transition to my successor. We discussed candidates to succeed me.

I checked in again in November and learned that a choice had been made: Heath Tarbert. A Baltimore native and University of Penn lawyer, Tarbert had clerked for Supreme Court Justice Clarence Thomas and had served as a White House associate counsel in the George W. Bush administration. I had been introduced to Tarbert during the early part of the Obama administration when he was with a prominent Washington law firm. I was impressed with his drive and determination. After the November 2016 election, I asked Tarbert to consider becoming CFTC general counsel. Instead, he accepted an opportunity to support Treasury Under Secretary David Malpass as Assistant Secretary of the Treasury for International Markets and Development. Upon Malpass's departure to run the World Bank, Tarbert had been promoted to acting Treasury under secretary for international affairs.

In December 2018, the White House announced its intention to nominate Tarbert to chair the CFTC. I knew Tarbert's international chops would be a great advantage for the agency. I issued a statement complimenting the "superb choice," who would "continue the work of transitioning the CFTC into a twenty-first-century digital regulator. . . to support strong economic growth and American prosperity." Tarbert did that and more.

Boca

In March 2019, a month before my commission expired, Regina and I flew to West Palm Beach and grabbed an Uber to the famous Boca

Raton Resort and Club. We drove through the palm tree–lined entryway, passed the coral pink gatehouse, and turned into the busy *porte cochère*, where a bellhop took our bags. We entered the stately Spanish-style pink palazzo built a century ago, now part of the Waldorf Astoria chain. "Boca," as it is known, has long been the site of the annual conference of the Futures Industry Association (FIA). This year was the 44th and would be one of the most well-attended ever, with over a thousand participants.

I had started coming to this event sometime around 2004 and had always enjoyed it. Few other conferences so perfectly combine the right time of year with a great location and a broad array of industry participants. FIA Boca has all the most influential people of the derivatives industry—"C Suite" officers, senior regulators, the press, investment bankers, and dealmakers. I recall many memorable moments here, from negotiating acquisitions by GFI to meeting overseas regulators as a CFTC Commissioner.

Perhaps my most memorable moment at Boca happened two years earlier in 2017 during a dinner hosted by the respected law firm of Katten Muchin. As acting CFTC chairman, I was seated at the head table with the firm's well-regarded senior partner Arthur Hahn and Futures Industry Association president and CEO, Walt Lukken. Also with us was a good friend and former CFTC chairman, Jim Newsome. As the appetizer was served, Newsome turned to me and said, "Congratulations on being nominated as full chairman." I said, "Thanks, Jim, but nothing's been announced yet." He said, "It has. Congratulations!"

I checked my email and, sure enough, there was the announcement from the White House. There was a buzz in the room, and Hahn stood up, clinked his glass with a spoon and announced my nomination. The room broke out in applause, and I stood to say a few words.

Since then, two years had passed by quickly. This would be last time I would give the traditional chairman's keynote address, which opens the first day of the conference. I was up early that morning and in the pool for a swim before sunrise. I then had breakfast in the Palm Court with members of my staff. Shortly after, I went down to the large auditorium and mic'd up. Walt Lukken began his introduction and welcomed me onto the stage.

I took a good look at the room. It held about 600, and I could see that there were another 100 or so people standing and still arriving through the doors. I thanked the audience and gave my remarks, including a review of things done and things still to be done. I then summed up by saying that I had tried to do "what my parents taught me: to leave any place I visited in better condition than when I arrived." In the case of the CFTC, that meant better run, better funded, more transparent, more accountable, and more market intelligent.

With a slight choke in my voice, I said, "You know, I have been coming to Boca for over a decade, yet this is the last time I will address you as CFTC chairman." I thanked the audience for the honor of serving them and the American people. The audience's reaction overwhelmed me.

One journalist covered the speech under this headline:

How Chris Giancarlo Helped the Futures Industry Get Its Groove Back

Chris Giancarlo will go down as perhaps the most popular regulator in industry history. The CFTC chairman, who will step down this year. . . , gave his farewell address at the FIA Boca conference this year with a focus on the agency's achievements during his term.

Giancarlo breathed new optimism and life into the industry at the FIA Boca conference two years ago with a speech calling for a practical and cooperative approach to regulation. His approach, a stark contrast with prior CFTC chairmen, drew what is thought to be the first ever standing ovation for a CFTC chairman. And his final speech to the audience at FIA Boca that year garnered a second standing ovation.

He recounted several accomplishments, including CFTC's Technology lab, aimed at working with the FinTech community. . .

He also secured an increase in CFTC funding for the agency, the first in six years that he said was "solely on the merits of our funding request." Giancarlo said more money for better technology is absolutely critical for the agency as markets become more technologically driven and complex. . .

Ultimately, Giancarlo will be remembered as the CFTC chair who changed the tone of the agency and its interaction with the industry.[2]

Taking Leave

There were a few other farewells to bid, including to Congress. In May, I testified for the last time before the House Agriculture Committee in the Longworth building. Collin Peterson, Democratic chairman—and leader of our 2017 Midwest music tour—said, "Welcome back to the committee. I think the last time we were in this room, we were playing guitars, right?"

He was right. A few months before in that very room, he and I and his 2nd Amendments band had entertained an audience from across party lines for the bipartisan "Congressional Rock and Roll Caucus" gathering. This morning, the room was the setting for compliments from both sides of the aisle for the CFTC's work and progress.

Two weeks later, I was on the other side of the Capitol testifying before the Senate Appropriations Subcommittee on Financial Services. I was testifying once more beside SEC Chairman Clayton. The hearing was quite routine in many respects.

However, Louisiana Senator John Kennedy, the committee chairman, made a point of thanking me for my service: "Five years is a long time to give of your life. And I know it's not a job, it's sort of a lifestyle that you take on as chairman. . ."

Senator Coons, the ranking member, spoke directly to Regina, seated behind me:

> "And to your wife, Regina, if I might just express our gratitude for your support for his service. And I'll join with Chairman Kennedy in our thanks to you both for the time you've dedicated to our nation in your role as chairman of the CFTC."

After an hour and a half of testimony, the meeting came to an end with a bit of humor, when Senator Kennedy said:

> "Chairman [Giancarlo], we're going to miss you, I mean that. You've done an extraordinary job."

With a smile, I replied:

> "I never thought I would ever say this Senator, but I'm going to miss you, too!"

(LAUGHTER)
The gavel came down and the meeting was over.

Another important farewell was to the crypto community. Sparked by a conversation with CFTC senior economist George Pullen, I published an online open letter to coincide with New York's 2019 Blockchain Week. It was entitled, "Free Markets and the Future of Blockchain."

It began:

> It has . . . been my honor to work on so many issues close to the hearts and minds of the crypto community, not least of which are: virtual currencies, distributed ledger technology (DLT) and fintech broadly. I am appreciative for the time I had to serve as chairman and especially humbled by the moniker of "CryptoDad" that I was given by this fantastic community of vibrant, bright, ambitious people.
>
> I could not have predicted at the time [I first joined the CFTC] that virtual currencies, DLT and FinTech would become such a major part of the conversation for our agency. I feel fortunate to have been at the helm during this time to be a voice in government to quiet some of the fears and calls to dismiss or squash this new technology.
>
> It has been a core belief during my tenure as Chairman that in order for the CFTC to remain an effective regulator, it must keep pace with these changes, or our regulations will become outdated and ineffective. I am pleased to say that over the last two years, the CFTC has been no bystander to the digitization of modern markets.[3]

I mentioned the 500th anniversary of the death of Leonardo da Vinci and the Renaissance's exploration of innovation. Now a new era of exploration had begun, I suggested. I called for the new era to be founded in enduring ideals: free enterprise and democratic capitalism.

With farewells almost complete and final rulemaking proposals headed to the commission, Mike Gill and members of my staff planned a farewell celebration. The event was held in the agency's conference center, which was filled to capacity with staff and honored guests. The speakers included Federal Reserve Chairman Powell; Andrew Bailey, now governor of the Bank of England; SEC Chairman Clayton; former House Financial Services Chairman Mike Conaway; and my former CFTC compatriot, Sharon Bowen. I was especially touched by remarks by my four fellow commissioners, including Dan Berkovitz, who referenced Theodore Roosevelt's famous paean to the "Man in the Arena":

"It is not the critic who counts; not the man who points out how the strong man stumbles, or where the doer of deeds could have done them better. The credit belongs to the man who is actually in the arena, whose face is marred by dust and sweat and blood; who strives valiantly; . . . and who at the worst, if he fails, at least fails while daring greatly, so that his place shall never be with those cold and timid souls who neither know victory nor defeat."[4]

Commissioner Quintenz teased me about my CFTC writing output. He estimated that in my five years on the commission, I had authored three white papers, nine Congressional testimonies, 63 speeches, and 103 public statements. He calculated a sum total of 469,197 published words—"just shy of *War and Peace!*" Yet Quintenz touched me by saying that my work at the agency reflected the admonition of Ralph Waldo Emerson: "Do not go where the path may lead, go instead where there is no path and leave a trail."

As I took the agency podium for the final time, I remembered the important adage to dance with the one who brought you. The last of my farewells would be to those who got me there and the agency staff—the people who had made possible whatever success I had enjoyed. I said that no leader, whether in government, business, or any walk of life can achieve much without the support of family, friends, and colleagues. I thanked Regina, my parents, and my children. I thanked my regulatory peers and my commission colleagues. But mostly, I thanked the rank-and-file staff: serious, hardworking, and dedicated people in federal government service. I said that wherever life took me, I would always be proud that I had the opportunity to lead the good men and women of the CFTC.

Welling up with tears, I crossed the room, stepped up onto the bandstand and joined Collin Peterson and the 2nd Amendments. Joined by two hometown friends and musicians, I sang a song that I dedicated to the CFTC.

It was Neil Young's "Long May You Run."

Chapter 15

The Winding Crypto Road

What is that feeling when you're driving away from people and they recede on
the plain till you see their specks dispersing?
It's the too-huge world vaulting us, and it's good-bye.
But we lean forward to the next crazy venture beneath the skies.
—Jack Kerouac (novelist), On the Road

Beside Still Waters

I was physically and emotionally exhausted when I stepped down from the CFTC. I had put every bit of energy I had into the job from the day I started until the day I left. I felt drained as I closed the chairman's office door behind me late in the evening on Sunday, July 14, 2019. Health Tarbert would enter that office at 9 a.m. the next morning.

My first bit of extended relaxation came in early September when Regina and I spent eight perfect summer days in Whipsaw Cottage at the Waldheim Resort on Big Moose Lake in the western Adirondacks. We swam in the early morning, took long walks in the mountains, and read by the fire in the evening. It provided plenty of time for rejuvenation, as well as reflection.

As I sat one morning beside Big Moose's north bay reading the news on my mobile phone, I thought about how the Internet had transformed the distribution of news and the business of journalism. In fact, over the course of much of my professional career, the Internet had transformed so many industries, from music (think Pandora and Spotify) and television (YouTube and Netflix), to retail shopping (Amazon and eBay) and local transportation (Uber and Lyft), from travel and leisure (Expedia and Travelocity) and photography (Flickr and SmugMug), to communications (Twitter and FaceTime), social networking (Facebook and LinkedIn), and business meetings (Zoom and BlueJeans).

It struck me that the Internet was not finished spinning its gray magic. Like a whirlwind, it continued to expand and disrupt everything in its path. It had developed far beyond an Internet of Information easily culling the morning's global news on my smartphone. It had evolved into an Internet of Things that provided my mobile device with a "health check" on the status of brake fluid, coolant, and motor oil levels on my Volvo S-90 after the six-hour drive up to the Adirondacks. Now, the Internet was morphing again into an Internet of Value in which ownership of that automobile would be represented by something much better than an easily lost paper title. Rather, it would be recorded on an immutable digital ledger that I could access anytime from anywhere and confirm with every other computer in the world that I, and only I, owned the vehicle. And, better, if I wanted, I could sell a portion of that vehicle to my next door neighbor to share.

The first wave of the Internet had empowered global communication between humans and the second wave had enabled communications among electronic devices. The third wave would power autonomous interaction and exchanges of value among people and commercial enterprises. This wave had in its direct sights dealings in the most important commodity of all: money and the banks and financial institutions that handle it.

The Nature of Money

To understand the scale of the change ahead, let's answer this question: what is money?

In essence, money is trust. It is a societal construct. It is a shared notion of value, a "shared fiction."[1] Money is what we all agree it is. It has value because we agree it has value. Money may have government authorization and backing, but without social trust, money is worthless. Its value is entirely derived from society's acceptance of its value. In the words of Mark Carney, former governor of the Bank of England, "money is more of an art grounded in values of trust, resilience, dynamism, solidarity and sustainability. Central banks are its curator."[2]

This is so with the US dollar, which, contrary to common misunderstanding, has not been backed by gold or silver for the past 50 years. The dollar is not a legal claim on anything at all. Its value is entirely derived from its widespread domestic and international acceptance and use as a medium of exchange, store of value, and unit of account. That widespread use is a matter of social trust.

Money is also inconstant. It goes through long periods of stability and then suddenly morphs into something different.[3] "Some wild genius has a new idea, or the world changes in some fundamental way that demands a new kind of money, or a financial collapse causes the monetary version of an existential crisis. The outcome is a profound change in the basic idea of money—what it is, who gets to create it, what it's supposed to do."[4]

From what I have seen firsthand, I believe we are today going through one of those profound changes in the basic idea of money. To understand why, let me take you on a very short history of money.

Money has evolved over the span of human civilization. Initially trade was through barter: a chicken for a clay pot. However, what does a society do when a person wants to trade a chicken, but doesn't need a clay pot in return? The answer was a token that society recognized as representing value. It could be traded for any good, whether a clay pot, a chicken, or a blanket.

The first tokens may have been shells or beads. They evolved into things that carried some inherent value, such as salt, which was the currency of the Roman army.[5] Other tokens with innate value were coins minted from precious metals like silver and gold. In more recent times, tokens of currency are based on intangible items of little intrinsic value, such as paper or, increasingly, polymer notes. The paper dollars in circulation today are tokens. Humans intuitively understand tokens of value; it is hardwired into their DNA. That is why, as societies evolve into the future, so will their tokens.

The drawback of physical tokens to date is that they are local instruments. Their use is limited to physical transactions between a payer and payee who are both physically present. Physical tokens are awkward to transport and are, therefore, impractical for large value payments. Physical tokens also have diminishing value outside of their zone of issuance and acceptance. Importantly, physical token money does not work in modern eCommerce.

The local aspect of tokenized money became an increasing hindrance during the Age of Discovery when European merchants sought to expand global trade and commerce. In the early 1600s, the Amsterdam Exchange Bank permitted individuals to place token money on deposit in return for tradable drafts representing transferable liabilities of the bank that could be easily transported and used outside the local area.[6] Other European banks serving mercantile interests followed suit and expanded this service. They accepted deposits of physical money and issued their own notes and bills known as "banknotes."

The innovation of banknotes was highly successful. Most money used today in the global economy is bank-issued money. Bank money is an obligation of a particular financial institution, not an obligation of a government or central bank, although the account holder may benefit from some degree of government deposit insurance. Everyday payments made by credit or debit cards or by check are examples of bank money facilitated by commercial banks and other financial institutions. The money shown on your bank statement is bank money and your bank is unlikely to hold an equivalent stock of tokenized government money to back it up.

Bank money is also known as "account-based" money because it exists not in the form of a token, but as an account liability on the balance sheet of a particular bank or financial institution. The account-based system is a product of double-entry bookkeeping. With account-based money, unlike with physical tokens, value is denominated in account entries where the account holder's credit balance is matched by the bank's liabilities to the depositor.

In terms of technology, there is a major difference between token-based and account-based money. It relates to the process of verification. With token-based money, e.g. a dollar bill, verification is primarily performed by the recipient confirming that the bill is authentic and not counterfeit. The parties to the transaction need not be identified. When you purchase a sandwich with a ten dollar bill, you don't need to tell anyone your name, where you bank or how much is in your account. Account-based money, on the other hand, requires third-party authentication of the identity of each party to the transaction, confirmation of the adequacy of funds in the transferor's account, and confirmation of the receipt of funds by the transferee. When you pay for a sandwich with a debit or credit card or a check, someone somewhere or some algorithm knows who you are, where you bank and how much is in your account. These are distinctive and significant characteristics.

If you use Zelle and Venmo, you are still using account-based money. The transaction is effected through a series of electronic messages instructing movement of account-based money by third parties. With these cashless payments—whether by card, wire, check, or digital app, including Venmo—the deal isn't fully settled (meaning it could still be reversed) until the banks involved have identified the parties and recorded, reconciled, and settled their respective debits and credits. When you swipe your smartphone against a reader for an Apple Pay transaction, it triggers another series of electronic messages. You are not actually transferring value. Some commercial enterprise somewhere will do that later upon receipt of those messages and—here's the rub—usually collect a fee from you or someone else for doing so.

So, while the shortcoming of tokenized money is that its use is limited in both physical space and cyberspace, the shortcoming of account-based money is that it is exclusionary, expensive, and slow. Why do I say that?

Unlike token-based money, transactions in account-based money require identification of the individual parties to the transaction. Identification is necessary in every transaction to pinpoint the parties' respective bank accounts to confirm that there is enough money in the payor's account to be debited and the correct amount has been received by the recipient. Without first identifying the parties, that account-based process cannot happen. That process also takes time to complete. And it requires fees to be paid to the third parties to do all that identification and handle all those debits and credits.

Without question, these three characteristics of account-based money—exclusiveness, slowness, and cost—have been remarkably reduced since the seventeenth century. In fact, dramatic progress continues at reducing the restrictiveness, latency, and expense of account-based money.[7] Yet they have not been reduced all together. The use of account-based money is still exclusive. A little over 5% of Americans[8] and 21% of people around the globe[9] lack a bank account and have to rely on physical cash. Account-based money is still slow. It typically takes several days in the United States to clear a check and settle a securities transaction. And it is still expensive. It is estimated that fees for credit cards and other payment services cost Americans 2.3% of gross domestic product[10] or over $400 billion each year. The average cost of sending a few hundred dollars overseas is 6.38% percent of the transaction.[11]

The Crypto Revolution

So, how will the Internet of Value revolutionize money? Very simply, for the first time in human history, money will be able to transcend time, space, and social class. Cryptocurrency solves both the local limitation of tokenized money and the exclusivity, latency, and cost of account-based money. Unlike physical cash, cryptocurrency can make transferring value as simple, immediate, and cost-free as sending a text message, whether across a supermarket counter or around the globe.

Value transfer will no longer be limited by geography and, unlike account-based money, will take place directly, person to person, without the need for third-party intermediaries to validate identity, account sufficiency, and receipt of funds and the cost and time to do so. And, because it is transfer of a token, there is no need to give up or even have identity as a first step. Verification is primarily performed by the recipient's digital wallet, which algorithmically confirms the authenticity of the cryptocurrency token, rather than the identity of the transacting party. There is no need to find out what is in someone's bank account or even if they have one. With cryptocurrency, transferring money across the globe is no longer just for those with identities and who can afford it.

In Chapter 7, I explained what cryptocurrency is and how it functions. In a sentence, cryptocurrency is a digital representation of value built upon a decentralized computer network in which transactions are verified and records maintained using cryptography to avoid forfeiture and consensus mechanisms in place of centralized authorities. Because it generally uses a consensus method to confirm validity, rather than individual validators, crypto is said to be "censorship resistant,"[12] facilitating financial privacy and economic liberty.

Today, there are thousands of different cryptocurrencies that each have distinctive characteristics and fall into different categories. Many perform distinct financial and other services: some enable payments or foreign exchange transactions; others facilitate lending or hedging.[13] They generally do so without any single entity operator. One cryptocurrency, Filecoin, enables users to store data on global peer-to-peer networks of computers instead of in centralized, Big Tech file storage services like AWS and Google Cloud. Filecoin incentivizes entities to share excess hard drive space with the network.[14]

"Filecoin demonstrates how being able to program money—to instantly, automatically send microtransactions across the world—can create economic incentives that enable entirely new technologies."[15] Many other cryptocurrencies are also "programmable." That is, they enable the coupling of digital tokens with smart contracts, embedding the most complex business and process logic into the tokens themselves. Just as you can program a new smart device to raise the temperature or lower the lights in your home for future events, so too can you program certain cryptocurrencies to make payments or convert themselves into other forms of money upon some future occurrence. To some, the very essence of crypto is its enablement of programmable, decentralized software applications.[16]

Not only does cryptocurrency enable the autonomous movement of things of value from place to place, but—for the first time in human experience—it also equips value to move autonomously across time. That is, coupled with algorithmically, self-executing smart contracts, things of value, especially, money will now be able to be programmed to conduct future transactions without the traditional services of professional validators. In the not too distant future, you will be able to program your money to do something far into the future, perhaps after you are gone—say, present itself as a wedding gift for your grandchild or help fund purchases of science equipment at your alma mater—without hiring hosts of lawyers, trustees, and executors.

Stablecoins

Programmability is an especially attractive feature of a rapidly emerging type of cryptocurrency known as "stablecoins." Stablecoins are cryptocurrencies that attempt to achieve price stability by pegging their value to reserve currencies, such as the US dollar. They represent financial obligations of non-banks that are generally collateralized with either fiat currency deposits at a bank or with short-term government bonds held at a custodian in order to trade at par with a sovereign currency.[17] You might think of stablecoins as something similar to prepaid debit cards or travelers checks.[18]

Stablecoins provide greater settlement certainty by being irreversibly recorded on a blockchain. In an increasing number of global currency transactions, stablecoins serve as an efficient bridge between sovereign fiat currencies and cryptocurrencies. They also are increasingly being used to make domestic and international payments that can settle around the clock in minutes rather than hours and days as with US dollar transactions. This greatly accelerates the velocity of transactions, an important economic efficiency. It is estimated that annualized stablecoin trading volume is already $16 trillion compared to the US wholesale payment volume of $25 trillion.[19] In only a short period of time, stablecoins have become a faster, cheaper, and more programmable way to move value.

Stablecoins are a rapidly growing part of the digital asset ecosystem. Popular stablecoins include Tether, USDC, Binance, DAI, Paxos, and Gemini Dollar. Demand comes primarily from digital asset traders and investors who seek stable valuations alongside the instant processing and settlement abilities of cryptocurrencies. Regulators and central banks around the world are paying closer attention to stablecoins. One knowledgeable observer believes that programmable stablecoins tied to instantaneous securities settlement could provide regulators with comprehensive visibility into broad counterparty credit exposure of financial institutions that was missing in the 2008 financial crisis and is still sought today.[20]

Nevertheless, stablecoins raise some concerns. My former colleague, Tim Massad, views stablecoins as the economic equivalent of money-market funds—their true value depends on the market value of the port-folio of investments backing them.[21] He notes that there is no US legal framework for regulating them, no requirements on how reserves must be invested, and no requirements for audits or reporting.[22] Massad pru-dently points out that if the value of stablecoin holdings were to become widely in doubt, then "a sudden wave of withdrawals could be signifi-cant in the larger crypto ecosystem."[23] One suggestion is for stablecoins to be managed by a currency board and pegged and 100% backed by a major reserve currency.[24] Another would be some well-crafted and not overreaching rules for providing greater transparency in the holding of stablecoin reserves.

In fact, the catchall term *stablecoin*, though somewhat unavoidable, is not helpful. It obfuscates material design differences, such as the degree to which leading stablecoins are designed for compliance and low-friction Internet payments or to provide prudential care, custody, and control of currency reserves supporting the instrument's stable value. Not all stablecoins are created equal.[25] In truth, some are more equal than others.

DeFi

At the same time as crypto is freeing money from the bounds of space and time, the Internet of Value is spinning out another transformative innovation: decentralized finance, popularly shorthanded to "DeFi."

In simple terms, DeFi organizes financial services over the world wide web in a way that is open to anyone to use, rather than going through intermediaries like banks, brokerages, oddsmakers, or exchanges. DeFi replaces intermediaries with transparent computer code written on blockchains that empowers individual lenders, borrowers, wagerers, buyers, and sellers to interact directly with each other rather than going through central intermediaries. DeFi uses cryptocurrency and distributed ledger technology to draw upon the computing power of a giant global network of dispersed computers to conduct business processes that are normally done by large, single business enterprises to provide a full spectrum of financial services from banking and lending to securities trading and wagering. One emerging type of DeFi application enables direct lending from crypto holders to traders for substantial yield.[26]

Though in its infancy, DeFi presents a considerable challenge for public policy. That is because the traditional path of regulation generally begins with policymakers looking at any commercial ecosystem to be regulated and identifying the key actors and intermediaries. In the case of financial markets, they are the exchanges, clearinghouses, underwriters, dealers, and market makers. The next step is to register and regulate those entities, organize them in self-regulatory bodies, and deputize them to provide data and other reports to regulators. Intermediaries perform these duties in return for certain privileges, barriers to entry, and quasi-monopolies.

This form of "entity-based" regulation is not an unreasonable regulatory method in an analog world. Through it, regulators have long and often successfully supervised ecosystem conduct, behavior, and orderliness. But this traditional regulatory approach of co-option and deputization is directly challenged by the potential of DeFi, which disintermediates the intermediaries and puts front and center the direct action of the individual market participants.[27] It calls for a consideration of a new "activities-based" rather than the traditional "entity-based" regulatory approach.

With its likely continued evolution, DeFi has the potential to test this traditional regulatory method of intermediary co-option in the same way that the Internet has challenged so many other venerable regulatory frameworks, such as taxicab regulation following the development of ride-sharing services such as Uber.[28] That is: reduce costs and latency, increase competition, and improve accessibility for consumers while upending traditional forms of supervision for regulators.

To enable those social benefits, policymakers are going to have to act differently than just the same old way of doing things. They must avoid the regulatory temptation voiced by SEC Commissioner Hester Peirce to, "grab hold of this and make it like the markets I already regulate."[29]

This is especially so for legacy approaches to countering money laundering and tax evasion. It is widely known that the current approach of commercial bank administered, anti-money laundering (AML) and "know your customer" (KYC) checks is highly inexact yielding a preponderance of false positives. One study indicates that the current system has less than 0.1% impact on criminal finances, compliance costs exceed recovered criminal funds more than a hundred times over, and banks, taxpayers, and ordinary citizens are penalized more than criminal enterprises.[30] Unquestionably, the current AML/KYC process leaves a lot to be desired. Maintaining such an ineffective system in its present form cannot be a reason to thwart further development of DeFi and digital token technology. We must find more effective ways to counter illicit financial activity. An answer may be found in new technologies of big data analysis, automated pattern recognition and artificial intelligence.

In late spring 2021, I attended a late-night party on a rooftop in Manhattan's stylish meatpacking district. There with my two sons and a crowd of their peers, we talked to dozens of young DeFi innovators celebrating the first anniversary of a leading DeFi venture, a consensus-based, decentralized data exchange for predicting future events. I was inspired by the freewheeling inventive energy of these entrepreneurs. They represented the spirit of creative choice that remains the source of most new jobs and economic growth.[31] Given a chance, they are the ones who will point the way to the digital future of finance, one that is less static and more dynamic, one that may be better suited to serve the needs of tomorrow and not just today.

Undoubtedly, the continuing evolution of this new Internet of Value will be uneven with fits and starts. There will be bubbles, reversals, mistakes, and successes as with any profound change. There will be fiascos and criminality. There may even be one or more spectacular crypto market crashes. Both supporters and detractors will push regulators and lawmakers to take sides. Conflicts of interest and self-serving hype will remain rampant. The status quo will be strongly attacked and defended. Invariably, there will be public calls for both suppression and supplication of crypto.

Yet, the technology will not be stopped, whatever the regulatory policy response. Suppression in any one jurisdiction will just move the evolution to another. The direction of travel for this innovation is increasingly clear and, frankly, amazing. Bitcoin is just the tip of the iceberg. Like the first Internet wave, this third wave of the Internet will produce so much business disruption and business innovation and value destruction and value creation that cannot now even be imagined.

The challenge for policymakers is to have the courage to let the creative entropy of the Internet of Value take place in their backyards and not try to constrain it to happen elsewhere. As I said to the world's financial regulators in that strange white room in Basel in 2017, this innovation is not going away. It's like a roaring wind. "You can take shelter from it, get blown away by it or hitch a sail and ride it."

Peer-to-Peer Oversight

One justification for an aggressive regulatory response to cryptocurrency and DeFi innovation is cybercrime. In Chapter 7, I recounted some of the odious usage of cryptocurrency and efforts of regulators to stamp it out. Yet, by 2020, the criminal share of all cryptocurrency activity fell to just 0.34%, or $10.0 billion in transaction volume,[32] a drop in the ocean of $2 trillion in annual proceeds of illicit activities around the globe.[33] Even ransomware in cryptocurrency is a small proportion of annual cryptocurrency transactions.[34] In April 2021, Internet criminals were paid 75 Bitcoin in ransom following their successful hack of computers operating the Colonial Pipeline oil and gasoline pipeline system. A few weeks later, however, the FBI was able to retrieve 64 of the ransomed Bitcoin by gaining control of a Bitcoin wallet used by the cybercriminals. In an interview with CNBC, I said that it was a good precedent for acceptance of cryptocurrency. "It proves that the Bitcoin blockchain is not hostile ground for law enforcement. It also proves that it is not a perfect tool for criminal activity."[35] If the criminals and their accomplices had taken their ransom in physical cash rather than Bitcoins, they might all still have it today.

In fact, "Bitcoin's transparency may do more to mitigate fraud and theft than traditional banking and currency ever could."[36] That is because rather than being anonymous, Bitcoin and many other crypto transactions are generally pseudonymous, meaning users' address on many cryptocurrency blockchains are designated alphanumerically rather than by personal identity. Pseudonymity serves to shield identity, while the underlying transactions remain traceable. By anticipating new criminal schemes, financial regulators can come up with crime fighting techniques using big data analysis, pattern recognition and other technologies that are better suited to crypto and DeFi to thwart money laundering, tax evasion and the inevitable criminal conduct in the digital future of money.[37]

In his final address in January 2021, then Assistant Attorney General Makan Delrahim of the Department of Justice proposed the establishment of the Digital Markets Rulemaking Board, a regulatory body of industry and government officials with substantive rulemaking authority over issues of market integrity and investor protection within the digital marketplace.[38] This public–private approach to governance, Delrahim contended, could serve as a complement to the "rigid" and "static" rules imposed by traditional regulatory agencies, which often lack the nimbleness to effectively regulate the swiftly evolving digital economy.

While Delrahim's remarks were concerned with antitrust in the broader digital marketplace, the necessity of self-regulation is perhaps most pronounced in the context of cryptocurrency. As I have described, no federal market regulator has comprehensive jurisdiction over cryptocurrency trading in the United States. The SEC regulates issuance and trading of cryptocurrencies categorized as securities, but not commodities. The CFTC fully regulates trading of derivatives of those cryptocurrencies that are categorized as commodities. Yet, the CFTC has only limited enforcement authority over spot trading of the underlying crypto. As a result, a patchwork of intersecting, and often conflicting regulatory approaches has emerged, spanning the SEC, the CFTC, federal bank regulatory authorities, and other federal, state, and international bodies. While such regulatory overlap is regrettably not uncommon in the United States, the lack of a comprehensive crypto-specific regulatory scheme has hampered greater crypto innovation and economic development.

This patchwork also leaves a significant regulatory gap. No federal agency has direct jurisdiction over US trading platforms for spot trading in non-security cryptocurrency. As a result, there are no nationally required investor protection measures against fraud, manipulation, and abuse in spot crypto markets of the kind that are common in US securities and derivatives markets.

It is time to consider how to foster best practices and suitable investor protections in the burgeoning cryptocurrency industry. Some have proposed expanding SEC and CFTC jurisdiction to cover cryptocurrency spot markets. While this is well worth considering, it must take into account that the SEC has no legal authority over commodities. Also, the SEC has too often been reluctant to guide financial market development with anything other than the blunt cudgel of enforcement action depriving it of any significant operational regulatory expertise over crypto. Meanwhile, the CFTC has now served for over three and a half years as the world's only regulator of major markets for Bitcoin and Ethereum derivatives. The CFTC's crypto knowledge and regulatory expertise is unsurpassed by any other regulator, here or abroad. Yet, the CFTC does not have a primary mandate for US retail investor protection.

Other federal alphabet soup regulatory agencies have similarly proscribed authority and ability in relation to crypto. One proposal would have the Financial Stability Oversight Council regulate crypto. That is not a solution, however, that would enhance either crypto oversight or economic growth and development. FSOC has no operational capacity or institutional competence to conduct crypto market oversight. As a systemic risk–monitoring body, FSOC would be hard-pressed to justify legal jurisdiction over the relatively nascent crypto industry.

Instead, policymakers should initially consider crypto industry self-regulation.[39] In the most basic terms, a self-regulatory organization or SRO is a private or quasi-governmental organization that has the power to set rules and standards over its members. SROs often derive their authority from a statutory basis and remain subject to the ultimate oversight of a principal regulatory agency. Participation in an SRO may be voluntary, though it is often effectively mandated by statutory or regulatory requirements, as is the case for the Financial Industry Regulatory Authority (FINRA), which oversees securities brokers and broker-dealer firms.

The United States has a long and successful experience with self-regulation.[40] American futures exchanges, such as the Chicago Board of Trade (now part of CME Group), have successfully operated as self-regulatory organizations since 1859, decades before the advent of federal regulation in the 1920s.[41] They continue to operate as self-regulatory bodies today. In addition, other participants in the futures markets are overseen by the National Futures Association (NFA), a highly effective

SRO. Unlike the banking sector that is directly regulated by a multiplicity of federal regulators, the self-regulated futures industry did not falter or fail during the 2008 financial crisis. It is hard to deny the significant connection between long-standing self-regulation and the systemic stability and outstanding global competitiveness of the US futures industry.

There is broad support and momentum for formal self-regulation within the cryptocurrency industry, including among current and former federal policymakers and industry leaders.[42] Appetite for self-governance is demonstrated by the number of voluntary cryptocurrency industry organizations that in recent years have recommended best practices and promulgated codes of responsible crypto conduct.[43]

Interest in self-governance is perhaps unsurprising given the advantages that an SRO-based regulatory framework yields over exclusive government oversight. Most notably, SROs place greater authority in the hands of industry experts who are most familiar with market practices and emerging issues. SROs promote the specialization of knowledge, focusing solely on cryptocurrency-related issues, as opposed to monitoring all aspects of a federal agency's significantly broader jurisdiction. Given the early evolution of cryptocurrency and the complexity of its underlying technologies, substantial technical input from stakeholders is important for the development of sound investor protections.

Authorizing a crypto SRO would also support regulatory efficiency, allowing government agencies to conserve limited resources for highest-priority concerns. Member funding would ensure that taxpayers bear no cost for SRO oversight. Moreover, the work of a cryptocurrency SRO could yield additional fiscal savings by reducing redundancies of overlapping state and federal regulatory initiatives.

Finally, a cryptocurrency SRO would serve as a hub of resources for members and the public not provided under current regulatory regimes. SROs like the NFA not only promulgate and enforce industry standards, they also offer training, prepare market reports, educational materials, and compliance guides that allow investors to conduct diligence on member firms. In addition, SROs importantly serve as a forum for arbitration and mediation, allowing conflicts involving members to be resolved without the need for litigation. A cryptocurrency SRO would provide a centralized and specialized source for such services and information.

Crypto Native Regulation

It is increasingly clear that a better-defined US regulatory framework for cryptocurrency is necessary to preserve the integrity and stability of the marketplace and guide further development. Federally supported self-regulation of the cryptocurrency industry presents a promising and complementary path forward that can be readily initiated. It has certainly been a winning formula for innovation and economic growth in US futures markets.

Ultimately, however, with the continued growth of crypto and its related innovations of blockchain and DeFi, a Federal regulatory construct will be needed. To select the right regulatory framework for crypto, Congress will need to first identify the public policy to be achieved. In doing so, it must heed the advice of Aquinas, "The art of sailing must govern the art of shipbuilding."[44] By that, Aquinas meant that the way in which human activities are ordered should be based on the ultimate good desired, not by any preferred form of construction.[45]

Starting with first principles, let's ask ourselves: what is US public policy regarding crypto, primarily and blockchain and DeFi, secondarily? What public good should be served? If US public policy for crypto is largely one of investor protection, then a leading role undoubtedly should be played by the SEC with its statutory mission of investor protection. If so, however, then the SEC itself needs to be innovative. For the past few decades, the SEC's approach to investor protection has been to protect ordinary investors from participating in the upside opportunity of the most promising new business ventures that the SEC limits to wealthy and sophisticated "accredited investors." This restrictive regulatory approach cuts across the cultural grain of crypto that has attracted more interest and excitement from ordinary, everyday investors than Wall Street has enjoyed in a generation. If investor protection is the imperative, than the SEC must put forth new models of oversight that spur responsible market conduct without locking out the very generation that has spurred crypto from inception or punishing them for innovating new business models that challenge legacy regulatory procedures.

On the other hand, if public policy for crypto is to have robust and well-regulated crypto derivatives markets where global prices are increasingly set (as with so many key global commodities), then a leading role should be played by the CFTC. It has been walking that walk now for almost four years.

Perhaps there is also a role for the Digital Assets Sprint Initiative recently launched by the OCC, FDIC, and Federal Reserve to further US leadership in exploring the internet of value, fintech, crypto and defi to expand investment opportunity and modernize legacy payment and financial systems.

Sooner or later, Congress must establish what is US public policy concerning crypto. I suggest that policy is a national interest in fostering healthy development of crypto innovation, well ordered crypto trading markets and their contribution to the modernization of the existing financial payment system to make it less exclusionary and more accessible, less costly and more dynamic for all Americans. If so, then Congress should assign responsibility and adequate funding to one or more Federal regulators that are well suited to accomplish the mission. One approach for consideration is the formation of a new US Federal "Crypto Market Bureau" staffed jointly by the SEC and CFTC to draw upon the resources of the two agencies and perhaps others to come up with a practical and "crypto-native" regulatory framework with clear paths forward for US innovation and retail participation. Adequate consideration should be given to recommendations for crypto "safe harbors"[46] and other guidelines for crypto firms to operate in a responsible manner without undue regulatory risk.

One regulatory approach that is not conducive to healthy American financial innovation is the continuation and, even, expansion, of policymaking by aggressive regulatory enforcement. The growth and development of cryptocurrency hardly presents a financial crisis to be headed off, rampant fraud to be curbed, and widely-held "mom & pop" retirements to be protected through extraordinary, scorched earth regulatory tactics. Undoubtedly, the crypto industry needs to continue to take determined steps to enhance its best practices, including safeguards against ransomware, anti–money laundering, and tax evasion. Those efforts can be furthered with well-designed self-regulatory and state and federal supervisory structures. With such sound oversight, great US innovation can continue to evolve and offer new solutions to latent, expensive, and exclusive financial infrastructure. As I said in my 2018 Senate testimony, we owe it to this new generation of innovators to respect their enthusiasm about cryptocurrency and financial innovation with a thoughtful and balanced response, not an uncompromising one. It is time for Congress to reduce the regulatory risk hazarded by this dynamic new cohort of financial innovators by enacting a comprehensive and salutary regulatory framework specifically designed for crypto.

Bitcoin Rally 2.0

Early in this book, I taxed the reader with a fairly lengthy explanation of how derivatives work. I did so for a reason. It was to explain how derivatives provide an efficient and undistorted way to establish market prices for underlying commodities. I gave that explanation to help the reader appreciate how essential to the long-term development of cryptocurrency was the CFTC's 2017 decision not to block the launch of Bitcoin and Ether futures and other crypto derivatives. In doing so, professional, institutional investors can now discover reliable market pricing and transact in transparent and orderly markets regulated by a premier global regulator, the CFTC. Without the existence of professional markets for crypto derivatives, the underlying spot markets would have remained small and immature.[47]

The progenitor of all cryptocurrency, Bitcoin, began 2021 with another enormous price rally. In the first quarter, Bitcoin rose to a new high of over $60,000 per coin. Then, by the end of the second quarter, Bitcoin's price dropped almost 50% driven in part by an extensive Chinese crackdown on Bitcoin mining and payments.[48] Then, in July 2021, Bitcoin began another rally as this book was going to print. The high price volatility of Bitcoin is not unexpected for a commodity with a fixed supply. Basic economics explains that for a commodity with a set quantity, the rising or falling of demand can only result in one thing: immediate and pronounced price action.

The market volatility of Bitcoin and other cryptocurrencies is of greater concern when combined with the high level of trading leverage deployed on some non-US crypto trading platforms.[49] Some overseas platforms have offered leverage trading of as much as 125–1. When traders use margin, they basically borrow from the crypto platform to take large positions. Leverage trading can compound both profits and losses. If prices go up, the trader pays off the small amount of margin and keeps the profits. If prices go down, the trader has to pay the platform back. To ensure payback, platforms often trigger selling at a set price in order to make sure they are repaid. When combined with high volatility, leverage is a powerful tool for professional traders and a dangerous one for amateurs.

The 2021 Bitcoin rally and subsequent rout sparked another round of maddening praise and criticism. Bitcoin is indeed all things to all people: a technological revolution unlocking myriad economic innovations, exponentially appreciating financial asset, censorship-resistant digital gold, a hedge against monetary depreciation, and a rebuke to the existing financial system. For others, Bitcoin is highly volatile and speculative, environmentally destructive, serves no socially useful function, and, worse, can be used to evade law or conduct illicit finance.

There is one thing, however, that Bitcoin is not. Bitcoin is not a government construct. It is a societal one. It bears no sovereign imprimatur, travels on no government payment rails, and settles no government fiscal or tax obligations (except in El Salvador). Perhaps most crucially, it is not subject to government monetary control. This freedom from monetary "colonialism,"[50] intermediary censorship, or central bank devaluation at a time of spiking inflation[51] may be what most excites Bitcoin's champions and alarms its critics.

Many people confuse Bitcoin's worth with its price. Yet, Bitcoin's worth has been enduringly established as the chief herald of the digital future of money.

So what of Bitcoin's current price? Clearly, the opposing views of the utility of Bitcoin stir opposing views of its value. Fortunately, CFTC regulated US Bitcoin futures and options marketplaces operate to resolve those competing views by aggregating liquidity, distributing bids and offers, matching buyers with sellers, and settling trades in both cash and physical Bitcoin, all in regulated, transparent markets. In June 2021, total Bitcoin futures open interest across derivatives exchanges was close to $12 billion down from $19 billion in the first quarter.[52] This pool of derivatives trading liquidity provides essential price discovery. It allows both sides of the Bitcoin debate to express their opinion of its worth, up or down. One need not be a Bitcoin "maximalist" to take comfort knowing that price of Bitcoin is determined not by the heavy hand of government, but increasingly by active commercial give-and-take in well-regulated and liquid futures markets.

Miami Vice

A pleasant surprise since leaving Washington has been returning to the practice of law. In January 2020, I became senior counsel to the renowned firm of Willkie Farr & Gallagher. Founded in New York in 1888, "Willkie" has a distinguished history with many prominent alumni. It also has a proud tradition of bringing in noted government officials after the completion of their public service. They include the firm's namesake, Wendell Willkie, the Republican candidate for president in 1940, as well as New York Governor Mario Cuomo and Federal Energy Regulatory Commission Chairman Norman Bay. Today, Willkie's practice is exceptionally strong in the junction between financial markets, law, and technology. One of its senior lawyers, Jeff Poss, had advised my former business, GFI Group and, after I left the CFTC, recruited me to come aboard. In 2021, we formed an internal practice group of several dozen lawyers called "Willkie Digital Works" to concentrate the firm's extensive work in crypto, FinTech, and DeFi.

During the first weekend in June 2021, one of my Willkie partners, Justin Browder, and I hopped a flight to Miami to attend a conference called Bitcoin 2021. It was my first business travel since the COVID lockdown and it felt good to move. The conference was a frenzied affair, the largest Bitcoin conference in history and attended by over 12,000 people, mostly young and wildly enthusiastic. Still, we noticed the engagement of an important cadre of Wall Street bankers, institutional investors, and serious entrepreneurs, signs of the maturation of Bitcoin as an investment asset class. They were up early in the Florida sunshine and out late at night at the countless parties on Collins Avenue rooftops overlooking the shoreline. Miami has become the Palo Alto of crypto.

After a late breakfast on Friday in Miami Beach with Senator Cynthia Lummis, who had just launched a seminal Senate Financial Innovation Caucus, we headed back downtown and went backstage in the enormous conference hall. There, we first watched Tyler and Cameron Winklevoss describe Bitcoin as digital gold and predict it will eclipse physical gold in value. We then watched Jack Dorsey, chief executive of both Twitter and payments provider Square, say: "If I were not at Square or Twitter, I would be working on Bitcoin."

I then went on stage with my friend, the voluble Brian Brooks, former acting comptroller of the currency. During his short but action-packed tenure, Brooks served as a highly effective agent of regulatory reform and receptiveness to financial technology.

Before a Miami audience of thousands of Bitcoiners, Brooks and I talked about how as federal regulators we were each able to take forward-leaning positions on FinTech, crypto, and DeFi because of the absence of comprehensive policy positions on those topics during the Trump administration. I said that I sensed shifting ground and expected the Biden administration to be more assertive of broad and perhaps restrictive regulatory authority over financial innovation. Brooks and I encouraged the Bitcoin audience and industry to better establish its voice in Washington so that when broader crypto regulation came, it would be sensible and salutary. I said it would be far better for the crypto community to play a role in sculpting the coming regulatory response than to have it imposed upon them.

For a moment, I knew I had seen this movie before. It was back in 2009 when I was encouraging the swaps industry to articulate constructive reforms to its business practices in the lead up to Dodd–Frank. It was déjà vu all over again.

On Saturday, the conference played a video of Nayib Bukele, the president of El Salvador, announcing a bill to make Bitcoin official legal tender in the country.[53] The audience leapt to a roaring standing ovation. Some saw it as "an important step toward a world where money is sound, not subject to the vagaries of politics."[54] Some saw it as national ruination.[55] The IMF observed it with F.U.D.[56]

Inexorable Motion

Indeed, the CFTC's greenlighting of Bitcoin futures in 2017 continued to reverberate. With the success of CME's cash-settled Bitcoin futures and options, cryptocurrency derivatives trading has mushroomed.[57] True to its nature, the US futures industry has been bold in innovating around this new technology. In 2019, ICE's Bakkt exchange inaugurated Bitcoin futures contracts that settle in actual delivery of Bitcoin rather than in US dollars.[58] LedgerX, an independent firm, had begun offering Bitcoin options and futures,[59] and CME had kicked off both Ether futures[60] and micro-Bitcoin futures.[61] ErisX launched bounded futures in Bitcoin and Ether that seek to protect traders from large price movements.

By 2021, the CFTC's steady oversight of the world's only transparent, liquid, and fully regulated markets for cryptocurrency futures has fostered an enormous ecosystem of retail and professional crypto traders, market makers, hedge funds, custodians, prime brokers, benchmark administrators, deposit and lending firms, retirement plan operators, crypto credit cards, trade surveillance services, trade associations, advisers, and specialist lawyers and accountants. Cryptocurrency has increasingly become part of the modern financial landscape. The venerable BNY Mellon (est. 1784) is now handling Bitcoin; Citigroup (est. 1812) is considering Bitcoin futures for its institutional clients, Mass Mutual (est. 1851) has put $100 million of Bitcoin into its general account; and Mastercard (est. 1966) is integrating crypto into its payments systems. The sector has grown into a multi-trillion-dollar global industry.

The CFTC was a key catalyst for today's crypto ecosystem. By braving the political risk of greenlighting the self-certification of Bitcoin futures, the CFTC provided the marketplace with greater certainty for innovation, free enterprise, and economic development. Hester Peirce of the SEC has written approvingly of the "healthy bitcoin futures market" fostered by the CFTC, admonishing that "regulators should commit themselves to providing regulatory clarity so that traditional financial market participants can engage with crypto with confidence that they are complying with their regulatory obligations."[62] In contrast, the political risk aversion of many contemporary regulators in the United States and abroad has only reinforced uncertainty and the risk of regulation by enforcement that stymies rather than stimulates economic development.

Earlier I explained how I had come to see the generational aspects of crypto. I described how Millennials and Generation Z view technology as an agent of social change away from an uncongenial banking industry and its governing institutions that increasingly struggle to earn their confidence. Studies show that cryptocurrency enjoys significant acceptance amongst the broad population led by Millennials.[63] Nine percent of US adults overall own Bitcoin, but 16% of Millennials do, preferring it over traditional investments like stocks, bonds, and real estate.[64]

I am proud of the sympathy and encouragement we gave at a critical juncture to a new generation's interest in financial innovation. There is something extraordinarily dynamic and creative about the crypto and DeFi communities. A generation that rarely sets foot in a bank branch, but downloads music anytime day or night, listens to podcasts by the hour, and sends texts and photos around the world in seconds is unwilling to wait three days—during bankers hours—to settle a financial transaction. From their own experimental work, more direct and efficient financial models will emerge. Some efforts will fail and others will succeed. Yet, ultimately, they point the way to the future of money and finance. Treating them with disdain is foolish and arrogant.

Undoubtedly, I was able to lead the CFTC's forward-leaning approach to crypto innovation because I was unrestrained by a White House that had no set policy on FinTech or crypto of any kind, positive or negative. While President Trump denounced Bitcoin several times, his view was never taken as administration policy or direction. Thus, it was left to the leadership of each of the several federal financial regulators to respond within their institutional purview to the digital revolution in finance. I certainly drew encouragement from the CFTC's unmatched tradition of market and product innovation. I had the cooperation of an agency staff and clear-sighted commissioners uniquely comfortable with product innovation and new market development. If any major global market regulator was going to be the first mover in crypto regulation, it would have been the CFTC.

As of Independence Day, 2021, the Biden administration has not announced a comprehensive policy for FinTech and crypto. This is despite sympathetic encouragement to do so.[65] Some commentators view the current Biden approach to crypto as quite defensive and reactionary, focused on externalities like market volatility and crypto's use in illicit trade, but with little impetus to advance national interests in innovation and growth.[66] It is especially disappointing that, more than six months into the administration, President Biden has not nominated a chairperson for the CFTC, despite the highly competent work of Acting Chairman Behnam and the presence of other ready candidates. Such lackluster attention to leadership of the CFTC, the world's most experienced and accomplished crypto authority, does not bode well for needed regulatory clarity for American financial innovation. In fact, it is insupportable that, at time when the nation needs a smart policy response to the growth of crypto, there is no Senate confirmed head of the only US agency with any experience regulating derivatives trading markets for Bitcoin and other cryptocurrencies.

During my time at the helm of the CFTC, many government officials were downright hostile to cryptocurrency development. I recall a meeting in New York of the G-20 Financial Stability Board a few months before my departure. Gathered together in the tall, wood-paneled and -beamed Benjamin Strong room at the New York Federal Reserve's august Wall Street offices were most of the senior officials of the global financial system—distinguished central bank governors, important securities regulatory chairs, dour finance ministers from dozens of major global economies, plus representatives of IOSCO, the BIS, the World Bank, the Organization for Economic Cooperation and Development, the European Central Bank, the European Commission, the Basel Committee on Banking Supervision, the International Association of Insurance Supervisors, the International Accounting Standards Board, and the Committee on Payments and Market Infrastructures.

As the group turned to a discussion of initial coin offerings, the finance minister of one of the world's largest economies asked the group, "Are we regulating cryptocurrencies to let them exist or make them to go away?"

It was an interesting question. A few of the delegates looked down into their laps. There was no direct answer and the conversation moved on. However, I was certain that if I polled the room, "make them go away" would have been the majority choice.

Yet, within a year, government sector opinion was changing. Following digital currency announcements from Facebook's Libra and the People's Bank of China—and, perhaps, as in response to them—researchers at more than 60 central banks began considering digital versions of their central bank money. Not a few of them regard it as an opportunity to promote or defend the international utilization of their currencies. The BIS went from dismissing central bank digital currency, or "CBDC," as it is known, to giving it full attention. In 2019, the BIS formed its first European Innovation Hub to study CBDC,[67] naming as its director, Benoît Cœuré, a smart French banker for whom I have enormous respect from his service on the executive board of the European Central Bank. By June 2021, the BIS established its fourth Innovation Hub in London.[68]

It was clear that while central bankers did not invent cryptocurrency or even much like it, a number of them were not blind to its value proposition. Very soon, their interest would increase exponentially.

Chapter 16

Digital Dollars

Discovery consists not in seeking new landscapes, but in having new eyes.
—Marcel Proust (novelist), *Remembrance of Things Past*

Fight for the Future of Money

I am writing this final chapter in June 2021 just after giving formal testimony before Senator Elizabeth Warren and the Economic Policy Subcommittee of the Senate Banking Committee. Having testified in front of Congress thrice before joining the CFTC, around a dozen times during my term of office and, now, four times since departing, this latest hearing felt familiar, almost routine. Still, it marked an important milestone along another unique journey since returning to the private sector.

This new endeavor began almost two years before. Not long after handing over the keys to the CFTC chairman's suite, my two sons and

I departed the District of Columbia bound for a short driving and sailboat vacation around the Chesapeake Bay. Along the way to board our charter, we took a side trip down Virginia's Yorktown Peninsula. Our destination was the battlefield where George Washington's Continental Army and Comte de Rochambeau's French force drove the surrender of General Cornwallis's British regulars, spawning American independence.

My mobile phone rang. I answered on the car's hands-free speaker. It was my brother Charlie. After some warm greetings to me and the boys, he asked if I had given any thought to central bank digital currency, or "CBDC" as it was known.

I had indeed. My view was simple and certain. As I've explained, the ever-evolving Internet was decentralizing financial services and money in the form of cryptocurrency. It was only a matter of time before sovereign governments would create their own digital currencies. I was certain it would happen with the US dollar. As we drove along, we talked about the impact of cryptocurrencies on the dollar at home and abroad.

We later called Daniel Gorfine, who had just departed the CFTC and brought him into the discussion. Over the next few weeks, we continued to research the subject and kick around ideas. In October 2019, Daniel and I drafted an op-ed that ran in *The Wall Street Journal* evocatively entitled, "*We Sent a Man to the Moon. We Can Send the Dollar to Cyberspace.*"[1] We argued that China's pending launch of its digital currency was the cyberspace equivalent of the Sputnik launch. We sounded the alarm about US government complaisance in the face of China's rapid progress in developing a digital version of its currency, known as the Yuan or Renminbi. We argued that standing idly by while its major overseas economic competitor deployed a sovereign digital currency could someday put the dollar's primary reserve currency status at risk.

The article drew wide attention and positive reaction. The day the article appeared in print, I was having a post-workout breakfast in the New York Athletic Club's vaulted dining room overlooking Central Park. I was able to share a newspaper copy with Tim Massad unexpectedly seated at the next table. Later, my old colleague Gary Cohn texted: "Great piece in the WSJ."

A few weeks later, I was at the annual FinTech Festival in Singapore, one of the major global venues for digital finance, where I met up with David Treat. He's the brilliant but disarmingly affable managing director and global head of the Capital Markets Blockchain practice for Accenture, the global consultancy firm. David was leading Accenture's CBDC advisory services for several important central banks. He complimented our advocacy for exploring a digital dollar and offered to support it with Accenture's immense global resources. Because of its market leadership in CBDC, Charlie, Daniel, and I decided to engage Accenture as our lead architect and technology innovation partner.

In January 2020, David Treat and I attended the World Economic Forum in Switzerland, the annual winter gathering of influencers of the world's ruling elites. In the high altitude and, for this one week, in the high-human density town of Davos, we announced the creation of the Digital Dollar Project (DDP).[2] The Project is a think tank devoted to the public discussion of the merits of a tokenized form of the US central bank digital currency, or—as we termed it—a "Digital Dollar." The Project's mission is to encourage research into a US digital currency, to convene private sector thought leaders and actors to advise on the topic, and to propose possible models to support the public sector.[3]

Determined to bring many perspectives and professional disciplines to bear, we assembled an extraordinarily experienced advisory board that we announced in mid-March 2020. It includes economists, business leaders, technologists, innovators, lawyers, academics, consumer advocates, and human rights experts.[4] We began a series of public and private briefings for interested stakeholders, including policymakers, global bodies, nonprofits, academics, and private sector entities. Later, the highly accomplished Adrienne Harris, former Special Assistant for Economic Policy to President Obama, joined the Project's executive board.[5]

Central Bank Digital Currency (CBDC)

CBDC is digital money issued by a central bank and backed by its sovereign government. That distinguishes it from Bitcoin and cryptocurrencies, which are not backed by a sovereign government. There are several forms that CBDC could take from digital account-based systems to fully digital tokens verified through government-sanctioned consensus mechanisms. For consumers, CBDC wallets would offer essential payment functionalities integrated with existing banking services. Payments at points of sale could still be effected through conventional credit card–style terminals, including fully contactless solutions. The difference is that real and immediate money would flow through those terminals, not electronic messages to third parties as they are under the current system.

A Digital Dollar

At the end of May 2020, the Digital Dollar Project released its initial white paper.[6] It proposed a tokenized form of the US dollar enjoying the full faith and credit of the US government. It would effectively be an American government digital currency that would operate alongside existing forms of money, including physical cash. Its value would be the same as that of a paper dollar; it would just have a different format—a digital one.

The Digital Dollar Project's proposal seeks to preserve the existing two-tier banking system and the important work of commercial banks in personal and business lending.[7] It proposes that the issuance, distribution, and redemption of US digital currency would work the same as coins or dollar bills; the Federal Reserve would distribute it to domestic banks or regulated entities against reserves. Banks would then distribute Digital Dollars to domestic end-users' digital wallets. With careful design choices, including perhaps limits on holdings,[8] CBDC should not be a threat to the practice of fractional banking. People and businesses will still need credit to make purchases and invest in opportunities.

Commercial and retail banks should be able to attract deposits from non–interest bearing digital wallets into insured, interest bearing digital bank accounts.

Digital Dollar

The Digital Dollar Project uses the phrase "Digital Dollar" to refer to a US dollar CBDC. We chose that title because it is catchy. However, it might be a little misleading. The dollar already exists in digital forms, like the electronic bank accounts held by financial institutions. But what the Digital Dollar Project proposes is tokenized fiat money—not account-based money. Unlike digital account-based money, a tokenized, digital dollar would make sending money as simple, immediate, and cost-free as sending a text message without going through verifying intermediaries.

The Digital Dollar Project is officially agnostic about the continued development of non-sovereign cryptocurrency, whether commercial or decentralized. The Digital Dollar Project's proposal is also monetary policy neutral, taking no view on issues of money supply. A digital dollar would be a policy tool, not a policy expression. It is reasonable to expect that prudent central banks will be no less prudent in originating CBDC than they are in printing fiat currency and that profligate central banks will be uniformly profligate in all forms of money.

A US Digital Dollar would not share the drawbacks of Bitcoin in environmental sustainability. A Digital Dollar would not need to be "mined," consuming large amounts of energy to demonstrate proof of work and earn newly minted coins. Instead, Digital Dollars would be created cryptographically by the Federal Reserve and distributed electronically. Such distribution would make a digital dollar environmentally superior even to the current use of fiat money that has often ignored, but not insignificant, environmental costs in the operation of electronic ATMs and the physical mining, minting, and distribution of notes and coins.

Drivers of Interest

As I have explained, the private sector has a decade's head start on governments and central banks in exploring digital money. It is one of the reasons we started the Digital Dollar Project—to rouse the US official sector and the American public into action.

In fact, over the past year, governments have begun to catch up. The Bank for International Settlements recently reported that almost 90% of central banks said they were considering the pros and cons of issuing digital fiat, while three-fifths of central banks are now actively experimenting with CBDC.[9]

There are at least seven drivers for central bank interest in CBDC.

The first is data capture. In the twenty-first century, the world's most valuable resource is data,[10] and financial data may be the most valuable data of all. What likely caused the People's Bank of China initially to consider CBDC was concern over the potential for two of its fast-growing and widely popular mobile-device payment providers, AliPay and WeChatPay, to gain proprietary access to financial data of Chinese citizens. In Communist China, finance is the exclusive instrument of the Chinese Communist Party (CCP) and financial data is too essential to be outside of CCP control. Moreover, CBDC has great potential as an instrument of state surveillance. It can be used as an effective tool of China's "social credit" system, by which individuals and businesses are tracked and evaluated for political trustworthiness.[11]

Yet, the Chinese central bank was not alone in concern over proprietary control of financial data. Policymakers in London, Brussels, and Washington had similar concerns about consumer privacy when the social media giant Facebook announced in 2019 the launch of its own virtual currency, Libra (subsequently renamed "Diem"), to enable digital payments.[12]

The second driver of central banks' interest in CBDC is modernization of financial market infrastructure. This is especially important for economies that depend heavily on financial services. For example, Singapore has led the way in a multiyear multiphase project aimed at exploring the use of distributed ledger technology for clearing and settlement of payments and securities with the eventual goal of developing simpler-to-use and more efficient alternatives to existing systems based on central bank issued digital tokens.[13] The Swiss National Bank and the Banque de France will soon trial Europe's first cross-border payments in CBDC.[14]

China is also deeply focused on financial infrastructure modernization. It is quite advanced in exploring distributed ledger technology.[15] It has launched a national Blockchain Service Network (BSN) to lead blockchain innovation and set global standards.[16] China's BSN is an infrastructure platform that allows private entities, especially small and medium-sized businesses, to overcome the two biggest barriers to entry—prohibitive costs and interoperability with existing financial system infrastructure.[17] By April 2021, the BSN had attracted 20,000 users and more than 2,500 projects across the world.[18] No other country, including the United States, has anything like it.

At the same time, China is particularly far along in developing a sovereign digital currency, working on what it calls the Digital Currency Electronic Payment system or DCEP to modernize its financial infrastructure. An analysis by the US Chamber of Digital Commerce indicates that China has filed more than 80 patents related to its digital currency.[19] DCEP is an enormous data processing and payment system. A number of large, important Chinese businesses have joined this initiative as partners in technology and payments implementation.

The conventional international symbol for the Chinese Yuan is "CNY." China refers to its new electronic currency as eCNY. Today, both Chinese citizens and noncitizens can download digital wallets from six major Chinese banks and fund them with eCNY.[20] The design of China's digital currency wallets is highly sophisticated with four categories of functionalities for different levels of use, including one for smaller amounts for which no identification is claimed to be required.[21] People can download eCNY to the new digital wallets at 3,000 Chinese ATMs and shop in tens of thousands of stores in major cities like Beijing and Shanghai.[22] The new eCNY is also programmable, featuring an initial utility for paying for city subway and bus tickets and urban bike sharing.[23]

The third driver of central bank interest in CBDC is financial inclusion. Digital currency holds great promise in expanding financial access to unbanked populations. In fact, China intends to use its eCNY to address a chronic situation of financial under-inclusion for approximately 400 million Chinese citizens. Yet, the Bahamas has beat out China in launching a digital currency for that purpose. The "sand dollar," a digital version of the Bahamas Dollar, is meant to improve financial inclusion for a young Bahamian population well equipped with smartphones, but scattered on 700 islands over 180,000 square miles without easy access to bank branches.

In the United States, roughly 14 million American adults lack a bank account.[24] A Digital Dollar might help expand financial inclusion for underserved populations due to lower system costs and the ready availability of digital wallets. A Digital Dollar wallet on a smartphone could possibly be an "on ramp" to a broader range of financial services. In fact, development of a US CBDC may be only the starting point for financial service providers to better serve populations that have historically been excluded. As Georgetown University Law Professor Chris Brummer, has written:

> The potential advantages of a tokenized dollar from the standpoint of financial inclusion are impossible to ignore. . . . The supporting rails for a digital dollar could be opened up to other kinds of applications that could help contribute holistically to a transformation of the very model of financial inclusion . . ., [including] services like government sanctioned digital IDs, alternative credit scoring tools, and savings programs . . . even robo-advising and financial education services for low-income people.[25]

The fourth driver of central bank interest in CBDC is precision monetary policy. This need became apparent in the US government's initial response to the COVID-19 pandemic, when tens of millions of Americans had to wait a month or more to receive relief payments by paper check, while over a million payments were made to people who were dead.[26] The crisis exposed fundamental shortcomings in the US government's capacity to swiftly channel financial resources to the unbanked public using paper checks during a national pandemic lockdown. Had a digital dollar been in circulation during the COVID-19 crisis with a means of personal identification, it would have enabled the sending of monetary relief instantaneously to the digital wallets of targeted beneficiaries. More broadly, a digital dollar could also be used to immediately distribute such US government assistance payments as social security benefits, school meal vouchers, and food stamps.

The fifth driver of central bank digital currency is the rapid rise of stablecoins. In the previous chapter, I described concerns voiced by former CFTC Chairman Massad about the impact of stablecoins on financial stability. The concern is that private operators of non-sovereign stablecoins will fail to meet their undertakings with detrimental impact on financial markets and the broader economy.

Yet, financial stability is not the only reason central bankers are closely eyeing stablecoins. It is also the remarkably improved settlement speed and certainty of stablecoins compared to account-based transactions. As they gain market share, stablecoins could become a primary means of transacting for many users.[27] The concern of central banks is that money will circulate almost exclusively within these private systems, beyond the central bank's control.[28] "Central to that rationale is that if the central banks don't do [digital currency], Big Tech will."[29] Villeroy de Galhau, governor of the Banque de France, a leader in CBDC exploration, recently said that the EU risked loss of sovereign control over its money if it did not push ahead with plans for a digital Euro.[30] Mark Carney, the former governor of the Bank of England, expressed a preference for central bank digital currencies over private stablecoins, saying that while central banks consider and prepare for possible CBDCs, private stablecoins could become massive and the consequent "uberization" of money could be hard to unwind.[31]

This remarkable rise of stablecoins has brought central bankers to a "fight or flight" moment, that is, whether to suppress or hijack stablecoin success. China appears to be doing both. In the early summer of 2021, China implemented a sweeping ban on cryptocurrency mining, staggering domestic production of over half of global Bitcoin production. Chinese miners shut down, sold, or moved their computer mining operations to such places such as Texas and Kazakhstan. China also prohibited banks and online payment providers from facilitating cryptocurrency transactions. At the same time, China continued to appropriate the infrastructure of its successful domestic mobile payment giants AliPay and WeChatPay to facilitate the accelerating rollout of China's eCNY.[32] For Western developed economies, the Bank for International Settlements has begun to deride stablecoins as "ancillary" at best to the existing financial system,[33] while accelerating its own development efforts at central bank digital currency.

Olympic Gold

The sixth driver of CBDC interest is geopolitical influence and economic power. Western national security agencies are increasingly concerned about China's global ambitions for its eCNY. It is no secret that China is positioning the eCNY for international use and designing it to operate outside the global financial system. To jump-start that process, China plans to distribute eCNY wallets to athletes and spectators at the 2022 winter Olympics to use during the games and later when they return home to almost every country in the world.[34] By early 2022, China will have seeded eCNY into the four corners of the globe.

China would likely integrate eCNY into its high-priority global infrastructure development strategy known as "one belt, one road."[35] Such integration could encourage dozens of participating economies to make payments using eCNY. Such use would allow Chinese client states to bypass much of the outdated, glacially slow, and often ineffectual banking systems that poorly serve underdeveloped parts of the globe.[36] China is already evaluating the feasibility of a pan-Asian CBDC payments network through the "multiple central bank digital currency bridge" project among the central banks of Hong Kong, Thailand, China, and the United Arab Emirates.[37] In addition, China may lure client states throughout Southeast Asia and Africa to peg their digital domestic currencies to that of China.

Consider an example of how the eCNY might eventually operate in an international context. Imagine a large African city with a Chinese-built and -financed water filtration station. The facility's construction features Chinese-developed electronic sensors that recognize when reserves of chlorine or other components or materials are running low. Using China's leading 5G telecommunications technology, that Chinese-built sensor will instruct a computer to automatically order supplies from a Chinese supplier. In return, the supplier will receive direct payment in eCNY with little to no human management. The payment will be transmitted completely outside the global, account-based bank system.

While such a digital money transfer mechanism would undoubtedly bring efficiency gains to cities, supply chains, and electricity grids, it would also generate a virtuous cycle for the eCNY. The more counterparties and countries that benefit from immediately, cheaply, and directly settling accounts in eCNY, the greater the network effect in further expanding the orbit of Chinese economic influence.[38] It would enable cross-border payments to bypass SWIFT, the messaging network used in money transfers between commercial banks that is monitored by the US government. It would diminish the universality of economic sanctions as a geopolitical policy tool.[39]

Cutting Edge of Money

Throughout recorded history, sovereign and non-sovereign currencies have competed for patronage in global commerce. Many factors enabled some currencies to trade at discounts or premiums to others, especially social trust based on the issuers' economic strength and stability. Technological enhancements sometimes gave an edge to one currency over another, such as China's innovative paper currency during the Tang Dynasty or the instrument from which the US currency derives its name: the Spanish dollar that from the fifteenth to eighteenth centuries was easily divisible into "pieces of eight" for greater commercial convenience.[40]

From my time at the CFTC, I am keenly aware of global economic competition in commodity trading. The fact that prices for most of the world's key tradable commodities—such as wheat, soybeans, and crude oil—are today set in deep, transparent, and CFTC-regulated US commodity futures markets—and settled in US dollars—is an enormous American advantage. It means that those global commodities are paid and accounted for around the world in US dollars. It means American farmers and energy producers do not bear risk of changes in foreign exchange rates. Perhaps more importantly, it means overseas trading partners need to hold US dollars to pay for global commodity imports. This dynamic is an important pillar of the US dollar's primary reserve currency status.

China recognizes this US advantage. As the world's largest consumer of key commodities, such as soybeans, crude oil, and iron ore, China would derive great economic advantage if they were priced in Chinese currency rather than in US Dollars. That is one of the reasons why in the past few years China partially opened to overseas traders its futures trading markets, including contracts on iron ore and crude oil.[41] It is why China recently passed new laws further opening its futures markets to outside investment and clearing.[42]

It is also why China is asserting leadership in developing blockchain technology. As I told the Senate in early 2018, the Louis Dreyfus corporation had conducted the first large shipment of American soybeans to China entirely using distributed ledger technology.[43] All contractual aspects of the shipment from bills of lading and receipt of shipment were conducted by the parties on one universal distributed ledger. It was just the beginning.[44]

Technological capacity of monetary systems is as important a differentiator today as it was in earlier times for paper money and pieces of eight. Technological change in money is inevitably driven by the financial incentives of a market economy.[45] One can imagine a time when China looks to combine its new eCNY with its growing lead in distributed ledger technology and its opening futures markets to facilitate the entire process of logistics, payment, and price hedging for key world commodities in one Chinese-controlled currency network. It is already happening. Reports out of China in the summer of 2021 say that the new eCNY is being used in China's commodity futures markets for the first time.[46] The result will be extraordinary in its economic and financial efficiency.

Undoubtedly, the prospect that the CNY, digital or otherwise, will soon become a dominant global currency that rivals the dollar is implausible.[47] China's crude capital controls and inconstant enforcement of commercial contracts do not help the CNY's service as a reserve currency. The US dollar remains the world's primary reserve currency at 59.5% of central bank foreign currency reserves compared to 2.5% for the CNY.[48] It is also the currency of 39% of cross-border payments compared to 1.9% for the CNY.[49] The prominence of the dollar as the primary world reserve currency rests on many durable network elements, including the strength and size of the US economy; extensive trade linkages between the United States and the rest of the world; deep financial markets, including for US Treasury securities; the stable value of the dollar over time; the ease of converting US dollars into foreign currencies; the rule of law and strong property rights in the United States; and last but not least, credible US monetary policy.[50] These elements provide the US dollar with currently unsurpassed "network effects."

None of these are likely to be threatened by just any foreign currency, and certainly not because that foreign currency simply has the technological advantages of a CBDC.[51]

Yet, fully appreciating the strategic potential of the Chinese digital currency requires a sea change in assessing the potential of what China is doing. CBDC should be viewed as only one (though a key) component of entirely new digital financial system: a massive networked payment and data-processing financial structure.[52] Of China's 84 CBDC patents reviewed by the US Chamber of Digital Commerce, virtually all of them relate to integrating a system of digital currency into the existing banking infrastructure.[53] The system would constitute an interoperable, distributed ledger of all financial functions and programmable transactions in eCNY at home and abroad, including borrowing and lending, domestic and global payments, securities and commodities trading, retail and business payments, and monetary policy. At the center of this system would be China's central bank, the People's Bank of China (PBOC), putting within its purview and central command all important financial functions and transactions in its national currency. This networked and integrated system could generate its own network effect, an unprecedented, new type of network: instantaneous, low-cost, global, and entirely outside the Western-dominated, global banking system. The potential for reduced latency, lower transaction costs and financial velocity could send an already vibrant Chinese economy into hyperdrive.[54]

The question needs to be asked how will the US dollar fare if it remains an analog instrument, while other major reserve currencies, such as the eCNY and, as looks to be the case, a digital Euro, are recorded on accessible distributed ledgers, made programmable, and networked with other core financial market infrastructure. Lael Brainard, the keenly intelligent and serious Federal Reserve Board Governor, has said she "cannot wrap her head around the idea of the US not having a digital currency" for this very reason.[55]

Will the US dollar's enviable analog network effect have the same value in a digital tomorrow? Or will tomorrow's reserve currency balance rest on a new type of network in which national digital currencies are integrated with all worldwide financial functions and programmable transactions conducted in that currency? China clearly aims to find out.

Competing CBDC Networks

Yet, as important as are the first six drivers of CBDC that I have described, the seventh may be most important. That is leadership in setting the global standards for CBDC interoperability.

The world we know today is one of competing currency zones in which monetary systems, banking, and foreign accounts are generally oriented to one reserve currency or another, such as the US dollar zone and the "Eurozone." I envision that in the future those old currency zones may well be superseded by fully networked CBDC distributed ledger zones. There likely will be a Chinese eCNY blockchain zone and a Digital Euro blockchain zone. In these zones, national digital currencies will be deployed upon CBDC distributed ledgers of all significant financial functions and transactions, including banking, market trading, clearing and settlement, and monetary policy execution.

China aims to be a leading developer of CBDC infrastructure and blockchain technology to power these CBDC financial networks.[56] Over time, countries seeking to implement their own CBDCs may adopt Chinese DCEP technology rather than engineer the technology themselves. This will provide China with an opportunity to be a leading exporter of CBDC technology, including features designed for domestic financial surveillance for the world's too many regimes that aspire to have such power.

Perhaps more crucially, China intends to take the lead in setting the standards and protocols for a world of such bisecting and competing CBDC blockchain zones. It already has first-mover advantage. Last year, Chinese General Secretary Xi Jinpin is reported to have told Chinese party leaders to "take advantage of the trend of China's position as a global leader in the online economy . . . [and] proactively participate in the formulation of international rules for digital currency and digital taxation and create new competitive advantages."[57] Since then, PBOC officials have stepped forward in international discussions to propose new measures for CBDC interoperability, policy coordination, and transaction monitoring.[58] The potential power of such Chinese leadership in integrated CBDC financial networks is enormous.

Now the reader can begin to glimpse the stakes of the contest for the future of digital money. Those stakes are at least as high as those engendered by competitions to lead any of the transformational technological revolutions of the past 100 years. The balance of geopolitical power hinges on the outcome.

All Together Now

Like it or not, we are entering a new world. It would be nice to think that the United States and other developed economies can just tinker with the existing financial system with a bit more urgency to make it faster and somewhat more convenient and it will continue to serve for another generation or so. Perhaps it very well can. But is it wise to chance it? The US is the leading player and architect of the existing account-based financial system. Yet, the US' own domestic patch of that system has fallen behind the curve. It fails to move money in a relatively low cost, convenient and timely manner compared to its Western economic rivals.[59] Is it prudent to focus most efforts on propping up this legacy financial system while yielding leadership in this new Internet of Value to major economic and geopolitical competitors? To cite an overused cliché, should we not "skate to where the puck is going, rather than where it is?" China intends to sit at the head of the innovation table. Europe also appears to want to have a seat with its recent announcement that it will start work on a digital Euro.[60] But what of the United States?

Federal Reserve Chair Jay Powell has increasingly asserted the national importance of exploring a US CBDC. He has appropriately stressed that it is more important to get a US CBDC right than to be the first major country to develop one. He has said that both benefits and risks of a US CBDC need to be weighed, including the need to protect a CBDC from cyberattacks, counterfeiting and fraud, its impact on monetary policy and financial stability, and its ability to counter illicit activity while also preserving user privacy and security. In response to an April 2021 announcement about the continued rollout of the eCNY, Powell said the public and Congress must be closely involved in plans for a digital dollar.[61]

Under Chairman Powell's leadership and with particular attention from Governor Lael Brainard,[62] the Federal Reserve is looking thoughtfully at central bank digital currency. In February 2021, several members of Powell's senior team outlined five preconditions for a US CBDC: clear policy objectives, broad stakeholder support, strong legal framework, market readiness, and robust technology.[63] The technology piece is being tackled by a group of experienced researchers at the Federal Reserve Bank of Boston that are working with the Massachusetts Institute of Technology.[64] Those efforts are primarily focused on core technological CBDC architecture.[65] The results of their important work are expected to be published in September 2021.

That leaves four preconditions to examine. The Digital Dollar Project intends to help explore three of the remaining four: policy objectives, broad stakeholder support, and market readiness. To do so, the Digital Dollar Project announced in May 2021[66] the launch of a neutral, open, and collaborative forum to conduct pilot programs to explore those policy challenges and opportunities.[67] This research platform is meant to serve as a "testing ground" for collaboration by a wide range of commercial and noncommercial stakeholders. The DDP's efforts are intended not to conflict, but to be complementary to the work of the Boston Fed and MIT, other regional Federal Reserve Banks and the Federal Reserve Board.

US Pilot Projects

The Digital Dollar Project's pilot programs will explore, analyze, and understand technical and functional requirements, test applications and approaches, and consider promising use cases for both retail and wholesale commercial utilization. The projects and participating institutions will be selected and designated according to criteria approved by the Project's nonpartisan advisory group. The projects will be designed with an unbiased and nonprofit perspective that seeks to uncover and present the raw data unencumbered by commercial influence or priorities. Initial funding for the projects will be made possible through the generous financial support of Accenture. The Project will release the results of the pilots to the public for use in academic study, as well as policy consideration by Congress, the Federal Reserve, the US Treasury, and the wider stakeholder community.

Crafting a well-designed, durable, and universal US CBDC will be an enormous and complex undertaking. Something as complex and worthy of the US dollar's global importance should not be completed in a hurried manner. It will take time and seriousness to get it right.

Nevertheless, now is the time to get started. The recent launch of SpaceX reminds us that the United States once explored outer space and the lunar surface through a series of pilot programs known as Mercury, Gemini, and Apollo. So too, the US should explore a digital dollar in a series of well-conceived and -executed pilot programs in partnership between the public and private sectors. The Digital Dollar Project is highly motivated by the opportunity to assist in exploration of the public policy challenges and opportunities of CBDC through broad stakeholder participation and discussions.

Expectation of Digital Privacy

China views CBDC as a key element in building a modern, more inclusive, blockchain based, financial system. Its success in that endeavor will present the US and other democratic governments with significant challenges that should not be ignored. Yet, it should also not be overstated or feared. The goal of a free society cannot be to emulate a closed one. The United States did not vanquish the Soviet Union to "the ash heap of history" [68] by emulating the USSR's failed centrally controlled economy. Rather, the United States outperformed and better served its citizenry though the efficiency and dynamism of its free market, incentive-based private sector economy. The challenge of the eCNY calls for a similar return to free society fundamentals. If the US is to assert a leading role in setting global standards for CBDC, just as it was a leader in setting the standards for the first wave of the Internet, then it must expand its exploration of CBDC itself. But, it must do so in a way that is consistent with democratic values.

The dollar's ascendance during the post–World War Two period was accompanied by a historical rarity: the birth of a truly global market for goods and services. That, in turn, helped millions of historically impoverished people lift themselves into the middle class. Between 1981 and

2019, the world's poverty rate was cut from 42.3% to 8.2%, an 80% reduction in less than four decades.[69] Today, more people than ever before in history enjoy improved health, child welfare, and all the educational and civil liberty benefits that accompany material wherewithal.[70]

I believe this remarkable late-twentieth-century flowering of human well-being is related to the global adoption of democratic ideals of individual liberty, freedom of speech, personal privacy, limited government, the rule of law, and the aspirational nature of democratic societies. These ideals are encoded in the US dollar.

Some of those ideals are also set out in America's Constitution. One in particular is the Fourth Amendment's right to personal privacy. From it stems a body of jurisprudence defining the balance between an individual's right to privacy and the federal government's limited ability to abridge that privacy in pursuit of legitimate law enforcement, national defense, or other overriding objectives.

Although a right to financial and information privacy is not specifically established by the Fourth Amendment, for the last half-century courts have generally protected privacy using a doctrine called "reasonable expectation of privacy." Even so, Fourth Amendment privacy protections have been eroded considerably since the attacks of September 11, 2001. In fact, no account-based financial transactions are truly private because, as I have previously explained, in every case they require personal identity as a prerequisite step. The Fourth Amendment's jurisprudence needs to evolve further in this digital era to renew the balance between economic privacy with other societal priorities. Privacy protections, constitutional or otherwise, must clearly apply to data generated by legal use of CBDC if it is to enjoy societal support.

Privacy is essential in a free society that respects individuals and their civil rights. In the American Constitutional framework, people may enjoy privacy—keeping personal information to themselves—for any reason or no reason. Such civil authority over oneself, one's information, and one's relationships strengthens and empowers people in many ways, including by preserving their political and legal independence. Privacy reinforces individual freedom to support controversial causes. Privacy protects victims of stalking and harassment. Privacy gives people autonomy and choice as to how they engage with others and society. Privacy, especially economic privacy, enables a sovereign people to remain sovereign and a free society to remain free.

The Digital Dollar Project believes[71] a well-functioning CBDC should be:

- **Private:** People should be able to use a US CBDC without making themselves subject to undue corporate tracking or government surveillance. People should benefit from aboveboard, contractual sharing of information with providers of financial and other services, or they may refuse it. US law enforcement access to CBDC usage data should be controlled by applicable US law, including the Fourth Amendment and the subpoena process.
- **Secure:** A US CBDC should improve and not degrade people's security against theft, hacking, illegal seizure, unauthorized data mining, and fraud. It should provide people with more secure ways to handle money individually, on a system that is secure against attacks and legally protected, with money-handling tools that protect against the frauds that an unfamiliar technology might otherwise allow. A Digital Dollar should ensure that people's financial data is secure from exploitation by both commercial actors and government authorities.
- **Accessible:** A US CBDC should improve Americans' and global dollar users' access to financial services. Because it is a more efficient system, it should cost less to engage in basic CBDC transactions. And as an open system, it should enhance competition into financial services that produces better services at lower costs.
- **Transparent:** CBDCs should run on systems that are operationally transparent so that a variety of system users, including the public, can assure themselves independently about its technical functioning, its security, and its resistance to impermissible monitoring, data mining, or other exploitation.

With the proper Fourth Amendment jurisprudence and thoughtful design choices relating to anonymity and individual privacy, a digital dollar could well enjoy superior privacy protections than many competing instruments—whether provided by commercial interests or other sovereigns. Coding traditional democratic ideals of economic freedom and privacy into a digital dollar will surely enhance its global appeal. Hundreds of millions of people in the developing world may well be reluctant to surrender their growing economic security and autonomy to authoritarian state surveillance simply for the convenience of digital payments. As it has so often in its history, the US has the opportunity to lead in a way consistent with its finest ideals.

Safety in Numbers

It is said that "war is too important to be entrusted to the generals."[72] Similarly, money, especially digital money, is too important to be left to central bankers. While Chairman Powell's recognition of the need to preserve user privacy and security is reassuring, it is hard to think that privacy rights will be adequately protected in CBDCs if the design work is conducted solely by central banks, the key enforcers of Know-Your-Customer and Anti-Money-Laundering rules. Left to their own devices, many central banks may opt for account-based rather than token-based CBDC designs that are more easily surveilled and data mined.

That is why it is so important that advocates for economic privacy be fully engaged and heard as a US Digital Dollar is being considered and constructed. That is part of why the Digital Dollar Project was created—to bring the perspective of the private sector to the design of a US CBDC. After all, money is at least as much a social construct as it is a government one, if not more so. Social values that are enshrined in the dollar today—values like individual liberty, freedom of speech, personal privacy, free enterprise, and the rule of law—must be encoded in the Digital Dollar of the future.

I will, however, confess a fear. The early promise of the Internet of information was to bypass media gatekeepers to enable borderless, peer-to-peer exchange of information. For a time, the Internet provided essential "radio contact" among individuals struggling against state control and, in some cases, was a fountainhead of social media revolutions in the early twenty-first century.[73] Yet today, the freedom of the Internet of information is in question. In the United States, a handful of media oligarchs, encouraged by political partisans, control what online speech is aired and what speech disappears down an Orwellian "memory hole." We see glaring examples of this, including social media's muzzling of politically incorrect discussions about the origin of COVID-19[74] and the removal of videos of Congressional hearings on COVID-19 treatment protocols.[75] We see it, perhaps most powerfully, in the recent social media banishment of a former president.[76]

Regardless of what one thinks of the origins of COVID-19, alternative medical treatments, or Donald J. Trump, the prodigious power of social media to censor and expunge public dialogue is without precedent. What if it were your speech, point of view, or candidate that was similarly censored?

When it comes to our financial liberty, it is hard to imagine that the US government would use a digital dollar to do something so obvious and direct as to surveil the spending of everyday Americans or restrict transactions for otherwise lawful purposes.[77] Yet, a digital currency could be corrupted in more subtle ways. In recent years, numerous US federal government agencies have regularly circumvented constitutional privacy protections by obtaining sensitive personal data from commercial vendors.[78] It has been reported that the Biden administration is considering using private firms to track activity of American citizens in order to get around the Fourth Amendment and other laws that protect Americans from unreasonable searches and surveillance.[79] Even my former agency, the CFTC, took a far too cavalier approach in 2016 toward obtaining private source code without a subpoena, sparking the tussle I described earlier.

It is entirely foreseeable that sponsors of non-sovereign cryptocurrencies and stablecoins or even commercial servicers of Digital Dollars, such as wallet providers and others, could be put under political pressure to disable financial transactions with disfavored groups in a similar way as is being done today with political speech. Under political pressure, digital wallet providers might bar transactions with out-of-favor industries, such as firearms manufacturers or abortion providers, depending on which position's advocates held political power.

What if digital currency network operators or stablecoin sponsors could decide what financial transactions could be made and which would be prevented? What if they could surveil or restrict your ability to support political candidates and causes they disapproved of or activities and pastimes they disfavored? What if you were prevented from donating to advocacy groups for such causes as LGBT+ rights or second amendment freedoms depending on your point of view? After all, one group's respected liberties and celebrated causes may be another party's antagonists and prohibited activities.

All of this may sound so Orwellian that some readers may say, "I'll stick to cash." But what if cash is discontinued (as it is being done in some countries)? Even now, try using cash to support important social or charitable causes.

And if data is truly the most precious twenty-first century commodity of all, then we must ask the question, "Who owns our financial data?" This question is particularly relevant as more and more of our transactional and personal data streams from individuals to corporations and government agencies. The more data that we give away, the more that it can be mined, analyzed, and used to manipulate us and make decisions on our behalf.[80] If we want to prevent a small group of technocratic and government elites, however enlightened their intentions, from consolidating power over the rest of us, the answer must be "hands off." A sovereign people must be secure in their economic privacy and monetary holdings.

That is why, in addition to privacy rights, CBDC must feature censorship resistance as a core feature for use in a free society. A digital dollar and other sovereign and non-sovereign digital currencies must be free of any politically or socially imposed limitations on its ability to purchase legal goods and services in a free market economy. That is why it is so important that supporters of economic privacy in a free society must speak up as central bank digital currency is being developed. In many ways, that is why I have written this book—to explain that money is changing right before our eyes and urge the public to take hold of that change. We can't let the promise of the convenience of digital money blind us to the threat of the loss of our liberty.

Without inviolable protections for such civil liberties as freedom of speech, free enterprise, and individual economic privacy, a digital dollar would be no more worthy of a democratic society than the currency of an authoritarian one. The American people—and free people every-where—have everything to gain by encoding into a digital dollar stout protections for individual liberty and privacy. The free world has every-thing to lose by neglecting it. The issue is essential to the future of true democracy.

From a civil liberty perspective, a US central bank digital currency may have advantages over non-sovereign stablecoins if the CBDC is properly bound by constitutional Fourth Amendment protections, to which private stablecoins would not be subject. In this way, we might think of such a digital dollar as a "public option" for payments with con-stitutional protections of privacy.[81]

On the other hand, the best protection against impermissible gov-ernment surveillance of economic activity or restrictions on otherwise lawful transactions may be robust competition from well-constructed stablecoins and other non-sovereign digital money. "You can envision a jigsaw approach to privacy, where no entity has all of the information about a transaction, so that the CBDC doesn't become a tool of financial surveillance."[82] In short, broad choice between sovereign and non-sovereign digital currency may be the most effective guarantor of eco-nomic liberty and individual privacy.

Author and commentator William F. Buckley Jr. famously quipped that he would rather be governed by "the first 2,000 people in the Boston telephone directory than by the Harvard University Faculty."[83] It applies to the process of protecting economic privacy in the digital future of money. We can't leave it to elite functionaries in Basel, Brussels, Washington, Seattle, or Silicon Valley to adequately protect individual privacy from big tech and government usurpation. The impetus and, indeed, the demand must come from a free citizenry.

Which brings me back to where all this started: Bitcoin. You can be sure that if a reasonable expectation of financial privacy is not reliably embodied into sovereign digital money, Bitcoin and similarly censorship resistant forms of crypto will continue to thrive and succeed. And this will not be just for illicit use, but for use of ordinary citizens who simply and rightfully want their financial affairs to remain private and who have lost faith in governing institutions to make it so.

The same applies to monetary value. The more governments and central banks allow inflation to tax savings, reduce economic growth, and increase economic inequality, the greater Bitcoin's attraction and global proliferation. As I have said, the United States and other democracies have everything to gain by exploring well-designed, private-enhanced, and prudently managed CBDCs—and their citizens have everything to lose if they fail to do so.

Back on the Mound

I mentioned earlier that I was called to testify before the Economic Policy Subcommittee of the Senate Banking Committee as I was completing this manuscript. The hearing was initiated by Louisiana Senator John Kennedy and chaired by Massachusetts Senator Elizabeth Warren.

I began my testimony on June 9, 2021, with this oral statement:[84]

"Many thoughtful commentators, including members of this committee, are rightly concerned with the risks of. . .a Digital Dollar, including its impact on: fractional banking and financial stability, energy consumption, current payment models, economic privacy and the reserve currency status of the dollar.

"As a former chief regulator, I share the inclination to look at what could go wrong with new innovation, including digital money.

"However, as a thought experiment, I would also like to consider for just a moment what could *go right*.

"First, some worry that a Digital Dollar might *decrease* money held in commercial banks.

"But, what if *the opposite* happens? What if *more* money moves into the banking sector, especially if previously un-or-under-banked communities shift Digital Dollars into bank accounts because of the ease of doing so? What if mobile devices and digital wallets provide attractive on-ramps to banking services offering interest on deposits and government insurance? And, what if greater ease in converting commercial bank money into Digital Dollars would make people less likely to do so in a panic?

"Second: Many of you are rightly concerned with energy consumption. But, what if a Digital Dollar used *much, much* less energy than Bitcoin and other decentralized "proof of work" digital assets? And, what if a Digital Dollar even used less energy than is currently used for physical mining, minting and distribution of paper dollars and metal coins?

"Third, some are concerned that a Digital Dollar could negatively impact current business models for payments. But what if a Digital Dollar actually lowers payment costs and bank fees for consumers and small businesses? What if it provides instantaneous settlement, reducing cash flow stress that plagues small businesses and American consumers with costly overdraft and other fees? And, what if the economic benefit of increased activity from digital money results in expanding economic opportunity, small business formation and productivity?

"Fourth, all of us are rightly concerned about infringing individual privacy through mass surveillance of digital money. But what if a Digital Dollar was carefully engineered from the outset to incorporate Americans' reasonable expectations of individual privacy consistent with the Fourth amendment? What if we strike the right balance between the legitimate needs of law enforcement with Constitutional protections of individual privacy? And, what if a Digital Dollar with such American legal and due process limitations provides *superior* protection of individual privacy compared to many other sovereign and, indeed, non-sovereign, commercial digital currencies?

"Finally, some argue that the dollar's status as the world's reserve currency is well entrenched and requires no further innovation. But, what if a Digital Dollar improves financial stability, productivity and efficiency while enhancing the dollar with new functionality, ease of use and smart contract programmability? What if we add these enhancements while preserving the dollar's recognized competitive advantages: the backing of a robust and strong economy, good governance, openness, and rule of law?

And, what if we do all of this while protecting individual privacy in faith to our finest national ideals? Would we then have not done our duty to prepare the US dollar to serve our fellow citizens in the coming digital future of money?"

The hearing was a good one. Understanding of digital money had come a long way since I testified the year before. It is clear that some Senators are connecting the dots for the future of money. Committee members were generally supportive of greater exploration of a US CBDC and its potential to increase financial inclusion and modernize the payments system.

Somewhat to my surprise, Senator Warren launched into a sharp attack on cryptocurrency, including stablecoins, saying that the innovation's promise of boosting the lot of everyday Americans has not materialized. The criticism was echoed in a June report of the Bank for International Settlements which dismissed cryptocurrencies as, "speculative assets rather than money that in many cases are used to facilitate money laundering, ransomware attacks and other financial crimes. Bitcoin in particular has few redeeming public interest attributes when also considering its wasteful energy footprint."[85] The report went on to describe stablecoins as "an appendage to the conventional monetary system and not a game changer."[86]

Extending an observation from Gustave Flaubert,[87] you can probably judge the success of an innovation by the vehemence of its opposition. The fervor of the BIS attack on Bitcoin and stablecoins is remarkable coming from an organization that only began paying formal attention to the Internet of Value a decade after the Satoshi Nakamoto White Paper. Its criticism fails to acknowledge that without Bitcoin and its progeny, the world's central bankers would not even be considering CBDC. Surely, some central bankers and government representatives, having either ignored or derided Bitcoin and the emergence of cryptocurrency for the past decade, ought to be humble and learn from the private sector's substantial leadership as they rush to jump on the CBDC bandwagon.

While the US government is largely still considering its policy response to CBDC, the America private sector continues to make enormous strides in cryptocurrency development, especially in the area of stablecoins. So far, these efforts are far more advanced than US government efforts. Taking into account the combined efforts of both public and private sectors, it may be argued that, rather than being a global laggard, the United States could be considered to be "already winning the race for the future of money and payments."[88] That, of course, assumes the US public and private sectors are actively working together. They are not. They need to do so.

There is no reason to view development of digital money as necessarily pitting the private and public sectors against each other. Government has much to learn from private sector innovation. In fact, the official sector should draw extensively upon the private sector in its attempt to accelerate its work. Consumer advocates like Senator Warren may come to see that an effective ally in reforming the legacy banking industry may be the competitive challenge of non-sovereign cryptocurrency and decentralized finance. There is a sound argument that central bank leadership should come not in form of assembling its own CBDC instrument, but in laying out core principles for "open Internet-based financial services" to which private sector actors can construct innovative digital currencies.

In a series of recent blog posts, a group of thoughtful economists at the IMF and the New York Federal Reserve considered how sovereign and non-sovereign cryptocurrencies—CBDC and stablecoins—might work together in the digital future of money.[89] They note that central banks can foster the development of digital currencies either indirectly, by supporting the public provision of safe, privately issued digital currencies like stablecoins, or directly, by issuing publicly issued central bank digital currencies. They make clear that these approaches are not mutually exclusive. They suggest that a central bank digital currency may be designed to encourage the private sector to innovate on top of it, much like app designers or, in fact, the early Internet itself.[90]

What does seem to be commonly agreed is that the private and public sectors need to work together. Whenever the United States has led the world in technological innovation—whether exploring outer space in the last century or cyberspace in the turn of this century—it has done so through public/private partnerships.[91] In these partnerships, the US government has directed central policy frameworks to further the public interest while the private sector supplied technological innovativeness, large project management capability, and competitive urgency. Without the blending of the two, exploration of the lunar surface and cyberspace may have slipped beyond the twentieth century into the twenty-first.

It may be argued that developing a dollar CBDC is so important to the national interest that it should be the exclusive work of the public sector and not involve the private sector. I disagree. It is because the development of a dollar CBDC is so important to the national interest that it must involve collaboration by both. Without social trust, a digital dollar, like every form of money, will not succeed. The public must be deeply engaged in the creation of a digital dollar. That is why we have launched the Digital Dollar Project: to foster private sector engagement in the Dollar's digital future.

In the words of former governor of the Bank of England, Mark Carney, "Modern money is backed by a series of institutions, mostly housed in central banks. Its value rests on confidence. The value of money requires not just the belief of the public at a point in time but, critically, the *consent* of the public at all times. That dictates not just what the central bank does to maintain the value of money but how it does it and how it accounts for its actions. When it comes to money, the consent and trust of the public must be nurtured and continually maintained."[92]

This global wave of digital currency innovation is quickly gaining momentum. The questions for the United States are what role it will play in this wave of the Internet and to what degree its core values will be brought to bear. The United States—both public and private sectors—must take a leadership role in this next wave of digital innovation or be prepared to accept that the innovation will incorporate the values of America's global competitors.

It is naïve to think that the Internet, in its continuing evolution, will not transform money in the same way it has transformed information, social networking, retail shopping, local transportation, travel and leisure, photography, and the music and entertainment industries. It is going to happen. For money itself, that transformation has already begun. The pace of innovation will never again be as slow as it is today. It is incumbent upon policymakers to consider modernizing the dollar for the same reason we must modernize all economic and commercial infrastructure—to keep pace and benefit from advanced, new architectures of technology and innovation. It is about pursuing less friction, less cost, better policy tools, and broader social inclusion. It is about exploring new digital monetary architecture alongside a long serving, account-based foundation.

We should modernize the dollar to make sure that the values that are enshrined in the dollar today—values like freedom of speech, individual privacy, free enterprise, and, yes, censorship-resistence—are embraced in the digital future of money.

The time has come to explore the opportunities and challenges of a US CBDC in thoughtful partnership between the public and private sectors in the best tradition of American innovation.

Conclusion
Roadside Thoughts[1]

The only freedom which deserves the name, is that of pursuing our own good in our own way, so long as we do not attempt to deprive others of theirs, or impede their efforts to obtain it.

—John Stuart Mill, "On Liberty" (1859)

Philosophy of Value

I close this book with a brief reflection on the life of John Stuart Mill, the proponent of utilitarianism, a philosophy that commends action that creates the greatest amount of happiness for the greatest number of people.[2] I do so to lay out a philosophical approach to the digital future of money, a future of greater financial inclusion, economic liberty, and enduring democratic values for generations to come.

There is an important side to the life of British utilitarian philosopher John Stuart Mill that many people forget: He was a longtime official of the East India Company. That's the British monopoly that controlled India and much more of the world two centuries ago.[3]

Headquartered in London, the East India Company was a global juggernaut involved in commerce, trade, developing markets, and territorial acquisition throughout the world. Most of its trade focused on the Indian subcontinent. The company was multinational, powerful, and global—long before globalization was even a concept. Chartered by Queen Elizabeth I in 1599, it was given exclusive trade rights "with all countries east of the Cape of Good Hope and west of the Straits of Magellan." Eventually it would become a military power and empire-builder in Great Britain's name.

The East India Company was an opaque, private corporation spawned by political machination and controlled by a select few, selling stock only to its own chartered members. Yet the company also advanced official British interests, to the point where the interests of the Britain and company shareholders were often one and the same. The British government followed the Company into India. One historian labeled the company "both regulatory body and sole operator."[4] It oversaw the markets where it traded, and had a virtual monopoly over them.

In short, because of its profitability and contribution to the British economy through trade and taxation, the East India Company was effectively both private and public. It was a business and quasi-governmental entity unaccountable to anyone other than itself.

Notoriously, the Company ran South India with an iron fist. It committed untold abuses in its quest for domination and wealth. Excessive taxes backed by a colonial army brought Indian society to near-collapse. When famine struck India's rural millions, the East India Company did nothing to alleviate the misery. Instead, it continued to shake down the populace for taxes. It ran roughshod over India, answering to no one—with catastrophic results.

Mill saw a chance to offset some of the "externalities" of the East India Company's bloody governance. He joined the company in 1823, and was employed there until 1858—for 35 years. Much has been written about his work on utilitarianism, developing the ideas of his father, James Mill, and Jeremy Bentham. Yet almost nothing has been written about John Stuart Mill's time at the East India Company. While there, he remarkably became a voice for economic and judicial reform, women's rights, and universal suffrage.

Mill was, in effect, a vice president of external communications for one of the nineteenth century's most powerful business enterprises. This circumstance allowed him the opportunity to expound the utilitarianism of his philosophical writings.

Imagine analogous situations today. What if philosophers ran Fortune 500 companies? Or regulatory agencies? Or central banks? Imagine if Socrates had conducted internal audits at Goldman Sachs or Simone de Beauvoir had been a governor of the Federal Reserve. What if Regis Debray or Ayn Rand had held my job at the CFTC?

Why not, after all? As I have said, public affairs and government need the open air and diversity of experience of men and women from all walks of life and society. It is certainly true about the governance of finance.

I mention Mill for two reasons. First, it's cool to think of a great philosopher holding down a day job. But second, his example demonstrates that reformist ideas, résumés, and good intentions aren't enough to produce a great result. It takes something more.

Freedom and Responsibility

As a lawyer, business executive, and now former regulator, I find fascinating the scope of activities of the East India Company. A business should not supplant the role of broadly representative government in the way it did. The work of the East India Company will always be haunted by secrecy, greed, unseemly self-enrichment, and ultimately failure. (It closed its doors in 1874.) In the same vein, regulators should not set the commercial or social priorities of the very businesses they are regulating. Nor should they be captured by them. We need a proper but not impermeable zone of separation between business and government defined by the right balance of freedom and responsibility.

Finding that balance of freedom and responsibility was never far from my mind during my five years at the CFTC. I went to Washington with a conviction—seared into my fiber by the 2008 financial crisis—of the need for reforms in the way financial swaps were traded, cleared, and reported. I believed that Congress got the reforms framework right in the Dodd–Frank Act, but that the CFTC was misapplying some of the implementation. I worked to help get it right.

Yet I gradually came to see that the agency was driving through the rearview mirror. It was preoccupied with preparing for the last crisis and inattentive to the myriad challenges ahead. Dodd–Frank says nothing about contemporary concerns of cybersecurity, algorithmic trading, dealer concentration, disappearing market liquidity, distributed ledger technology, or cryptocurrency. Consequently, too little was being done, and what little was being done was based on groupthink and guesswork.

Thanks to the surprising results of the 2016 election, I became an accidental CFTC chairman. I set a new course, pointing the agency in a forward-facing direction as an increasingly competent, twenty-first-century regulator for twenty-first-century digital markets. With the support of a great executive team, open-minded fellow commissioners, and a rank and file hungry for clear leadership, we reinvigorated the CFTC as a regulator rightly recognized as market intelligent, technologically astute, principles-based, and open to innovation.

The outcome of these efforts was not an accident. It required design and execution. It was a conscious choice that hazarded some political risk and engendered some derision. It took some courage. Its success was born of the desire to match the innovativeness of America's free and open markets with intelligent and responsible regulation worthy of a dynamic, aspirational society.

Like John Stuart Mill, market regulators bring moral frameworks to their work. I certainly did. Of course, the work of an agency must proceed within the limits set by law, not individual will. But within that legal gamut, there is scope for discretion and judgment. My choices derived from my background. I am not unique in being a great-grandchild of humble immigrants who came to the United States in search of economic opportunity. They prospered in America's private sector–driven economy with its free market economic incentives and emphasis on personal discipline and fiscal responsibility. They embraced and contributed to America's pluralist culture, civil society, representative democracy, and rule of law. They absorbed the values of these institutions and instilled them in me.

Together, these values make up what is known as democratic capitalism, a system that is a proven success. It is not a matter of opinion, but a matter of economic fact, that everywhere there are free and competitive markets—combined with free enterprise, personal choice, voluntary exchange, civil society, and legal protection of person and property— you find broad and sustained prosperity and human advancement.

In free markets, millions of consumers, following their own self-interests and individual needs, make the decisions that direct the future. They don't have those decisions made for them. "Capitalism is the only economic/political system that allows individuals the freedom to think for themselves and rewards those who create the most productive ideas, products or services as determined by the actions of other productive people in purchasing those ideas, products or services."[5] For an emerging generation fascinated by crowdsourcing, free capital markets are the ultimate in crowdsourced decision making.

I have on my shelf a valuable volume titled *The Spirit of Democratic Capitalism*, by the theologian Michal Novak.[6] He argues that "of all the systems of political economy which have shaped our history, none has so revolutionized ordinary expectations of human life—lengthened the life span, made the elimination of poverty and famine thinkable, enlarged the range of human choice—as has democratic capitalism."[7]

Spirit of Democratic Regulation

It is worth borrowing Novak's title to propose an ethical approach to regulatory power over financial markets. That would be one based on these advanced economic, social, and political values. We should think of market regulation as something driven by more than just economics, but also by a set of moral counterweights aimed at balancing freedom and responsibility.

The first principle would be the Golden Rule. There is a reason, as C.S. Lewis observed, that the Golden Rule appears in every great civilization.[8] It is the foundation for civilization. Its absence is barbarism.

We should treat each other in the marketplace with the respect and regard we would want for ourselves—and with the business practices that we want for ourselves. That's how market regulators should treat market participants. It is how market participants should respond to appropriate regulation.

Next, democratic capitalism requires that regulators vigorously enforce the laws that protect market integrity. There must be no tolerance for fraud, deception, or manipulation in financial markets. Criminality abuses freedom for the personal gain of the few. Market integrity is essential to fostering robust trading and responsible risk taking. Enforcing the law is necessary to preserving economic freedom.

Third, there must be fairness. Regulators must not take sides, nor favor one set of market actors over another. They must not pick winners and losers. Regulators are not free agents or rogue actors, but must operate within the limits set by Congress. They must follow the law. They must be perceived as fair and just agents. They must have what is called "moral capital." Personal and institutional character matters.

Fourth, market regulation in the spirit of democratic capitalism respects the exercise of civil freedom, the foundation of our constitutional republic. We each have inalienable rights. Life, liberty, and the pursuit of happiness are about the freedom of the individual, and I believe that it is not just about moral and political freedom but also economic freedom. This is the "freedom of creative choice" that allows the individual to live a life and pursue work of his or her choosing, not chosen by government elites.

Accordingly, market regulators must not limit economic freedom without serious justification. In fact, regulators swear an oath to support and defend the US Constitution and the limitations on government power enshrined in the Bill of Rights. Accordingly, market regulators are duty bound to protect Constitutional freedoms and civil liberties, including economic and market activity.

That is why, as a general approach, good regulation must address demonstrable problems, not mere incidents of bad behavior; rely on solid evidence, not assumptions; represent an optimal approach among alternative courses of action; measure success through rigorous econometric analysis; and advance innovation and competition through flexible and technology-neutral rule frameworks.

There is no such thing as too much or too little regulation; those phrases are just political rhetoric. The 2008 financial crisis was not caused by too little regulation. More regulation would not have prevented it. It is not regulatory quantity that matters, but quality. There is only good regulation or bad regulation, well-calibrated regulation or poorly calibrated regulation. The question is always whether the regulation is actually effective in enhancing the environment being overseen.

Fifth, free markets facilitate exercise of our civil freedoms. Free markets should foster innovation, productivity, job creation, better health, and progress. But this freedom is not unlimited. It cannot be used to create monopolies, defraud others, manipulate markets, or engage in other actions that ultimately undermine free markets. Free markets must not be exploited in ways that can destroy free markets. That is where market regulators come in. In the spirit of democratic capitalism, the regulatory mission is to prevent such exploitation through well-developed market intelligence and carefully calibrated action.

The 2008 financial crisis posed a legitimate question: "Where were the regulators during the expansion of the credit bubble? Why didn't they pop the bubble when they could have?" There is no need to revisit the failures that led to the 2008 crisis. Yet, after that crisis, when the first significant asset bubble arose in 2017, the CFTC acted. And it acted in a way that was market centric. The CFTC did not suppress market activity in Bitcoin, as some market participants and central bankers would have had it do. Rather, the CFTC allowed the market to be broadened with more diversified investors—both long and short, retail and institutional. In so doing, the Bitcoin market self-balanced. It became a bit less fragile and more imperturbable to shocks. It became more *anti-fragile,* a concept of organic durability conceived by the market philosopher Nassim Taleb.[9] Bitcoin matured and thrived. Danger was averted. CFTC market regulation enhanced free markets; it did not suppress them.

Sixth, market regulation in the spirit of democratic capitalism encourages professionalism. Qualifications matter. Regulators must be prepared for their jobs. They must be knowledgeable with real-world experience—not just academic study—in the subject matter. At the same time, regulatory agencies like the CFTC must have funding adequate to recruit such qualified professionals to fulfill their missions. It is a matter of public trust.

We live in a polarized society where the mass media and the political class cheer on division. You may be surprised to hear a product of the private sector say this: I worked with many brilliant and talented people at the CFTC and elsewhere in the federal government. They are a credit to the nation. Too many mock government employees as underworked and overpaid and out of touch with the concerns of ordinary Americans. Well, I spent 30 years in the private sector and 5 in the federal government. Let me tell you, my CFTC colleagues served—and serve—this nation earnestly and well. They are professionals. They bring expertise, intelligence, and commitment to complex markets in the global economy. They are proof that American public service remains a noble calling, well worth a young person's consideration.

America's founders created a unique type of representative government—a participatory democracy. Unlike others, the US government was called into being by its citizenry, was limited in its powers to infringe on civil society, and yet welcomed the active participation of capable people in the conduct of public affairs. This participatory democracy was perfectly suited to the generations of determined immigrants who came to this country with their dreams and ambitions and, with hard work, perseverance, and determination, succeeded beyond their imaginings.

And so it is still to this day. America and its government—a participatory government—welcomes, indeed relies on and is strengthened by the contributions of an increasing diversity of everyday citizens who have something of value to share. Government service must not be restricted to persons from certain walks of life approved by politicians—such as academics, former Senate staffers or other existing politicians, as worthy as they are—and barred to those from commerce and industry. Government and regulation is made more responsive by private sector talent joining its ranks and, thereafter, returning to the private sector with appreciation for the challenges, responsibilities, and honor of public service.

Seventh, democratic capitalism treats individuals as important, by themselves and for themselves. In his writings, Mill sometimes talks about human "dignity." Markets should not exploit a worker or trader or participant. Human dignity must be protected, not overlooked, in our regulatory efforts. People matter. They are not numbers, categories, files, or social media accounts. Far too much of our saturated, online world dehumanizes us and takes away our dignity. In a world of almost 8 billion people, each one is a unique, singular person, and must be treated that way.

Human dignity encourages thinking and education, not propaganda or dogma. Regrettably, conformity, rather than intellectual diversity, is too often the state of today's pedagogical and journalistic institutions. Groupthink and fear of ridicule by the press and social elites impede regulatory modernization.

Intellectual conformity is anathema to democratic capitalism, healthy and dynamic markets, and the sound market regulation on which they depend. Regulators cannot be effective if they are fearful of political or media ridicule. Hyper partisanship, press attacks, and criminalizing of business behavior can breed cowed, conformist public officials. At times, the land of the free and the home of the brave appears more like the land of F.U.D. and the home of the afraid. Timidity and self-regard may cripple the United States in its efforts to confront the challenges of the digital future.

John Stuart Mill wrote:

> "Like other tyrannies, the tyranny of the majority was at first, and is still vulgarly, held in dread, chiefly as operating through the acts of the public authorities. But reflecting persons perceived that when society is itself the tyrant — society collectively, over the separate individuals who compose it — its means of tyrannizing are not restricted to the acts which it may do by the hands of its political functionaries."[10]

Instead of fretful conformity, we need courage. Democratic capitalism requires regulators with grit and the strength of their convictions. Sometimes poets and philosophers or simply outsiders like accidental regulators can see things that insiders miss. Today, I am concerned that the insiders are missing the fact that this new Internet of Value is much more than a new form of money—as exciting and transformational as that is—but may provide new frameworks to upgrade our antiquated financial system that I talked about at the beginning of this book, rendering it into a more inclusive, less costly, faster, and cheaper global system unlimited by time, social class, and centralized censorship. The insiders may believe that their first duty is to defend the existing financial system, protect incumbent institutions, preserve familiar ways of doing business, and shelter existing forms of regulation and political control of regulatory turf rather than to examine this new wave of the internet to see how it can improve the existing financial system to better serve humankind. Worse, they may look to avoid this opportunity because of a lack of respect for a new generation that has once again taken up the cry, "the times they are a changing"[11] with a new spirit of economic aspiration and financial freedom. A generation that has lost faith in the institutions of the old financial order and its purveyors is seeking a new and more open and durable system to build a brighter tomorrow.

Douglas Adams, author of *The Hitchhiker's Guide to the Galaxy*, said:

> "Anything that is in the world when you're born is normal and ordinary and is just a natural part of the way the world works. Anything that's invented between when you're fifteen and thirty-five is new and exciting and revolutionary and you can probably get a career in it. Anything invented after you're thirty-five is against the natural order of things."[12]

Whether the subject is crypto or the Digital Dollar, Adams's injunction seems to apply to a financial technology generation gap that today is as wide as the social and civil rights generation gap of 55 years ago.

It is time to transcend today's financial innovation generation gap. Throughout its history, the United States has been a world leader in technology development through public and private cooperation. Whether launching the space program or guiding the first wave of the Internet, the United States has launched bold technological endeavors reflecting long-standing American values of free enterprise, economic stability, technological innovation, individual liberty and privacy, and the rule of law. It is how America does big things.

It is time again to do big things. We must rebuild not only our physical infrastructure but our financial infrastructure using these new state-of-the-art tools and technologies. The Internet of Value is gaining momentum. We must take advantage of it. We must take a leadership role in this next era of digital innovation and do so with the values of a free society. Otherwise, the future of money will incorporate the anti-democratic values of our global competitors.

Free Markets and Free Peoples

Free market capitalism is not a source of misery and oppression; it is the antidote. It is unmatched in alleviating global poverty and unlocking human potential. Whatever the flaws and mistakes of market capitalism, they are best addressed through the free enterprise of daring and representative democracy.

The shortcomings of free markets are not fixed through government-run economies. In fact, whenever capital, goods, and services are allocated by government agencies, there are black markets and bread lines. Government-dominated markets always turn abundance into scarcity and inequality. Abandoning free markets devastates economies. It supplants equality of opportunity with equality of misery. During the twentieth century, approximately 70 million people perished from famine in countries with centrally planned food-procurement systems.[13] In our own times, these systems produce starvation and disease right before our eyes.[14]

Even European-style "social democracy"—beguiling to many American baby boomers—is a stifling polity. Unlike the vibrancy of capitalism, "Socialism is an insurance policy bought by all the members of a national economy to shield them from risk. But the result is to shield them from knowledge of the real dangers and opportunities in any economic environment. Rather than benefiting from a multiplicity of gifts and experiments, the entire economy absorbs the much greater risk of remaining static in a dynamic world."[15] With their high unemployment, slow growth, and sclerotic bureaucracy, social democracies fail to attract the world's keenest and most enterprising, who still harken to the hills of Silicon Valley, alleyways of Brooklyn, and rooftops of Miami Beach. It is no surprise that 5 of Europe's top 10 billionaires inherited fortunes earned long ago, while in America, 9 of the top 10 got rich solely from companies they founded and the hundreds of millions of jobs and careers created.[16]

We must disabuse our children of the notion that there is anything attractive or aspirational about political domination of commerce and human enterprise. Everywhere it has been tried, it has been a fraud and a failure. Socialism crushes human liberty and society. It steals power from individuals and families and gives it to government and government elites. It enables abuse by a select few who exercise unbridled power over many. For young people, politically driven economies are dream destroyers. Youth around the globe are ever in flight away from socialism toward free markets and free societies.

We must assert confidence in the value of free market capitalism. Free markets should be the natural choice of today's youth, who—today and always—aspire to bright and self-actualized futures.

This brings us full circle—back to the Golden Rule. We must see ourselves in each other, finding a mirror that reflects the soul. "Life is not just a succession of events or experiences. It is a search for the true, the good, and the beautiful."[17] Financial markets must be an arena where people can responsibly achieve their aspirations and further the social good. There must be honesty, integrity, and reliability in our dealings with others. For those who seek it, business and innovation must be a place to find satisfaction and spirituality in our work. It must make us better as family members, colleagues, citizens, businesspeople, market participants, and regulators. Aristotle felt that the regulation or polity, if moral, should ennoble us, make us better.[18] They are the foundation for a better tomorrow. The freedom to fearlessly pursue "our own good in our own way" is a gift from God.

A Future of Human Potential

My journey from the Palisades of New Jersey to the halls of Parliament and from Wall Street to the nation's capital has returned me to where I started: a quiet suburban home. I went to Washington to address problems of the past. I wound up facing challenges of the future. It is a future of digital things of value, including the most coveted thing of all: money.

I am certain that this digital future of money and finance is coming and coming fast. I know that it will lay bare the shortcomings of America's aged, analog financial infrastructure and its regulatory frameworks. It is already doing so. We must not fear it. We must harness it.

What I do not know is what the ultimate impact of this revolutionary change will be. Will this new Internet of Value decentralize things of value, in the way that Wikipedia has decentralized knowledge and information? Or will it do the opposite? Will it centralize things of value the way that social media purloins our personal data and manipulates our minds? If the latter vision prevails, governments and political elites may monitor and ultimately control the money we have and what we do with it, a means of overwhelmingly oppressive government power and a grimly static future.

Rather, we must take a stand for the future of human liberty. We must harness this wave of digital innovation—the Internet of Value—to advance greater financial inclusion, capital and financial freedom, and economic growth for generations to come. We must resist and counter-act those who would deploy this innovation for increased political control and surveillance. To make the right choice we must be bold, not fearful. Ultimately, the choice will be made by a free society of fearless people, philosophers and farmers, teachers and musicians, market regulators and market traders, men and women alike.

We must renew faith in the future for ourselves and our children. We must not be intimidated, but be confident. In so doing, we best encourage and reward the initiative, productivity, drive, and dreams of everyone on this planet . . . not just for elites in Washington, Brussels, and Basel, but for soybean growers in White Cloud, Kansas; dairy farmers in Melrose, Minnesota; or cotton producers in Bardwell, Texas; but also for commodity traders in Chicago, swap dealers in New York and London, and FinTech developers in Austin Texas, crypto entrepreneurs in Wyoming, and Bitcoin maximalists in Miami, and indeed for all people. We must do so for the sake of tomorrow's citizens here at home and abroad, in developed economies and developing ones.

With the proper balance of sound policy, regulatory oversight, private sector innovation, and, yes, a little bit of courage, new technologies and global trading methodologies will lead our markets to evolve in responsible ways. They will continue to grow the economy and create a future of untethered aspiration—one where creativity and economic expression is a social good in its own right and a source of human growth and advancement.

Postscript

August 8, 2021

As this book is going to print, the US Senate has just passed bipartisan bill to fund modernization of national infrastructure. The work would be paid for, in part, by $28 billion in taxes proposed to be raised from crypto transactions through broad tax information reporting obligations. The legislation inaptly sweeps up into its coverage a wide range of peripheral crypto servicers including software developers, hardware manufacturers, and miners.

Earlier, I said that in order to select the right regulatory framework for cryptocurrency, Congress will need to first identify the public policy to be achieved. It appears that Congress has now identified its first policy priority for crypto: taxing it. After decades of neglect of the nation's physical underpinnings, Congress now intends to upgrade America's physical infrastructure by, among other things, taxing and burdening its nascent crypto industry, an industry that likely offers solutions to America's similarly aged financial infrastructure. As it has so often, Congress appears to be mortgaging America's future to pay for political failures of the past.

Appendix
Remarks of CFTC Chairman

J. Christopher Giancarlo
To the ABA Derivatives and Futures Section Conference, Naples, Florida,
January 19, 2018

Introduction

Thank you. Good afternoon.

I'd like to recognize my fellow Commissioners Behnam and Quintenz, and the CFTC staff who are at this conference. They are formidable, knowledgeable public servants. I am proud to work with them. Their ideas enhance and enlarge any discussion. Dan Davis, Matt Kulkin, Jamie McDonald, Eric Pan, Vince McGonagle . . . all of you . . . thanks for your presence and participation.

And, I would like to thank the conference organizers for inviting me and putting on such a great program. It is also good to see so many fine colleagues, like Rita Molesworth, Ken Raisler, and so many others.

Ken reminded me that your annual search for the sun was very timely this year, given the temperatures elsewhere.

Members of the ABA Derivatives Section know each other well. It's a relatively small section, though larger than it used to be. Every year you meet together and assess the current state of derivatives. The potential of your meetings is evident, the results enormous. There is much power and influence here. In many ways, this meeting is the equivalent of the Fed's annual "Jackson Hole" meeting for derivatives lawyers.

I want to tap into that power and influence today.

As you know, before Dodd–Frank, the size and scope of this section was determined by the Commodity Exchange Act (CEA) regulatory jurisdiction being limited to exchange-traded derivatives. Your meetings before 2008 reflected this limitation.

However, with the passage of Title VII of Dodd–Frank and expanded Federal regulation of all derivatives—and with no initiative of any kind to repeal Title VII—the scope of issues to be considered, debated and sensibly addressed by this ABA section became more expansive, substantial and lasting.

Now, we need to move forward again, expanding our scope once again. This section must rise to the opportunity, attract the best and the brightest of the next generation of lawyers, and make further contributions to the jurisprudence of derivatives law and practice.

In fact, we meet at a time when the world is changing ever more rapidly, transforming, as the Internet and other exponential digital technologies are having an increasing impact on everything in the early twenty-first century from information transfer to retail shopping to personal communications.

It is no surprise that those technologies are having an equally transformative impact on US derivatives markets. They have altered trading, markets and the entire financial landscape with far ranging implications for capital formation and risk transfer. They include algo-based trading and automated data transfer, "big data" information analysis and interpretation, artificial intelligence driving dynamic trade execution, "smart" contracts valuing themselves and calculating payments in real-time, and distributed ledger technology, more commonly known as blockchain, that is challenging traditional market infrastructure.

In recent years, a number of these technologies have turned from several tributaries into one river, which recently became a surging torrent, a gulf stream. You can see it . . . read about it: virtual currencies.

Challenges and Opportunities of Virtual Currencies

In the waning months of 2017, virtual currencies, especially Bitcoin, took the world by storm. *The Wall Street Journal* estimates that Bitcoin's value increased 1,375% in 2017.[1] Stories about it and other virtual currencies moved rapidly from online chatter to the back pages of the financial press to the front pages of the national press to quarterly analysts' calls of bank CEOs and to White House press briefings.

They are sweeping us rapidly, day by day, hourly, into a new future. And that torrent is bumping up against some of the established frameworks of futures regulation, including the obligation of futures exchanges to ensure that virtual currency futures are not susceptible to manipulation, and of futures clearinghouses to ensure that such products are adequately risk managed.

That is why I wanted to speak with you. Virtual currencies demand the focused attention of this group. We cannot ignore them. This is not the time or place for denial or misunderstanding or personal preference. This is the time for recognition, reflection, and wisdom . . . a time to set the course for the future . . . navigating through new waters. Not tomorrow. Today.

In the past, this ABA section has produced some important and timely responses to changes in the derivatives market. And, we need you now. We need this section now.

Much interest in virtual currencies is driven by an emerging generation whose lives are increasingly lived in a global, interconnected, on-line world. It is a generation in which many would sooner invest in digital assets through their mobile phones than in corporate bonds through a stockbroker.

Among other things, the attraction of digital currency lies in the potential of an algorithmic, decentralized store of value, unit of account and medium of exchange that disintermediates the traditional banking system and its associated transaction fees and charges.[2] Further attraction lies in the enormous promise of distributed ledger technology that underpins many virtual currencies, including Bitcoin, a promise that has the attention of leaders of both governments and industry.

Supporters of virtual currency point to Bitcoin's innovative technological solution to the age-old "double spend" problem—which has always driven the need for a trusted, central authority to ensure that an entity is capable of, and does, engage in a valid transaction. Bitcoin replaces the central authority with a software rules-based, open consensus mechanism.[3] Indeed, an array of thoughtful business, technology, academic, and policy leaders have extrapolated some of the possible impacts that derive from such an innovation, including how market participants conduct transactions, transfer ownership, and power peer-to-peer economic systems.[4]

Yet, many of the virtues claimed for Bitcoin itself seem at present to be quite scant: it is fairly unstable as a store of value, highly volatile as a unit of account and relatively expensive as a medium of exchange. Critics argue that the current interest in Bitcoin is overblown and resembles a fever, even a mania. They have declared Bitcoin's heightened valuation to be a bubble similar to the famous "Tulip Bubble" of the seventeenth century.[5] They say that virtual currencies perform no socially useful function and, worse, can be used to support illicit activity.[6] Some assert that Bitcoin should be banned, as a few nations have done.[7]

There is clearly no shortage of opinions on virtual currencies such as Bitcoin. In fact, virtual currencies may be all things to all people: for some, potential riches, the next big thing, a technological revolution, and an exorable value proposition; for others, a fraud, a new form of temptation and allure, and a way to separate the unsuspecting from their money.

Whatever one's opinion, an objective perspective helps. As of the morning of January 16, the total value of all outstanding Bitcoin was about $200 billion based on a Bitcoin price of $12,000.[8] The total value of all outstanding virtual currencies was about $577 billion. The Bitcoin "market capitalization" is comparable to the stock market capitalization of a single "large cap" business, such as Intel or Citigroup (both around $200 billion). Because virtual currencies like Bitcoin are sometimes considered to be comparable to gold as an investment vehicle,[9] it is important to recognize that the total value of all the gold in the world is estimated by the World Gold Council to be about $8 trillion which continues to dwarf the virtual currency market size. Clearly, the column inches of press attention to virtual currency far surpasses its importance in today's global economy.

Yet, despite being a relatively small asset class, virtual currency presents both significant opportunities and challenges for regulators. The CFTC has alerted the public to the considerable risks of virtual currencies, such as Bitcoin. These include:

- **operational risks** of unregulated and unsupervised trading platforms;
- **cybersecurity risks** of hackable trading platforms and virtual currency wallets;
- **speculative risks** of extremely volatile price moves; and
- **fraud and manipulation risks** through traditional market abuses of pump and dump schemes, insider trading, false disclosure, Ponzi schemes and other forms of investor fraud and market manipulation.

Indeed, as a believer in America's free market economy and commercial and economic liberty, I am disinclined to set regulatory policy from personal value judgments as to the social utility of a lawful, emerging technology, however considerable the inherent risks. In fact, I agree with former CFTC commissioner and acting chair, Sheila Bair, who wrote recently specifically about Bitcoin that, "value—like beauty—is in the eye of the beholder."[10]

One thing is certain: ignoring virtual currency trading will not make it go away. Nor is it a responsible regulatory strategy. I also agree with Ms. Bair that, "instead of making value judgments about Bitcoin, what government should do is . . . . take steps to help ensure that the bitcoin price—wherever the market assigns it—is reflective of investors making informed decisions, free of fraud and manipulation . . . ."[11]

Federal Oversight of Virtual Currencies

As you well know, United States law does not provide for direct, comprehensive federal oversight of underlying Bitcoin or virtual currency spot markets. As a result, US regulation of virtual currencies has evolved into a multifaceted, multi-regulatory approach that includes:

- State banking regulators;
- The Internal Revenue Service (IRS);
- The Treasury's Financial Crimes Enforcement Network (FinCEN); and
- The Securities and Exchange Commission (SEC).

The CFTC also has an important role to play. And, we have not been idle. As early as 2014, my predecessor, Chairman Timothy Massad, discussed virtual currencies and potential CFTC oversight under the CEA.[12] Since then, the CFTC has:

- declared virtual currencies to be a commodity (2015)[13]
- enforced the laws prohibiting wash trading and prearranged trades of a virtual currency swap on a swap execution facility (2015);[14]
- taken action against unregistered Bitcoin futures exchanges (2016);[15]
- issued proposed guidance on what is a derivative market and what is a spot market in the virtual currency context (2017);[16]
- issued warnings about valuations and volatility in spot virtual currency markets (2017);[17] and
- taken enforcement action against a virtual currency Ponzi scheme (2017).[18]

Why has the CFTC acted? The CFTC believes that the responsible regulatory response to virtual currencies involves the following:

1. First, educating consumers. Over the past six months, the CFTC has produced an unprecedented amount of consumer information concerning virtual currencies, including the CFTC's Virtual Currency Primer,[19] its Bitcoin consumer advisory,[20] its market advisory,[21] its dedicated Bitcoin webpage,[22] its proposed guidance on what is a spot market in the virtual currency context,[23] and its weekly publication of Bitcoin futures "Commitment of Traders" data.[24]

2. Second, coordinating with other Federal regulators, especially the SEC, the Fed, and the Treasury through its recently formed virtual currency working group, but also, where appropriate, the FBI and the Justice Department.

3. Third, asserting CFTC legal authority over virtual currency derivatives in support of anti-fraud and manipulation enforcement, including in underlying spot markets.

4. Fourth, increasing regulatory visibility into markets for virtual currency derivatives and underlying settlement reference rates through the gathering of trade and counterparty data.

5. Fifth, prosecuting perpetrators of fraud, abuse, manipulation or false solicitation in markets for virtual currency derivatives and underlying spot trading.

In the past several days the CFTC has filed a series of civil enforcement actions against perpetrators of fraud and market abuse involving virtual currency. These actions and others to follow confirm that the CFTC, working closely with the SEC and other fellow financial enforcement agencies, will aggressively prosecute those who engage in fraud and manipulation of US markets for virtual currency.

Virtual Currency Products: A Review and Compliance Checklist

The CFTC's five objectives respond to the surging tide of global interest in virtual currency. Yet, that surging tide has also brought with it the world's first Bitcoin futures products.

Much has been written in the press about the CFTC's approach to the launch of Bitcoin futures, so a little perspective is also in order. The Bitcoin futures markets are relatively small with open interest at the CME of 6,290 Bitcoin[25] and at Cboe Futures Exchange (CFE) of 4,901 Bitcoin (as of Jan. 12, 2018). At a price of approximately $12,000 per Bitcoin,[26] this represents a notional amount of about $135 million. In comparison, the notional amount of the open interest in CME's WTI crude oil futures was more than one thousand times greater, about $170 billion (2,640,000 contracts) as of Jan. 12, 2018 and the notional amount represented by the open interest of Comex gold futures was about $75 billion (575,000 contracts).

Recently, CFTC staff undertook its review of CME and CFE's Bitcoin futures products with great care and thoughtfulness. The uniqueness of these products impelled staff to carefully consider CME's and CFE's responsibility under the CEA and Commission regulations to ensure that their Bitcoin futures products and their cash-settlement process are not readily susceptible to manipulation,[27] and the risk management of the associated Derivatives Clearing Organizations (DCOs) to ensure that the products are sufficiently margined.[28]

In this regard, the staff obtained the voluntary cooperation of CME and CFE with a set of steps that is unprecedented in scope. It includes seven elements:

1. Designated contract markets (DCMs) setting exchange large trader reporting thresholds at five Bitcoins or less;
2. DCMs entering direct or indirect information sharing agreements with spot market platforms to allow access to trade and trader data;
3. DCMs agreeing to engage in monitoring of price settlement data from cash markets and identifying anomalies and dispropor-tionate moves;
4. DCMs agreeing to conduct inquiries, including at the trade settle-ment and trader level when anomalies or disproportionate moves are identified;
5. DCMs agreeing to regular communication with CFTC surveillance staff on trade activities, including providing trade settlement and trader data upon request;
6. DCMs agreeing to coordinate product launches to enable the CFTC's market surveillance branch to monitor minute-by-minute developments; and
7. DCOs setting substantially high initial[29] and maintenance margin for cash-settled instruments.

The first six of these elements were employed to determine that the new product offering complies with the DCM's obligations under the CEA core principles and CFTC regulations and related guidance, including ensuring that a product is not readily susceptible to manipula-tion and monitoring the cash-settlement process under the staff's "heightened review" process for virtual currencies. The seventh element, setting high initial and maintenance margins, was designed to ensure adequate collateral coverage in reaction to the underlying volatility of Bitcoin.

In crafting its process of "heightened review" for compliance with core principles, CFTC staff prioritized visibility and monitoring of markets for Bitcoin derivatives and underlying settlement reference rates. Staff felt that in gaining such visibility, the CFTC could best look out for Bitcoin market participants and consumers as well as the public interest in Federal surveillance and enforcement. This visibility greatly enhances the agency's ability to prosecute fraud and manipulation in both the new Bitcoin futures markets and in its underlying cash markets.

As for the interests of clearing members, the CFTC recognized that major global banks and brokerages that are DCO clearing members are able to look after their own commercial interests by choosing not to trade Bitcoin futures (as some have done), requiring substantially higher initial margins from their customers (as many have done), and through their active participation in DCO risk committees.[30]

The CFTC has received some criticism from large market participants for not holding public hearings prior to self-certification of Bitcoin futures.[31] Yet, unlike the rule self-certification process, there is no provision in statute for public input into CFTC staff review of new product self-certifications. Neither statute nor rule would have prevented CME and CFE from launching their new products before public hearings could have been called.

Nevertheless, staff is attentive to concerns raised by a few clearing members of at least one of the associated DCOs of the self-certifying DCMs of a lack of consultation and input before the DCOs began clearing these Bitcoin futures contracts.

I do believe it is right that interested parties, especially clearing members, have an opportunity to raise appropriate concerns for consideration by regulated platforms proposing virtual currency derivatives and DCOs considering clearing new virtual currency products. This is especially so because of the nascent state of the underlying virtual currency markets and the unique challenges posed by this emerging asset class.

Therefore, I have recently asked CFTC staff to add an additional, eighth element to its review checklist. For all reviews of new virtual currency derivatives, DCMs and SEFs will be asked to disclose to the CFTC what steps they have taken in their capacity as self-regulatory organizations to gather and accommodate appropriate input from concerned parties, including trading firms and FCMs. Further, I have asked staff to take a close look at DCO governance around the clearing of new products and to consider recommendations for possible further action.

Next Steps

Although there is ready legal support in statute and CFTC regulation for many of the elements of the virtual currency review checklist, the staff will continue to work with exchanges on a voluntary basis at present. Nevertheless, it is worth discussing specific rule changes to accommodate the virtual currency review checklist in its own right.

I have asked the CFTC's General Counsel to be prepared to discuss with members of the Commission the statutory support for codifying the various elements of the review checklist. I have also asked him to propose for Commission consideration possible regulatory and/or statutory steps to better support the staff's approach to virtual currency product review.

Some press reports concerning Bitcoin futures would suggest that the issue is about the overall process of product self-certification. While I am neither an apologist nor opponent, but rather an inheritor, of the current process of self-certification, I do feel that these reports miss the point. As explained, I believe the real issues are: (a) whether a DCM's responsibility under the CEA and Commission regulations to ensure that virtual currency derivatives are not readily susceptible to manipulation is sufficiently robust given the nascent state of this emerging asset class and (b) whether a DCO has fulfilled its responsibility under the CEA and Commission regulations to ensure that virtual currency derivatives are sufficiently margined.

Nevertheless, I do want to make a brief comment on the CFTC's product self-certification process. As some of the longer-serving members of this section know, Congress and prior Commissions deliberately designed the product self-certification framework to give DCMs, in their role as self-regulatory organizations, the ability to design and certify new products. Congress framed the self-certification process deliberately so that development of new and innovative derivatives products would not be hampered by cautious regulators conscious of the political risks of approving new products. The CFTC's current product self-certification framework is consistent with public policy that encourages market-driven innovation that has made America's listed futures markets the envy of the world. Whatever the market impact of Bitcoin futures, I hope it is not to compromise the product self-certification process that has served so well for so long.

The Choice

I believe that the CFTC's response to the spectacular rise of virtual currencies has been a balanced one. Doing nothing would have been irresponsible. Had it even been possible under law or regulation, blocking these new futures products would not have stopped the rise of Bitcoin or other virtual currencies. Instead, it would have ensured that the virtual currency cash markets continue to operate without federal regulatory surveillance for fraud and manipulation.

Conclusion

History has placed us in this moment in time. New uses of technology, such as virtual currencies, expand our horizons and introduce new ways of thinking, new temptations, new risks, and new opportunities.

But, as with all new ideas, there may be—indeed, there will be—surprises and challenges. Predictions of certain boom or definite bust are common and of little value. It is more complicated than that.

I started this speech by asking for your input and comment. I will end on the same note. Thanks to Commissioners Quintenz and Benham and their advisory committees, we have the chance for input and feedback.

We turn to you. Circumstances have placed your subject area in the crossing currents of technology, economics, law, and regulation. This is a time to increase your visibility, your engagement, and your action. This is your time to step forward.

This is a moment for the section's best work, to rise to a significant challenge, perhaps some of the most significant challenges of a lifetime. We need to attract the best and the brightest to the field, through example, guidance, placement and reward.

We need more conversations, more writing, and a more robust flow of ideas. We need visionary thinking, best practices, and creative intellectual products.

And we need this intellectual power not just to meet the challenge of virtual currency and complex cross border rule compatibility. We need it to meet the broader challenge of furthering sound and efficient regulation of global financial markets essential for economic growth and prosperity at a time of transformational digital technologies and complex international regulatory geo-politics.

As this moment in history reveals itself, we need to be ready and even pro-active, anticipating events and ready for the unexpected. We are being propelled into a future that is unknown, a future that requires more expertise, more thoughtfulness, more creativity and more commitment.

In short, a future that needs more of you.

Thank you.

Notes

Introduction

1. Chris Giancarlo & Ken Hasimoto, "Looking for a Road," unpublished song lyrics, 1975.
2. For thoughtful discussions of the Internet of Value, see: Tapscott, Don, Tapscott Alex, "Blockchain Revolution: How the Technology Behind Bitcoin and Other Cryptocurrencies is Changing the World," Portfolio Penguin (January 1, 2018) and Casey, Michael J and Vigna Paul, "The Truth Machine: The Blockchain and the Future of Everything," St. Martin's Press (February 27, 2018).
3. Conventionally, the word "Bitcoin" is often capitalized when referring to the cryptocurrency as a concept, but lower-cased when referring to its individual tokens, or units of value. Since I will discuss Bitcoin as a concept, I will always use the upper case form in this book.
4. Mr. Smith Goes to Washington is a 1939 political comedy-drama film directed by Frank Capra starring Jean Arthur and James Stewart about a newly-appointed and naive US Senator who fights to reform a tainted political system.

Chapter 1

1. The Dodd–Frank Wall Street Reform and Consumer Protection Act (Pub.L. 111–203, H.R. 4173, commonly referred to as Dodd–Frank) was signed into US federal law by US President Barack Obama on July 21, 2010. It was the largest revamp of the US financial regulatory framework since the Depression, affecting all federal financial regulatory agencies and almost every part of the nation's financial services industry. Among other mandates, Dodd–Frank substantially expanded the jurisdiction of the Commodity Futures Trading Commission (CFTC) to regulate over-the-counter derivatives.
2. Robert J. Shiller, *Finance and the Good Society* (Princeton University Press, 2012), 76.
3. Leo Melamed is an American attorney, finance executive, and Chairman Emeritus of the CME Group who pioneered numerous financial instruments, including futures on US Treasury bills, Eurodollars, and stock index futures. See, generally, *Leo Melamed, Man of the Futures: The Story of Leo Melamed & the Birth of Modern Finance* (Harriman House, 2021).

4. Richard L. Sandor is an American businessman, economist, entrepreneur, and Chairman and CEO of the American Financial Exchange who pioneered interest rate futures. He also founded the world's first exchange to facilitate the reduction and trading of greenhouse gasses, earning the title "father of carbon trading." See *Good Derivatives: A Story of Financial and Environmental Innovation* (Wiley, 2012).

5. Anatoli Kupriyanov, *2009 ISDA Derivatives Usage Survey*, International Swaps and Derivatives Association (ISDA) Research Notes, No. 2 (Spring 2009), 1–5 available at https://www.isda .org/a/SSiDE/isda-research-notes2.pdf

6. The Milken Institute found the following economic benefits to the US economy from derivatives: "[b]anks' use of derivatives, by permitting greater extension of credit to the private sector, increased U.S. quarterly real GDP by about $2.7 billion each quarter from Q1 2003 to Q3 2012; [d]erivatives use by non-financial firms increased U.S. quarterly real GDP by about $1 billion during the same period by improving their ability to undertake capital investments; [c] ombined, derivatives expanded U.S. real GDP by about $3.7 billion each quarter; [t]he total increase in economic activity was 1.1 percent ($149.5 billion) between 2003 and 2012; [b]y the end of 2012, employment had been boosted by 530,400 (0.6 percent) and industrial production 2.1 percent." *See* Apanard Prabha et al., "Deriving the Economic Impact of Derivatives," Milken Institute (Mar. 2014), 1, available at http://assets1b.milkeninstitute.org/assets/Publication/ ResearchReport/PDF/Derivatives-Report.pdf

7. For a practical view of the role of derivatives products in everyday life, see: Dawn Stump, "Maybe Mom's Job Is Cool After All: Derivatives Get a Bad Rap, but They Keep Hamburgers Affordable," Roll Call, March 8, 2021, available at https://www.rollcall.com/2021/03/08/maybe-moms-job-is-cool-after-all/

8. Food and Agriculture Organization of the United Nations, International Fund for Agricultural Development, World Food Programme, "The State of Food Insecurity in the World 2014: Strengthening the Enabling Environment for Food Security and Nutrition," 2014, available at http://www.fao.org/publications/card/en/c/56efd1a2-0f6e-4185-8005-62170e9b27bb/

9. United States Census Bureau, International Data Base World Population: 1950–2050, available at http://www.census.gov/population/international/data/idb/worldpopgraph.php

10. David Pilling, "The Real Price of Madagascar's Vanilla Boom," *The Financial Times* (June 5, 2018), illustrating how the absence of a functioning market for vanilla futures was producing a cycle of boom and bust in Madagascar's vanilla crop, exacerbating poverty and violent gang activity on the African island. Available at https://www.ft.com/content/02042190-65bc-11e8-90c2-9563a0613e56

11. The Cosmos Club, founded in 1878, is a Washington social club distinguished in science, literature and the arts, a learned profession, or public service. Members come from virtually every profession that has anything to do with scholarship, creative genius, or intellectual distinction. Among its members have been three presidents, two vice presidents, a dozen Supreme Court justices, 36 Nobel Prize winners, 61 Pulitzer Prize winners and 55 recipients of the Presidential Medal of Freedom.

12. The most notable and perhaps most important CFTC commissioner to advocate for reform of swaps markets was former Chair Brooksley Born (in office: August 26, 1996–June 1, 1999), who called on Congress and the Clinton administration to authorize the CFTC to regulate over-the-counter swaps and who resigned as chair as a matter of principle when those calls were rejected.

13. Reporting, clearing, exchange trading, price discovery, and transparency have been the hallmarks of the (well-regulated) futures industry for over 100 years.

14. It is estimated that following the 2008 Financial Crisis, minimum global clearing rates were about 40% for interest rate swaps and 8% for credit default swaps. By 2017, about 85% both of new interest rate swaps and new credit default swaps were being cleared. See generally, CFTC

Chairman J. Christopher Giancarlo, "Cross Border Swaps Regulation Version 2.0: A Risk-Based Approach with Deference to Comparable Non-US Regulation" at https://www.cftc.gov/sites/default/files/2018-04/oce_chairman_swapregversion2whitepaper_042618.pdf

15. Giancarlo, Cross Border Swaps Regulation Version 2.0.
16. See Commissioner J. Christopher Giancarlo, "Pro-Reform Reconsideration of the CFTC Swaps Trading Rules: Return to Dodd–Frank" (Jan. 29, 2015), available at https://www.cftc.gov/sites/default/files/idc/groups/public/@newsroom/documents/file/sefwhitepaper012915.pdf (Hereinafter, "Giancarlo, Pro-Reform Reconsideration.")
17. Giancarlo, "Pro-Reform Reconsideration"
18. Giancarlo, "Pro-Reform Reconsideration"
19. J. Christopher Giancarlo, "Flawed US Rules Fragment Swaps Market: Avoiding US Rules Is Now the Driving Force in Global Swaps Market," Comment, *Financial Times* (November 10, 2014), available at https://www.ft.com/content/e70bbdfc-666f-11e4-8bf6-00144feabdc0
20. Katy Burne, "CFTC's Giancarlo: New Rules Divide Swaps Market: Rules Threaten Wall Street Jobs and Could Destablize Financial Markets, He Says," *Wall Street Journal*, (November 11, 2014) at https://www.wsj.com/articles/cftcs-giancarlo-says-new-rules-are-dividing-swaps-market-1415744134
21. For insight into Gary Cohn's remarkable personal story, see generally: Malcolm Gladwell, *David and Goliath: Underdogs, Misfits, and the Art of Battling Giants* (Little Brown, 2013).

Chapter 2

1. eSecurities, *Trading and Regulation on the Internet* (American Lawyer Media, Published September 1998 - January 2003).
2. He is suspected by some to be the alter ego of the celebrated British recording artist Mike Marlin. See https://en.wikipedia.org/wiki/Mike_Marlin
3. "The Great Recession was made possible by the mobilization of most of the governments and associated banks of East and West in a mad rush to pump money into securitized mortgages on the margins of the middle class and below. Inequality in a top-heavy, slow growing economy inspired a drive to substitute credit for real income and wealth. The result was a huge overhang of debt in the middle class and a swelling of assets at the top." George Gilder, *The Scandal of Money: Why Wall Street Recovers but the Economy Does Not* (Washington, DC: Regnery Publishing, 2016), 90–91.
4. See, www.wmbaa.org
5. Micah Green had previously served as president and co-CEO of the Securities Industry and Financial Markets Association (SIFMA), which was formed by a merger between The Bond Market Association and the Securities Industry Association. Today, he is a partner in the distinguished law firm of Steptoe & Johnson.
6. Many restaurants use the "Delmonico's" name. The original and, I believe, the best is at 56 Beaver Street in lower Manhattan where it has been since the nineteenth century. That restaurant introduced the concept of fine dining to America and is said to have created such dishes as Delmonico steak, Chicken à la King, Eggs Benedict, Lobster Newberg, and Baked Alaska.

Chapter 3

1. US Federal oversight of commodity futures began in 1922 with the Grain Futures Act and was reinforced with the 1936 Commodity Exchange Act.
2. Commodity Exchange Act (ch. 545, 49 Stat. 1491, enacted June 15, 1936).
3. Steven Lofchie, "CFTC Commissioner Giancarlo Calls for Progress on Swaps Trading Rules," Commentary, *Cadwalader Cabinet* (August 4, 2015), available at https://www.findknowdo.com/news/08/04/2015/cftc-commissioner-giancarlo-calls-progress-swaps-trading-rules

4. Mike Kentz, "Swap Auctions Gain CFTC Favour: Regulator Gives in to Controversial Broker Execution Protocols," *IFR* (August 8, 2015), available at http://www.finregalert.com/swap-auctions-gain-cftc-favour/

5. It was the place "where the music died," in the words of singer Don McLean from his classic anthem, "American Pie."

6. See generally, Statement of Commissioner J. Christopher Giancarlo on Proposed Rule for Position Limits for Derivatives, December 5, 2016, available at https://www.cftc.gov/PressRoom/SpeechesTestimony/giancarlostatement120516

7. "The New Mediocre Is Not Good Enough," Keynote Address of the Author Before the Cato Summit on Financial Regulation (June 2, 2015), available at https://www.cftc.gov/PressRoom/SpeechesTestimony/opagiancarlos-7#P36_9523, henceforth, "Giancarlo, "The New Mediocre."

8. Labor Force Participation Rates, US Department of Labor, Bureau of Labor Statistics, http://data.bls.gov/timeseries/LNU01300000 (last visited Jun. 1, 2015).

9. Richard Fry, "A Rising Share of Young Adults Live in Their Parents' Home," Pew Research Center (Aug. 1, 2013), available at http://www.pewsocialtrends.org/2013/08/01/a-rising-share-of-young-adults-live-in-their-parents-home/

10. News Release, "Employment Characteristics of Families—2014," US Department of Labor, Bureau of Labor Statistics (Apr. 23, 2015), available at http://www.bls.gov/news.release/pdf/famee.pdf.

11. W. Mark Crain and Nicole V. Crain, "The Cost of Federal Regulation to the U.S. Economy, Manufacturing and Small Business," National Association of Manufacturers, (Sept. 10, 2014), 1, available at http://www.nam.org/Data-and-Reports/Cost-of-Federal-Regulations/Federal-Regulation-Full-Study.pdf

12. Crain and Crain, "The Cost of Federal Regulations."

13. Crain and Crain, "The Cost of Federal Regulations."

14. "Follow Up Report: Review of the Commodity Futures Trading Commission's Response to Allegations Pertaining to the Office of the Chief Economist," CFTC (January 13, 2016), posted to the CFTC website on February 18, 2016, at https://www.cftc.gov/sites/default/files/idc/groups/public/@aboutcftc/documents/file/oig_oce011316.pdf

Chapter 4

1. IOSCO is an association of over 100 national regulatory organizations that oversee the world's securities and futures markets. IOSCO's mandate is to: (a) develop, implement, and promote high standards of regulation to enhance investor protection and reduce systemic risk; (b) share information with exchanges and assist them with technical and operational issues and (c) establish standards toward monitoring global investment transactions across borders and markets. IOSCO's headquarters is in Madrid, Spain. https://www.iosco.org

2. James Rickards, *The Death of Money: The Coming Collapse of the International Monetary System* (New York: Portfolio, 2014), 19–28. Rickards posits that Osama Bin Laden anticipated widespread panic and value destruction in US financial markets following the World Trade Center attacks to the extent that his cadre of operatives probably shorted the stocks of US air transportation companies to benefit from their inside knowledge of the coming attack.

3. Journalist Gillian Tett has insightfully examined why people working in modern institutions collectively act in ways that blind them to both risks and opportunities. Gillian Tett, *The Silo Effect* (New York: Simon and Schuster, 2015).

4. See generally, "Sharp Price Movements in Commodity Futures Markets: A Report," Market Intelligence Branch, Division of Market Oversight, Commodity Futures Trading Commission, (June 2018), available at https://www.cftc.gov/sites/default/files/2018-06/SharpPriceMovementsReport0618.pdf

5. Tommy Stubbington, "Banks Turn to Blockchains to Reform Costly Bond Market," *Financial Times* (July 1, 2021), available at https://www.ft.com/content/8b1005ed-5d70-4a31-b577-6c7f1f507c60

6. For a fascinating exploration of the possible range of DLT uses, see generally, William Mougayar, *The Business Blockchain* (Hoboken: Wiley) 2016.
7. J. Christopher Giancarlo, "Special Address Before the Depository Trust & Clearing Corporation 2016 Blockchain Symposium," March 29, 2016, available at https://www.cftc.gov/PressRoom/SpeechesTestimony/opagiancarlo-13
8. Leo Melamed, *Man of the Futures*, 179.
9. J. Christopher Giancarlo, "21st Century Markets Need 21st Century Regulation," Address to the American Enterprise Institute, September 21, 2016, available at https://www.cftc.gov/PressRoom/SpeechesTestimony/opagiancarlo-17
10. Giancarlo, "The New Mediocre."
11. "Gross Domestic Product, Percent Change from Preceding Period," US Department of Commerce, Bureau of Economic Analysis, available at https://www.bea.gov/national/xls/gdpchg.xls (last visited Jun. 1, 2015).
12. Crain and Crain, "The Cost of Federal Regulations."
13. Crain and Crain, "The Cost of Federal Regulations."
14. Ernst & Young, "UK Fintech: On the Cutting Edge," 2016, 7 (Commissioned by H.M. Treasury) available at http://www.ey.com/Publication/vwLUAssets/EY-UK-Fintech-On-the-cutting-edge-Executive-summary/$FILE/EY-UK-Fintech-On-the-cutting-edge-exec-summary.pdf.
15. Ernst & Young, "UK Fintech: On the Cutting Edge," 51, note 18.

Chapter 5

1. Daniel James Brown, *The Boys in the Boat: Nine Americans and Their Epic Quest for Gold at the 1936 Berlin Olympics* (New York: Penguin Books, 2014).
2. See "Statement of Commissioner J. Christopher Giancarlo on the Implementation Date for Margin on Uncleared Swaps," (August 31, 2016), available at https://www.cftc.gov/PressRoom/SpeechesTestimony/giancarlostatement083116
3. See "CFTC Charges MF Global Inc., MF Global Holdings Ltd., Former CEO Jon S. Corzine and Former Employee Edith O'Brien for MF Global's Unlawful Misuse of Nearly One Billion Dollars of Customer Funds and Related Violations," CFTC Release Number 6626-13 (June 27, 2013), available at https://www.cftc.gov/PressRoom/PressReleases/6626-13
4. Consent Order for Permanent Injunction, Civil Monetary Penalty and Other Equitable Relief Against Defendant Jon S. Corzine, Civil Action No. 11=cv-7866, United States District Court Southern District of New York (January 4, 2017), available at https://www.cftc.gov/sites/default/files/idc/groups/public/@lrenforcementactions/documents/legalpleading/enfcorzineorder010517.pdf
5. Consent Order for Permanent Injunction, Civil Monetary Penalty and Other Equitable Relief Against Defendant Jon S. Corzine.
6. Hester Peirce and Benjamin Klutsey (eds.), Reframing Financial Regulation: Enhancing Stability and Protecting Consumers (Mercatus Center, George Washington University: 2016), available at https://www.mercatus.org/publications/financial-markets/reframing-financial-regulation
7. South Dakota's Iron Mountain Road features 314 curves, 14 switchbacks, 3 pigtails, and 3 tunnels.
8. Italy's Strada Statale 163 is famous for its hairpin bends, zigzags, and amazing views over the Tyrrhenian Sea.

Chapter 6

1. Opinion: "Another Last-Minute Regulation: The Feds Want to Seize Trade Secrets Without Due Process," *Wall Street Journal*, November 7, 2016, available at https://www.wsj.com/articles/another-last-minute-regulation-1478563886
2. Britannica, "Leadership in War of Abraham Lincoln," available at https://www.britannica.com/biography/Abraham-Lincoln/Leadership-in-war

3. Also known as the "Pareto principle" after Italian economist Vilfredo Pareto, who in 1895 postulated that for many phenomena 80% of the result comes from 20% of the effort, including in business where it is often said that 80% of output is generated 20% of the staff.

4. Remarks of Acting Chairman J. Christopher Giancarlo before the 11th Annual Capital Markets Summit: Financing American Business, US Chamber of Commerce, "Transforming the CFTC," (March 3, 2017), available at https://www.cftc.gov/PressRoom/SpeechesTestimony/opagiancarlo-21

5. Norm Champ, Going Public: My Adventures Inside the SEC and How to Prevent the Next Devastating Crisis (New York: McGraw-Hill, 2017).

6. The Risk Desk (Scudder Publications), July 28, 2017.

7. Established in 1789, Durrants Hotel is one of the last remaining privately owned hotels in London. www/durrantshotel.co.uk

8. The Risk Desk, October 17, 2021, Scudder Publications.

9. Open Letter: "Response to Vatican Bollettino, 'Oeconomicae et Pecuniariae Quaestiones,'" CFTC website, Washington, DC, (Jul. 21, 2018), available at https://www.cftc.gov/pressroom/speechestestimony/giancarloresponsetobollettino072118

10. "CFTC Summary of Performance and Financial Information, Fiscal Year 2016," available at https://www.cftc.gov/sites/default/files/reports/summary/2016/index.htm

11. Richard Hill, Market Intel at Heart of CFTC Reorganization, Lawyers Say, Bloomberg BNA, March 27, 2017, available at http://www.finregalert.com/market-intel-at-heart-of-cftc-reorganization-lawyers-say/

12. In 2017, we used one of those monthly market review "deep dives" to learn about the process of Bitcoin "mining."

13. US Department of the Treasury, "Financial Stability Oversight Council," available at https://home.treasury.gov/policy-issues/financial-markets-financial-institutions-and-fiscal-service/fsoc

14. Since its creation in 2017, LabCFTC has published educational primers on Digital Assets, Virtual Currencies, Smart Contracts and Artificial Intelligence in Financial Markets, see: https://www.cftc.gov/LabCFTC/Primers/index.htm

15. "Registration Open for CFTC First Fintech Conference" (September 10, 2018), available at https://www.cftc.gov/PressRoom/PressReleases/7782-18

16. Fintech Cooperation Arrangements provide a framework for regulatory cooperation, data sharing and referrals, see generally: https://www.cftc.gov/LabCFTC/FinTechCoopArrangements/index.htm

17. Andrew Ackerman, "Trump Nominates J. Christopher Giancarlo as CFTC Chairman, Wall Street Journal (March 14, 2017), available at https://www.wsj.com/articles/trump-nominates-j-christopher-giancarlo-as-cftc-chairman-1489538771

18. Committee on Agriculture, Nutrition, and Forestry, United States Senate, Nomination of J. Christopher Giancarlo of New Jersey to be Chairman, Commodity Futures Trading Commission (June 22, 2017), available at https://www.agriculture.senate.gov/imo/media/doc/Nomination%20of%20Giancarlo.pdf

Chapter 7

1. See generally: "A CFTC Primer on Virtual Currencies," October 17, 2017, available at https://www.cftc.gov/sites/default/files/idc/groups/public/documents/file/labcftc_primercurrencies100417.pdf

2. According to Coinmarketcap as of June 30, 2021, available at https://coinmarketcap.com/charts/

3. See generally, Coinbase, "Where Can I Spend Bitcoin?" available at https://help.coinbase.com/en/coinbase/getting-started/crypto-education/where-can-i-spend-Bitcoin

4. Available at https://bitcoin.org/bitcoin.pdf

5. Paul Veradittkat, "A Different View on Bitcoin's Energy Consumption," TabbForum (May 17, 2021), available at https://www.linkedin.com/pulse/different-view-bitcoins-energy-consumption-paul-veradittakit/

6. Marcus Lu, "Visualizing the Power Consumption of Bitcoin Mining," *Visual Capitalist* (April 20, 2021), available at https://www.visualcapitalist.com/visualizing-the-power-consumption-of-Bitcoin-mining/

7. Marcus Lu, "Visualizing the Power Consumption of Bitcoin Mining."

8. Marcus Lu, "Visualizing the Power Consumption of Bitcoin Mining."

9. Steven Zheng, "CoinShares Report: Renewable Energy Accounts for 77.6% of Total Bitcoin's Energy Usage," November 30, 2018, at: https://www.theblockcrypto.com/daily/4271/coinshares-report-renewable-energy-accounts-for-77-6-of-total-bitcoins-energy-usage

10. TQ Tezos, "*Proof of Work vs. Proof of Stake: the Ecological Footprint,*" Medium.com (March 16, 2021), available at https://medium.com/tqtezos/proof-of-work-vs-proof-of-stake-the-ecological-footprint-c58029faee44

11. Yvonne Lau, "Ethereum Founder Vitalik Buterin Says Long-Awaited Shift to 'Proof-of-Stake' Could Solve Environmental Woes," *Fortune* (May 27, 2021, available at https://fortune.com/2021/05/27/ethereum-founder-vitalik-buterin-proof-of-stake-environment-carbon/

12. See generally, David Adler, "Silk Road: The Dark Side of Cryptocurrency," *Fordham Journal of Corporate and Financial Law* (February 21, 2018), available at https://news.law.fordham.edu/jcfl/2018/02/21/silk-road-the-dark-side-of-cryptocurrency/

13. Emily Flitter, "FBI Shuts Alleged Online Drug Marketplace, Silk Road," *Reuters* (October 2, 2013), available at https://www.reuters.com/article/us-crime-silkroad-raid/fbi-shuts-alleged-online-drug-marketplace-silk-road-idUSBRE9910TR20131002

14. Danny Nelson, "Silk Road Programmer Pleads Guilty to Making False Statements," CoinDesk (September 21, 2020), available at https://www.coindesk.com/michael-weigand-silk-road

15. Gemini is the third sign in the zodiac and originates from the Latin word for "twins."

16. I was especially influenced by Casey, Michael and Vigna, Paul, "The Age of Cryptocurrency: How Bitcoin and Digital Money Are Challenging the Global Economic Order," (St. Martin's Press, New York, 2015)

17. "CFTC Orders Bitcoin Options Trading Platform Operator and Its CEO to Cease Illegally Offering Bitcoin Options and to Cease Operating a Facility for Trading or Processing of Swaps without Registering," CFTC press release (September 17, 2015), available at https://www.cftc.gov/PressRoom/PressReleases/7231-15

18. David Siegel, "Understanding the DAO Attack," CoinDesk (June 25, 2016), available at https://www.coindesk.com/understanding-dao-hack-journalists

19. "CME and Crypto Facilities Announce Bitcoin Reference Rate and Index," Markets Media (May 2, 2016), available at https://www.marketsmedia.com/cme-crypto-facilities-announce-bitcoin-reference-rate-index/

20. "CFTC Orders Bitcoin Exchange Bitfinex to Pay $75,000 for Offering Illegal Off-Exchange Finance Regtail Commodity Transactions and Failing to Register as a Futures Commission Merchant," CFTC press release (June 2, 2016), available at https://www.cftc.gov/PressRoom/PressReleases/7380-16

21. "CFTC Orders Bitcoin Exchange Bitfinex to Pay $75,000."

22. In February 1996 Congress recognized that "the Internet . . . ha[d] flourished, to the benefit of all Americans, with a minimum of government regulation" and thus sought to ensure that Internet-access services would remain "unfettered by Federal or State regulation." The Telecommunications Act of 1996 together with the ensuing Clinton administration "Framework for Global Electronic Commerce" are well recognized as the enlightened regulatory underpinning of the Internet that brought about profound changes to human society.

23. Telecommunications Act of 1996.

24. CBOE, owned by CBOE Global Markets, is the largest US options exchange offering options on over 2,200 companies, 22 stock indicies, and 140 exchange-traded funds (ETFs). www.cboe.com

25. Prior to the changes made in the Commodity Futures Modernization Act of 2000 (CFMA) and the Commission's subsequent addition of Part 40, exchanges submitted products to the CFTC for approval. From 1922 until the CFMA was signed into law, less than 800 products were approved. Since then, CFTC regulated exchanges have certified over 12,000 products. For financial instrument products specifically, the numbers are 494 products approved and 1,938 self-certified. See generally, "Written Testimony of Chairman J. Christopher Giancarlo before the Senate Banking Committee, Washington, D.C." (February 6, 2018), *Introduction: Virtual Currency*, available at https://www.cftc.gov/PressRoom/SpeechesTestimony/opagiancarlo37#P59_18438

26. The CME Group is one of the world's leading financial innovators, having played a formative role in the creation of financial futures and cash settled derivatives that are foundational to the global economy. Today CME Group comprises four major futures exchange—the Chicago Mercantile Exchange (CME), the Chicago Board of Trade (CBOT), the New York Mercantile Exchange (NYMEX), and the Commodity Exchange (COMEX)—and offers the widest range of benchmark futures and options products available by any consolidated exchange. www.cmegroup.com

27. "CME Group Announces Launch of Bitcoin Futures," October 31, 2017, at: https://www.cmegroup.com/media-room/press-releases/2017/10/31/cme_group_ announceslaunchofbitcoinfutures.html

Chapter 8

1. Pierre Isaac Isidore Mendès-France (January 11, 1907–October 18, 1982) was a French politician who served as President of the Council of Ministers of the French Fourth Republic for eight months from 1954 to 1955.

2. Federal Register / Vol. 82, No. 243, Wednesday December 20, 2017, available at https://www.govinfo.gov/content/pkg/FR-2017-12-20/pdf/2017-27421.pdf

3. "CFTC Issues Final Interpretative Guidance on Actual Delivery for Digital Assets," press release (March 24, 2020), available at https://www.cftc.gov/PressRoom/PressReleases/8139-20

4. J. Christopher Giancarlo, "The Importance of Large Trade Size Liquidity in U.S. Financial Markets," Third Annual Conference on the Evolving Structure of the US Treasury Market, Federal Reserve Board of New York (November 28, 2017), available at https://www.cftc.gov/PressRoom/SpeechesTestimony/opagiancarlo-33

5. Disappointingly, the CFTC ultimately received limited spot market data (e.g. during the product settlement period when we raised concerns) in a format that was quite difficult to use.

6. "Statement on Self-Certification of Bitcoin Products by CME, CFE and Cantor Exchange," CFTC Release Number 7654-17, December 1, 2017, available at https://www.cftc.gov/PressRoom/PressReleases/7654-17

7. Alexander Osipovich, "First U.S. Bitcoin Futures to Start Trading Next Week," *Dow Jones Newswire*, Fox Business (December 4, 2017), available at https://www.foxbusiness.com/features/first-u-s-bitcoin-futures-to-start-trading-next-week-update

8. On numerous occasions in the months that followed, Mnuchin and President Trump publicly referred to cryptocurrency with significant skepticism.

9. See *Cryptocurrency a Response to Financial Crisis, Says CEO*, *Wall Street Journal* (June 14, 2016), statement of Blythe Masters, available at https://www.wsj.com/video/cryptocurrency-a-response-to-financial-crisis-says-ceo/D28A8012-413F-447E-AA5A-F1911BA64FC3.html

10. Sheila Bair, "Why We Shouldn't Ban Bitcoin," *Yahoo Finance* (December 26, 2017), available at https://www.yahoo.com/entertainment/former-fdic-chair-sheila-bair-shouldnt-ban-Bitcoin-141019569.html

Chapter 9

1. The G-20 countries are Argentina, Australia, Brazil, Canada, China, the European Union, France, Germany, India, Indonesia, Italy, Japan, Mexico, Russia, Saudi Arabia, South Africa, South Korea, Turkey, the United Kingdom, and the United States. Spain is a permanent guest invitee.

2. Jay Clayton and J. Christopher Giancarlo, "Regulators Are Looking at Cryptocurrency: At the SEC and CFTC We Take Our Responsibility Seriously," *Wall Street Journal* (Jan. 24, 2018) (hereafter, Clayton and Giancarlo, "Regulators Are Looking at Cryptocurrency"), available at https://www.wsj.com/articles/regulators-are-looking-at-cryptocurrency-1516836363

3. Robert Schmidt and Benjamin Bain, "Who Wants to Be Bitcoin's Watchdog?" Bloomberg (January 12, 2017), available at https://www.bloomberg.com/news/articles/2018-01-12/who-wants-to-be-bitcoin-s-watchdog

4. Schmidt and Bain, "Who Wants to Be Bitcoin's Watchdog?"

5. Schmidt and Bain, "Who Wants to Be Bitcoin's Watchdog?"

6. J. Christopher Giancarlo, "Remarks to the ABA Derivatives and Futures Section Conference, Naples, Florida," CFTC (January 19, 2018), available at https://www.cftc.gov/PressRoom/SpeechesTestimony/opagiancarlo34

7. Alain de Botton, "The News: A User's Manual," *Pantheon* (February 2014).

Chapter 10

1. See "Cryptocurrency a Response to Financial Crisis, Says CEO," video statement of Blythe Masters, *Wall Street Journal* (June 14, 2016), available at https://www.wsj.com/video/cryptocurrency-a-response-to-financial-crisis-says-ceo/D28A8012-413F-447E-AA5A-F1911BA64FC3.html

2. See Eric Sammons, "10 Types of Crypto Fans—Which Are You?" Dashforcenews.com (Sept. 27, 2017), available at https://www.dashforcenews.com/10-types-of-crypto-fans-which-are-you/

3. US Senate Committee on Banking, Housing and Urban Affairs, Hearing: "Virtual Currencies: The Oversight Role of the U.S. Securities and Exchange Commission and the U.S. Commodity Futures Trading Commission" (February 6, 2018) (hereafter: Virtual Currency Hearing), available at https://www.banking.senate.gov/hearings/virtual-currencies-the-oversight-role-of-the-us-securities-and-exchange-commission-and-the-us-commodity-futures-trading-commission

4. Virtual Currency Hearing.

5. Clayton and Giancarlo, "Regulators Are Looking at Cryptocurrency."

6. Virtual Currency Hearing.

7. "U.S. Soy Cargo to China Traded Using Blockchain," *Reuters* (Jan. 22, 2018), available at https://www.reuters.com/article/grains-blockchain/u-s-soy-cargo-to-china-traded-using-blockchain-idUSL8N1PG0VJ

8. "Giancarlo, the Man, the Legend, the Meme," Trustnodes (February, 7, 2018), available at https://www.trustnodes.com/2018/02/07/giancarlo-man-legend-meme

9. Joon Ian Wong, "How an American Commodities Regulator Became the Unlikely Star of 'crypto Twitter,'" Quartz (March 2, 2018), available at https://qz.com/1220027/the-cftcs-j-christopher-giancarlo-giancarlocftc-is-an-unlikely-hero-of-crypto-twitter/

10. Mark Krieger, "Chairman of the CFTC Made Surprisingly Thoughtful Comments about Bitcoin Today, Liberty Blitzkrieg.com, February 6, 2018, at https://libertyblitzkrieg.com/2018/02/06/chairman-of-the-cftc-made-surprisingly-thoughtful-comments-about-bitcoin-today/

11. Marketplace Staff, "Biden: Yellen Needs a 'Hamilton' Musical. Dessa: Here You Go., January 21, 2021, at https://www.marketplace.org/2021/01/21/yellen-hamilton-musical-biden-dessa/

Chapter 11

1. Interpretative Guidance issued by the CFTC in 2013 imposed CFTC transaction rules on swaps traded by US persons even in jurisdictions committed to implementing G-20 swaps reforms and was vehemently and almost universally resented by overseas market regulators. See 17 CFR Chapter I. Interpretive Guidance and Policy Statement Regarding Compliance With Certain Swap Regulations, *Federal Register Vol.* 78, No. 144 (Friday, July 26, 2013), available at

https://www.cftc.gov/sites/default/files/idc/groups/public/@lrfederalregister/documents/
file/2013-17958a.pdf Commissioner Jill Sommers colorfully referred to the guidance as the
"Intergalactic Commerce Clause." See CFTC Commissioner Jill E. Sommers, Commissioner,
Statement of Concurrence: (1) Cross-Border Application of Certain Swaps Provisions of the
Commodity Exchange Act, Proposed Interpretive Guidance and Policy Statement; (2) Notice of
Proposed Exemptive Order and Request for Comment Regarding Compliance with Certain Swap
Regulations (June 29, 2012), available at https://www.cftc.gov/PressRoom/SpeechesTestimony/
sommersstatement062912

2. See, Anu Bradford, *The Brussels Effect: How the European Union Rules the World* (New York: Oxford University Press, 2020).
3. Giancarlo, "Deference is the Path Forward in Cross-Border Supervision of CCPs," *Les Echos,* Paris, France, Sep. 11, 2017 at https://www.lesechos.fr/2017/09/regulation-financiere-poursuivre-lharmonisation-des-chambres-de-compensation-181467; Giancarlo, "Cross-Border Swaps Regulation Version 2.0: A Risk-Based Approach with Deference to Comparable Non-U.S. Regulation" (Oct. 1, 2018), at https://www.cftc.gov/sites/default/files/2018-10/Whitepaper_CBSR100118_0.pdf
4. "CFTC Approved Final Cross-Border Swaps Rule and an Exempt SEF Amendment Order at July 23 Open Meeting," July 23, 2020, at: https://www.cftc.gov/PressRoom/PressReleases/8211-20

Chapter 12

1. For a gripping account of the origin of Ethereum see, Matthew Leising, *Out of the Ether: The Amazing Story of Ethereum and the $55 Million Heist That Almost Destroyed It All* (Hoboken: Wiley, 2020).
2. William Hinman, "Digital Asset Transactions: When Howey Met Gary (Plastic)," Remarks at the Yahoo Finance All Markets Summit: Crypto (June 14, 2018_, available at https://www.sec.gov/news/speech/speech-hinman-061418
3. A market's durability and resistance to manipulation derives from both depth and breadth of participation. See, generally, Barney Frank and J. Christopher Giancarlo, Opinion: "Manipulation Helped Kill Libor. Its Replacement Needs to be Stronger" *Barron's* (Aug. 28, 2020), available at https://www.barrons.com/articles/when-libor-transitions-out-will-sofr-be-any-better-51598629759
4. A riveting account of the manipulation of LIBOR is provided by David Enrich, "The Spider Network: The Wild Story of a Math Genius, a Gang of Backstabbing Bankers, and One of the Greatest Scams in Financial History," March 21, 2017 Custom House, New York.
5. See generally, Galina Hale, Arvind Krishnamurthy, Marianna Kudlyak and Patrick Schultz, "How Futures Trading Changed Bitcoin Prices," Federal Reserve Bank of San Francisco Economic Research, *FRBSF Economic Letter* 2018-12 (May 7, 2018), available at https://www.frbsf.org/economic-research/publications/economic-letter/2018/may/how-futures-trading-changed-bitcoin-prices/
6. It is a style that current apostles of big government no longer wish to emulate. See James Panero, "Biden's Architecture of Power," *Wall Street Journal* (May 26, 2021), available at https://www.wsj.com/articles/bidens-architecture-of-power-11622065951?mod=searchresults_pos1&page=1
7. The Federal Open Market Committee sets US monetary policy through key decision about interest rates and money supply. The committee consists of the seven members of the Federal Reserve Board, the president of the New York Fed and 4 of the other 11 regional Federal Reserve Bank presidents. It is invariably chaired by the chairman of the Federal Reserve Board.
8. Letter from Jack Kingston, Congressman and Chairman of the House Subcommittee on Agriculture, Rural Development Food and Drug Administration, and Related Agencies, to Gary Gensler, Chairman of the Commodity Futures Trading Commission (June 8, 2012) (on file with the Commodity Futures Trading Commission).

9. Tuckman's work on "Entity Netted Notionals" was subsequently published in a scholarly journal written with other outstanding CFTC economists. Lee Baker, Richard Haynes, John Roberts, Rajiv Sharma, and Bruce Tuckman, "Risk Transfer with Interest Rate Swaps," *Financial Markets, Institutions & Instruments,* New York University Salomon Center and Wiley Periodicals, Volume 30, Number 1, 2021: 30, 3–28.

10. "Impact of Automated Orders in Futures Markets," Report by Staff of the Market Intelligence Branch, Division of Market Oversight, CFTC, March 2019, at https://www.cftc.gov/sites/default/files/2019-03/automatedordersreport032719.pdf

11. Ram Charan, *The Attacker's Advantage: Turning Uncertainty into Breakthrough Opportunities* (New York: Public Affairs, 2015).

12. Nick Chong, "CFTC Chair: Cryptocurrencies Have a Future, They Are Here to Stay," CNBC, October 2, 2018, available at https://www.newsbtc.com/tech/cftc-chair-cryptocurrencies-have-a-future-they-are-here-to-stay/

13. Nick Chong, "CFTC Chair."

14. Jean Eaglesham, Dave Michaels, and Danny Dougherty, "Regulators' Penalties Against Wall Street Are Down Sharply in 2017—Business-Friendly Shift Under President Trump Is Only One Factor, as Enforcement Actions from the Financial Crisis Wind Down," *Wall Street Journal* (August 6, 2017), available at https://www.wsj.com/articles/regulators-penalties-against-wall-street-are-down-sharply-in-2017-1502028001

15. Eaglesham, Michaels, and Dougherty, "Regulators' Penalties Against Wall Street Are Down Sharply in 2017."

16. Eaglesham, Michaels, and Dougherty, "Regulators' Penalties Against Wall Street Are Down Sharply in 2017."

17. Eaglesham, Michaels, and Dougherty, "Regulators' Penalties Against Wall Street Are Down Sharply in 2017."

18. J. Christopher Giancarlo, "Regulatory Enforcement & Healthy Markets: Perfect Together," Remarks at Economic Club of Minnesota, Minneapolis, Minnesota (October 2, 2018), available at https://www.cftc.gov/PressRoom/SpeechesTestimony/opagiancarlo56

19. Giancarlo, "Regulatory Enforcement & Healthy Markets."

20. Giancarlo, "Regulatory Enforcement & Healthy Markets."

21. "CFTC Division of Enforcement Issues Report on FY 2018 Results," CFTC press release (Nov. 25, 2018), available at https://www.cftc.gov/PressRoom/PressReleases/7841-18

22. "Enforcement Manual, CFTC Division of Enforcement," CFTC press release (May 20, 2020), available at https://www.cftc.gov/media/1966

Chapter 13

1. "Advisory with Respect to Virtual Currency Derivative Product Listings," CFTC Staff Advisory No. 18-14 (May 21, 2018), available at https://www.cftc.gov/PressRoom/PressReleases/7731-18

2. In fact, my successor, Heath Tarbert, used the title Chairman and Chief Executive.

3. See https://www.cftc.gov/PressRoom/PressReleases/7936-19

4. Tom Zanki, "CFTC Head Seeks Bigger Budget, But Trump Wants It Flat," Law360 (May 23, 2014), available at https://www.law360.com/articles/927470/cftc-head-seeks-bigger-budget-but-trump-wants-it-flat

5. "CFTC and Kansas State University Announce 2018 Agriculture Commodity Futures Conference," CFTC press release (Nov. 15, 2017), available at https://www.cftc.gov/PressRoom/PressReleases/7646-17

6. "Swap Execution Facilities and Trade Execution Requirement Proposed Rule," *Federal Register*, Volume 83, Issue 231 (Nov. 30, 2018), available at https://www.cftc.gov/sites/default/files/2018-11/2018-24642a.pdf?utm_source=govdelivery

7. J. Christopher Giancarlo, "Address to the ABA Business Law Section, Derivatives & Futures Law Committee Winter Meeting," American Bar Association (Jan. 25, 2019), available at https://www.americanbar.org/content/dam/aba/events/business_law/2019/01/derivatives/jcg_speech.pdf

8. The CFTC's role as a primary regulator of several key overseas derivatives clearinghouses comes in the context of the oversized role in global transactions of the US dollar based clearing collateral and US banks as clearing members and trading liquidity providers.

9. The Intercontinental Exchange (NYSE: ICE) well known as "ICE" is an American Fortune 500 company that operates global exchanges, clearing houses, and provides mortgage technology, data, and listing services worldwide. Among other exchanges, ICE owns the New York Stock Exchange. www.intercontinentalexchange.com

10. J. Christopher Giancarlo, "The Future of the City of London: Global, European Financial Center, Remarks at Guildhall, London" (June 4, 2019), available at https://www.cftc.gov/PressRoom/SpeechesTestimony/opagiancarlo74

11. Available at https://montypython.fandom.com/wiki/The_Ministry_of_Silly_Walks

Chapter 14

1. *House of Cards*, Season 1, Episode 2, Chapter 2.

2. Jim Kharouf, "How Chris Giancarlo Helped the Futures Industry Get Its Groove Back," johnlothian.com (March 14, 2019), available at https://johnlothiannews.com/how-chris-giancarlo-helped-the-futures-industry-get-its-groove-back/

3. J. Christopher Giancarlo, "Free Markets and the Future of Blockchain," CoinDesk (May 15, 2019), available at https://www.coindesk.com/christopher-giancarlo-cftc-future-of-blockchain

4. Theodore Roosevelt, "Citizenship in a Republic" speech delivered at the Sorbonne, Paris, France (April 23, 1910), available at https://www.leadershipnow.com/tr-citizenship.html

Chapter 15

1. Jacob Goldstein, *Money: The True Story of a Made-Up Thing* (New York: Hachette Books, 2020).

2. Mark Carney, "The Art of Central Banking in a Centrifugal World," Andrew Crockett Lecture, Bank for International Settlements, June 28, 2021, at https://www.bis.org/events/acrockett_2021_speech.pdf

3. Goldstein, *Money.*

4. Goldstein, *Money.*

5. The word "salary" derives from the Latin word for "salt": *salis.*

6. Niall Ferguson, *The Ascent of Money* (New York: Penguin Books, 2018), 2nd ed., 45–46.

7. Tony McLaughlin, "Two Paths to Tomorrow's Money," Citi Digital Policy, Strategy and Advisory (October 2020), available at https://www.citibank.com/icg/bcma/psg/assets/docs/Tomorrow-Money-Citi.pdf

8. FDIC, "How American Banks: Household Use of Banking and Financial Services" (Oct. 19, 2020), available at https://www.fdic.gov/analysis/household-survey/index.html

9. The World Bank, Global Findex Database 2017, available at https://globalfindex.worldbank.org

10. Darrell Duffie, "Testimony Before U.S. Senate Committee on Banking, Housing and Urban Affairs Subcommittee on Economic Policy," June 9, 2021, available at https://www.banking.senate.gov/imo/media/doc/Duffie%20Testimony%206-9-21.pdf, citing McKinsey & Company, "The 2020 McKinsey Global Payments Report," available at https://www.mckinsey.com/~/media/mckinsey/industries/financial%20services/our%20insights/accelerating%20winds%20of%20change%20in%20global%20payments/2020-mckinsey-global-payments-report-vf.pdf

11. Darrell Duffie, "Testimony Before U.S. Senate Committee."

12. Adam Ludwin, "A Letter to Jamie Dimon," October 16, 2017, at http://www.ceresaig.com/wp-content/uploads/2017/11/A-Letter-to-JP-Morgan-Jamie-Dimon-—-Block-Chain-Crypto-FX.pdf

13. Brian P. Brooks, "Crypto Is the Future. More Banks, Regulators Need to Embrace It," *American Banker* (May 26, 2021), available at https://www.americanbanker.com/opinion/crypto-is-the-future-more-banks-regulators-need-to-embrace-it

14. Id.

15. Marta Belcher, "Testimony to Senate Committee on Banking, Housing and Urban Affairs, Crptocurrencies, What Are They Good For?," July 27, 2021 at https://www.banking.senate.gov/imo/media/doc/Belcher%20Testimony%207-27-21.pdf

16. Ludwin, Id.

17. For a good overview of the current state of Stablecoins, see generally: FTSE Russell and Digital Asset Research, "*Stablecoin Ecosystem Primer*" (May 2021), available at https://content.ftserussell.com/sites/default/files/stablecoin_ecosystem_primer_final.pdf?_ga=2.216755473.682178879 .1623967329-913208021.1623967329.

18. Brooks, "Crypto Is the Future."

19. Caitlin Long, "Ten Stablecoin Predictions and Their Monetary Policy Implications" (citing figures from Coinmarketcap.com and Mastercard), *Cato Journal* (Spring/Summer 2021), available at https://www.cato.org/cato-journal/spring/summer-2021/ ten-stablecoin-predictions-their-monetary-policy-implications

20. Long, "Ten Stablecoin Predictions."

21. Timothy Massad, "Can a Cryptocurrency Break the Buck?" Bloomberg (May 31, 2021), available at https://www.bloomberg.com/opinion/articles/2021-05-31/stablecoins-like-tether-should-face-regulators-scrutiny

22. Massad, "Can a Cryptocurrency Break the Buck?"

23. Massad, "Can a Cryptocurrency Break the Buck?"

24. Steve H. Henke and Robert J. Simon, "Beyond Bitcoin, Its Time for Cryptocurrency Boards," *National Review* (March 19, 2021), available at https://www.nationalreview.com/2021/03/ beyond-bitcoin-its-time-for-cryptocurrency-boards/

25. Marcus, David, "Good Stablecoins, A Protocol for Money and Digital Wallet: the Forumula to Fix Our Broken Payment System," August 18, 2021, Medium.com, at: https://medium.com/@ davidmarcus/good-stablecoins-a-protocol-for-money-and-digital-wallets-the-formula-to-fix-our-broken-payment-f11f59fc92d7

26. Justina Lee, "Crypto Die-Hards Built a $90 Billion Wall Street on the Internet," Bloomberg (June 16, 2021), available at https://www.bloomberg.com/news/articles/2021-06-16/defi-platforms-with-names-like-sushiswap-aim-to-be-nasdaq-for-crypto

27. CFTC Commissioner Dan Berkovitz recently addressed the subject of DeFi in US derivatives markets questioning the legality of DeFi under the CFTC's governing law and asserting that it would be a "bad idea" to allow unregulated, unlicensed derivatives markets to compete side by side with fully regulated and licensed derivatives markets. Dan M. Berkovitz, "Climate Change and Decentralized Finance: New Challenges for the CFTC," Keynote Address before FIA and SIFMA-AMG, Asset Management Derivatives Forum 2021 (June 8, 2021), available at https://www.cftc.gov/PressRoom/SpeechesTestimony/opaberkovitz7

28. Samuel R. Staley, Catherine Annis, and Matthew Kelly, "Regulatory Overdrive: Taxi Regulations, Market Concentration and Service Availability," Institute for Justice (October 18, 2018), available at https://ij.org/wp-content/uploads/2018/10/Taxi-WhitePaper.pdf

29. Carla Mozee, "SEC Commissioner Hester Peirce Worries That Stricter Rules by US Officials Will Hurt the Crypto Market," *Markets Insider* (June 9, 2021), available at https://markets.businessinsider.com/currencies/news/sec-commissioner-hester-pierce-worries-rules-cryptocurrency-market-gensler-bitcoin-2021-6-1030508646

30. Ronald F. Pol, "Anti-Money Laundering: The World's Least Effective Policy Experiment? Together, We Can Fix it," Policy Design and Practice, Volume 3, February 25, 2020, at: https://www.tandfonline.com/doi/full/10.1080/25741292.2020.1725366

31. Citing US Census Bureau's Busines Dynamics Statistics, George Gilder asserts that between 1996 and 2009, virtually all new jobs came from start-ups; see George Gilder, *Knowledge and Power: The Information Theory of Capitalism and How It Is Revolutionizing Our World* (Washington: Regnery, 2013), 33.

32. *The Chainalysis 2021 Crypto Crime Report*, available at https://go.chainalysis.com/2021-Crypto-Crime-Report.html

33. See United Nations Office on Drugs and Crime, available at https://www.unodc.org/unodc/en/money-laundering/overview.html

34. *The Chainalysis 2021 Crypto Crime Report*.

35. MacKenzie Sigalos, "The FBI Likely Exploited Sloppy Password Storage to Seize Colonial Pipeline Bitcoin Ransom," CNBC (June 8, 2021), available at https://www.cnbc.com/2021/06/08/fbi-likely-exploited-sloppy-password-storage-to-seize-colonial-ransom.html

36. Ezra Galston, "Untraceable Bitcoin Is a Myth," *The Wall Street Journal* (June 16, 2021), available at https://www.wsj.com/articles/untraceable-bitcoin-is-a-myth-11623860828

37. Yaya J. Fanusi, "Central Bank Digital Currencies: The Threat from Money Launderers and How to Stop Them," *The Lawfare Podcast* (Dec. 15, 2020), available at https://www.lawfareblog.com/lawfare-podcast-yaya-fanusie-central-bank-digital-currencies-threat-money-launderers-and-how-stop

38. Makan Delrahim, "A Whole New World: An Antitrust Entreaty for a Digital Age" (Jan. 19, 2021), available at https://www.justice.gov/opa/speech/assistant-attorney-general-makan-delrahim-delivers-final-address

39. See generally, Giancarlo, Bahlke, and Pittman, "Peer-to-Peer Governance: Why Cryptocurrency SROs Can Work," Bloomberg Law (Feb. 11, 2021), available at https://news.bloomberglaw.com/us-law-week/peer-to-peer-governance-why-cryptocurrency-sros-can-work

40. CFTC "US Futures Trading and Regulation Before the Creation of the CFTC," available at https://www.cftc.gov/About/HistoryoftheCFTC/history_precftc.html

41. Jonathan Lurie, *The Chicago Board of Trade, 1859-1905: The Dynamics of Self-Regulation* (University of Illinois Press, 1979).

42. *See e.g.*, CFTC Commissioner Brian Quintenz, *Keynote Address Before the DC Blockchain Summit* (Mar. 7, 2018), https://www.cftc.gov/PressRoom/SpeechesTestimony/opaquintenz8

43. Several voluntary cryptocurrency SROs that have been formed or proposed in recent years, including the Virtual Commodity Association and the Association for Digital Asset Markets, and cryptocurrency trade associations, such as the Blockchain Association, the Chamber of Digital Commerce, and the Crypto Rating Council. Similar concepts have already been formalized in other countries such as the United Kingdom, Japan, and South Korea.

44. Saint Thomas Aquinas, *The Summa Contra Gentiles* (The English Dominican Fathers trans., Burns Oates & Washbourne Ltd., 1924).

45. Hence, shipbuilding should be conducted to allow for safe and efficient navigation. Sailing should not be jeopardized by aesthetically pleasing but unseaworthy ship designs.

46 SEC Commissioner Hester Peirce has put forth well considered "safe harbor" proposals. See generally, "Token Safe Harbor Proposal 2.0," April 13, 2021 at: https://www.sec.gov/news/public-statement/peirce-statement-token-safe-harbor-proposal-2.0

47. Saheli Roy Choudhury, "Bitcoin Is Breaking Records Because Bigger Investors Are Buying It Now, Says PwC," CNBC (Jan. 4, 2021), available at https://www.msn.com/en-us/money/markets/bitcoin-is-breaking-records-because-bigger-investors-are-buying-it-now-says-pwc/ar-BB1crW8I?ocid=FinanceShimLayer

48. Xie Yu, Chong Koh Ping, and Joe Wallace, "Bitcoin Price Extends Drop After China Intensified Crypto Crackdown," *The Wall Street Journal* (June 21, 2021), available at https://www.wsj.com/articles/china-orders-ant-group-state-banks-to-root-out-cryptocurrency-related-activities-11624282695

49. Chris Morris, "Big Short Investor Says Bitcoin Is in a Speculative Bubble," *Fortune* (March 1, 2021), available at https://fortune.com/2021/03/01/bitcoin-bubble-michael-burry-big-short-investing-btc/

50. Alex Gladstein, "Fighting Monetary Colonialism with Open-Source Code," Nasdaq (June 24, 2021), available at https://www.nasdaq.com/articles/fighting-monetary-colonialism-with-open-source-code-2021-06-23?amp

51. Gwynn Guilford, "Inflation Jumps to 13-Year High as Prices Surge 5%," *The Wall Street Journal* (June 11, 2021), available at https://www.wsj.com/articles/us-inflation-consumer-price-index-may-2021-11623288303

52. Omkar Godbole, "*Open Positions in CME-Based Bitcoin Futures Slump to 5 ½ Month Low*," CoinDesk (June 4, 2021), available at https://www.coindesk.com/open-positions-in-cme-based-bitcoin-futures-slump-to-5-1-2-month-low

53. Nelson Renteria, Tom Wilson, and Karin Strohecker, "In a World First, El Salvador Makes Bitcoin Legal Tender," Reuters (June 9, 2021), available at https://www.reuters.com/world/americas/el-salvador-approves-first-law-bitcoin-legal-tender-2021-06-09/

54. Max Raskin, "A Global First: Bitcoin as National Currency," *The Wall Street Journal* (June 15, 2021), available at https://www.wsj.com/articles/a-global-first-bitcoin-as-national-currency-11623796143

55. James Crawley, "Adopting Bitcoin as Legal Tender Could Ruin El Salvador's Economy, Economist Says," CoinDesk, June 16, 2021, available at https://www.coindesk.com/hankebitcoin-el-salvador

56. Rodrigo Campos, "*World Bank Rejects El Salvador Request for Help on Bitcoin Implementation*," Reuters, June 16, 2021, available at https://www.reuters.com/business/el-salvador-keep-dollar-legal-tender-seeks-world-bank-help-with-bitcoin-2021-06-16/

57. Juntina Lee, "Ex-Wall Street Quants Net 78% Return in Crypto Options Boom," Bloomberg, June 21, 2021, available at https://www.bloomberg.com/news/articles/2021-06-21/a-130-million-crypto-quant-nets-big-returns-as-options-boom

58. Nikhilesh De, "*Bakkt Says It's 'Clear to Launch' Bitcoin Futures Next Month*," CoinDesk, August 16, 2019, available at https://www.coindesk.com/bakkt-says-its-cleared-to-launch-bitcoin-futures-next-month

59. "CFTC Approves LedgerX to Clear Fully-Collaterlised Futures and Options on Futures," Hedgeweek (March 9, 2020), available at https://www.hedgeweek.com/2020/09/03/289180/cftc-approves-ledgerx-clear-fully-collateralised-futures-and-options-futures

60. "CME Group Announces Launch of Ether Futures," CME Group press release (February 8, 2021), available at https://www.cmegroup.com/media-room/press-releases/2021/2/08/cme_group_announceslaunchofetherfutures.html#

61. "CME Group to Launch Micro Bitcoin Futures on May 3," CME Group press release (March 30, 2021), available at https://www.cmegroup.com/media-room/press-releases/2021/3/30/cme_group_to_launchmicrobitcoinfuturesonmay3.html

62. Hester Peirce, "Paper, Plastic, Peer-to-Peer," Remarks at the British Blockchain Association's Conference: Success Through Synergy, Next Generation Leadership for Extraordinary Times (March 15, 2021), available at https://www.sec.gov/news/speech/peirce-paper-plastic-peer-to-peer-031521

63. Spencer Bogart, "Bitcoin Is (Still) a Demographic Mega-trend: Data Update," Blockchain Capital Blog (Dec. 2, 2020), available at https://medium.com/blockchain-capital-blog/bitcoin-is-still-a-demographic-mega-trend-data-update-c50df59a6cb3

64. Bogart, "Bitcoin Is (Still) a Demographic Mega-trend."

65. See, Don Tapscott, Anthony Williams and Kirsten Sandberg, "New Directions for Government in the Second Era of the Digital Age: Strategy, Action and Policy for the Biden-Harris Administration," Foreword by Tony Scott, Blockchain Research Institute (Feb. 9, 2021), available at https://app.hubspot.com/documents/5052729/view/226751718?accessId=18087e

66. Donna Redel and Olta Andoni, "Has the Biden Administration Lost the Plot on Crypto Regulation?" CoinDesk July 1, 2021, available at https://www.coindesk.com/biden-administration-loses-plot-on-crypto-regulation

67. Bank for International Settlements, "About the BIS Innovation Hub," (n.d.), available at https://www.bis.org/about/bisih/about.htm

68. Bank of England, "Bank for International Settlements and Bank of England Launch Innovation Hub London Centre," BIS press release (June 11, 2021), available at https://www.bankofengland.co.uk/news/2021/june/bank-for-international-settlements-and-boe-launch-innovation-hub-london-centre

Chapter 16

1. J. Christopher Giancarlo and Daniel Gorfine, "We Sent a Man to the Moon. We Can Send the Dollar to Cyberspace," *The Wall Street Journal* (Oct. 15 2019), available at https://www.wsj.com/articles/we-sent-a-man-to-the-moon-we-can-send-the-dollar-to-cyberspace-11571179923

2. Helen Partz, "Davos: Giancarlo's Digital Dollar Project Will Focus on Benefits of a US CBDC," CoinTelegraph (Jan. 22, 2020), available at https://cointelegraph.com/news/davos-giancarlos-digital-dollar-project-will-focus-on-benefits-of-a-us-cbdc

3. The Digital Dollar Project is not a commercial venture. It is self-funded and has no commercial product or service to advance. Its sole mission is serving the public interest.

4. See: https://digitaldollarproject.org/advisory-group/

5. See: https://newsroom.accenture.com/news/digital-dollar-project-to-launch-pilot-programs-to-explore-designs-and-uses-of-a-us-central-bank-digital-currency.htm

6. See The Digital Dollar Project, "Exploring a US CBDC," May 2020, at: www.digitaldollarproject.org/exploring-a-us-cbdc

7. *Id.*

8. Some analysts have proposed caps on CBDC holdings to avoid cannibalizing commercial banking, Joanna Ossinger, "JPMorgan Says Digital Currencies Must Balance Inclusion, Banks," Bloomberg, August 6, 2021, at: https://www.bloomberg.com/news/articles/2021-08-06/jpmorgan-says-digital-currencies-must-balance-inclusion-banks?sref=008H7iJP

9. Codruta Boar and Andreas Wehrli, "Ready, steady, go? Results on the Third BIS Survey on Central Bank Digital Currency," Bank for International Settlements (BIS), *BIS Paper No. 114* (Jan. 27, 2021), available at https://www.bis.org/publ/bppdf/bispap114.pdf

10. "The World's Most Valuable Resource Is No Longer Oil, but Data," *The Economist* (May 6, 2021), available at https://www.economist.com/leaders/2017/05/06/the-worlds-most-valuable-resource-is-no-longer-oil-but-data

11. Criticism of Chinese government policy or CCP doctrine may one day result in one's Chinese CBDC being disabled from paying for, say, access to electronic media, transportation outside of one's village, or even necessities like food. Communist governments have a long and murderous tradition of using food deprivation as a means of social control. See, Pierre Yared, "Nothing to Celebrate: A Century After the Bolshevik Revolution, We Should Remember Communism's Stark Legacy—Including Mass Starvation," *City Journal* (Winter 2018), available at: https://www.city-journal.org/html/nothing-celebrate-15660.html

12. See Taylor Telford, "Why Governments Around the World are Afraid of Libra, Facebook's Cryptocurrency," Washington Post, July 12, 2019, at: https://www.washingtonpost.com/business/2019/07/12/why-governments-around-world-are-afraid-libra-facebooks-cryptocurrency/

13. "Project Ubin: Central Bank Digital Money Using Distributed Ledger Technology," Monetary Authority of Singapore (n.d.), available at https://www.mas.gov.sg/schemes-and-initiatives/Project-Ubin

14. John Revill, "French and Swiss Central Banks to Trial Wholesale Digital Currencies," Reuters (June 10, 2021), available at https://www.reuters.com/business/finance/french-swiss-central-banks-trial-wholesale-digital-currencies-2021-06-10/

15. McKinsey & Company, "China's Digital Economy: A Leading Global Force," August 2017, available at https://www.mckinsey.com/~/media/mckinsey/featured%20insights/China/Chinas%20digital%20economy%20A%20leading%20global%20force/MGI-Chinas-digital-economy-A-leading-global-force.ashx

16. James T. Adreddy, "Beijing Tries to Put Its Imprint on Blockchain," *The Wall Street Journal*, May 11, 2021, available at https://www.wsj.com/articles/beijing-tries-to-put-its-imprint-on-blockchain-11620735603

17. Alexander Zaitchik, Jeanhee Kim, and Kelly Le, "Special Series: China Bets on the Blockchain," Forkast News (June 28, 2021), available at https://forkast.news/video-audio/part-i-china-bets-on-the-blockchain/

18. Zaitchik et al., "Special Series: China Bets on the Blockchain."

19. Hannah Murphy and Yuan Yang, "Patents Reveal Extent of China's Digital Currency Plans," *Financial Times* (Feb, 12, 2020), available at https://www.ft.com/content/f10e94cc-4d74-11ea-95a0-43d18ec715f5

20. SMSH, "Yes, Foreigners Can Use China's New E-CNY Digital Currency: Alipay and WeChat Pay Are So 2020," Smart Shanghai/*Shanghai Life* (May 21, 2021), available at https://www.smartshanghai.com/articles/activities/how-to-use-china-digital-yuan-cbdc

21. Mu Changchun, "Opinion: China's Digital Yuan Wallet Designed to Meet Everyone's Needs," Caixin (June 16, 2021), available at https://www.caixinglobal.com/2021-06-16/opinion-chinas-digital-yuan-wallet-designed-to-meet-everyones-needs-101727437.html?rkey=pAgjKe3ecjJNiwQ6B8r4EPFL%2FE7ci4pKefjbMYLjiCXABf4EEUJQDA%3D%3D

22. Changchun, "Opinion: China's Digital Yuan Wallet."

23. Wolfie Zhao, "China's New Digital Yuan Test Shows It Can Be Programmed to Confine Utility," The Block Crypto (July 2, 2021), available at https://www.theblockcrypto.com/post/110377/china-digital-yuan-test-programmable-chengdu

24. "2017 FDIC National Survey of Unbanked and Underbanked Households," Federal Deposit Insurance Corporation (Oct. 2018), available at https://www.fdic.gov/householdsurvey/2017/2017report.pdf

25. Chris Brummer, *Thinking Big on Fed Accounts, Digital Dollars and Financial Inclusion*, Medium.com (June 23, 2020), available at https://chrisbrummer.medium.com/thinking-big-on-fed-accounts-digital-dollars-and-financial-inclusion-622733baacba

26. Erica Werner, "Treasury Sent More Than 1 Million Coronavirus Stimulus Payments to Dead People, Congressional Watchdog Finds," *Washington Post* (June 25, 2020), available at: https://www.washingtonpost.com/us-policy/2020/06/25/irs-stimulus-checks-dead-people-gao/

27. "Digital Disruption: The Inevitable Rise of CBDC," Morgan Stanley Research (April 12, 2021), available at https://www.morganstanley.com/ideas/central-bank-digital-currency-disruption

28. Werner, "Treasury Sent More Than 1 Million Coronavirus Stimulus Payments."

29. Claire Jones and Izabella Kaminska, "CBDCs Now Seem a Matter of When, Not If," Opinion FT Alphaville (June 23, 2021), at: https://www.ft.com/content/adc2130e-0f46-4da2-ae3f-3b4b0cacbeda

30. "Monetary Sovereignty at Risk in Push for Digital Euro—French Central Banker," Reuters (June 29, 2021), available at https://www.reuters.com/business/monetary-sovereignty-risk-push-digital-euro-french-central-banker-2021-06-29/

31. Carney, "The Art of Central Banking in a Centrifugal World."

32. Jing Yang, "China's Digital Yuan Puts Ant and Tencent in an Awkward Spot," *The Wall Street Journal*, July 25, 2021, at https://www.wsj.com/articles/chinas-digital-yuan-puts-ant-and-tencent-in-an-awkward-spot-11627210802

33. Bank for International Settlements, Annual Economic Report 2021, June 29, 2021, at: https://www.bis.org/publ/arpdf/ar2021e.htm

34. Issaku Harada, "China Aims to Launch Digital Yuan by 2022 Winter Olympics," *Nikkei Asia* (May 27, 2020), available at https://asia.nikkei.com/Spotlight/Cryptocurrencies/China-aims-to-launch-digital-yuan-by-2022-Winter-Olympics

35. For an overview of the enormity of China's Belt and Road project, see Andrew Chatzky and James McBride, "*China's Massive Belt and Road Initiative*," Council on Foreign Relations Backgrounder (Jan. 28, 2020), available at https://www.cfr.org/backgrounder/chinas-massive-belt-and-road-initiative

36. Zaitchik et al., "Special Series: China Bets on the Blockchain."
37. "Central Banks of China and United Arab Emirates Join Digital Currency Project for Cross-Border Payments," Bank for International Settlements press release (Feb. 21, 2021), available at https://www.bis.org/press/p210223.htm
38. .Zaitchik et al., "Special Series: China Bets on the Blockchain."
39. Whatever one's opinion of specific instances or frequency of utilization of economic sanctions, they are certainly less widely destructive than a key alternative of statecraft: warfare.
40. Shepard Pond, "The Spanish Dollar: The World's Most Famous Silver Coin," The President and Fellows of Harvard College, *Bulletin of the Business Historical Society Vol. 15*, No. 1 (Feb., 1941) available at https://www.jstor.org/stable/i356449.
41. Kirsten Hyde, "China Opens Futures Markets Further to Outside World," FIA (Nov. 25, 2020), available at https://www.fia.org/marketvoice/articles/china-opens-futures-markets-further-outside-world
42. FIA, "FIA Supports China's Historic Futures Law, May 21 2021, available at https://www.fia.org/resources/fia-supports-chinas-historic-futures-law
43. "U.S. Soy Cargo to China Traded Using Blockchain," Reuters (Jan. 22, 2018), available at https://www.reuters.com/article/grains-blockchain/u-s-soy-cargo-to-china-traded-using-blockchain-idUSL8N1PG0VJ
44. It is somewhat ironic that this innovative blockchain transaction between the United States and China took place in the middle of an American administration that was looking to disentangle and decouple the complex US/China trade relationship.
45. Bordo, Michael D, "Central Bank Digital Currency in Historical Perspective: Another Crossroad in Monetary History," National Bureau of Economic Research, Working Paper 29171, August 2021, at: https://www.nber.org/papers/w29171
46. Sebastian Sinclair, "Digital Yuan Used in China's Domestic Futures Market for First Time: Report," Yahoo Finance, August 21, 2021, at: https://www.yahoo.com/now/digital-yuan-used-china-domestic-033927042.html
47. Eswar S. Prasad, *Gaining Currency: The Rise of the Renminbi* (New York: Oxford University Press, 2017), 245.
48. International Monetary Fund, available at https://data.imf.org/?sk=E6A5F467-C14B-4AA8-9F6D-5A09EC4E62A4
49. International Monetary Fund.
50. Randal K. Quarles, "Parachute Pants and Central Bank Money," Speech AT the 113th Annual Utah Bankers Association Convention, Board of Governors of the Federal Reserve System, June 28, 2021, available at https://www.federalreserve.gov/newsevents/speech/quarles20210628a.htm
51. Quarles, "Parachute Pants."
52. Matthew D. Johnson, "China's Digital Renminbi Initiative Is a Network, Not a Currency," Blogpost: The Strategist (June 16, 2021), available at https://www.aspistrategist.org.au/chinas-digital-renminbi-initiative-is-a-network-not-a-currency/
53. Hannah Murphy and Yuan Yang, "Patents Reveal Extent."
54. In the *Star Wars* movies, hyperdrive is a propulsion system that allows a starship to reach lightspeed and traverse the void between stars in the alternate dimension of hyperspace. As a consequence, the hyperdrive was a key instrument in shaping galactic society, trade, politics, and war. Wookiepedia, at https://starwars.fandom.com/wiki/Hyperdrive
55. Ann Saphir, "Fed's Brainard: Can't Wrap Head Around Not Having U.S. Central Bank Digital Currency," Reuters, July 30, 2021, at: https://www.reuters.com/technology/feds-brainard-cant-wrap-head-around-not-having-us-central-bank-digital-currency-2021-07-31/
56. Adam Zarazinski and Christina Tkach, "China Digital Currency Scorecard: What You Need to Know," TabbForum (May 4, 2021), available from https://tabbforum.com/opinions/china-digital-currency-scorecard-what-you-need-to-know/

57. Garnaut Global, "The Truth About Digital Currency and De-Dollarisation, April 1, 2021.

58. Johnson, "China's Digital Renminbi Initiative Is a Network."

59. Catalini, Christian and Lilley, Andrew, "Why is the United States Lagging Behind in Payments?," SSRN, July 27, 2021 at: https://papers.ssrn.com/sol3/papers.cfm?abstract_id=3893937

60. Silvia Amaro, "The ECB Starts Work on Creating a Digital Version of the Euro," CNBC (July 14, 2021), available at https://www.cnbc.com/2021/07/14/the-ecb-starts-work-on-creating-a-digital-version-of-the-euro-.html

61. Craig Torres, "Powell: Need for Digital Dollar Is an Issue for Congress, Public," Bloomberg (April 11, 2021), available at https://www.bloomberg.com/news/articles/2021-04-12/powell-need-for-digital-dollar-is-an-issue-for-congress-public

62. Lael Brainard, "Private Money and Central Bank Money as Payments Go Digital: An Update on CBDCs," Board of Governors of the Federal Reserve System (May 24, 2021), available at https://www.bloomberg.com/news/articles/2021-04-12/powell-need-for-digital-dollar-is-an-issue-for-congress-public https://www.federalreserve.gov/newsevents/speech/brainard20210524a.htm

63. Jess Cheng, Angela N Lawson, and Paul Wong, "Preconditions for a General-Purpose Central Bank Digital Currency," Board of Governors of the Federal Reserve System, *Federal Notes* (Feb. 24, 2021), available at https://www.federalreserve.gov/econres/notes/feds-notes/preconditions-for-a-general-purpose-central-bank-digital-currency-20210224.htm. This Federal Reserve note identifies the following five broad preconditions: "clear policy objectives, broad stakeholder support, strong legal framework, robust technology, and market readiness."

64. Treacy Reynolds, "The Federal Reserve Bank of Boston Announces Collaboration with MIT to Research Digital Currency," Federal Reserve Bank of Boston (Aug. 13, 2020), available at https://www.bostonfed.org/news-and-events/press-releases/2020/the-federal-reserve-bank-of-boston-announces-collaboration-with-mit-to-research-digital-currency.aspx

65. Eric S. Rosengren, "Central Bank Perspectives on Central Bank Digital Currencies," Remarks of President and CEO Eric S. Rosengren, Federal Reserve Bank of Boston (May 21, 2021), available at https://www.bostonfed.org/news-and-events/speeches/2021/central-bank-perspectives-on-central-bank-digital-currencies.aspx

66. Digital Dollar Project, "Digital Dollar Project to Launch Pilot Programs to Explore Designs and Uses of a US Central Bank Digital Currency," May 3, 2021, available at https://digitaldollar-project.org

67. Id.

68. Ronald Reagan, "Address to the British Parliament," June 8, 1982, at https://www.historyplace.com/speeches/reagan-parliament.htm

69. Federal Reserve Bank of Dallas, "Globalization and Monetary Policy Institute, 2014 Annual Report," available at https://www.dallasfed.org/~/media/documents/institute/annual/2014/annual14.pdf

70. Georges Clemenceau, French Premier.

71. The author credits the work of the Digital Dollar Project Advisory Group's Privacy Subcommittee: Elizabeth Gray, Jim Harper, and Sigal Mandelker.

72. For a poignant depiction of the role of the Internet in effecting social change, see, generally, Emily Parker, *Now I Know Who My Comrades Are: Voices from the Internet Underground* (New York: Sarah Crichton Books/Farrar, Straus and Giroux, 2014).

73. Bret Swanson, "Big Tech and Big Finance Breed Hubris," *The Wall Street Journal,* Opinion (July 6, 2021), available at https://www.wsj.com/articles/big-tech-and-big-finance-breed-hubris-11625520108

74. World Bank Poverty Homepage, available at https://www.worldbank.org/en/topic/poverty

75. Ron Johnson, "YouTube Cancels the U.S. Senate," *The Wall Street Journal,* February 2, 2021, at https://www.wsj.com/articles/youtube-cancels-the-u-s-senate-11612288061

76. Nick Clegg, "In Response to Oversight Board, Trump Suspended for Two Years; Will Only Be Reinstated If Conditions Permit," Facebook (June 4, 2021), available at https://about.fb.com/news/2021/06/facebook-response-to-oversight-board-recommendations-trump/

77. Although, perhaps, not as hard as it should be. The June 2021 leak of personal IRS tax filings suggests a staggering criminal invasion of privacy in service to a political agenda. Opinion: "Return of the IRS Scandal," *The Wall Street Journal* (June 8, 2021), available at https://www.wsj.com/articles/return-of-the-irs-scandal-11623191964

78. Numerous US federal government agencies regularly circumvent constitutional privacy protections by obtaining sensitive consumer data from commercial vendors. See Laura Hecht-Felella, "Federal Agencies Are Secretly Buying Consumer Data," Brennan Center for Justice (April 16, 2021), available at https://www.brennancenter.org/our-work/analysis-opinion/federal-agencies-are-secretly-buying-consumer-data

79. Zachary Cohen and Katie Bo Williams, "Biden Team May Partner with Private Firms to Monitor Extremist Chatter Online," CNN (May 3, 2021), available at https://www.cnn.com/2021/05/03/politics/dhs-partner-private-firms-surveil-suspected-domestic-terrorists/index.html

80. According to one widely read historian, those who own the data own the future," Yuval Noah Harari, *21 Lessons for the 21st Century* (New York: Penguin Random House, 2018).

81. Joe Weisenthal and Tracy Alloway, "Interview with Hyun Song Shin, Economist, Bank for International Settlement," Bloomberg Odd Lots Newsletter, June 25, 2021.

82. Weisenthal and Alloway, "Interview with Hyun Song Shin."

83. https://www.youtube.com/watch?v=2nf_bu-kBr4

84. The author credits Daniel Gorfine for the idea and rhetorical appeal of asking what could go right in adopting CBDC rather than the far more common inquiry of what could go wrong.

85. "CBDCs: An Opportunity for the Monetary System," Bank for International Settlements Annual Economic Report (June 23, 2021), available at https://www.cnn.com/2021/05/03/politics/dhs-partner-private-firms-surveil-suspected-domestic-terrorists/index.html

86. "CBDCs: An Opportunity for the Monetary System."

87. Gustave Flaubert, nineteenth-century French novelist, is said to have observed that "You can calculate the worth of a man by the number of his enemies."

88. Dante Disparte, "A Central Bank Digital Currency Would Be Bad for the US," CoinDesk (May 17, 2021), available at https://www.coindesk.com/a-central-bank-digital-currency-would-be-bad-for-the-us

89. Tobias Adrian & Tommaso Mancini-Griffoli, "Public and Private Money Can Coexist in the Digital Age," IMF Blog (Feb. 18, 2021), available at https://blogs.imf.org/2021/02/18/public-and-private-money-can-coexist-in-the-digital-age/ and Tobias Adrian, Michael Lee, Tommaso Mancini-Griffoli, and Antoine Martin, "Central Banks and Digital Currencies," Liberty Street Economics (June 23, 2021), available at https://libertystreeteconomics.newyorkfed.org

90. Adrian and Mancini-Griffoli, "Public and Private Money Can Coexist; Adrian et al., "Central Banks and Digital Currencies"

91. In the 1960s, NASA partnered with a host of private sector vendors, engineering firms, and contractors to land a man on the moon and accomplish America's then highest priority. Also in the 1960s, the Pentagon's Defense Advanced Research Projects Agency (DARPA) contracted to the private sector development of key Internet components while, later in the century, the National Science Foundation created NSFNET to contract with both private companies and public universities to lay the groundwork for the Internet as we know it today.

92. Carney, "The Art of Central Banking in a Centrifugal World."

Conclusion

1. The author credits Daniel Gorfine for the idea and rhetorical appeal of asking what could go right in adopting CBDC rather than the far more common inquiry of what could go wrong. April 9, 2018, at: https://www.cftc.gov/PressRoom/SpeechesTestimony/opagiancarlo43

2. See John Stuart Mill, "On Utilitarianism" (1861) in *Utilitarianism*, Mary Warnock ed. (Glasgow, Scotland: William Collins Sons, 1962) containing other important works by Mill, including "On Liberty" (1859), and works by Jeremy Bentham and John Austin. For background, see John Skorupski, *John Stuart Mill* (Routledge, London, 1989). Skorupski focuses primarily on Mill's philosophy, analysis, and inductive arguments.

3. See John Keay's *The Honorable Company: A History of the English East India Company* (New York: Harper Collins, 1991) and Niall Ferguson, Empire: How Britain Made the Modern World (New York: Penguin 2004).

4. John A. Allison, *The Financial Crisis and the Free Market Cure* (New York: McGraw Hill, 2013), 253.

5. Michael Novak, *The Spirit of Democratic Capitalism* (New York: Madison Books, 1982).

6. Novak, *The Spirit of Democratic Capitalism*, 13.

7. See generally, Nassim Nicholas Taleb, *Antifragile: Things That Gain from Disorder* (New York: Random House, 2012).

8. C. S. Lewis, *The Abolition of Man* (1943). Mill also endorses the Golden Rule in On Utilitarianism at 268.

9. Niall Ferguson, *The Great Degeneration: How Institutions Decay and Economies Die* (New York: Penguin Press, 2013), 72, reviewing the lessons of Walter Bagehot's *Lombard Street* and the successful administration of the Bank of England.

10. On Liberty, Id.

11. Bob Dylan, 1964, Columbia Records.

12. Douglas Adams, "The Salmon of Doubt: Hitchhiking the Galaxy One Last Time" (2002, William Heinemann Ltd.).

13. Today in socialist Venezuela, hospital emergency rooms are overwhelmed by children with severe malnutrition, a condition that was rarely seen in that country rich in natural resources before its socialist takeover. See "As Venezuela Collapses, Children Are Dying of Hunger," Meridith Kohut and Isayen Herrera, *New York Times* (Dec. 17, 2017), available at https://www.nytimes.com/interactive/2017/12/17/world/americas/venezuela-children-starving.html. It is estimated that by May 2018 approximately 5,000 people per day were leaving Venezuela in search of food. At this rate, 1.8 million people will have left by the end of 2018, joining 1.5 million who have already fled. This is over 10% of Venezuela's population of 32 million. See Rhoda Howard-Hassmann, "Famine in Venezuela," World Peace Foundation (Aug. 21, 2018), available at https://sites.tufts.edu/reinventingpeace/2018/08/21/famine-in-venezuela/

14. George Gilder, *Knowledge and Power* (Washington, DC: Regnery, 2013), 282.

15. Minerva Research, Sunday Briefing (June 13, 2021), available at https://minerva-intelligence.com/sunday_briefing/

16. Pope Benedict XVI, Papal Welcome, World Youth Day 2008, held in Australia (July 17, 2008), available at https://www.vatican.va/content/benedict-xvi/en/messages/youth/documents/hf_ben-xvi_mes_20070720_youth

17. See Aristotle, "The Politics." A recent version is edited by Johnathan Barnes, "The Politics," [Introduction by Melissa Lane, translated originally by Benjamin Jowett] (Princeton, NJ: Princeton University Press, 2016).

18. Yared, "Nothing to Celebrate."

Appendix

1. Paul Vigna, "For Bitcoin: A Year Like No Other," *The Wall Street Journal* (Jan. 2, 2018), available at https://www.wsj.com/articles/for-bitcoin-a-year-like-no-other-1514721601

2. Milton Friedman spoke about the prospects of a disintermediated Internet payment system as far back as 1999. See National Taxpayers Union, "Milton Friedman Full Interview on Anti-Trust and Tech (1999)," YouTube video (Aug. 9, 2012), available at https://www.youtube.com/watch?v=mlwxdyLnMXM&feature=youtube

3. See generally, "CFTC Talks," Episode 24 (Dec. 29, 2017), Interview with Coincenter.org Director of Research Peter Van Valkenburgh, available at http://www.cftc.gov/Media/Podcast/index.htm

4. See Marc Andreessen, "Why Bitcoin Matters," *New York Times* DealBook (Jan. 21, 2014), https://dealbook.nytimes.com/2014/01/21/why-bitcoin-matters/; Jerry Brito and Andrea O'Sullivan, *Bitcoin: A Primer for Policymakers* (Arlington, VA: George Mason University Mercatus Center, 2016), https://www.mercatus.org/publication/bitcoin-primer-policymakers; Christian Catalini and Joshua S. Gans, "Some Simple Economics of the Blockchain," Rotman School of Management Working Paper No. 2874598, MIT Sloan Research Paper No. 5191-16 (last updated Sept. 21, 2017), https://papers.ssrn.com/sol3/papers.cfm?abstract_id=2874598; Arjun Kharpal, "People are 'underestimating' the 'great potential' of bitcoin, billionaire Peter Thiel says," CNBC (Oct. 26, 2017), https://www.cnbc.com/2017/10/26/bitcoin-underestimated-peter-thiel-says.html; Hugh Son, "Bitcoin 'More Than Just a Fad,' Morgan Stanley CEO Says," *Bloomberg* (Sept. 27, 2017), https://www.bloomberg.com/news/articles/2017-09-27/bitcoin-more-than-just-a-fad-morgan-stanley-ceo-gorman-says; Chris Brummer and Daniel Gorfine, "Fintech: Building a 21st-Century Regulator's Toolkit," Milken Institute (Oct. 21, 2014), available at http://www.milkeninstitute.org/publications/view/665

5. See generally, Bronwyn Howell, "Is Bitcoin the Tulip Craze of the 21st Century, or Something Else?" American Enterprise Institute: *AEIdeas* (Jan 5, 2018), available at http://www.aei.org/publication/is-bitcoin-the-tulip-craze-of-the-21st-century-or-something-else/

6. Virtual currencies are not unique in their utility in illicit activity. National currencies, like the US dollar, and commodities, like gold and diamonds, have long been used to support criminal enterprises.

7. Countries that have banned Bitcoin include Bangladesh, Bolivia, Ecuador, Kyrgyzstan, Morocco, Nepal, and Vietnam. China has banned Bitcoin for banking institutions.

8. See https://coinmarketcap.com/ for latest numbers.

9. See, e.g. http://openmarkets.cmegroup.com/12749/bitcoin-gold-growth-comparison

10. Sheila Bair, "Former FDIC Chair: Why We Shouldn't Ban Bitcoin," *Yahoo Finance* (Dec. 26, 2017), available at https://finance.yahoo.com/news/former-fdic-chair-sheila-bair-shouldnt-ban-bitcoin-141019569.html

11. Bair, "Former FDIC Chair."

12. Testimony of CFTC Chairman Timothy Massad before the US Senate Committee on Agriculture, Nutrition and Forestry (Dec. 10, 2014), available at http://www.cftc.gov/PressRoom/SpeechesTestimony/opamassad-6

13. In re Coinflip, Inc., Dkt. No. 15-29, CFTC (Sept. 17, 2015), available at http://www.cftc.gov/idc/groups/public/@lrenforcementactions/documents/legalpleading/enfcoinfliprorder09172015.pdf

14. In re TeraExchange LLC, Dkt. No. 15-33, CFTC (Sept. 24, 2015), available at http://www.cftc.gov/idc/groups/public/@lrenforcementactions/documents/legalpleading/enfteraexchangeorder92415.pdf

15. In re BXFNA Inc. d/b/a Bitfinex, Dkt. No. 16-19, CFTC (June 2, 2016), available at http://www.cftc.gov/idc/groups/public/@lrenforcementactions/documents/legalpleading/enfbfxnaorder060216.pdf

16. "Retail Commodity Transactions Involving Virtual Currency," 82 Fed. Reg. 60335 (Dec. 20, 2017), available at www.gpo.gov/fdsys/pkg/FR-2017-12-20/pdf/2017-27421.pdf

17. CFTC, "A CFTC Primer on Virtual Currencies" (Oct. 17, 2017), available at http://www.cftc.gov/idc/groups/public/documents/file/labcftc_primercurrencies100417.pdf

18. On September 21, 2017, the CFTC filed a complaint in federal court in the Southern District of New York against Nicholas Gelfman and Gelfman Blueprint, Inc., see http://www.cftc.gov/idc/groups/public/@lrenforcementactions/documents/legalpleading/enfgelfmancomplaint09212017.pdf

19. CFTC, "A CFTC Primer on Virtual Currencies."

20. CFTC, "Customer Advisory: Understand the Risks of Virtual Currency Trading" (Dec. 15, 2017), available at http://www.cftc.gov/idc/groups/public/@customerprotection/documents/file/customeradvisory_urvct121517.pdf

21. CFTC, "Statement on Self-Certification of Bitcoin Products by CME, CFE and Cantor Exchange" (Dec. 1, 2017), available at http://www.cftc.gov/PressRoom/PressReleases/pr7654-17

22. CFTC, "Bitcoin," http://www.cftc.gov/Bitcoin/index.htm

23. "Retail Commodity Transactions Involving Virtual Currency."

24. CFTC, "Commitments of Traders," available at http://www.cftc.gov/MarketReports/CommitmentsofTraders/index.htm

25. Each CME contract represents 5 Bitcoin.

26. The price changes day to day. As of January 17, 2018, *The Wall Street Journal* is reporting that the price has fallen below $11,000 for the first time since early December. See Mike Bird and Gregor Stuart Hunter, "Bitcoin Sinks as More Regulation Looms," *The Wall Street Journal* (Jan. 17, 2018), B130, available at https://www.wsj.com/articles/just-another-day-for-bitcoina-20-plunge-1516103459

27. See CEA Section 5(d)(3), 7 U.S.C. 7(d)(3); Section 5(d)4), 7 U.S.C. 7(d)(4); 17 C.F.R. 38.253 and 38.254(a), and Appendices B and C to Part 38 of the CFTC's regulations.

28. CEA Section 5b(c)(2)(D)(iv), 7 U.S.C. 7a-1(c)(2)(D)(iv) ("The margin from each member and participant of a derivatives clearing organization shall be sufficient to cover potential exposures in normal market conditions").

29. In the case of CME and CFE Bitcoin futures, the initial margins were ultimately set at 47% and 44% by the respective DCOs. By way of comparison, that is more than 10 times the margin required for CME corn futures products.

30. One clearing member called for the CFTC to force DCOs to establish a separate clearing system for virtual currencies. However, the CFTC's "hands were tied" by statute and regulation from requiring a separate clearing system or guaranty fund as a condition to Bitcoin futures product self-certification. The CEA does not require a self-certification process for clearing new futures products. Where separate guaranty funds have been established at DCOs in the past, they have come about through independent negotiations between clearing members and DCOs, not by CFTC action.

31. FIA, "Open Letter to CFTC Chairman Giancarlo Regarding the Listing of Cryptocurrency Derivatives" (Dec. 7, 2017), available at https://fia.org/articles/open-letter-cftc-chairman-giancarlo-regarding-listing-cryptocurrency-derivatives

32. "Leaders' Statement from the Group of 20" (G-20). Pittsburgh Summit, Treasury.gov (Sept. 24–25, 2009), available at https://www.treasury.gov/resource-center/international/g7-g20/Documents/pittsburgh_summit_leaders_statement_250909.pdf

33. J. Christopher Giancarlo, "Op-Ed in Les Échos: Deference Is the Path Forward in Cross-Border Supervision of CCPs," CFTC.gov, available at http://www.cftc.gov/PressRoom/SpeechesTestimony/giancarlooped091117

34. "Comparability Determination for the European Union: Margin Requirements for Uncleared Swaps for Swap Dealers and Major Swap Participants," 82 Fed. Reg. 48394 (Oct. 18, 2017), available at http://www.cftc.gov/idc/groups/public/@lrfederalregister/documents/file/2017-22616a.pdf

35. "Comparability Determination for the European Union," 48398-99.

36. "Comparability Determination for the European Union," 48413.

37. CFTC, "CFTC Comparability Determination on EU Margin Requirements and a Common Approach on Trading Venues," CFTC.gov, Release PR 7629-17 (Oct. 13, 2017), available at http://www.cftc.gov/PressRoom/PressReleases/pr7629-17

38. CFTC, "CFTC Approves Exemption from SEF Registration Requirement for Multilateral Trading Facilities and Organized Trading Facilities Authorized Within the EU," CFTC.gov, Release PR 7656-17 (Dec. 8, 2017), available at http://www.cftc.gov/PressRoom/PressReleases/pr7656-17

Acknowledgments

Book acknowledgments are the literary counterpart of acceptance speeches at the Academy Awards. They are both meant to thank the very people who made everything possible. They both have the same common fault line: do not leave out those who really matter.

There are, however, differences between the two. The winner of the award ceremony does not know in advance if they will get to give the speech. And, if they do, they will only have a few brief minutes to say what they have to say. It is understandable if they leave out an important friend or two.

A writer, on the other hand, knows well in advance that the book will be published. A writer has the time and space necessary to recall all the worthy people and influences that deserve recognition. Thus, there is no possible excuse for a writer not to thank everyone whose support, encouragement, and help contributed to the book and its story.

So, with that pressure top of mind as I write these acknowledgments, there are no excuses if I forget anyone (but please forgive me if I do). Here goes my most sincere thanks to the people who made this book and this journey possible.

Bill Falloon at Wiley liked the concept of this book from the start, never wavered, and saw it through with enthusiasm. My sincere thanks to Purvi Patel, Samantha Enders, Sindujaabirami Ravichandiran, Donna J. Weinson, and the rest of the Wiley team.

My thanks also to Tim Hays, my ever-enthusiastic and irrepressible literary agent. Elise Daniel spent hours generously advising me on how to get off to the right start, as did Norm Champ. Herb Schaffner, a true and straight shooter, and Roger Parloff, a superb journalist and exacting reader, painstakingly edited and, in so doing, contributed enormously. Both John Sodergreen and Chris Ferrari made sure I got the history right. Myles Thompson helped me frame the subject. Steve Adamske made certain that I was fair in its telling. Eric Pan, Amir Zaidi, Daniel Gorfine, Mike Gill, and Erica Richardson read portions and gave me their thoughtful advice. John Shosky helped me develop a unique voice as a public official for which I am forever grateful. Israel Pollack and Kyle Commerford ably assisted with many of the citations herein.

I am grateful to Cameron and Tyler Winklevoss for first opening my eyes and keeping them open, a wonderful foreword, and a delightful dinner in St. Moritz. My gratitude and respect goes to so many great crypto OGs: Jeremy Allaire, Yoni and Ronen Assia, Sam Bankman-Fried, Brian Brooks, Chad Cascarilla, Michael Casey, Shayne Coplan, Meltem Demirors, Dante Disparte, Jan van Eck, Avichal Garg, Elad Gil, Matt Goetz, Kathryn Haun, Tom Jessop, Amy Devine Kim, Joey Krug, Stuart Levey, Caitlin Long, Joseph Lubin, Flori Marquez, Blythe Masters, Asaf Meir, Dan Morehead, Richard Olsen, Ari Paul, Anthony Pompliano, Zac Prince, Donna Redel, Matthew Roszak, Yuval Rooz, David Rutter, Marco Santori, Dan Schulman, Cuy Sheffield, Laura Shin, Colleen Sullivan, Don & Alex Tapscott, Sheila Warren, and Changpeng Zhao.

I can never repay the debt I owe to Mickey Gooch and his fabulous creation, GFI Group, for a great ride with a purpose and terrific colleagues with whom I worked, laughed, and managed wholesale markets for a decade and a half: Herve Alfon, Nick Brown, Tom Cancro, Marisa Cassoni, Robert Crossan, Michael Cosgrove, Clay Davis, Darryl Denyssen, Michel Everaert, Dudley Fishburn, Scott Fitzpatrick, Richard Giles, Chris Ann Grimmett, John Healy, Colin Heffron, Helena Jarabakova, Ron Levi, James Martin, Prash Naik, Mark Pasquale, Jim Peers, John Piluso, Scott Pintoff, Marc Souffir, Doug Steele, Julian Swain, Dana Urschler, Matt Woodhams, and so many others. GFI was more than a business, it was Good Fun Indeed.

My road to Washington began in Hanover Square, New York, following a financial crisis with a meal shared among business competitors who became lifelong friends. I am grateful to my WMBAA cofounders: Sean Bernardo, Chris Ferreri, Julian Harding, Steve Merkel, Bill Shields, and our trusty guide, Micah Green.

I have so many people to thank for supporting my government service including two very different presidents with little in common. Yet, I am grateful to both President Barack Obama and Donald J. Trump for each having nominated me to serve. I am also grateful to New Jersey Governor Chris Christie for encouraging President Obama in 2013 to announce my nomination and Gary Cohn in 2017 for calling me to the attention of the president-elect.

I most heartily thank my fellow CFTC Chairmen: Russ Behnam, Sharon Brown-Hruska, Gary Gensler, Walt Lukken, Tim Massad, Jim Newsome, and Heath Tarbert, and CFTC commissioners: Dan Berkovitz, Sharon Bowen, Michael Dunn, Fred Hatfield, Brian Quintenz, Scott O'Malia, Jill Sommers, Dawn Stump, Mark Wetjen, and the late Bart Chilton. The nonpartisan and workmanlike tone from the top provided by these fine men and women makes the CFTC one of the best functioning and most professional agencies in Washington.

If the CFTC accomplished anything during my time as chairman, it was thanks to its over 500 dedicated public servants. They include a remarkable group of leaders and professionals: Jeff Bandman, Andy Busch, Brian Bussey, Mary Connelly, Matt Daigler, Dan Davis, Rich Danker, Phyllis Dietz, Eileen Donovan, Nancy Doyle, Donna Faulk-White, Eileen Flaherty, Wes French, Aitan Goelman, Ward Griffin, Mel Gunewardena, Venita Hill, Rosemary Hollinger, Shonneice Jones, Shivon Kershaw, Christopher Kirkpatrick, Matt Kulkin, John Lawton, Michael Locante, Gretchen Lowe, Jamie McDonald, Vince McGonagle, Nicole McNair, Chuck Marvine, Lyle Munroe, Eric Pan, Kevin Piccoli, Chelsea Pizzola, George Pullen, Phillip Raimondi, Erica Richardson, John Rogers, Bella Rosenberg, Rob Schwartz, Maggie Sklar, Tom Smith, Sarah Somerville, Sayee Srinivasan, Manal Sultan, Tony Thompson, Charlie Thornton, Bruce Tuckman, David Van Wagner, Rahul Vharma, Kevin Webb, Scott Williamson, Tracey Wingate, Ann Wright, Margie Yates, Amir Zaidi and so many more. I am also grateful to Marcia Blase for getting me through my rookie season and to Jason Goggins for always speaking freely. By the time they handed me off to Mike Gill, I was ready for his constant balance, good nature, and caritas.

I consider myself remarkably fortunate to have served beside and collaborated with some skilled senior US officials and their staffs: Federal Reserve Board Chairs Janet Yellen and Jerome Powell; Federal Reserve Board Governors Lael Brainard and Randy Quarles; Regional Federal Reserve Presidents Bill Dudley, Charlie Evans, Esther George, Neel Kashkari, and John Williams; NEC Directors Gary Cohn and Larry Kudlow; Treasury Secretary Steve Mnuchin; Securities and Exchange Commission Chairs Mary Jo White and Jay Clayton and Commissioners Troy Paredes, Dan Gallagher, Kara Stein, Mike Piwowar, and Hester Peirce; Comptrollers of the Currency Thomas Curry, Joseph Otting, and Brian Brooks; Federal Deposit Insurance Corporation Chairs Martin Greunberg and Jelana McWilliams; Directors of the Consumer Finance Protection Bureau Richard Cordray and Kathy Kraninger; and Directors of the Federal Housing Finance Administration Mel Watt and Mark Calabria. I am equally grateful to such dedicated public servants as David Bowman, Corado Camera, Neil Chatterjee, Alan Cohen, Brent Macintosh, David Malpass, Sigal Mandelker, Justin Muzinich, Andrew Olmem, Morgan Ortagus, Nate Wuerffel, and my dear friend Tony Sayegh. Their service to our country and its citizens merits the highest praise.

I remain deeply grateful to Supreme Court Justice Clarence Thomas for administering my oath of office as a solemn and sacred undertaking. I am also indebted to numerous current and former members of Congress for their courtesy and engagement on matters affecting US financial markets, including former House Speaker Paul Ryan and Representatives Mike Conaway, Warren Davidson, Tom Emmer, Scott Garrett, Anthony Gonzalez, Vickey Hartzler, Jim Himes, Bill Huizenga, Frank Lucas, Blaine Luetkemeyer, Stephen Lynch, Patrick McHenry, Collin Peterson, David Scott, Austin Scott and Darren Soto as well as Senators John Boozeman (Arkansas), Shelly Moore Capito (West Virginia), Chris Coons (Delaware), Tom Cotton (Arkansas), Mike Crapo (Idaho), Steve Daines (Montana), Joni Ernst (Iowa), Bill Hagerty (Tennessee), John Kennedy (Louisiana), James Lankford (Oklahoma), Cynthia Lummis (Wyoming), Mitch McConnell (Kentucky), Jerry Moran (Kansas), Rob Portman (Ohio), Pat Roberts (Kansas), Mitt Romney (Utah), Debbie Stabenow (Michigan), John Thune (South

Dakota), Thom Tillis (North Carolina), Chris Van Hollen (Maryland), Mark Warner (Virginia), Elizabeth Warren (Massachusetts), and Richard Shelby (Alabama).

I also benefited from working with some extraordinary global leaders and their staffs, among whom were British Chancellor of the Exchequer Philip Hammond, Her Majesty's Treasury senior officials Charles Roxburgh and Katherine Braddick, Governors of the Bank of England Mark Carney and Andrew Bailey and Deputy Governors Sir Jon Cunliffe and Sam Wood, European Commission Vice President, Valdis Dombrovskis and Commission colleagues, Olivier Guersent, John Berrigan and Mario Nava, Bank for International Settlements Director Benoit Coeure, European Securities and Markets Authority Executive Director Steven Maijoor, Ontario Securities Commission former Chair Maureen Jensen, French Autorite des Marches Financiers President, Robert Ophele, German Federal Financial Services Authority Presidents Felix Hufeld and Mark Branson, Hong Kong Securities and Futures Commission Chief Executive Ashley Alder, Central Bank of Ireland Director General Derville Rowland, Italian Commissione Nazionale per le Societa e la Borsa Chairman Paolo Savona and Condirectore Nicoletta Giusto, Autorite des Marches Financiers of Quebec President Louis Morisset, Singapore Monetary Authority Managing Director Ravi Menon and Japanese Financial Services Agency Chairman Ryozo Himono and Deputy Director Jun Mizuguchi. I am also grateful to the leadership of the NFA: Tom Sexton, Karen Wuertz and Ed Dasso and of the FIA: Walt Lukken, Allison Lurton and Jacqueline Mesa.

The Digital Dollar Project has been a remarkable journey. When we began work in December 2019, US officials saw little reason to consider CBDC; 18 months later, they are racing to get ahead. Our voices rang true in that call to action. I am grateful to its first-rate advisory group and my fellow board members Charlie Giancarlo, Daniel Gorfine, Adrian Harris, and David Treat; and the fabulous team at Accenture: Amanda Brino, Denise Berard, Alison Geib, Luke Giancarlo, Michael Greco, Robert Hoffman, Geoff Kahn, Osumene Mandeng, Danielle Martell, Vincent Mele, Juliet Meyer, Dominic Paolino, Leslie Wong, Alissa Worley, and John Velissarios.

It is satisfying to be able to continue my public service in a minor way as chairman of Common Securitization Solutions. I am appreciative of the support of Acting Director Sandra Thompson and fellow board members:

Tony Renzi, David Benson, Dylan Glenn, Andy Higginbotham, Lynette Kelly, Mike Piwowar, Ramon Richards, and Jerry Weiss. It is a pleasure to work with the indomitable Perianne Boring and a honor to serve on the Advisory Board of the Chamber of Digital Commerce.

American businessman, economist, and entrepreneur Richard L. Sandor, chairman and CEO of the American Financial Exchange, is an inspiration to me. So are my fellow AFX board members, Barbara G. Novick, Art Kelly, Robert Albertson, Andy Lowenthal, and the late Carole L. Brookins. It is similarly a privilege to serve on the board of Nomura Securities and support the work of its forward-thinking chief executive, Kentaro Okuda-san.

Joining Willkie Farr & Gallagher has been terrific. The firm does everything right from the little things in the way it treats its people, to the big things in how it treats its clients. I clearly saw that during COVID-19, when the firm seemed never to miss a beat on both counts. I am deeply grateful to Jim Anderson, Scott Arenare, Conrad Bahlke, Margo Bailey, Barry Barbash, Norman Bay, Matthew Berger, Karystyna Blakeslee, Justin Browder, Brant Brown, Georgia Bullitt, Jim Burns, Tom Cerabino, Eugene Chang, Nan-I Chen, Ruby Cherry, Henrietta de Salis, Michael DeNiro, Athena Eastwood, Wes Eguchi, Archie Fallon, Matt Feldman, Elizabeth Gray, Eric Halperin, Mickey Hartz, Benedict Hur, Jorge Kamine, David Katz, Neal Kumar, David McCabe, Rita Molesworth, David Mortlock, Margery Neale, Thomas Obersteiner, Paul Pantano, Chris Peters, Graham Pittman, Jeff Poss, Arty Rogov, Bill Rooney, Michael Schachter, Heather Schneider, Claudia Seyer, Chris St. Jeanos, Bill Stellmach, Neil Townsend, Deborah Tuchman, Adam Turteltaub, Kimberly Wachtler, Martin Weinstein, and the late Jack Nussbaum.

I have been blessed with many great teachers, both in and out of school, to whom I owe so very much: the selfless Sisters of Charity of St. Elizabeth of Convent Station, Dwight-Englewood's Malcom Duffy, Albert Greco, Gene Wojtyla, and Anita Liskin; Skidmore's Phyllis Roth, Henry Galant, Erwin Levine, Mary Ellen Fischer, Patricia Ann Lee, and Tad Koroda; Vanderbilt's John Marshall, Don Langevoort, and Hal Meyer; Curtis Mallet-Prevost's Townsend Knight, Albert Francke, Jerry Mulligan, Mark Barth, Larry Goodman, and Geoffroy Lyonnet; and intellectual influences Chris Brummer, Darrell Duffie, Niall Ferguson, George

Gilder, Peggy Noonan, Maureen O'Hara, Hal Scott, and the great Leo Melamed. I am grateful to Chris Guthrie, Yesha Yadev, and Morgan Ricks at Vanderbilt Law School and Professors Flagg Taylor and Catherine Hill at Skidmore College, especially past president Phillip Glotzbach, Wendy Anthony, and Joe Porter, for hosting me for a week in the special collections library in 2019 while I organized my CFTC papers in preparation for this book.

I am doubly blessed with many dear colleagues and friends, near and far, from whom I have learned so much and to whom I owe so much: Mike Adam, Joe Allegro, John Ashcroft, Paul Atkins, Marvin Bader, JoAnn Barefoot, Charles Baugh, the Beyels, Fred Crosnier, the de Torres family, Bruce DiCicco, Jamie Dittrich, Terry Duffy, Bryan Durkin, Chris Edmonds, Joseph Englehard, Willie Falkenstern, Brendan Foley, Salvatore Giampiccolo, Angela Giancarlo, Ed Gillespie, Paul Gleiberman, Matthew Goetz, Jay Grushkin, Kyle Hauptman, Chris Hehmeyer, David Hirschmann, Chris Iacovella, Mel Immergut, Eric and Amy Kamisher, the Keegans, Mike Kelly, Ken Kurson, Ed & Cora Koch, Jeff Levoff, Drew Maloney, Catherine McGuinness, Ryan McKee and Jonathan Jachym, Dennis "Mac" McKinley, Kevin McPartland, Anne McMillen, Sean Neary, Jim Newsome, Art O'Connor, Sandie O'Connor; Bill Palatucci, Scott Parsons, Ed Peterson and the Peterson family, Michelle Price, Ken Raisler, Linda and Peter Rich, the Sanchez and Scaglione families, Mark and Patti Schmitz, Michael, H.J. and Pace Schwarz, Kaivan Shakib, Marnie Simpson, John Smart, Jeff Sprecher and Kelly Loeffler, Annette Sutherland, Jim Tabacchi, Larry Tabb, Ed Tilly, Mark Tucker, Roy Tumpowski, Adam Varney, John Voigt, Sheila K. Wills, Don Wilson, and John Wotton. I am grateful to David Gillies, who insisted that I write it all down, and the Gueguen family (Jean-Francois, Anne-Sophie, Malo, Arthur, Lola, and Maya) who remind me of the sacrifices generations have made to succeed in America. I am indebted to the Martin/Pratt family for an incomparable place of reflection. I am also grateful to Sister Joanne Picciurro and Reverends Luca Caveada, Stephen Fichter, Ashley Harrington, Jack O'Connell and Robert Wolfee and Cursillistas Ken Bransfield, Peter Fusco, Joseph Genco, Dr. Michael Giuliano, Lou Mondello, Tom Kearney, Jack O'Grady, Doc Peterson, Pat Ferrara, Vincent Shea, and many others for being the wind beneath my wings. I'll be back soon. DeColores!

They are gone now, but I am who I am because of my grandparents, Florence and Henry Schwarz and Fiorina and Charles Giancarlo. I wish they were around so I could tell them what a wonderful life it has been. . .just as they said it would be. I am fortunate to have found myself in the happy embrace of my in-laws, Harry and Tina Beyel and their wonderful brood. They have shared with me their unconditional love since I first sat down at their kitchen table and announced that I was marrying their beautiful daughter. I am grateful to be the recipient of four generations of cross Atlantic affection by wonderful European cousins including my lifelong friend Marisa Cassoni, as well as, Marisa Gesualdo, on whose Roman rooftop the White House located me to confirm my nomination. I am also grateful for the powerful lessons, good and bad, of my father and some quiet words of love before his passing. My mother remains a source of light and laughter in so many lives. She inspired my love of books and writing. This work is my gift to her. My brothers are the distant chords of memory of a childhood of promise and adventure. Charlie has ever been my polestar and remains so today. Mike and Tim have traded turns holding the fort and the family honor. They and their families are dearer to me than I ever manage to say. My children, Emma, Luke, and Henry, are my brightest pride and greatest joy. Seeing them spiritedly set foot in this world is another treasure in this life of mine, for all of which I thank God most singularly.

Penultimately, I thank John, Paul, George, and Ringo for Sgt. Pepper, Mr. Cella for teaching me the chords, Ricky Flynn for song writing and lead licks, Bruce Springsteen for Thunder Road, Tony Cutrupi, Howie Gordon, Alan Saperstein, and Kydus for Stairway to Heaven, Jay Shulman for singing in Saratoga, Joe Allegro and Dave Gillies for harmonies on the back porch, Mike Marlin for "Forgive Me Yet," the Slacks for night music at the Stone Pony, Westhampton and Rob Norden's '76 House, the Precedents for London, the Second Amendments for Michigan, Missouri, and Amarillo by Morning, and most essentially, Neil Young for the Harvest Moon that continues to shine in her eyes.

And those eyes, of course, belong to you, Regina, my bride of 32 years. I am grateful that you are with me for the ride. I love you from the bottom of my heart.

About the Author

J. Christopher Giancarlo

Dubbed "CryptoDad" for his celebrated call on Congress to respect a new generation's interest in cryptocurrency, the Honorable J. Christopher Giancarlo served as 13th Chairman of the United States Commodity Futures Trading Commission.

Considered one of "the most influential individuals in financial regulation," Giancarlo also served as a member of the US Financial Stability Oversight Committee, the President's Working Group on Financial Markets, and the Executive Board of the International Organization of Securities Commissions. Giancarlo was first nominated as a CFTC Commissioner by President Barack Obama and unanimously confirmed in June 2014. He was subsequently nominated as CFTC Chairman by President Donald Trump and again unanimously confirmed in August 2017.

Giancarlo is Senior Counsel to the international law firm, Willkie Farr & Gallagher. He is also a board director, advisor, and angel investor in numerous technology and financial services companies. In addition, Giancarlo is a co-founder of the Digital Dollar Project, a not-for-profit initiative to advance exploration of a US Central Bank Digital Currency.

Mr. Giancarlo received his J.D. in 1984 from Vanderbilt University School of Law and graduated *Phi Beta Kappa* with a B.A. in 1981 from

Skidmore College. Mr. Giancarlo is a member of the bar (1985) of the State of New York. Among other honors, Mr. Giancarlo has been awarded: "*Contribution to Regulatory Reform*" by IFLR Americas (2020); "*The Freedom of the City*," from The City of London (May, 2019); and "*Person of the Decade*," from The French American Academy (October 2017). Twitter: GiancarloMKTS

Index

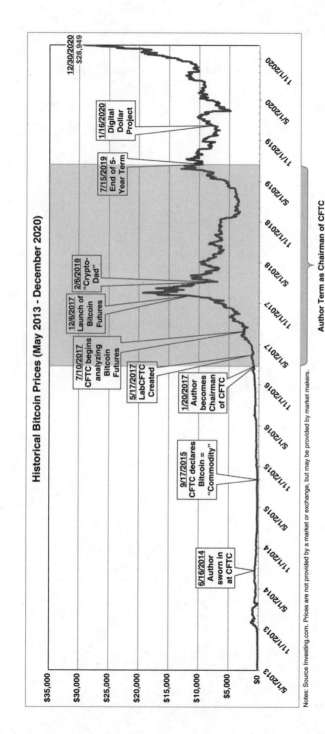

Historical Bitcoin Prices (May 2013 - December 2020)

12/30/2020 $28,949

1/16/2020 Digital Dollar Project

7/15/2019 End of 5-Year Term

2/6/2018 "Crypto-Dad"

12/6/2017 Launch of Bitcoin Futures

7/10/2017 CFTC begins analyzing Bitcoin Futures

5/17/2017 LabCFTC Created

1/20/2017 Author becomes Chairman of CFTC

9/17/2015 CFTC declares Bitcoin = "Commodity"

6/16/2014 Author sworn in at CFTC

Author Term as Chairman of CFTC

Notes: Source Investing.com. Prices are not provided by a market or exchange, but may be provided by market makers.

386